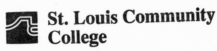

The Biology of
Science Fiction Cinema

The Biology of Science Fiction Cinema

MARK C. GLASSY

McFarland & Company, Inc., Publishers

Jefferson, North Carolina, and London

Library of Congress Cataloguing-in-Publication Data

Glassy, Mark C., 1952–
    The biology of science fiction cinema / Mark C. Glassy.
      p.   cm.
    Includes index.
    ISBN 0-7864-0998-3 (illustrated case binding : 50# alkaline paper)
    1. Science fiction films— History and criticism.   2. Biology in
motion pictures.   I. Title.
PN1995.9.S26 G56   2001
791.43'656 — dc21
                                   2001030076

British Library Cataloguing data are available

Manufactured in the United States of America

*McFarland & Company, Inc., Publishers
  Box 611, Jefferson, North Carolina 28640
    www.mcfarlandpub.com*

To Jason, Matt, and Dawn,
my three Nobel Prizes.
My sons made me a father
and my daughter made me a daddy.

Table of Contents

Introduction

My love affair with science fiction started in 1956 when I was four years old. Prior to that I had a fairly mundane childhood. That changed abruptly when I saw *Earth vs. the Flying Saucers* at the Adler Theater in Marshfield, Wisconsin. When I walked (or floated) out of that theater, the power of the imagination had taken me over, infused in me a sense of wonder and awe, and left me craving more. The seeds of my imagination were well fertilized by that wonderful film and I have thanked my parents numerous times for taking me to see it.

Since that fateful viewing I have tried to see just about every SF film available, and read countless books and short stories, as well. More often than not compromises had to be made to accommodate what was going on in my life so I could see the film du jour. Even through the 20 years I spent in school I allocated enough time to satisfy my film habits. After I married, I took my wife to SF movies, and as our three children arrived, we brought them along, too. This habit or life style has continued during my tenure as a faculty member and in my involvement in the biomedical companies I established in cancer therapeutics. Irrespective of how busy I was, I always made time for SF.

Though at first blush science fiction and science may seem diametrically opposed (and in some cases they certainly are), after a closer analysis they present many elements in common, chief of which are creativity and imagination. It is the glue of imagination which holds them together. The best science and the best science fiction are the most creative and imaginative. A scientist may know many facts, read many books, cite volume, chapter, and verse of every scientific paper within his or her field of specialty — but what matters most is novel thought, original ideas, and creativity. The most important activity we humans can do is use our imaginations, to think and ponder. Without it nothing would change. In this respect, Einstein was correct when he said imagination is more important than knowledge.

I am a professional scientist with extensive study in biochemistry and molecular immunology. My specialty is human antibodies, especially in their application to cancer therapeutics, i.e., human monoclonal antibodies to cancer. And so my life's work has involved both extensive scientific knowledge and its imaginative and creative application.

1

Both science and science fiction give me great joy, and together they have brought me to this book. As a scientist I have an understanding of the fundamental concepts of life and the biological sciences. I am trained to observe details, make conclusions, and interpret facts. By applying this rigor to the biological sciences presented in SF cinema, I hope to offer the reader a powerful tool for understanding some interesting facts and concepts by being able to distinguish "reel" science from real science. Perhaps the reader will be enlightened and enriched in the many wonders that countless scientists have tirelessly worked to uncover for decades. At the very least, I hope the reader of this book will have fun and enjoy SF cinema more thoroughly. I intend to answer some questions often posed by an SF film audience, such as, "Is that true?" "Is that how they do it?" "Could that really happen?"

SCIENCE AND FICTION IN CINEMA

The most dominant art form of the twentieth century has been the cinema. Film critics usually judge movies by how well the actors and their scenes are presented, either individually or together, and the implied meanings, montage, symbolisms, and metaphors found within the scenario. Was a particular actor right for a particular part? Did a certain thematic structure justify its existence? More often than not, many scenes were done simply because they *could* be done.

Science fiction films are subject to the same scrutiny, but critics must also consider two other elements: the verisimilitude or accuracy of the science (otherwise they would not be "science" fiction) and the success of the special effects. The former generally takes a back seat to the latter. A viewing of just about any Georges

Méliès film from the beginning of the twentieth century will show you that special effects superseded science, though not by much.

My purpose here is not to be hypercritical of SF cinema. Quite frankly, that is too easy and too unproductive, and too many books are already available which do exactly that. I do not believe in criticism for criticism's sake; you must have a reason, and it's even better if you can suggest improvements as you criticize. Besides, others have made careers out of these sorts of analyses, and I do not want to rehash what has gone before. I love SF films and I do treat them with respect. Ridicule is not my aim. These films, no matter how good or "bad," have given me enormous pleasure since I started watching them in 1956.

Over the years I have come across several definitions of what makes a film science fiction, and all of them, for one reason or another, have been unsatisfactory. The science in SF cinema, either bluntly stated or subtly implied, covers a lot of ground, thereby making any plausible definition difficult and often times cumbersome. This is very much like the definition of pornography: You don't know what it is but you know it when you see it.

Science is a straightforward word; it means the analysis and measurement of our surroundings—essentially, discovery.

But the key word in SF is "fiction," which is something imaginary or speculative by the standards of its time. There are many examples of yesterday's science fiction becoming today's science.

I personally prefer the word "speculative" over "imaginary" because speculative implies limitations and a basis in something real. For example, many films in this book *speculate* on the many possibilities of DNA and what can go wrong with it. No matter how imaginative that speculation may be, DNA has certain chemical, physical, and biological limitations to it, so speculations about DNA tend to be based on reality. In contrast, "imaginary" is essentially limitless. A writer or filmmaker can *imagine* time travel or teleportation, but at present there is no physical or real basis for either one.

The world of SF attempts to make the impossible possible, and there is much to be learned from this, especially as it applies to the biological sciences. We can glean significant insight this way. What biological science is necessary to make a werewolf or create a zombie? Can the hair of a werewolf come and go, can their teeth elongate and then shorten? Can organs and limbs be taken from cadavers and reused? Can DNA really be mutated at will to create new species? If skin is so pliable and flexible then can we really alter it to take new forms? Contemplation of these interesting questions constitutes the core of this book.

The collective brain trusts of SF cinema want you to believe these things happen all the time, and more often than not, what they propose is certainly credible. This credibility sets up an intriguing situation. Much of the moviegoing public views SF cinema as containing some element of realism, if only because what they see on the screen becomes real to them. They tend to trust the film's creators to say intelligent and "correct" things. In fact, however, much of the perceived real science is in a sense misinformation — mere pseudoscience or, as I prefer to call it, "reel" science. The main purpose of this book is to separate the *reel* from the *real* in science.

It is important to realize that in moviemaking, biological science always takes a back seat to the budget. Show business is more "business" than "show." The primary job of filmmakers is to make money on their movies, and if they also create art, then fine and dandy. And if they happen to educate the audience, then the cynic in me says it was an accident! It is unreasonable to assume that the creators

of SF movies are bona fide scientists or even had a passing interest in the subject. Even in cases where the moviemakers had an expert science consultant involved, many times what was shown or said was just enough science to move the plot along and attract a paying public. Filmmakers never sacrifice plot, pacing, or dialogue for fact; they make up their own facts to suit their particular cinema needs.

Since many of the SF filmmakers were uninformed about the real limitations of biological science, they in essence were bound by no rules and could be as inventive and creative as they wanted (within their budgets, of course). It is this inventiveness and creativity which induces professional scientists like myself to analyze what was shown on the silver screen and ponder the "what ifs" in life. What if the biological "science" portrayed in the movies could really happen? What if bone structures could grow like that? What if glands and hormones could transform animals into new species? What if DNA could really enhance and accelerate new cell growth? What if these unusual genetic mutations could really survive? What if brains could be transplanted between different species?

By analyzing the biological science in these movies we will be able to see how well the filmmakers handled the material. How well did the story, the screenplay, the individual lines uttered by the various actors represent the presented (or implied) biological science, and how well have some of these withstood the test of time?

SELECTION OF FILMS

The films presented in this book are not just random examples of SF cinema. They were chosen because they represent examples of interesting and thoughtful biological science — which unfortunately does not always mean interesting and thoughtful cinema. Quite frankly, some of the movies are dreadful. However, the biological science was the sole criterion for selection, regardless of whether the film could boast the best (or worst) script, acting, flow of dialogue, actors or creatures, or special effects. As the book progressed and I began organizing material according to the various scientific disciplines presented, I asked a further question: Which SF movies best fit each category? Which ones best exemplified, say, molecular biology, or which ones best handled the use of hormones, pharmaceuticals, and so on? The answer depended upon what decade the film was made.

When looking at all the films in chronological sequence, and noting the science discussed and the physical set-up of laboratories, on a decade by decade basis, some interesting observations can be made. In the 1930s and 1940s, a practical understanding of DNA was a long way off, so the biological science tended to center on glandular and hormonal effects. During the 1950s the Atomic Age was in full force, and most of the biological science during this decade centered on radiation-induced mutations. During the 1960s and 1970s some sophisticated biological science concepts began to appear in SF films, such as immunology, cryobiology, biochemistry, endocrinology, and virology. The 1980s and 1990s clearly belong to the DNA age, when the phrase "DNA" is frequently mentioned in movies without really knowing what it is.

The laboratory sets of the 1930s and 1940s varied little; the filmmakers were apparently satisfied as long as there were plenty of exotic-looking glass containers with bubbling fluids. Over the decades the lab sets have become more sophisticated, and it will be interesting to see how well a 1990s SF lab will compare to a 2050s SF lab. Perhaps it will look as "primitive" as a 1930s lab does in the 1990s.

Many of the films described in this book were based on a prior existing novel or story, but I will not comment on these original sources. My comments will be limited to what was shown on the screen. I will not even comment on the extant screenplays, since these were often altered in the filming. Some of the lines were ad-libs that the film's brain trust (the writers, producers, directors, and editors), for whatever reason, saw fit to leave in. Sometimes the lines were flubbed but the mistakes were kept in because the producers could not afford to reshoot the scenes. For these reasons I focus only on what actually made it to the screen. After all, this is what the paying public saw, and this is what has stuck in their minds, for better or worse. If some snippet of science was uttered that was factually incorrect though thematically sound, still it is what the public remembered.

And this is where my interest lies: When the viewers left the movie theater or rewound the video, they may have learned some biological science, and that is what they remembered. Was what they learned 100 percent correct, 100 percent incorrect, or somewhere in between? In other words, how accurate was the biological science both spoken and visual (such as the laboratory settings, set decorations, off-camera "implications," etc.), which made it to the screen? This is where I will distinguish between real and reel biological science.

Each film is broken down and analyzed in six sections: *Synopsis; Biological Science Principles Involved; What Is Right with the Biological Science Presented; What Is Wrong with the Biological Science Presented; What Biological Science Is Necessary to Actually Achieve the Results in the Film;* and *Could It Actually Happen.* The films are presented chronologically in each section, except in the case of remakes, which immediately follow the originals.

An overview of each scientific discipline provides evidence that the creators of SF films have reasonably kept up with current developments in the biological sciences. When something new was more or less understood by the general public (glands in the '30s and '40s, radiation in the '50s, DNA in the '80s and '90s), this information soon found its way onto the silver screen. In this respect, aspects of the biological sciences have been kept fresh and interesting throughout the history of SF cinema.

In summary, SF cinema has had a dramatic effect on how science is perceived by the general population. The world of SF makes everything look easy, and with everything easy, then when something goes wrong, people tend to be impatient and act accordingly. Though much of what transpires in SF cinema can actually happen it is nowhere near as easy as often presented. Missed are the countless hours of scientists toiling away in their laboratories, where failures peppered with a few successes are more the norm. In this respect, the life of a scientist has been "glamorized" into something more romantic than the day to day grind, drive, and passion required to do good and interesting science. It would be so nice if it were truly that easy.

Then again, who wants insects growing to the size of cars, or alien species draining our blood, or a giant blob absorbing the human race? *Could it happen?*

Read on, gentle reader, and learn.

Scientific Principles: An Overview

My interests are in the biological sciences and not in the physical sciences. (For that, I will refer the reader to Professor Lawrence Krause's outstanding book *The Physics of Star Trek*.) In order to more fully appreciate what I have to say about the SF films I have chosen for discussion in this book, I will provide a somewhat simplistic background in the scientific principles involved. Many of the details and minutiae of the biological disciplines are not required to appreciate the biology in the selected films.

The best place to start in discussing biological science is life itself. According to the trusty *American Heritage Dictionary* in my computer, life is "the property or quality that distinguishes living organisms from dead organisms and inanimate matter, manifested in functions such as metabolism, growth, reproduction, and response to stimuli or adaption to the environment originating from within the organism." That was a mouthful. In the simplest terms, life is that interval between birth and death. Others prefer an even simpler definition, which is the ability of an organism to reproduce. Not meaning to split hairs here,

but with this definition ("the ability of an organism to reproduce"), the mule, a product of a male donkey and a female horse (or a hinny, a product of a male horse and a female donkey) is sterile and not capable of reproduction, and therefore would not be considered life — which is nonsense. However, the sterile mule concept is an important one which I will get back to, since many of the life forms in SF films are essentially one-shot sterile creatures. In the SF film realm I prefer to define life as whatever exists between birth (or creation) and death, irrespective of how "it" was born, and whether it can reproduce itself.

Scientists understand life through experiment. In the strictest sense, an experiment is a study in which the investigator intentionally alters one or more factors under certain controlled conditions and monitors the resulting effects. This covers a lot of territory. Experiments can be very simple (such as just watching what is in front of you) or very complex. In SF films we have an even different set of circumstances. I would call these reel experiments, as compared to real experiments. Looking at it another way, real experiments are typically done in stages; you ask a question, get an answer, reformulate your question and get a different answer. You start with an hypothesis, which is a tentative answer to some question, obtain facts which support or refute the hypothesis, then ask additional questions to discern the correct answer. In essence, this is the Scientific Method. In reel experiments there is usually only one shot at it, and it usually works—"perfectly" (at least perfectly to a cinema-scientist)! And more often than not, with disastrous results.

Life itself is organized on many structural levels. There is a hierarchy of biological organization which is important. The smallest is the molecular, followed by the cellular, the multicellular, then the organismal (or species), and finally a biological community which is composed of several different species. Each one of these levels is important in the context of SF films, and there are many examples of movies which deal with each level. These will be discussed in due time.

Some of the general properties of life which I will discuss in more detail during the SF film section of this book are: order, reproduction, growth and maintenance, energy utilization, response to the environment, homeostasis (regulatory mechanisms), and evolutionary adaptation. Order is the characteristics of an organism which allow it to exist; reproduction allows individual organisms to reproduce its own kind; growth and development are the heritable programs in the form of DNA which allow an individual species to remain that species; energy utilization is the ability of an organism to take in energy and transform it into work; response to the environment allows organisms to optimally assimilate their surroundings to effectively carry out their functions; homeostasis is the ability of an organism to regulate and maintain its internal environment, such as temperature, even in a broad external environment; evolutionary adaptation is

how organisms evolved as a result of their interaction with their environment.

As a whole, organisms are greater than the sum of their parts. A dissected animal, for instance, will no longer function when broken down into its individual components, such as heart, liver, or muscle. This also applies to individual cells. They too will no longer function when broken down into individual components, like the nucleus, cytoplasm, membrane, mitochondria (the energy generator of cells), and so on. Furthermore, this also applies to the molecular level. Individual proteins will no longer function when broken down into their individual amino acids, the building blocks of proteins. This is where the concept of "vital forces" or "humors" of life originated centuries ago. Scientists at the time knew that all of life's components were necessary to work together in harmony for an organism to carry out its vital functions. This "vital force" is what separated living from non-living beings. In modern terms, we understand these forces to mean how well or efficiently an organism's structural arrangement is critical to sustaining life in any given environment. This is best seen with carbon atoms. In one form it is the basis of life; in another form it is the hardest element on earth, the diamond; and in an even different form it serves as the newly discovered "buckey balls" or buckminsterfullerene (a shape of carbon resembling soccer balls) which has very interesting properties. Depending upon the form, the same atom, carbon, can have radically different functions.

The general topics I will cover can be readily divided into three major categories or disciplines: biology, biochemistry (or molecular biology), and medicine. These three categories can, in turn, be further subdivided into anatomy, cell biology, physiology, microbiology, immunology, hematology, endocrinology, pharmacology, molecular biology, surgery, neurobiology, entomology, and, for lack of appropriate scientific terms, areas I call shrinkology and CULFology. Shrinkology is the term I will use which deals with body shrinking (hence the name), miniaturization, and tissue resorption. CULFology is an acronym which stands for the study of "Creating Unusual Life Forms," which probably applies to just about every SF film. (Another term for CULFology is cryptozoology, which is the scientific term for improbable beasts, such as the Yeti or Bigfoot. Many of the beasts in SF films are indeed improbable!)

To better appreciate what these terms mean as applied in this book, I will define them for you so there is no need to dash to the dictionary. Anatomy is the science of the morphologic structure of an animal's (or monster/alien's, as the case may be) body and the relation of its parts. Biochemistry, simply put, is the study of the chemistry of life. Cell biology is the study of how individual cells work and contribute to the overall organism's structure and function. Physiology is the science of how the vital functions and processes of living organisms normally function together. Microbiology is the study of micro organisms such as bacteria and viruses, earth-bound or otherwise. Immunology is the study of how organisms secure and protect themselves against diseases and infections. Hematology is the study of blood and blood forming tissues. Endocrinology is the study of internal or hormonal secretions and their behavior on cells and tissues. Pharmacology is the study of drugs, their sources, appearance, chemistry, actions, and uses. Neurobiology is the study of the nervous system. Entomology is the study of insects, small or big!

ANATOMY AND PHYSIOLOGY

We will first start with anatomy, how our body parts are assembled, how they work, and what life is composed of. One of the first biological "laws" scientists are taught is "form follows function," meaning the form of an organism or any of its parts is determined by how it must function. For example, respiration requires cells and tissues to capture oxygen (or an equivalent) and to release waste carbon dioxide. The structure of human lungs allows the function of respiration to perform very well. To protect the lungs we need to have them covered, and this is done with bones, skin, and muscle. Another important principle in the "form follows function" concept is that animal body forms are shaped by their interactions with their surrounding environment; certain forms will optimally interact with different environments in different ways. In colder climates bodies are protected by excess fur and feathers. On the molecular level there must be mechanisms which not only prevent individual cells from freezing, but also prevent the formation of ice crystals. When tiny ice crystals take shape they form as sharp spikes and are very deadly to our individual cells and tissues, and are the equivalent of a telephone pole going right through our bodies! (Nature has designed natural "anti-freeze"–like proteins that protect cells from the effects of freezing water. These anti-freeze proteins will be discussed later in this book.)

The simplest level of anatomical organization is the cell. Just in mammals, including humans, there are approximately 250 major different cell types, not to mention other multi-celled organisms such as insects, plants, mollusks, arthropods, fish, etc. Though each of these cell types has unique features which distinguish them from other cells, they do have many similar aspects. The primary similarities are a membrane (which contains the entire contents of the cell) the cytoplasm (the semi-fluid portion of the cell), and the nucleus (which contains the chromosomes and DNA, the genetic blueprints which make each cell). The differences in each cell type are primarily biochemical in nature and have to do with individual proteins and enzymes which carry on specialized functions (such as metabolism, cell structure, and cell physiology). It is these specialized functions that make, say, a muscle cell different from a lung cell, though they each have the same DNA; it is the expression of different bits of DNA which makes cells different from each other.

The science concerned with normal vital processes of organisms, primarily animals and plants, especially in regards to their normal body functions, is called physiology. The most intriguing aspect about physiology is how animals with quite diverse biology go about solving common problems. For example, how do single-celled organisms, mollusks, ants, and humans obtain energy from the environment and use oxygen? Also, the environments for these organisms do constantly change, so how do they adapt to carry on the same essential processes? The answer is anatomical and physiological adaptation, which solves the problems of searching for food, generating body heat, and responding to external stimuli.

Anatomy and physiology are dramatically intertwined in that the functions of animal tissues and organs are correlated with their structures. Animals have specialized cells, grouped into tissues and organs, which perform unique functions to help ensure the survival, maintenance, and reproduction of the species. The main organ systems in mammals are the digestive (mouth, pharynx, esophagus, stomach, intestines, liver, pancreas, anus), circulatory (heart, blood vessels, blood), respiratory (lungs, trachea, other breathing tubes), immune (bone marrow, lymph nodes, thymus, spleen, white blood cells), excretory (kidneys, bladder), endocrine (pituitary, thyroid, pancreas, thalamus, hypothalamus), reproductive (ovaries, testes),

nervous (brain, spinal cord, nerves, sensory organs), integumentary (skin, hair, claws, skin glands), skeletal (bones, ligaments, cartilage), and muscular (muscles).

Other physiological aspects which dramatically affect any given species are body size and metabolic rate. The amount of energy necessary to maintain an organism is inversely proportional to its body size. The smaller an organism the more energy needed to maintain its normal functions. A popular example is the comparison of a mouse to an elephant; though they have the same body parts and organs, the mouse consumes approximately 10 times the energy per gram of tissue than the elephant. Also, an animal's size, shape, proportions, and posture affect its interactions with the environment. Using the above mentioned example, imagine a mouse the size of an elephant. It would not be able to support its weight with its scrawny legs.

Another key feature of physiology is the homeostatic mechanisms each organism uses to regulate its internal environment. Even when exposed to diverse external environments, such as extremes of temperature, the animal's internal environments must stay the same for survival. In humans, whether in a valley, on a mountain peak, under water, in a hot and dry desert, or in icy snow, the body temperature is a relative constant 37°C, the blood circulation continues and remains at a pH of 7.4, digestion occurs unchanged, and breathing continues unabated.

DERMATOLOGY

Though on the surface skin seems simple, it is anything but. Much of what happens in the films described in this book pertains to skin, so it is only appropriate we spend some time talking about it. Actually, skin is one of my favorite organs. That's right, an organ. Believe it or not, skin is considered the largest organ of any vertebrate animal, whether on land, in the air, or in the sea. Though non-vertebrates, such as insects, have outer coverings which serve the same purpose as skin, those coverings are not skin in the technical sense.

For adult humans, the skin weighs an average of four kilograms and covers an area of approximately two square meters. Its major function is to act as a barrier against the surrounding environment, the outside world. Skin also serves as a shield to protect the delicate organs and tissues within our bodies. Skin is composed of three major layers of cells and tissues. The outermost layer is called the epidermis, and this serves three functions: It is a physical barrier, it protects against light (such as harmful radiation), and it is an immunologic organ (it helps fight off germs and bacteria). Subsequent layers, the dermis (or corium) and the subcutis, contain cells which perform specific functions that maintain the integrity and action of skin.

Each layer of skin has its own distinct specific cell types. The outermost layer, the epidermis is composed of the basal cell layer, primarily consisting of keratinocytes, melanocytes, and merkel cells. The next layer is called the squamous cell layer and is composed of Langerhans cells and the desmosome-tonofilament complex. Then comes the granular cell layer, the horny cell layer, the stratum lucidum, and the oral mucosa. The epidermal appendages consist of eccrine glands, apocrine glands, hair follicles, arrectores pilorum, sebaceous glands, and nails. The dermis contains collagen, elastin, ground substance, blood vessels, and nerves. The basement membrane zone contains ultrastructural components and chemical components. As you can see, skin is a complex and well organized structure.

In Western culture, the most important skin is that of the face. Because of the muscular complexity of the face and attached skin, great care is spent when doing alterations. However, in terms of genetic deformities, burns, or other accidents (such as chemical), potentially large sections of skin from the trunk and/or limbs needs replacing. There are several companies world wide specializing in methods to create artificial skin ("synthetic skin") and they have made great strides. Those most benefiting from this technology are burn victims requiring the immediate availability of large sections of skin. There is still substantial improvement yet to be made in this field, but the ready availability of actual and complete skin is rapidly approaching.

At first glance it may seem trivial, but the detail and nature of the sutures needed in closing skin cuts are quite sophisticated. Properly placed sutures are important to minimize such problems as skin-edge eversion, redistribution and minimization of tension, maintaining natural contours (especially around exposed and beauty areas), and the elimination of dead space, all while avoiding suture scars. The actual suture technique chosen for a specific skin wound closure depends upon which function of the skin is the most important, and the anatomical location of the specific area involved. Sutures are either interrupted, showing above the skin surface, or running, those which "snake" between tissue edges and are below the skin level. Furthermore, there are several different interrupted techniques, like vertical mattress suture, flask-shaped simple suture, horizontal mattress suture (with or without a bolster), and a half-buried horizontal mattress suture, as well as different running techniques, like a simple running suture, running locked suture, and a running subcuticular suture. Not all tissues, skins, locations, and sutures are alike. Mastery of them all is a remarkable accomplishment — an achievement many cinemascientists have easily attained.

Another major problem in dealing

with skin is what to do if the skin being closed or attached is not a perfect fit, or when too much tension at the attach site would cause tearing. What results are called skin flaps, which require small local tissue-movement procedures that fine tune and adjust the skin to the correct location, function, and cosmetic requirements of the individual. A local skin flap is a full thickness of skin transferred from one site to an adjacent site while still maintaining the blood supply. There are a variety of flaps and flap procedures, which are beyond the scope of this book. However, you get the idea that skin surgery, a necessary SF film component in attaching limbs, organs, faces, and other tissues, is a very complicated procedure.

HAIR

Now, a few words about hair follicles, since they do play a part in some SF films. Excessive hair growth in women is referred to as hirsutism. Otherwise, excessive body hair is called hypertrichosis. In either case, the underlying cause is typically hormonal and related to excessive testosterone, the male androgen hormone.

The growth of hair is cyclic in that there are distinct phases—referred to as growth (anagen), involution (catagen, when the hair follicle shortens and an anchored club hair is produced), and rest (telogen). Humans are born with approximately 100,000 hair follicles in the scalp. Each day approximately 100 hairs are shed from the scalp and about the same number of follicles enter the growth phase (anagen). It is the duration of growth which determines the length and volume of hair. The growth and rest cycles are regulated by complex interactions between the epithelium and the dermis skin layers in the scalp.

Hair on the body is called vellus hair, which is short, fine, and non-pigmented. These vellus hair follicles can become larger or smaller under systemic and other local influences which alter the length and time of growth (anagen) and the individual hair volume. Some sex hormones, such as the androgens (e.g., androsterone and testosterone) do regulate vellus hair growth, primarily on the face (beard), chest, and limbs.

The angle of growth of hair is coordinated in the same direction on various parts of the body. (This is important because the hair angle on humans is different than on, say, wolves; so for a werewolf to exist, his hair growth would probably have to change directions. Not an easy thing to do.) The rate of growth and type of hair are unique for specific body areas. Hair on the scalp is programmed to grow long, whereas that on the arm is rarely longer than one to two centimeters. Hair growth proceeds through distinct phases, namely, a prolonged growth or anagen phase, a short involutional or catagen phase, and a final resting or telogen phase. The hair cortex is produced by keratinization of cells in the hair bulb, and once keratinization has occurred, no amount of trimming or cutting or bleaching on the surface will have any effect on the rate or thickness of growth. Mature, thick hair is called terminal, while the fine hair growing over the body surface, as on the forehead and abdomen, is called vellus. Also, hair follicles have rapid metabolic rates.

Hair color is due to the amount and type of melanin cells present. Melanin cells produce color pigments. Dark hair contains more melanosomes (pigment producing cells) while light hair contains fewer. Red hair contains erythromelanin, while in gray or white hair the melanocytes in the basal layer of the hair matrix are greatly reduced in number.

MOLECULAR BIOLOGY / BIOCHEMISTRY

Biochemistry is the chemistry of living organisms and of the chemical, molecular, and physical changes which occur. There are five major chemical groups which comprise biochemistry. These are proteins (and enzymes), lipids (i.e., fats and cholesterol), carbohydrates (i.e., sugars), nucleic acids (such as DNA and RNA), and organics (such as vitamins and natural products). All cells and tissues of every life form on Earth are composed of these elements, and they impact, some more than others, every biological discipline discussed in this book.

Another area which will require some explanation, primarily due to the general population's misconceptions, is the area of molecular biology. Way too much pseudoscience surrounds this powerful and exciting area. At one time in the not too distant past, say, before 1972, molecular biology was considered the ugly sister of biochemistry. When genes were first cloned during the early 1970s, this marked the beginning of the current "Golden DNAge" of molecular biology. However, during the intervening years the discipline of molecular biology has essentially unified all of experimental biology and has come to mean the study of DNA, genes, and the proteins they make. These proteins determine the organization and functions of cells and tissues. The diverse fields of biochemistry, cell biology and cell physiology, developmental biology, genetics, and perhaps even neurobiology have all become unified under the umbrella of molecular biology. Quite a powerful discipline indeed. The fundamental rubric is that genes give rise to proteins, which give rise to organelles, which give rise to cells, which give rise to organs, which, in turn, give rise to organisms. You should also note that each one of these steps is also reversible; organisms make organs, which make tissues, which make cells, which make proteins, which make genes. Even though this appears to be circular, all life does revert back to genes. No ifs, ands, or buts about it, genes control everything. You mess with your genes and all sorts of bad things could happen. Much of the biological science discussed in this book can be related to good genes gone bad!

The essence of molecular biology can be divided into three separate phases, with each phase depending upon the complexity of what you are studying. The first phase is, simply put, the understanding of how gene expression is controlled so that everything is done at the right time for the right purpose. The second phase is how the structure and function of proteins, as determined by their own separate genes, carry out all the necessary biological functions, such as growth, metabolism, cell movement, muscle contraction, and the sending and receiving of chemical signals (as seen with nerve responses). Proteins are the workhorse molecules of cells. The third phase is the ability of proteins to cohesively dictate how cells, tissues, and individual organisms uniformly respond in the correct way to their individual environments. In essence, genes not only specify protein structure, they also specify the organization of cells and tissues.

The fundamental tenet of the molecular biologist is that the stunning diversity of life found in Nature is ultimately controlled by genes. The ability of genes to exert this control is elegantly determined by the simple chemistry of DNA (deoxyribonucleic acid) and its relative, RNA (ribonucleic acid). DNA is a double-stranded, helical nucleic acid molecule capable of replicating and determining the inherited structure of a cell's proteins. RNA is a single-stranded nucleic acid molecule involved in protein synthesis, the structure of which is specified by DNA.

DNA and RNA are linear polymers consisting of four types of nucleotide subunits. This "gang of four" is adenosine (A), guanosine (G), thymidine (T), and cytosine (C). (In RNA, the nucleoside thymidine is substituted by uracil [U]; the other three, A, G, and C, are the same.) The products of genes are proteins and linear polymers of 20 different types of amino acid subunits. (It should be noted that not all proteins contain all 20 different amino acids.) The properties of cells, tissues, and organisms are dependent upon the specific *sequences* of these 20 amino acids in proteins. In simple terms, genes (i.e., DNA) control these properties, their timing and amount of production, and the coordination of their synthesis with other proteins. The translator of all this DNA into proteins is RNA.

DNA molecules are extremely long unbranched polymers of the four nucleotide subunits (A and G are classed as purines; T and C are classed as pyrimidines), and each nucleotide contains a sugar group called a deoxyribose, a phosphate group linking the sugars together, and a purine or pyrimidine base in the middle. To help understand this, think of winding stairs. The handrails are the phosphate groups, the posts are the deoxyribose, and the stairs are the nucleic acids. An adenosine is bound to a thymidine and a guanosine is bound to a cytosine, so the "stairs" are composed of pairs of either A-T or G-C nucleotides.

In *each* cell in humans we have 23 pairs of chromosomes, for a total of 46. All in all, there are about six billion nucleotides, and each chromosome is about 50 to 200 million base pairs in length. (All of this is packed into each and every cell of our bodies!) The information in DNA is in its nucleic acid sequences, much like the sequences of letters to make up individual words. Sentences have structure, rules, and syntax, and so does DNA. Different sequences of letters make up different words, and different words make up different sentences. The same goes for DNA, in that its "alphabet" is the same but the sequence of letters (or nucleotides) distinguishes gibberish from, say, English. To continue with the same metaphor, the diagraming of sentences breaks them down into nouns, verbs, adverbs, adjectives, etc. Genes can also be broken down into analogous sections and moved around. The molecular biologist uses similar syntax principles in cloning DNA and genes.

Cell Biology

The cell is the smallest unit of living structure capable of independent life, composed of an outer membrane which surrounds protoplasm, internal organelles (if any), and a nucleus. The cell is as important to cell biology as the atom is to chemistry. All organisms from the single-celled creature to the multicellular of mammal, are composed of cells. Single-celled organisms are typically referred to as prokaryotes, and have no internal organelles ("little organs"); whereas multicelled organisms are called eukaryotes, and contain numerous organelles. In humans alone, there are over 250 different cell types. You have cells in your eyes which permit you to read this sentence, and different cells which allow you to turn the page. At some time during their existence cells must replicate their contents, utilize energy, interact with their environment, and reproduce themselves with exacting fidelity. This field of cell biology covers the areas of cell physiology and cell biochemistry. Needless to say, much of the cinemascience in this book involves cell biology.

Anatomically, the insides of eukaryotic cells are very complex, composed of such organelles as the prominent nucleus, mitochondria, Golgi apparatus, endoplasmic reticulum, ribosomes, vacuoles, lysosomes, peroxisomes, a cytoskeleton, and the extracellular matrix. As stated before the living cell is a unit greater that the sum of its parts. The nucleus contains the cell's genetic library; mitochondria are the main energy transformers; the Golgi apparatus finishes, sorts, and ships many of the products of cells; the endoplasmic reticulum manufactures membranes and performs other biosynthetic functions; ribosomes build cell proteins; vacuoles are involved in cell maintenance; lysosomes are digestive compartments; peroxisomes consume oxygen for metabolism; the cytoskeleton provides structural support and is involved in cell motility; and the extracellular matrix is involved in support, adhesion, movement, and development of cells.

Some SF films deal with cryobiology which is the ability to preserve individual cells at cold or sub-zero temperatures and achieve vascular stasis. Cold, as used in medicine, dates back to the Egyptians, around 2500 B.C., who used cold to relieve inflammation and treat injuries. Cryosurgery is a technique which removes heat from tissues by the application of cold, usually some cryogenic agent such as carbon dioxide ($-78°C$, solid) or liquid nitrogen ($-195°C$). When thinking about cryobiology and/or cryosurgery, note that the rate of temperature fall, the rate or rewarming, individual cell solute concentration, and the length of time cells are exposed to below-freezing temperatures in the $0°C$ to $-50°C$ range, are all key factors which determine a particular cell's or tissue's survival or destruction. Slow cooling produces extracellular ice formation, and rapid cooling leads to intracellular ice formation. Slow thawing also causes an increased concentration of cellular and local electrolytes.

Living organisms (and viruses, for that matter) have developed a number of mechanisms to enable them to survive freezing conditions. I am not referring to thicker skin or excessive hair, but rather to nature's creation of antifreeze proteins. These are special proteins created by nature to allow organisms to survive in freezing and very cold conditions, and serve the same purpose as antifreeze. All antifreeze proteins depress the freezing temperature of aqueous solutions, interact with ice surfaces, and inhibit ice crystal growth. In technological jargon, antifreeze proteins work by causing thermal hysteresis, which is the inhibition of ice recrystallization, and allowing the organism to supercool in the presence of ice without harming its life. Water molecules take on a certain form and shape as ice, which is detrimental to life. As I stated earlier, on a molecular scale, ice crystals in a living cell are the equivalent of a telephone pole going through your gut. And nature knew this, which is why these antifreeze proteins were created. These special types of proteins exist in such diverse organisms as bacteria, fish, and plants. Imagine a fish-sicle or a carrot-sicle! Scientists have cloned the genes which code for these antifreeze proteins and have inserted them into some plants, which in turn now survive in freezing temperatures. Typically, cold temperature slows metabolism, and antifreeze proteins allows metabolic steps to occur at speeds comparable to higher body temperatures.

All this is fine and well and is wonderful for individual cells or organisms which are not complex. However, when applied to humans there is a long way to go to have all cells in the body uniformly cryogenically protected. There are two common chemicals used to cryopreserve cells and tissues: glycerol and dimethylsulfoxide (abbreviated as DMSO). These chemicals work very well and adequately preserve the viability of cells. The problem is in rapidly getting these chemicals to all cells and tissues within the body before ice crystal formation destroys cells. This becomes a problem with deeply embedded cells and tissues that are harder to get to than those areas near the surface or near blood supply arteries and veins.

ENDOCRINOLOGY

Endocrinology is the science of hormones, which are chemical substances formed in one organ or part of the body and carried in the blood or circulation to another organ or body part. Hormones have the ability to alter the function and sometimes the structure of cells and tissues. There are three major varieties of hormones: those of females, those of males, and those gender neutral. Also, hormones come in a variety of chemical compositions, consisting of proteins, peptides, steroids, lipids, organic chemical forms, and combinations in between. Endorphins, the natural pain analgesic family of peptides, are also classed as hormones. Included in the world of hormones are various serums, glands and gland extracts, tissue extracts, cytokines, and other molecules which bring about cellular and tissue transformations.

The endocrine system, along with the nervous system, provides communication between cells and organs. Such systems are critical for the proper development and function of multicellular organisms such as humans. These systems regulate and permit growth and development; reproduction; homeostasis; and responses to stress, stimuli, and changes in the environment.

The term endocrine refers to the process of the secretion of biologically active substances into the body, and these biologically active substances are hormones. The targets of hormones are typically called receptors. These receptors have two functions. First, they must be able to distinguish one hormone from another. Second, the receptor must be able to transmit the information gained from the binding of the hormone into a meaningful biological response. For example, the hormone insulin is secreted by pancreatic cells, travels through the circulatory system, binds to its receptors on target cells, and triggers the metabolism of carbohydrates.

For proper homeostasis of hormonal control, a variety of mechanisms are available which regulate circulating hormone levels. There are mechanisms which stimulate production, cause spontaneous or basal release, cause feedback inhibition (natural suppression), synthesize, release, and inhibit other hormone production. Most of this activity is regulated by diet and the nervous system. In turn, hormones precisely regulate metabolic events. Alterations in hormonal levels, even subtle ones, can cause dramatic changes. Also, much hormonal regulation is controlled by circadian and hemi-circadian rhythms, with the best known being the menstrual cycle of females.

MICROBIOLOGY

This discipline primarily deals with microorganisms, including fungi, protozoa, bacteria, and viruses. Infectious agents, also classified as microorganisms, are composed of three major groups. The first is acellular and consists primarily of prions, virads, and viruses. The second is unicellular and consists of prokaryote (chlamydias, mycoplasmas, rickettsias, bacteria, and mycobacteria) and eukaryotes (fungi and protozoa). The third class is multicellular and consists of helminths (worms) and arthropods. More will be said during the individual SF films which deal with this aspect of biology.

Infectious diseases remain the leading cause of morbidity and mortality throughout the world, and the world's deadliest infectious disease is tuberculosis (or TB for short; one third of all people on Earth are infected with TB, and it kills about three million every year!). The overwhelming reason for this is that known measures of control and therapy are not applied. Just the simple task of washing your hands eliminates the vast majority of infections, including TB. Infectious agents may be defined as life forms that are capable of replication either free in the environment or in association with a host. Most, but not all, infectious agents are microorganisms; examples of large organisms are pathogenic worms, such as a gut-associated tape worm and blood flukes.

The host response to an infectious agent varies considerably and can include immunologic, inflammatory, or degenerative processes. For example, when humans are infected with *Mycobacterium tuberculosis* (tuberculosis), an immune response occurs which can cause serious damage to the host far and above anything the invading organism itself can cause. During an inflammatory response resulting from an invading infectious organism general manifestations of malaise and fever may result.

It is unknown just how many living agents are truly infectious to humans. Furthermore, new organisms and their method(s) of action are constantly being discovered and described. To be sure, the plagues of the Middle Ages are gone, but others (e.g., HIV/AIDS) are with us, and new ones will come in the future.

IMMUNOLOGY

Animals encounter a number of unwelcome intruders (collectively called antigens) in life and must have an adequate defense against them. Antigens are foreign substances that do not belong to the host organism and elicit an immune response. These intruders (antigens) are composed of life forms, such as viruses, bacteria, and parasites, and of certain chemicals, such as pollutants, allergens, and other pathogens. Though most are present in food and water, others are found in a variety of life forms. In addition, animals must also deal with abnormal cells and tissues within our own bodies and physiological problems here are called autoimmunity.

Immunology is the science primarily concerned with the various aspects of resistance to diseases referred to as immunity (active and passive), induced sensitivity, and allergy. There are a number of immune states, such as active, passive, acquired, innate, cell-mediated, humoral, maternal, and natural. Many of the cells that function in the immune response originate in lymphoid tissues. These cells mature and become competent in the body's defense by encountering antigens and destroying them.

Internal defense against pathogens includes nonspecific mechanisms, which are general defenses against a wide variety of pathogens, and specific mechanisms, such as antibody-mediated or cell-mediated immunity to specific antigens. The ability of our immune system to handle these antigens more or less determines the type of health animals experience. A healthy immune system usually means a healthy animal, and a poor immune system usually means poor health.

An integral part of the study of immunology, especially in light of what this book is all about, is the field of transplantation immunology. Many of the humans and creatures described and/or shown in the movies discussed in this book have had one transplant or another, either of an organ (brain, heart, lungs, etc.) or skin. Transplantation itself is the replacement of an organ or other tissue (such as bone marrow) with organs or tissues derived from another. Most transplants involve kidneys, livers, hearts, lungs, pancreas, intestines, bone marrow or skin (and in some of the films discussed in this book, brains). The easiest transplants are with "matched donors," in that the antigens of the cells and tissues of the donor are perfectly matched with the recipient; by matching the recipient's immune system, the donor's cells and tissues are not seen as "foreign" and therefore accepted. The most problematical transplants are between dissimilar organs and tissues, especially between significantly different species, such as between an animal and a human, and are called xenotransplants (xeno comes from Greek, meaning "other").

Each cell in our bodies has a type of antigen called histocompatibility antigens, abbreviated as HLA. When these HLA antigens are dissimilar in transplants (i.e., not matched) the organ or tissue is usually rejected. The mechanisms of transplant rejection are complex and consist of cell-mediated and/or humoral (antibody) aspects. For example, immediate or acute rejection of a kidney transplant is mediated by specific antibodies and takes place soon after the transplant is completed. Cell-mediated rejection mechanisms are chronic problems and performed by what we call T-lymphocytes, and principally occur during the first week after the transplant.

The consequences of cellular and humoral (antibody) immune responses to a transplanted organ or tissue may lead to a loss of function and necessitate the removal of the organ or tissue. Transplant rejection episodes occur in many transplant recipients and in some cases can be controlled by drugs that suppress the immune system. Once these immunosuppressive drugs wear off, the tissue or organ can still be rejected.

PHARMACOLOGY

Pharmacology is the science of drugs, their sources, appearance, chemistry, actions, and uses. I am one of those who believe in the concept of "better living through chemistry." The $300 billion global pharmaceutical industry thanks you very much for buying their products. Drugs are taken for both medical and nonmedical reasons.

A drug can be broadly classified. In essence, a drug is any therapeutic agent or substance (other than food, of course) used in the prevention, diagnosis, treatment, alleviation, or cure of disease or ailment. Moreover, a drug also refers to those agents which stimulate or depress, are habit forming or addictive, and used for health or recreationally. The most abused legal drug in the world is caffeine (the second is alcohol). Drugs can come from plants and are referred to as "natural products," or they can be made synthetically by chemical procedures (from the simple to the mind boggling complex).

Drugs essentially come in two varieties. Those which are agonists combine with certain receptors in the body to initiate the drug's actions; these receptors typically have high affinity or specificity for the drug. The other variety are called antagonists and oppose or resist the action of other substances; simply put, antagonists offer resistance. Examples of agonists are adrenaline and noradrenaline, which stimulate the heart and muscle. Antagonists of adrenaline are called beta-blockers, such as propranolol, which suppress heart and muscle activity.

The language of the pharmacologist involves a few words that deserve special focus. Ligand is a compound that activates a receptor and triggers its characteristic response. An agonist is a compound that interacts with a receptor to mimic the effects of the endogenous ligand. An antagonist is a compound that interacts with a receptor to inhibit its activation by an agonist or ligand. A partial agonist is an agonist that is unable to induce the maximum activation of a receptor. A nonselective agonist is a compound that activates a variety of receptors and is therefore nonspecific. These responses essentially summarize all the molecular effects of how drugs work.

HEMATOLOGY

One of the most interesting and dynamic parts of our body is blood, the "circulating tissue," which is composed of a variety of cell types, proteins, and other organic molecules. This fluid and its suspended elements circulate through the heart into the arteries, veins, and capillaries, transporting oxygen, nutritive molecules, and cells to the tissues and removing carbon dioxide and other waste products for excretion. In the average adult there are typically anywhere from six to eight liters of blood present. A unit of blood is about half a liter in volume, so an average adult would contain 12 to 16 units of blood.

Blood cells are typically classified into a variety of groups (or types), and currently there are 22 of these; the most familiar (and most common) are the "ABO" and the "Rh" groups. A blood group is a classification system based on genetically determined antigens located on the surface of erythrocytes (red blood cells). These groups or types become significant when considering blood transfusions, maternal-fetal problems, tissue and organ transplantations, disputed paternity cases, and genetic studies. Blood groups have even been found in ancient mummies and other anthropological specimens, such as Neanderthals, Cro-Magnon, and some dinosaurs! A blood sample taken from the Shroud of Turin, the disputed cloth which covered the body of Jesus Christ, was determined to be type AB.

The most common blood groups are the four "ABO" types, consisting of O, A, B, and AB. This classification depends upon the presence or absence of two distinct antigens: A or B. There is A positive, B positive, AB positive (when both are present), and the absence of these two is classed as type O. When considering all types within the 22 blood groups, there are a total of 192 different groups! In addition to these there are another 15 or so that are rare (and even more that are rarer still—

in that one individual or a small family are the only ones with that type!).

Normal blood cells have limited life spans and must be replenished in precise numbers by a continually renewing population of progenitor cells. In other words, our blood cells are controlled by a strict protocol of homeostasis. Each blood cell has its own rules and restrictions. Red blood cells must produce oxygen-carrying hemoglobin, and white cell B lymphocytes must produce antigen-recognizing antibodies. Blood clotting platelets come from another cell type, etc., etc.

NEUROBIOLOGY

Neurobiology is, simply enough, the biology of the nervous system. Nerves are whitish cord-like structures, composed of one or more bundles of myelinated or unmyelinated fibers coursing outside of the central nervous system (CNS), by which stimuli are transmitted from the CNS to a part of the body or back. It is the nervous system which distinguishes animals from all other forms of life, and there are over 230 different nerves in the human body.

The most intricately designed tissues on earth are those of the human nervous system. A single cubic centimeter of the human brain contains up to several million nerve cells, each of which may communicate with thousands of other neurons. All of this hard wiring allows us to learn, think, remember, and be aware of ourselves and our surroundings.

To maintain proper body physiology, our nervous system intimately interacts with our immune system (neuroimmunology) and our endocrine system (neuroendocrinology). However, our immune system and endocrine systems may take minutes, hours, or days to respond to a certain stimulus, whereas our nervous system takes only fractions of a second to respond. An impulse can travel down a neuron at over 200 mph! Therefore, information can go from our brains to our hands (or vice versa) in a few milliseconds. For animals to survive in their environment they must respond to stimuli immediately, and our nervous system handles that job very well. And it does this job very well via a combination of electrical and chemical signals that allows neurons to communicate with each other.

The nervous system receives and detects information from the external environment and transduces this information into electrical impulses. The cell types which do the lion's share of this processing are glial cells and neurons. Glial cells perform many functions in our bodies, chief of which are the transport of molecules from the blood supply to neurons, maintaining a constant external environment, and phagocytosis. Neurons transmit information to other neurons by use of electrochemical impulses and the release of neurotransmitters, which are small chemicals that cross a synapse to stimulate another neuron cell.

SHRINKOLOGY

The science of making cells, tissues, organisms, and bodies small (with intact control and normal functions) I've labeled "shrinkology." Smallness could be both qualitative and/or quantitative. The cell components can stay the same but the organism can physically be smaller (qualitative); or the components of the cell can be reduced in size, thereby making the cell — and subsequently the organism — smaller (quantitative). A qualitative change would be the comparison of a 400 pound man to a 200 pound man: They both contain similar organs, bones, etc. A quantitative change would be to make a 200 pound man the size of a mouse — with all the features of a man, only in miniature.

CULFOLOGY

This is the science of creating unusual life forms. (Another word for this is cryptozoology, which is the scientific term for the study of improbable beasts.) The size of the life form doesn't matter, whether a virus or a Godzilla — just the fact that what is created, in whole or in part, is not normally found in nature. For the purposes of this book, creating unusual life forms can range from body parts (such as a "living" hand) to intact organisms (such as a new species of silicon creatures) to altering the size and nature of an already existing organism or species (mostly through surgery). When I asked some non-scientists what they thought was meant by CULFology (after I explained the term), most responded with "Frankenstein's monster," so the general principles of this concept are present in people's consciousness. For a more detailed discussion of this topic I refer you to the section in this book which describes CULFology cinema.

ENTOMOLOGY

The science concerned with the study of insects is called Entomology. This involves their history, ecology, systematics, classification, biology, patterns, reproduction, etc. Most people know that a bug is a bug and an insect is an insect, but most also think that all bugs are insects and vice versa, which is not the case.

Insects outnumber all other forms of life on Earth. There are almost one million different species that have been classified, with many more estimated. No other life form even comes close to matching those numbers. Insects live just about everywhere — land, air, and (though rare) sea.

The Class Insecta is divided into more than two dozen orders, some of which are lice, beetles, earwigs, flies and mosquitoes, true bugs (such as the bedbug and chinch bug), ants, bees and wasps, termites, butterflies and moths, dragonflies, crickets, roaches, grasshoppers, fleas, and mantids. The largest order is Coleoptera, which is beetles and weevils, and is made up of over 500,000 species. Even the minor orders of earwigs (Dermaptera) and fleas (Siphonaptera) have over 1,000 species each! When man has left planet Earth, insects will still be here. The most telling aspect about the dominance of these animals is that in spite of the billions of dollars spent each year on insecticides, no single species of insects has ever been completely eradicated, merely controlled.

1 CELL BIOLOGY

This chapter on cell biology, and the following one on molecular biology, are the two largest chapters of this book. They are also the areas in which I have published the bulk of my scientific and medical research papers, so I am somewhat familiar with the topics. It is interesting how the creators of these films understood cell biology well enough to sell biology to the buying public. When examined in total (from 1936 to 1995), the area of SF cinema cell biology has done a good job in keeping interesting and entertaining biological science concepts on the screen.

The Man Who Lived Again (1936)

Synopsis: Dr. Laurience (Boris Karloff) is a "famous brain surgeon" who demonstrates a way to "swap" the thoughts between two brains. Laurience transfers his mind into another to not only obtain a younger body, but to also avoid the police. A colleague switches the minds back to their original bodies just before Laurience dies, thus saving the day.

Screenplay: L. Du Garde Peach, Sidney Gilliat, and John L. Balderston.

Biological Science Principles Involved: Cell Biology. Neurology. Psychiatry.

What Is Right with the Biological Science Presented: Dr. Laurience is presented as a careful scientist, and that is good. However, in the end, he wants to use his work for his own means, which is to transfer his mind into a younger, more vibrant body.

When Laurience shows the brain he keeps in a tank to his future colleague, Dr. Claire Wyatt, he rightfully comments, "The brain is dead. What I call the full content of the brain is gone forever." EEG (electroencephalogram) analysis would show a "flat line," indicating there is no brain activity. However, the individual cells could be metabolically alive and still be non-functional as complex brain tissue. This is an interesting concept, whether a brain is metabolically alive though "flat-lined." This brings up interesting possibilities should the procedure ever become available to instill brain activity in dead, diseased, or damaged brains. This is completely different from brain transplants, where a brain is put into a new body. Here we are talking about how to enhance or restore brain activity to an impaired brain.

Dr. Laurience (Boris Karloff, right) in his wonderfully equipped lab in *The Man Who Lived Again* (1936). The three-chambered glass vessel to Karloff's immediate left is a complex separatory funnel apparatus primarily used for solvent extractions. This glass funnel is seen on the benches of many SF films.

I like the idea of the female lead being a bright and intelligent scientist. More often than not, the females in SF films are nothing more than pretty window dressing, so having one as an interesting scientist (in 1936, no less) is refreshing. Many of my colleagues are females, and we are all enriched because of the tireless and enthusiastic work they do.

What Is Wrong with the Biological Science Presented: The movie's plot involves the simultaneous transfer of two people's thoughts into each other's body. The brain is composed of anatomically different regions, so which regions would be transferred first? Would the workings of, say, the medulla oblongata, be transferred first, and perhaps the substructures of the cerebellum next? If the frontal lobe is not as well connected in person one as in person two, what would the effect be?

Keeping a brain "alive" in a tank is difficult to accept. Laurience said, "Until now, it has never been possible to extract the thought content from a living brain and leave it alive but empty ... I can take the thought content from the mind of a living animal and store it as you would store electricity." Though the brain has electrical activity, it cannot be stored as in a battery. As we start the next century we still cannot extract and store thought content.

What Biological Science Is Necessary to Actually Achieve the Results in the Film: The human brain has an enormous capacity, and to have all thoughts (successfully) transferred to another brain would imply that each brain could handle each other's thoughts. It is interesting to contemplate transferring the thoughts of a genius into the physical brain tissue of someone who is not. In some respects, it would be like transferring the contents of a multi-volume encyclopedia into a short chap book (sort of like Frankenstein's Monster, who got the "abnormal brain" instead of the "normal" one). In this case, however, both brains would be viable...

If the capacity of the brain could be made to double (some experts say we use no more than 10 percent of our brains), which seems reasonable, then the ability to handle two independent thoughts may be possible. After all, there are psychiatric cases in which the individual has multiple personalities, so perhaps independent thoughts are possible.

Could It Actually Happen: The ability to capture thoughts, personality, the likes, the dislikes, etc., is one of mankind's favorite topics of contemplation. The mind gave rise to contemplation, and contemplation gave rise to the mind. Some have even considered the mind to be the "soul" of individuals, such as in the phrase, "body, heart, and soul." The mind is so complex that it is difficult to imagine technology existing which could completely "capture" the entirety of a person's being, though in the world of science and science

fiction one must never say never. The advantages of this would be interesting. Imagine being able to have the minds of, say, Albert Einstein, Walt Disney, and Groucho Marx forever captured to have around for future advice and entertainment. It would certainly impact society if this were available.

The Man with Nine Lives (1940)

Synopsis: Dr. Kravaal (Boris Karloff) is a scientist who develops a procedure called "Frozen Therapy" and accidentally freezes himself. Years later, Dr. Mason uses Kravaal's work as inspiration to continue to perfect the procedure. Mason visits Kravaal's cabin in the woods and, after finding the frozen Kravaal, successfully revives him. Kravaal tries to make some new freezing formula but can't exactly remember the steps. Kravaal is eventually shot for previous crimes.

Screenplay: Karl Brown, from a story by Harold Shumate.

Biological Science Principles Involved: Cell Biology. Cryobiology.

What Is Right with the Biological Science Presented: Cryobiology is a vibrant aspect of biology and medicine. Many labs throughout the world have the capacity to freeze and preserve cells and tissues from a variety of species. I myself have what we call "frozen down" thousands of cells and tissues and stored them in either ultra cold freezers ($-80°C$), or in liquid nitrogen ($-180°C$), with no difficulty reviving them years later. With small clumps of cells this is no problem. The real problem is with clumps of cells larger than a centimeter, since it would take too long for the cryoprotectant to effectively penetrate the inner cells and keep ice crystals from damaging the delicate cells and tissues. Once properly frozen, time is irrelevant, so cells and tissues can be kept for an indefinite period, as long as the proper storage conditions are not compromised. Some cells and tissues have been successfully kept frozen for decades, so no one really knows how long properly preserved cells will keep. Needless to say, only time will tell.

In the film, Dr. Bassett, the coroner, correctly states that, "No human being can live once his temperature drops below ten degrees of normal." This is correct. Temperatures much colder than that would slow too many vital processes for total recovery.

During the end sequences we see Dr. Kravaal mixing up some of his cryoprotectant and writing down the following formula: 80cc of one solution, 14cc of another, and 2cc of the "active agent." In reality, he gets pretty close to what we actually use in the lab for the cryopreservation of cells. Ever since my days as a graduate student, the actual "freeze-down" media I have used is composed of 80cc of growth media, 15cc of serum, and 5cc of the "active agent" (usually glycerol)! I would call Kravaal's statement a happy coincidence.

What Is Wrong with the Biological Science Presented: During the early part of the movie Dr. Mason is giving a demonstration of frozen therapy to his colleagues at the hospital. One of the doctors in the audience says, "The body is actually frozen. The kidney and digestive organs no longer function." Well, they certainly do continue to function, albeit at a much slower pace. If they did not function, they would be dead!

During this same demonstration Dr. Mason notes that the patient's body temperature has dropped to 88 degrees (normal is 98.6 degrees Fahrenheit) and says, "Metabolism at this time is practically nil. The only sign of life is the easy rhythm of the patient's heart beat. By subjecting the body to freezing temperatures, the repair

tissues of the body are greatly strengthened, while the malignant cells are retarded from growth." Nothing is right with those statements.

The most astonishing aspect of this same demonstration is the method Mason used to revive his patient, who is kept "frozen" (88 degrees is a long way from frozen!) for five days. Mason intubates her (puts a tube down her mouth) and pours hot coffee into her stomach! The patient then wakes up and says she felt no pain!

Later in the film Dr. Mason is talking to his nurse, Judy, in his office and reads the following passage from a book on frozen therapy written by Dr. Kravaal: "A mouse, heavily infected with cancer, was prepared for and subjected to freezing at 100 degrees below zero by means of liquid hydrogen. Revived at the end of two weeks, completely free of all cancerous growth." If only curing cancer were that easy! First of all, liquid hydrogen is more than 300 degrees below zero, not 100. And secondly, low temperatures would slow the metabolism of both cancerous cells and normal cells *the same way*, so there would be no advantage here.

Kravaal makes the following statement as to why his formula works: "The heart of the secret is that the protection (from death by freezing) must be given by inhalation, not by injection." There is no way the cryoprotectant could enter the body in sufficient quantities through the lungs. However, a combination of inhalation and injection would be more effective.

Finally, while attempting to duplicate his cryoprotectant formula, Kravaal says (after looking in a microscope), "blood sample taken from the subject after death shows blood corpuscles are being destroyed or disintegrating. A typical reaction to very heavy poisoning. Obviously, the solution is too strongly activated." Well, improperly preserved blood cells would certainly be "destroyed or disintegrated" when thawed, so that is correct. However, behaving as a typical reaction to poisoning because the solution is too strongly activated is chemistry I have never heard of!

What Biological Science Is Necessary to Actually Achieve the Results in the Film: Surprisingly, this is one of the few films discussed in this book where the reel science is very close to the real science of cryobiology. My hat goes off to the writers of the film.

Kravaal's freeze-down formula is essentially glycerol. Though it is the best general use cryoprotectant available for individual or small groups of cells, it would not be the best for an entire body, primarily because you could not get it to all cells and tissues fast enough (slow diffusion rates). If there is some way to carefully lower the body temperature (and there *are* ways to do this, though elaborate and expensive) in a rapid and uniform manner, then the concept of "frozen alive" is possible.

Could It Actually Happen: During the opening of the film the following words scroll across the screen: "Adding to the many miracles performed by modern [i.e., 1940] science that have accounted for the saving of thousands upon thousands of human beings comes its newest and most modern discovery — Frozen Therapy. Estimates of how long frozen therapy can produce a state of suspended animation range from days to years. But on the fact that disease can be arrested — that life can be prolonged, by freezing human beings in ice the medical world agrees. In research hospitals today men and women are alive and breathing — their bodies encased in ice." A body may be encased in ice, but it is not frozen. Furthermore, truly frozen bodies would not be breathing.

Donovan's Brain (1953)

Synopsis: Dr. Pat Corey, a brain scientist, conducts research on how to keep a brain alive without a body. A small plane crashes nearby and there is only one survivor, the wealthy Mr. Donovan. Since Donovan's body is crushed beyond repair, Dr. Corey removes the brain and keeps it alive. Donovan's brain slowly takes over Dr. Corey's body, forcing him to do everything that Donovan wants. Eventually, the brain is destroyed by a lightning bolt.

Screenplay: Felix Feist, adapted by Hugh Brooke, from the novel by Curt Siodmak.

Biological Science Principles Involved: Cell Biology. Neurobiology. Nutrition.

What Is Right with the Biological Science Presented: All in all, there isn't much right with the biological science presented here. However, an active brain does emit alpha waves, plus a few others.

The brain waves discussed in this movie can readily be detected with an electroencephalogram (or EEG). As a general rule, the less mental activity occurring in the brain, the more synchronous are the brain waves of an EEG. When a healthy person (Donovan is not a healthy person!) is lying quietly with closed eyes, then slow, synchronous alpha waves are present. When the eyes are opened and external stimuli is activating the brain, then faster beta waves are present. Beta waves indicate that the various parts of the brain are not in synchronization and mental activity is occurring. Even laying in a state of rest and trying to solve some sort of mental problem will activate strong beta waves.

Dr. Corey says to his staff, consisting of his wife (Nancy Davis; soon to be Mrs. Ronald Reagan!) and Dr. Frank Schrat, "In violent death, like the plane crash, organs of the body die at different times." This is quite true, not all organs "die" at a uniform rate.

What Is Wrong with the Biological Science Presented: This is a long list. In no particular order:

The brain inside the (non-sterile) fish tank is that of Mr. Donovan. This convincing laboratory setup from *Donovan's Brain* (1953) is in the home of Dr. Corey (Lew Ayres, left). The actress on the right, Nancy Davis, soon followed a different path and became Mrs. Ronald Reagan.

The monkey brain shown at the beginning of the film is seen in a fish tank-like setup with two bare wires coming out of the brain's cortical tissues, which are in contact with surrounding liquid. It is remarkable this did not short out!

Donovan's brain primarily emits alpha waves, characteristic of someone in a restful state. Donovan is anything but in a restful state, so this is wrong. If anything, Donovan should have strong beta waves!

Another major concern is that of the distance of the thought transference. Dr. Corey refers to this phenomena in the film as "clairvoyance." (Clairvoyance is the perception of objective events — past, present, or future — not ordinarily discernible by the senses; some may call this extrasensory perception or ESP.) Apparently, Donovan's brain could influence Dr. Corey from many miles away. Since this aspect of biology (and I am being kind) is beyond the scope of this book, I will not comment further.

Dr. Corey's colleague, Dr. Schrat, sums it up best regarding Donovan's brain by saying, "Impossible. It can't see, it can't hear, it can't feel." I agree.

What Biological Science Is Necessary to Actually Achieve the Results in the Film: Brain metabolism and physiology are in a delicate balance and would require sophisticated instrumentation and apparatus — more than what Dr. Corey had at his home — to keep a brain alive. Organ culture techniques have progressed significantly, and it is certainly possible to maintain intact organs in separate containers, even a brain. Necessary nutrients and other growth-promoting substances would have to be provided, a physiological temperature of 37°C would have to be maintained, and metabolic waste would have to be eliminated to assure survival of the organ. Such a setup is called a perfusion apparatus and pumps the necessary fluids to the organ's cells and tissues.

Could It Actually Happen: My comments on brain surgery/transplants found elsewhere in this book apply here as well. Quite frankly, I do not have a problem with keeping a severed brain alive. However, being able to mentally communicate with it is not likely to happen in our lifetimes.

Indestructible Man (1956)

Synopsis: Butcher Benton (Lon Chaney, Jr.) is sentenced to die in the San Quentin gas chamber and vows to kill the three men who framed him and sent him up. Dr. Bradshaw, a distinguished biochemist, revives Benton with electricity, which gives "The Butcher" incredible strength. Benton eventually dies from a massive charge from an electrical power plant.

Screenplay: Vy Russell and Sue Bradford.

Biological Science Principles Involved: Physiology. Biochemistry. Cell Biology.

What Is Right with the Biological Science Presented: Though a lot of biological science is either stated or implied, not much of it is right. However, I have to tip my hat to the screenwriters for having a wonderful imagination. In spite of the complete lack of scientific verisimilitude, this film is charming and entertaining.

After giving Benton his electrical shock, Bradshaw is seen contemplating whether he should also use adrenaline and amyl nitrate to help revive him. These compounds, especially adrenaline, are potent stimulators to get the heart going again, so at least they got something right.

What Is Wrong with the Biological Science Presented: Where to start? There is the cyanide poison, the excessive cell growth, the very dense skin, the ability to withstand bullets (and a bazooka shell, and fire), trying to obtain a blood sample from a dead body (no heart pumping means no blood flow which means no ability to remove blood from a standard arm venipuncture!), not to mention that terrific jolt of 287,000 volts of electricity! And finally, Bradshaw is doing research on finding a way to cure cancer, a good use of his time, so what did he want with Benton's body, which is apparently cancer free? This is never explained, and taken all together it boggles the mind.

Animals (and humans, in particular) need oxygen to survive. Oxygen binds to iron bound up with the hemoglobin proteins found inside our red blood cells (RBCs). The less hemoglobin we have the less oxygen we can use, thereby prohibiting physical activity (depending upon the degree of oxygen starvation). At higher altitudes there is less oxygen, which is why mountain climbers often have to bring tanks of oxygen along to supplement their activity. Physiologically, oxygen depleted RBCs enter our lungs to become reoxygenated by the inhaled air. Over the eons nature devised a very efficient mechanism to do all this. However, metabolically, there are many instances in which this entire process can go awry, one of which is poisoning by cyanide. As explained during a voice-over at the beginning of this movie, Butcher Benton is killed in the San

Quentin gas chamber for his crimes. The criminal is strapped into a chair inside a sealed chamber and a cyanide capsule is released into a container of acid, which causes the release of cyanide gas. This cyanide gas is inhaled into the lungs and quite efficiently inhibits respiration, thereby quickly causing death in a simple, painless manner. (For those of you who are metabolically inclined, cyanide inhibits the transfer of electrons down the respiratory chain to molecular oxygen by stopping the reoxidation of reduced cytochrome oxidase by oxygen. The action of cyanide is essentially an irreversible process.) For Bradshaw to revive Benton, the cyanide bound to the enzyme cytochrome oxidase must be completely washed out. And that, gentle readers, is no mean feat! And it's virtually impossible with a lifeless corpse.

Bradshaw hooks up a liter-sized bottle to Benton's arm vein and drains a liquid into his body. This liquid is never identified, and we can only guess it may be some mutated virus or bacteria cocktail which can gobble up cyanide and metabolically inactivate it, plus some growth factors and vitamins thrown in for good measure.

The 287,000 volts of electricity Bradshaw gave Benton would be enough to fry all the delicate tissues in the body. So much for the subtle approach. Even though Bradshaw says after giving the charge, "The heart muscle is simply responding to a terrific electrical shock … it does prove that the [heart] cells still function," it is amazing that there is any heart tissue left to function after that jolt!

It is interesting to note that while Benton is being revived after the jolt, the narrator explains, "Electrical voltage had burned out his vocal cords, yet it hadn't destroyed his brain. He [Benton] knew who he was. The tremendous electrical voltage that Dr. Bradshaw had given Butcher had increased his cellular struc-ture to the point where he was no longer a man. Dr. Bradshaw's experiment had created a vicious, brutal animal with an almost inconceivable amount of strength." I can accept the burnt out vocal cord bit (like I said, everything would be burnt and cauterized), but increasing his cellular structure is pure bunk. The severe electrical charge could have solidified his skin tensile strength by increased skin keratinization — but not to the point where it could inhibit the penetration of bullets; a 45 caliber slug would have easily penetrated even the toughest of skin.

If Benton's body cells truly did "multiply a hundred times, perhaps thousands" as stated by Bradshaw, then you could imagine the size of the end result. It would make Godzilla look small! What Bradshaw (and, of course, the screenwriters) actually meant is that the *density* of Benton's cells is increased, giving him better "armor" and strength. There is some evidence of this because Bradshaw later attempts to obtain some blood from an arm vein and the syringe needle bends when trying to puncture the skin on Benton's arm, causing Bradshaw to say, "The tissue must be a nearly solid mass of cells."

What Biological Science Is Necessary to Actually Achieve the Results in the Film: Ignoring all the electricity problems one still has to deal with, the deadly cyanide poisoned Benton's ability to utilize oxygen. This serious problem would have to be overcome first and foremost. Meanwhile, his brain is being robbed of oxygen, critical for normal brain function. There are what are called "chelating agents" which serve the purpose of binding up certain atoms and molecules. Some of these chelating agents have been designed to bind with cyanide, thereby making it harmless. Administering the chelating agent antidote is not really the problem here. Getting it to the person before significant metabolic damage occurs is.

After just a few minutes of being deprived of oxygen the brain begins to lose its normal functions. Anything after 10 minutes and the brain is no longer functional, effectively "brain-dead." By the time Benton's body arrives at Bradshaw's lab, several hours (at least) have transpired, and by then the brain would certainly have been beyond salvage. The only thing worth saying is that perhaps the massive jolt of electricity given to Benton had somehow rewired his neural and brain circuitry back to normal.

Administering the chelating agent presents another problem. Benton is dead and therefore has no pumping circulation system. With a normally beating heart, injected fluids rapidly disperse throughout the body, but when that heart is no longer pumping then it would be virtually impossible to effectively administer enough of the chelation agent to all body tissues. To do this, Bradshaw would have to connect the body to a heart/lung machine which could then artificially pump fluids and maintain the necessary physiological pressures for effective circulation. Then he could administer the chelation agent, absorb up all the cyanide, flush it out, and prepare him for the electrical charge.

For skin to become a "nearly solid mass of cells" would require extensive keratinization of the tissues. Keratin is a scleroprotein present predominantly in hair and nails. It contains a relatively large amount of sulfur, and there are at least 11 different protein forms known to exist. Keratinization is the excessive formation of keratin to form a horny layer, such as that found at the stratum corneum, the outermost layer of skin, composed of dead and fully keratinized cells. This outermost layer of skin is what sloughs off. Well known animals with very thick, keratinized skin are the rhinoceros and the crocodile. Again, the massive electrical charge may have somehow stimulated the layers of skin to differentiate and harden into keratin.

Could It Actually Happen: Perhaps you can revive people with electricity. After all, physicians do this with their cardiac paddles to restimulate the heart once it stops, so this really is not a stretch. As always, the issue is the amount of time between heart stopping and starting. However, at stated above, reviving someone loaded up with cyanide poison is out of the question. Having skin become very dense has been observed in some cases of psoriasis and eczema and other dermatological abnormalities.

Giant from the Unknown (1957)

Synopsis: Professor Cleveland, an archaeologist, and his daughter go up into the mountains of Southern California to look for traces of 500-year-old Spanish explorers. During his expedition, Prof. Cleveland discovers a Spanish Conquistador's burial ground. As a result, a giant conquistador, nicknamed the "Diablo Giant" awakens and kidnaps the professor's daughter. The Giant is eventually caught and ultimately dies by falling into the raging water of a dam, à la *The Amazing Colossal Man.*

Screenplay: Frank Hart Taussi and Ralph Brooke.

Biological Science Principles Involved: Cryobiology. Infectious Disease. Biochemistry.

What Is Right with the Biological Science Presented: Professor Cleveland, after discovering that the Giant is alive, comments, "...I have come to the conclusion that there is some unusual and unknown substance in the earth up here that acts as a preservative. Some high incidence, possible of tannic acid from oak leaves or from some other organic substance ... something that sustains life." Tannic acid has been used since antiquity and does indeed have some preservative properties if used in the right way. Its ability to preserve cells and tissues is a direct function of the amounts used, though how enough necessary to preserve a human body got there 500 years ago will have to remain a mystery.

What Is Wrong with the Biological Science Presented: Though tannic acid does, as discussed, have some preservative properties, it cannot "sustain life." When the Diablo Giant woke he has all his mental faculties intact, which just can't happen. Tannic acid would not be able to reach all the cells and tissues of the body in a uniform manner so the degree of preservation would vary widely throughout the body. The brain would certainly not be functional, not to mention capable of creative thought. For example, when the Giant kidnaps Cleveland's daughter she tries to get away in a Jeep, but it doesn't start. The Giant comes up to her from the passenger side, pushes the passenger seat up and grabs her. Well, how did the Giant know how to instantly deal with the Jeep's seat?

During one scene Professor Cleveland speculates to Wayne Brooks that the conquistadors "...arrived here and were stricken with an epidemic. All of the men died, but not Vargas [the giant]. His unusual strength sustained him, but he fell into a deep coma. Now the Indians mistook this for death and buried him at a spot near where we found the armor. Now, fantastic as it sounds, I believe that his body has been preserved for centuries." To add more outlandishness to this, Brooks further adds, "And during the electrical storm, a bolt of lightning struck near enough to rekindle the spark of life." No doubt this is inspired by the "birth" of Frankenstein's Monster.

The earlier scene where Brooks shows Cleveland the lizard found inside the geode deserves comment. The geological forces which are necessary to form geodes are so severe that in no way would any kind of organic material, no matter how well preserved, survive, not to mention be intact and alive! Brooks does recognize the significance of all this because he comments, "...that ugly little fellow [the lizard] is a leading character in a thesis I am preparing on the subject of physical antiquities." It is interesting that Brooks classifies an "extinct" lizard as a "physical antiquity." If it is extinct then how could it be alive?

What Biological Science Is Necessary to Actually Achieve the Results in the Film: There were a couple of things mentioned in this film which are of interest. The central plot of the movie involves the ability to (functionally) preserve a human. The writers suggest tannic acid as the main ingredient. However, what is more intriguing is Cleveland's mention that the conquistadors were stricken with an epidemic. Here is where some interesting biological science can be introduced. For the sake of argument let us assume that indeed the Giant did awaken and that some epidemic did put him in a coma-like state. What kind of epidemic would do that? This epidemic would have to be either a virus (or combination of viruses) and/or a bacteria (or combination of bacteria). It is doubtful that a bacteria would be involved, since they would need to survive and therefore consume the Giant's cells and tissues. This leaves us with some type of virus or viruses. There are not any known viruses which have these properties, though perhaps some day either nature will mutate one or some scientist somewhere could genengineer one which could do exactly this. The body's metabolism would have to slow down, similar to a hibernation mode, to conserve energy, and a virus could potentially do this. Another issue is the level of water needed to sustain life. If there is no evaporation, nor any sort of water loss, then vital fluids and tissues could be preserved. There would have to be some sort of virus that caused excessive buildup and retention of water. That too is possible.

Could It Actually Happen: There is no way a lizard (or any another form of life for that matter) could survive in a rock, not to mention a geode. What did the lizard eat? What about water?

Preserving a body and successfully reviving it with some jolt of electricity is certainly possible, though the conditions would have to be perfect. Physicians use electrical charges as a matter of routine when trying to restart the heart, so this is not really at all farfetched. Perhaps some sort of virus could bring about a type of hibernation.

The Blob (1958)

Synopsis (applies to both this and the 1988 versions): A small meteorite lands, and the blob-like content attaches itself to a man, eventually completely consuming him. Other humans are absorbed into the growing blob. Eventually it is learned that cold temperatures inactivate the blob, and it is taken to the Arctic for storage.

Screenplay (1958 version): Theodore Simonson and Kate Phillips, from an original idea by Irvin H. Millgate.

Biological Science Principles Involved: Cell Biology. Cryobiology. Infectious Disease.

What Is Right with the Biological Science Presented: Without knowing all the facts, the physician, when confronted with the blob digesting an arm of a man, tells his nurse, "There's a man here with some sort of parasite on his arm which is assimilating his flesh at a frightening speed." Because of its obvious gelatinous appearance, its pulsations, and the fact that it was literally crawling up the man's arm, calling the blob a parasite is a reasonable guess by a country doctor.

As the blob completely absorbs humans it grows in size and mass. Initially, after assimilating its first human, the blob is about three feet long, two feet wide, and about two feet tall. The physician (meal #3) sees the blob in his office and says to his nurse (meal #2), "I don't know what this is but it's got to be killed before it gets any bigger." The physician knew it completely absorbed the old man it first came in contact with, and also knew that this gelatinous mass could grow significantly larger. The doctor then blasts it with a shotgun which, unfortunately, has no effect.

When the physician and his nurse confront the blob in their office, the doctor tells the nurse to throw a bottle of "trichloroacetic acid" on the blob. After being doused with this acid the blob's naturally dark red surface briefly turned a lime-yellow color, pulsed some, then became normal. Trichloroacetic acid (or TCA for short; CCl_3COOH is the chemical formula) is a very common reagent in most medical and research labs throughout the world. Medically, it is used as an astringent (contracts tissues to help control bleeding) antiseptic in 1–5 percent solution or as an escharotic (a caustic or a corrosive) for venereal and other warts. In research labs it is primarily used to precipitate proteins for use in their characterization and purification.

TCA is a very mild acid, and having it splashed on your skin would cause no burn marks, no absorption, no dissolving. You should get it washed off as soon as possible, and certainly do not get any in your eyes, but there would be nothing permanent. Some with sensitive skin may experience a slight burning sensation or a local inflammatory response, but they would quickly recover after washing the area. Blob "skin" may act differently when exposed to TCA. After splashing the blob with TCA there is some sort of response, and the reagent did affect or irritate the blob surface, though it was short lived. What this suggests is that perhaps there may be other acids which could have an even stronger effect on the blob and be used as a defensive and/or controlling weapon.

To explain why the cold temperatures adversely affect the blob, some background information on what the blob is is needed. So, what is the blob? Or, more correctly, what could it be? Let us look at the facts. It first arrives inside a small meteorite and absorbs a human. Absorbing is a key piece in this. With enough mass the blob moves about by rolling on the ground and oozing under doors. The mechanism used to do this is simpler than you may think. Within our bodies cells are constantly moving about and being squeezed into the tightest of spots. There is a natural elasticity to our cells—the result of a web-like network of tiny tubes and scaffold-like structures within animal cells that can be taken apart and re-assembled with amazing speed and accuracy. At any one time these internal cellular structures can be solid-like (a "sol") or gel-like (fluid), and the alteration from sol to gel status is called "sol-gel transformation." Much cellular movement is attributed to sol-gel transformations that occur inside cells. To move, these tubules lengthen (sol state), thereby pushing out the membrane, and then shorten (gel state). In essence, this is the basis of amoeboid-like movements. It is a treadmill-like mechanism inside cells, and the lengthening and shortening of these parts help cell movement.

The blob moves by rolling around on the ground using sol–gel-like transformations on a massive scale. This would in-

volve an efficient sol-gel transformation mechanism that provides enough energy as momentum that movement is possible. Directed movement in this manner is called "taxis" and is usually directed to a food source or directed away from a potential threat. Taxis, or movement, occurs when a chemical signal is received by a receptor, thereby causing some type of action to occur. There are probably several types of chemical receptors on the blob's surface (food, irritation, cold, heat receptors) that are able to send some sort of signal to itself that make it move forward or retreat.

Cold temperatures disrupt sol-gel transformations and keep the cellular machinery in a gel-like state. The blob could have sensed the cold temperatures, and its sol-gel transformation instincts caused the blob to retreat from the cold meat freezer. This is one of the more interesting metabolic consequences of a life form which depends entirely upon a functioning sol-gel system and a friendly environment for survival. CO_2 extinguishers work by sending ultra-cold CO_2 gas towards the flame, depleting it of oxygen and thereby causing it to go out. The ultra-cold CO_2 also severely inhibits the blob's sol-gel transformations, it would have literally frozen had not the blob retreated.

The blob is shot at several times, all to no effect. There is no central nervous system in the blob, so minimal pain is felt with each shot. The blob also does not have a circulatory system, so a bullet would have no physiologically disrupting effects. After being shot, blob matter does not splatter off, so the blob must be composed of high tensile strength carbohydrate polymers, much like a thick jam.

What Is Wrong with the Biological Science Presented: When describing the way the blob absorbs flesh, the physician says to his nurse, "It absorbs flesh on contact, like an acid." Though the mixed metaphor imagery is effective, there is a difference between absorbing and dissolving. Some acids do indeed dissolve flesh on contact, and the chemical reaction which results is ultimately one of destruction; there is loss of mass. Absorbing, however, implies a metabolic benefit and definitely some sort of mass gain. You can have one or the other but not both.

Of all the acids to throw on the blob I would not have picked TCA (trichloroacetic acid), simply because it is too weak. The nurse grabs the bottle of TCA (when instructed to by the physician) and splashes it on the blob when there were other bottles, probably of a stronger acid (sulfuric, hydrochloric, nitric), available she could have used.

The surface tension of the blob is unacceptable. Surface tension is the intermolecular attraction of the surface of a liquid in contact with air and its tendency to pull the molecules of the liquid inward from the surface. As the blob rolls along its path there would be some sort of residue left on the ground, and we see none. Nor is there anything which gloms onto or sticks to the surface as it rolls along. The blob has a shine to its surface, so there must be some sort of liquid present. To have the surface tension seen in the film, the blob would have to be composed of some high tensile strength carbohydrate polymer capable of interacting with protein sol-gel transformations. All of this could function without a central nervous system, via the chemoreceptor system described. Another problem with the surface tension has to do with the size of the blob. When it became significantly larger than ten feet long and ten feet tall, there would have been some serious movement problems. Something of that size would collapse upon itself from the sheer weight and be more pancake-like than amoeboid-like.

The act of absorbing animals and humans would have metabolically given off a lot of heat, but none is seen. There is no steam rising from the blob, nor are there mucoid-like tracks left as the blob moves around.

What Biological Science Is Necessary to Actually Achieve the Results in the Film: Though understated in this film version, the first and most important thing is that the blob had all the necessary enzymology, the metabolic machinery to completely degrade human protein, DNA, fat, lipids, carbohydrates, bone, etc., and convert it to blob mass. This is very important because if all the blob needed was carbon, hydrogen, oxygen, nitrogen, minerals, etc., it could easily have consumed plants, trees, shrubs, grasses, etc., which were plentiful and everywhere. However, the blob is not a vegetarian but a flesh eater. Therefore, the blob could not metabolically handle the carbon-carbon biochemical bonds found in plants, but needed those found in earth animals. This would limit the biochemical basis of what chemistry makes up the blob, and would also provide some insight as to how to go about killing it. Perhaps some of its metabolic pathways could have been poisoned.

Since the blob could locate humans (animals) to absorb them, it must have some sort of chemoreceptor system on its surface to identify flesh (much the same way a bee knows where to fly to a flower for honey). Animals give off their own peculiar scents, and these blob chemoreceptors act like a nose (in that certain chemicals are detected as a scent, giving the blob a sense of direction for movement). As such, the blob would have highly sensitive chemoreceptors, because the identification of food sources is a high survival need.

Since the blob primarily absorbs humans then it absorbs what humans are composed of, which is primarily water. With that much water, the blob would be sloshing around too much, so it must have a system where it would eliminate the excess water. Therefore, there should be a liquid trail left behind its movements; there was not.

The level and degree of the sol-gel transformations would determine the movement and direction of the blob. This movement would be somewhat slow. At the leading edge of the blob the sol transformations would occur, causing outward movement. At the opposite end of the blob, gel transformations would simultaneously occur, causing retreating-like movement. The combined coordinated action would be treadmill-like.

Could It Actually Happen: No. It would not take much, but the blob's biggest problem would be its own weight. After attaining a not-very-large size, the blob would crush itself with its own weight. Also, at very large sizes it would spread out, pancake-like, and no longer be an amorphous mass. All in all, if the blob were real it would be a very weak life form.

The Blob (1988)

Screenplay (1988 version): Chuck Russell and Frank Darabont. (The major difference between the two films is the level and sophistication of special effects. In this area, the 1988 version is far superior. Even in terms of biological science the 1988 version is better. Otherwise, the essential plot is the same.)

Biological Science Principles Involved: Cell Biology. Microbiology. Cryobiology. Infectious Disease.

What Is Right with the Biological Science Presented: In keeping with the advances made in the area of special effects, the anatomical realities of a life form dissolving and absorbing humans is shown as it would most likely happen. Bits and pieces of humans would be absorbed at different rates. Also, it is made very clear that non-digestible parts, such as jewelry and parts of clothing, are left behind by the blob, as well as a trail of ooze indicating where it has moved.

The blob has a rough, gelatinous, irregular surface to its structure which would be appropriate for the composition it has. Though there is no central nervous system, there are also no visible internal organs, which would be in keeping with a blob-like structure.

The first man who came in contact with the blob is graphically shown during mid-absorption, and only his body above the diaphragm area is still intact. The rest is blob. The blob's ability to rapidly absorb indicates the presence of some very potent dissolving processes and fast metabolic pathways.

As in the 1958 version, this 1988 blob is also a carnivore, in that it travels through some woods and does not eat any of it. It too prefers animals and humans.

When frozen the blob crystallizes. Pieces that break off appear to have regeneration capabilities. This then begs the question, what is the smallest piece that can regenerate itself?

It was shown that the blob moves through water with relative ease. The blob is able to slither and snake its body around in water, thereby causing movement. This, plus some degree of buoyancy, contributed to its ability to "swim."

Finally, liquid nitrogen (about -180°C) is used to completely freeze and crystallize the blob. Liquid nitrogen would rapidly freeze the blob and would keep it frozen for a brief time. It would then have to be quickly disposed of before thawing took place.

What Is Wrong with the Biological Science Presented: This blob moves way too fast. This is not credible. The blob is seen climbing walls, which would have been *somewhat* credible when it was relatively small, but at the size seen, the blob's sticking ability should have been overwhelmed

To move, the blob must have internal proteins, similar to actin and myosin, the key components in muscle, which stretch and contract. A sol-gel mechanism is used to propel the blob's mass, in a treadmill–like fashion as it moves about. As seen in this photograph from the 1988 version of *The Blob*, the distinct surface convolutions indicate that the blob has internal structures (organs?). An internal protein meshwork is pulling and tugging on the surface membrane skin, giving it its distinctive appearance.

by its sheer weight, and bringing it crashing to the floor.

This 1988 blob is shown to deploy pseudopod-like tentacles on command. For this to actually happen would require a completely different anatomy — essentially the same as what an amoeboid life form would need. Separate muscles for the release, flex, and contraction of the tentacle to occur would be necessary. Related to this is the blob's ability to bend steel doors and break loose door hinges. The forces necessary to do this are far beyond what any mass of tissue can do. Near the end of the film the blob is in a sewer system and is able to break through the street blacktop and manhole covers. That stretches credibility too far.

An explanation brought forward in this film is that the blob originated from government biological weapons research. Two government officials have the following exchange.

Official #1: "We suspected that conditions in space would have a mutating effect on bacteria."

Official #2: "Its activity must be what threw the satellite out of orbit."

#1: "Correct. Our little experimental virus seems to have grown up into a plasmid life form that hunts its prey. A predator. It's fantastic."

#2: "The organism is growing at a geometric rate. By all accounts it's at least a thousand times its original mass."

First they talk about bacteria, then end up talking about viruses and plasmids. Conditions in space are indeed different from that here on Earth. In space there are a lot more harmful radiations; and though long term exposure may alter some bacteria, there are not enough data to support this (there eventually will be, but the mutations may not be harmful). A virus and a plasmid are distinct entities, though if you stretched things somewhat a virus and a plasmid could be interchangeable. All organisms grow at a geometric rate — only to a certain degree, then stop (usually as a result of space limitations and available food). "A thousand times its original mass" is an interesting statement. When we first see the blob emerge from the "meteorite" (aka satellite) it appears to have the mass of about two pounds. A thousand times that is two thousand pounds, or one ton. By the time this conversation takes place in the film the blob is many tons in mass, perhaps as much as 100 tons. (A hundred tons is 200,000 pounds. Assuming the average human weighs 180 pounds, then the blob would have had to consume about 1100 humans to weigh 100 tons.)

What Biological Science Is Necessary to Actually Achieve the Results in the Film: While on the ceiling, some drops ooze off the blob and fall onto the surface of a wood desk below it. The surface of the wood desk where the drops landed is immediately dissolved with acid-like effects. During the eating process humans produce a lot of low pH stomach acid that helps dissolve the food. This fluid is only present when eating. The blob could have had something similar, in that since it was in an eating frenzy all its digestive juices were flowing and it would therefore have been easy for a glob of digestive juices to drop off. Since the blob rapidly dissolves its food, it would have to have powerful digestive juices — and the results seen on the wood desk are excellent proof of the effectiveness of these juices.

To dissolve tissues and bones immediately would require the presence of a strong acidic environment, plus an environment capable of allowing large volumes of some powerful enzymes to work. Inside the blob would be machinery for the rapid degradation of protein found in tissues and cells. With all this internal activity, the surface membrane would have to be strong enough to be both an adequate barrier and a container.

As the blob consumes more humans and grows in size, it shows an ability to change its anatomy, a process which is called differentiation. A rapidly pulsing structure becomes visible, and tissue dissolving "acid" is extruded by tentacle tips. Finally, being so large, the blob develops an anatomically distinct "mouth." And the presence of a mouth would imply a digestive system. All of this different anatomy could certainly be possible and would be genetically controlled. Finally, the presence of anatomic structures would imply the presence of genes (to make them) and therefore cellular structure. Consequently, the blob is more than a jelly-like mass. It has internal cellular structure with sol-gel transformations, a variety of chemoreceptors to determine behavior, digestive and growth metabolism, and the genes to assure survival.

Could It Actually Happen: No. (See comments regarding the 1958 version.)

The Flesh Eaters (1964)

Synopsis: Dr. Peter Bartell, a marine biologist, is on an island in the mid–Atlantic conducting research on flesh-eating organisms. A small plane with three on board is stranded on the island because of a hurricane. Bartell develops a method of using electricity to destroy the flesh eating organisms; unfortunately, the electricity causes the organisms to grow and mutate into a giant amoebae. Hemoglobin is found to be poisonous to the creature, and this is used to eventually kill it.

Screenplay: Arnold Drake.

Biological Science Principles Involved: Infectious Diseases. Dermatology. Biochemistry. Cell Biology.

What Is Right with the Biological Science Presented: Flesh eating bacteria are real and do pose a serious threat. The worst of the bunch is the *Staphylococcus aureus* strain. Those unfortunates infected with these bacteria have a difficult recovery. Typically, *S. aureus* gets into muscle and slowly (and painfully) eats it. More often than not, surgeons have to remove large pieces of tissue to help "cure" the patients. If one bacterial organism is missed it can allow a regrowth and bring back the same problem.

Bartell accurately states, "There is the possibility the same parasite could be transferred to your body if you should touch them." Some infectious diseases do act in this manner.

Bartell collects a sample of the organism in a metal cigarette lighter (scientists use anything and everything at their disposal!) only to find out later that the organism eats its way through the metal. Bartell says he wants to perform some basic tests on the organism. If the organism can eat its way through the metal lighter, then this would also mean that the organism is capable of generating some very caustic acid which is strong enough to disrupt the chemical bonds of metal atoms. Bartell eventually collects a sample by putting some into a glass test tube. Apparently, the organism cannot eat nor dissolve silicon dioxide (i.e., glass). What is interesting is that there is a class of bacteria-like organisms known as "metalophiles" which do indeed "eat" metals. These microorganisms are very primitive in their structure and metabolism and are classed as Archaea. Perhaps some of Bartell's "protein eaters" were mixed with metal eaters, or had the metalophile biochemical enzymes to metabolize metals.

What Is Wrong with the Biological Science Presented: As presented in the film, these "protein eaters" eat off all the flesh, including all connective tissue, cartilage, and fatty or adipose tissues. This is a lot more than just eating protein. Even if we accept the idea that these "microscopic parasites" do eat *all* flesh, there is the problem of time. In the film, the eating occurs in a matter of seconds. This is simply way too fast to occur in real life.

Another significant problem is one of mass. If the "microscopic parasites" consume all the flesh, then these parasites should have significantly increased in numbers. We did not see this, so where did all that flesh, organs, and tissues go? Also, that much metabolism would have released an enormous amount of energy as heat.

Inside bone is the marrow, which is composed of cells and tissues that produce a variety of vital proteins and hormones necessary to carry on life's processes. Bone is primarily composed of calcium, and since these organisms do not eat bone, then they must not be able to process calcium compounds.

Later in the film it is shown that hemoglobin is toxic to the amoeboid organisms, so much so that it causes their death. This is an anomaly, since the organisms are capable of completely eating all flesh, which would include the heart, blood vessels, and blood itself—which is primarily hemoglobin. The organisms die by a "direct" injection of hemoglobin into their tissue, so perhaps oral digestion is not a problem.

The organism's enzymes are apparently capable of inactivating hemoglobin.

After Bartell conducts a small scale experiment with some of the organisms by giving them a mild electrical shock, these organisms coalesce together and form a much larger, amoeboid-like creature. Nature already has a system very much like this. The unicellular slime molds are single-celled creatures which, as soon as a food source is exhausted, come together and form a larger multicellular organism. Perhaps the electricity caused the unicellular flesh eaters to coalesce into this amoeboid creature. This is certainly plausible, though the explanation Bartell gives is not. Bartell, when he sees this amoeboid creature for the first time, says, "The charge of energy bound the amino acids together and it formed this." The electrical binding of amino acids together could have created a protein polymer, which has unique and interesting properties. In no way, however, would a protein polymer be even close to amoeboid life.

What Biological Science Is Necessary to Actually Achieve the Results in the Film: Enzymatic action is necessary to "eat" protein, not to mention carbohydrates, lipids (fat), and nucleic acid (DNA, RNA, etc.). Since not all proteins are created equal, then this organism must have a cornucopia of metabolic enzymatic activity, such as serine proteases, peptide proteases, nucleases, lipases, etc.

Why these organisms are sensitive to hemoglobin (Hb) deserves a closer analysis. What is in Hb that would give it these remarkable powers? Hb is primarily protein with a heme group that contains one iron molecule. Since we see these organisms "eat" through a metal cigarette lighter, then perhaps iron has no effect on them. However, the Hb is directly injected into the organism, so ingested iron is somehow inactivated; but inactivated iron in the organism's tissues could have been poisonous. This is an interesting concept. Another possibility is that the heme group itself, a flat porphyrin complex which binds an iron atom, is toxic to the organism. Finally, perhaps some portion of the actual protein structure of the Hb molecule has toxic effects on the organisms.

Could It Actually Happen: There is controversy over the nature and number of drugs prescribed by physicians. The problem here is that bacteria are capable of mutating; and if exposed to too many drugs, a bacteria will mutate ways to overcome the action of the drugs, thereby rendering them ineffective. With enough exposure to these pharmaceutical drugs, the bacteria would mutate and therefore continue to grow. This is how mutants form. Mutated flesh eating bacteria could be a real and continuing problem should our ability to effectively treat them fail. So, yes, this could happen.

Atom Age Vampire (1963)

Synopsis: Professor Levins develops a compound which regenerates and rebuilds abnormal cells and tissues. Levins tries his compound on Janet, a woman who has facial disfigurements. Janet's scars disappear but return later. Levins tries to make more and uses himself as a guinea pig, which causes him to turn into a monster. After Levins kills some people, he is eventually caught and dies. In death, Levins reverts to his normal self.

Screenplay: Anton Giulio Majano, with English dialog by John Hart.

Biological Science Principles Involved: Dermatology. Biochemistry. Cell Biology.

What Is Right with the Biological Science Presented: The motivating force behind Professor Levins' experiments is his desire to

Professor Levins (Alberto Lupo) is the *Atom Age Vampire* (1963), emerging from his atomic chamber, ready to go out and find his next victim. Note the escaping steam, which is radioactive. As such, his entire lab and surroundings would be heavily contaminated (for years!) and capable of killing nearby living forms, both animal and plant. In addition to altering his skin composition, the radiation also lengthened (and trimmed) his fingernails.

help those suffering from the effects of radiation. An admirable occupation. During one particular scene, Professor Levins explains that earlier in his life he spent eight months in Japan studying the effects of atom bomb radiation on people. This work inspired him to devote the rest of his life to radiation research. Furthermore, when explaining genetic mutations, Levins says, "Suppose that mutations could be made permanent or not as we please. Imagine if this were so, what extraordinary developments it could lead to." Yes, imagine that. His reasons and motivations for doing his research are sound and professional.

Some facial scarring, the kind Janet has, is often presented as keloids, which are nodular, firm, and movable masses of hyperplastic scar tissue, often tender and frequently painful. Keloids consist of irregular bands of collagen, the major protein of connective tissue, and occur in the dermis and adjacent subcutaneous tissues of the skin. Facial burns typically have numerous keloids. There are compounds available which may partially "repair" some keloid scarring, though the success would, of course, depend upon the nature and extent of the scarring. Facial scarring would be the worst, especially in Western society and particularly on women. The majority of the tissue repair medications currently available are either steroid or collagen based and are applied topically; they are not injected, as seen in this movie.

At one point Levins talks about using his developed compound as an anti-cancer vaccine. Anti-cancer vaccines are not something which would "restore cells," as suggested in the film. A true cancer vaccine would prevent the growth of tumors and not necessarily kill those already present. Such a vaccine would be used prophylactically after the patient has received whatever therapy is necessary for treatment.

What Is Wrong with the Biological Science Presented: Early on in the film Professor Levins is talking into a tape recorder, and he says, "I am not being immodest when I speak of a whole new era in the field of biology and therapy. The destructive and degenerative effect of atomic explosions have driven scientists more than ever before into research involving methods and processes of regeneration, rebuilding abnormal or totally destroyed cells. It is completely suggestful in correcting abnormal cell growth, as well as in restoring cells which have been destroyed. Just as good often grows out of evil, derma 28 has grown out of derma 25, the serum which provoked an accelerated abnormal development of cells. When I've finally succeeded in stabilizing its effects, I've produced the anti-cancer vaccine which for years has been the major goal of the most important scientific research. Repeated experiments using derma 28 and specimens deformed by injections of derma 25 proved its miraculous efficiency without a doubt." Certainly a mouthful. The expressed and implied motivations for doing his research are admirable. The ability to control and destroy particular cells is indeed a worldwide research effort being undertaken by the keenest scientific minds. However, having the same "serum" capable of regeneration, rebuilding, correcting, restoring, and serving as an anti-cancer vaccine is ludicrous.

After giving his subjects injections of either derma 25 or the more advanced derma 28, Levins places them in his "radiation chamber" to both help counteract and enhance the effects of his derma compounds. You cannot have it both ways.

Levins uses up all his derma 28 and does not feel he has the time to prepare any more ("every drop of derma 28 represents months of work and anxiety"). So he takes the "easy" way out and decides to "create a monster" by injecting himself with derma 25 so he can go out unrecognized (!) as a beast and attack and kill young women to get the "glands which produced derma 28." (And this is the *easy* way?) These glands are most likely extracts of the pituitary, adrenals, and hypothalamus. From a young female, interpreted as premenopausal (and post-puberty), a key ingredient of these glands would be estrogen and its derivatives. The supposition here is that female hormones would be better for skin.

After becoming a monster from the affects of derma 25 injections, Levins then enters his radiation chamber — which then fills with smoke. Apparently, this exposure to the radiation causes him to revert back to his normal self. That by itself is fraught with problems, which are compounded when he exits the chamber and releases the radioactive smoke into the lab, contaminating everything and clearly compromising both health and safety!

And this brings us to the actual title of the film. The "Atom Age" angle is understandable (since radiation is a key component of the plot), but the use of the word "vampire" is stretching it too much. Unless, of course, you consider the collection of female glands a vampire's habit.

What Biological Science Is Necessary to Actually Achieve the Results in the Film: If such compounds as derma 25 and derma 28 exist, then they would have to be hormone based (most likely composed of some sort of growth hormone, or what are collectively referred to as cytokines—proteins which modulate cell growth). There are a variety of these substances that either individually or in combination could bring out some of the effects described by Levins. However, to turn into the monster, a completely different set of biological substances would be needed. As the "monster," Levins' eyes bulge, his teeth grow, and his face becomes hairier. Quite a number of genes would have to be either turned off or turned on for all this to take place.

Radiation exposure typically causes cell destruction and is used, with a certain degree of success, in cancer patients to eradicate some cancer lesions. The radiation destroys portions of the DNA structure, making cell growth and duplication cease. For radiation to cause Levins to revert back to normal would mean that the radiation would selectively destroy the DNA in those cells causing him to become a monster in the first place. If all the "monster" DNA were destroyed then only the normal cells would remain. This could be possible, though not in the short amount of time shown in the film.

Could It Actually Happen: Controlling cell growth, differentiation, and proliferation is certainly possible, and research in these areas is actively being done in many top scientific and medical labs throughout the world. However, this is mostly done at the single cell level, and not at the entire organism level suggested in this film. Those days are still a long way off.

The "melting away of scars" is another area of active dermatological research, and there has been good progress made in this area. A combination of plastic surgery and application of appropriate chemical compounds will result in the effective removal of disfiguring scars.

The radiation aspect of "monster reversion" is difficult to understand. Way too

much hoping and praying that only the right DNA would be affected is necessary for this to actually happen, though it did make for interesting drama.

Frozen Alive (1964)

Synopsis: Dr. Frank Overton is a scientist at the "World Health Organization, Low Temperature Unit, Berlin Division" who develops a procedure to deep freeze animals and bring them back alive. He and his colleague, Dr. Helen Wieland, successfully experiment on chimpanzees. Overton volunteers to be the first human to be frozen and is successfully revived.

Screenplay: Evelyn Frazer.

Biological Science Principles Involved: Cryobiology. Cell Biology. Physiology.

What Is Right with the Biological Science Presented: The level of accuracy in the science throughout the film was refreshingly high, and I have nothing but praise for Evelyn Frazer, the writer of the film. She did a marvelous job and certainly did her homework.

Here are some examples. During a lecture at the institute, Dr. Wieland says, "Both the parent chimpanzees have been deep frozen and kept in the cold store at a temperature of minus 80 degrees centigrade for three months before they were mated. We've been carrying out very exhaustive tests. None of the experimental animals have suffered any damage to their brain or major nerve centers whatsoever. In conclusion, the great problem until now of all low temperature work with large animals has been how to stop the heart and then freeze the blood quick enough to prevent brain damage from oxygen starvation." These sentences demonstrate careful science, since they want to see if normal biological processes are left intact (which is why they want to mate the chimps; if they mate successfully, then this would imply that normal body functions were not harmed). Also, the problem of uniformly freezing all cells and tissues simultaneously was addressed, as well as adequately oxygenating the brain. It's all well written and all true.

Overton, when asked what the maximum period of successful cold storage is, responds with, "Well, our maximum is three months, but in theory, that can be extended to three years, 30 years, 300 years, just as long as you'd like. It makes no difference, they'd still come back as good as new. Where life is suspended, time has no meaning at all." All of it true and a pleasure to hear.

Here is some more scientific verisimilitude for you. During a demonstration of the procedure, the facility director, Sir Keith, notes that a test chimp "doesn't look frozen," and Wieland responds with, "She's absorbed about a gallon of glycerol. That's why she hasn't iced up yet." Keith then asks, "Why not pack her in dry ice straight away?" Dr. Wieland responds with, "The body surface would cool much quicker than the interior if we did that. Now this way [freezing carbon dioxide around her first], all the body processes are arrested simultaneously. Then she'll stay sweet and sound until we wake her up." What is particularly satisfying about this exchange is not only its correctness, but the fact that a female scientist, in a position of authority, is giving the accurate explanations.

What Is Wrong with the Biological Science Presented: Even though this film has a high level of scientific accuracy, there are some missteps. One of the reasons given for even developing the field of low temperature research was because it "opens up far reaching possibilities in human surgery." Well, not quite. If the patient is completely frozen then it would be very difficult to cut tissues with a scalpel, or any other knife for that matter, not to mention the problems involved with the natural healing processes. Also, Overton later stated that this technique "will free them [i.e., patients] of malignant disease," meaning cancer. It is very hard to imagine scenarios whereby freezing cells and tissues will "free them of malignant disease." Overton was probably thinking of the surgery angle here, in that they could freeze the patient and then operate at their leisure. This will not work.

What Biological Science Is Necessary to Actually Achieve the Results in the Film: In cryobiology, the reason for low temperature work is preservation, nothing else. To make cryosurgery feasible would require the invention of new instruments, equipment, and tools. That is not likely, since conventional surgery at room temperature is so much simpler. Properly frozen cells have little or no metabolism. The healing of scalpel cuts and sutures requires active metabolic wound healing mechanisms to occur. There would have to be some way to overcome this.

Could It Actually Happen: The comments made earlier about the film *The Man with Nine Lives* equally apply here.

The Creeping Flesh (1972)

Synopsis: On an expedition, archaeologist Professor Hildern (Peter Cushing) finds what he believes to be the "missing link" in human evolution and brings the fossil skeleton to his lab. When water touches the skeleton's bones, flesh begins to form anew. As a result of all this, Professor Hildern goes insane and ends up in an asylum run by his half-brother (Christopher Lee).

Screenplay: Peter Spenceley and Jonathan Rumbold.

Biological Science Principles Involved:

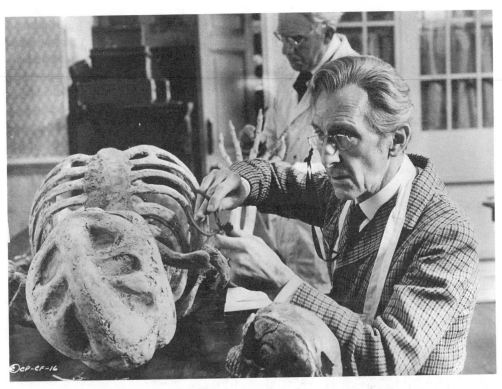

The Creeping Flesh (1972): This skeleton has enough "flesh" dry-preserved on its bones that when any part comes in contact with water, flesh begins to form immediately, including tendons, muscle, blood vessels (intact), skin, and fingernails. Note the interesting cranial indentations on the skull of the specimen. (Also, note the hole in the back of the smaller skull. An unfortunate end.)

Cell Biology. Dermatology. Infectious Diseases. Immunology.

What Is Right with the Biological Science Presented: Though there are no particular scientific facts per se that are discussed, there are some generalities and lab bench exercises performed by Prof. Hildern which are realistic looking. Cushing is such a good actor that when he is mixing and experimenting you actually believe what he is doing.

What Is Wrong with the Biological Science Presented: This is one of those films in which the reel science is far more interesting than the real science. This forces one to think of "what if" scenarios, and therein lies some intriguing insights into biology.

During Professor Hildern's opening monologue he tells another doctor, "My work is of the utmost importance for the survival of the human race. Do you believe in evil, doctor? I don't mean evil as it is commonly understood. I mean the existence of evil as an existing organism. As a plague, a disease, as it infects humanity like cholera, or typhoid. An epidemic slowly spreading until it infects the whole world. Evil is a disease. A disease which can be prevented or cured like many other." Evil is what you make of it and, to some people, infectious diseases, be they the plague, tissue eating *Staphylococcus*, cholera, or AIDS, would certainly be considered evil. However, being able to "cure" it is another matter entirely.

Professor Hildern also goes on to say (while analyzing a specimen on a microscope slide), "You are looking at the very essence of evil itself. I alone possess the knowledge of how to combat this terrible force which I stand guilty of unleashing upon the world…"

All this talk of "evil" comes about in an interesting manner. Hildern places a drop of blood obtained from the rejuvenated skeleton (more on that later) on a microscope slide and observes round black cells (!) with about a dozen very long pili (or what are called "micro whiskers," which are each about four times the diameter of the cells). Hildern comments, "Living blood cells, but not ordinary cells." It's an amazing understatement, since there isn't anything even remotely resembling that in nature. Hildern then mixes some of his own blood with that of the creature's, and the creature's blood cells attack Hildern's cells! This is actually shown, and is quite remarkable biology. In the lab, getting one type of cell to attack another cell is a relatively easy thing to do, but the way it is shown in this film is completely wrong. In our body the "cell wars" which are constantly waged do resemble this somewhat, but not completely black cells attacking completely red cells.

Furthermore, Hildern goes on to say, "Since evil is a disease, it would be possible to immunize man by some form of inoculation." In theory, this is correct and is the fundamental basis of immunity. Hildern continues with, "If a minute quantity of evil serum were introduced into the blood stream of an individual, that individual should be proof against contamination by the evils of this world for the rest of his or her life. We must prepare a serum from the evil cells and put it to a practical test." I do like how this guy thinks. If only it were that easy!

The good professor's concepts of immunology then take a radical turn. He takes about 5cc of blood from the skeleton creature's finger and places it in a flask, mixes it with another liquid (most likely some other serum), and finally places this mix over a lit Bunsen burner. Hildern then takes some other liquids, mixes them in, and places about 2cc into a (non-sterile!) syringe. He then injects this into a monkey, and a short time later removes a sample of the monkey's blood for analysis. There is no way a monkey's immune response could generate antibodies that fast; at best it would take a few days, and preferably a few weeks to months—with multiple immunizations—to generate a healthy, strong immune response. After obtaining the monkey serum, Hildern places it on a slide and examines it under a microscope, saying, "The serum has formed a protective film around each cell. Now the question is, can this protection withstand the forces of undiluted evil, withstand an attack from the blood taken from the newly formed flesh?" As you would expect, Hildern then wants to try this "anti-evil serum" on a human, and he ultimately chooses his own daughter. Hildern gives her a 3cc injection to "get rid of her evil," and as you can easily guess, something goes wrong, she goes berserk, and ends up in the insane asylum of Hildern's brother. It would be an interesting world if our immune systems behaved in this manner.

Now, finally, on to the "missing link" himself. Here lies the biggest problem with the cinemascience presented in this film. Professor Hildern finds this (complete) skeleton during an expedition to New Guinea and brings it back to his estate. The skeleton itself is huge, with a proportionately large skull about three times the size of *Homo sapiens*. Though not necessarily so, a large skull could suggest a large brain capacity; however, it should be noted that much larger dinosaurs often had brains the size of walnuts. The top of his skull has three indentations, indicating an out formed anatomy. Furthermore, the skeleton is clearly barrel chested. When some water gets onto a finger of the skeleton during its cleaning, flesh starts to appear, complete with veins, arteries, muscle, cartilage, etc. Hildern's brother (Lee) sums it up best when he says, "...how do you form living tissue around dead bone?" Well, once the good professor sees the new flesh, he cuts off the finger, which pulsates and bleeds(!), suggesting a functioning circulatory system. If Hildern only put water onto a finger, then how did pumping action occur? And where did the blood flow come from?

Later, while Hildern transports the skeleton, he is caught in a rain storm. The rain water soaks the skeleton, causing flesh to appear all over the body. After this we get a good look at the head, and no eyes are visible. However, since the creature is shown to have rudimentary thinking ability, then brain tissue must also have formed, suggesting that tissue formation is somewhat selective.

What Biological Science Is Necessary to Actually Achieve the Results in the Film: Comments on the immune response have already been made, so that need not be detailed again. However, one comment on the time it would take for the monkey (or a human for that matter) to generate "anti-evil" antibodies is necessary. For antibodies to appear as fast as implied in the film, it would require an already existing immune response with the appropriate antibody(ies) present in the serum. A re-exposure to the antigen would restimulate antibody production. If this were true, then the monkey would already be "immune" to Hildern's "disease of evil."

You would have to do a lot of hand waving to figure out a rational way for dead bone to grow fresh flesh. For this to even remotely work would require some layer(s) of desiccated skin to be present on the bones' surface, with the presence of

water simply rehydrating the skin cells. Since blood is clearly present, then it would also have to rehydrate. Since these cells are clearly red, then hemoglobin (containing both heme groups and atoms of iron) must also be present. This is asking too much of a thin layer of desiccated skin!

Even if all that were possible, the biggest problem yet is with pumping blood, which would imply a heart. Desiccated heart tissue must be present and then rehydrated in the presence of water to make it work. Even still, the heart would need some sort of electrical shock to get it to start pumping again. Though fun to watch, having a single finger actively bleed is utterly ludicrous.

Could It Actually Happen: If evil is able to be quantified in some sort of chemical way (all antigens are chemicals), then an immune response could be generated against it. As far as is known there is no immune response against something as subjective as evil.

Professor Hildern states in the film that the skeleton he found during his expedition in New Guinea is about 3000 years old. Scientists have been successful in obtaining functional blood cells from the 3000 to 4000 year old remains (skin and bones) of Egyptian mummies, so the possibility of reconstituting ancient cells is certainly real. Once skin has been dried it essentially becomes leather-like, so being able to reconstitute that is very doubtful, even with all the cytokines and hormones of modern science at your disposal.

NANOTECHNOLOGY

To better appreciate the next film, *Deep Red*, it would be best to provide a brief background on an interesting aspect of biology which will certainly change our futures.

Nano is a billionth of a meter, which

is about five carbon atoms wide, so we are talking very small here. The dream of nanotechnologists is to create molecular motors which can perform real work with 100 percent efficiency. Does that sound like science fiction? Well, nanotechnology is a reality, which may be surprising to some. There already exists in our bodies certain enzymes which form the basis of real, single protein machines that are "alive" and work. "Single molecule physiology" has advanced enough that molecular motors are being designed on the principles of how they work. Various nanolevers, nanogears, nanobearings, nanopulleys, nanopropellers, nanorods, nanoblocks, nanotubes, and nanospheres are being designed from the mechanisms of how enzymes behave.

Already the world's smallest rotary motor, an enzyme called ATPase, has been shown to work with near 100 percent efficiency! ATPase is an enzyme found in virtually all species on earth and makes ATP, the major currency of energy in the biological world. Every day our body synthesizes approximately its own weight in ATP, so this is one busy enzyme! One particular subunit of this enzyme rotates on an axis, and this has been actually visualized. Most motors have some sort of rotational motion, and this ATPase enzyme does just that. And fast? Some enzymes do their jobs in quintillionths of a second without wearing out!

Other enzyme systems, like the proteins actin and myosin of muscle, are being studied for potential applications in nanotechnology. Also, strands of DNA are being used as scaffolding-like supports to hold molecular motors. Furthermore, synthetic organic molecules are being created to behave as single motors; the molecules created here perform the function of a molecular bearing. All of this work opens the way to fabricate, spatially define, and test various proteins for the fabrication of molecular motors. To be sure, molecular devices will be incredibly important in the not too distant future.

Deep Red (1994)

Synopsis: A tiny space ship comes to earth and embeds itself in a little girl (Gracie), subsequently giving her "reds," the ability to heal tissues and reverse the aging process. Dr. Newmeyer wants the addictive reds, or "nanites," for immortality and kidnaps Gracie. A private investigator is brought in and eventually recovers the reds and the girl.

Screenplay: D. Brent Mote.

Biological Science Principles Involved: Biochemistry. Infectious Diseases. Cell Biology. Pharmacology.

What Is Right with the Biological Science Presented: Nanobiology research is a very active field occupied by the keenest minds throughout the entire world, and is essentially taking the proteins and mechanisms of biochemistry and making molecular motors of them. In the broadest definition, much of gene therapy can be thought of as nanobiology, since work, albeit gene function, is being done on the molecular scale.

As private investigator Mr. Joe Keyes describes it, "We've got a couple of Ph.D.s in biochemistry or some damn thing who are prowling around looking to kill each other over some high tech something or other that one supposedly stole from the other one's research lab." Though it is nice to think that scientists are above such petty squabbles, the reality is that scientists too have egos. Some have incredibly huge egos at that, are very competitive, and, unfortunately, at times very cutthroat. It just takes a couple to ruin it for everyone else, and Dr. Newmeyer's personality is, unfortunately, more common than perhaps thought.

As presented in the film, there are two types of reds. This is best explained by Mrs. Rickman, the wife of one of the Ph.D.s Newmeyer is after. She says, "Nanites [i.e., reds] come in two types. Reds, which are sterile drones that live for a few days, and deep reds, which are immortal and capable of infinite reproduction. Like a queen bee, there is only one deep red. Gracie has it. The problem is the more you use them [reds], the faster you use them up." This is just like a classic drug addiction where the more you use the more tolerant you become, which means you need bigger and bigger doses for them to still work. This addiction angle is quite accurate.

It is shown that reds can easily be passed from one person to another by skin contact, much like an infectious disease. Since this is by skin contact, then the nanites have the ability to bind to skin, penetrate the cells and tissues, then hone in on their target where they "set up shop" and change the host's molecular processes.

Once the reds are inside their hosts and begin to take over their metabolism, they get warmer, which suggests that their basal metabolic rate or BMR significantly increases, a physiological process which also occurs when you spike a fever. This too is accurate.

What Is Wrong with the Biological Science Presented: It is shown that those infected with reds have from time to time smoke appearing from their bodies, which would imply some sort of friction (molecular friction from the nano motors?). This is definitely smoke and not steam, such as sweat coming off of athletes during cold weather. The smoke appears to come out of the skin, which would have to come through pores. Though visually this looked cool, there is no rational way for that much smoke to come from the host body's pores.

Dr. Newmeyer has a monitoring de-vice/computer which scans the upper body area, the thoracic area, and if reds are present, the device indicates how many and where they are. If the reds are true molecular machines, then they would be protein based and therefore it would be impossible to distinguish them from the body's own proteins. If, however, there are some metal components to the reds, then perhaps the instrument Newmeyer has could detect low levels of metals in the body, most likely by magnetic resonance. All of this is doubtful with current technology.

During one particular experiment in Newmeyer's lab a computer screen is seen with a visual design of the lobes of the lungs and the following words: "engaging chymotrypsin," followed by "recording nucleophilic acyl substitution." Chymotrypsin is a protease enzyme synthesized in the pancreas and secreted into the small intestine that hydrolyzes (or degrades) the peptide bonds of ingested proteins into smaller fragments called peptides for further degradation and subsequent reuse in various metabolic salvage pathways. "Nucleophilic acyl substitution" is a phrase used to describe the actual chemical reaction mechanism of how chymotrypsin works, in which a pair of electrons from a carbon atom are bound up to two oxygen atoms, one from the enzyme and one from its substrate, and then removed. This is interesting and all that, but what it has to do with "reds" and nanotechnology is not clear. It is tempting to speculate that since those with reds have increased metabolism, perhaps they would need to process food stuffs more rapidly. Perhaps the script writer found some detail on chymotrypsin in a biochemistry textbook and thought it sounded good enough to foist on the paying public.

Newmeyer says he was born in 1920 and would therefore be in his 70s. Since he looks like he is in his early 40s, then his youth has been restored. Newmeyer also says he is a Nobel Prize winner, which all by itself is an extraordinary thing to say. If he is a prize winner then he would have been famous and recognizable. Don't you think that someone would have noticed? It serves no purpose to say he was a winner of the Nobel Prize, and this should have been avoided.

What Biological Science Is Necessary to Actually Achieve the Results in the Film: As discussed above, nanotechnology is a vibrant field still in its infancy, with its "golden age" yet to come. As Newmeyer presciently says, "Believe me when I tell you that deep red is our future. The enhancement of our genetic destiny." That, gentle readers, is money in the bank! To be sure, nanotechnology will change our lives.

While explaining some of the red technology, Mrs. Rickman asserts, "...reds control aging. The Hayflick limit. The number of times a cell can reproduce without going haywire [just as effective an explanation for the layman as any other], what we call aging. Dr. Newmeyer tested Gracie's blood to see what cured her club foot and cerebral palsy. Newmeyer found the 'nanites,' which are molecular protein machines capable of repairing or reshaping the body, cell by cell. They are the closest thing to immortality. Reds go through your body and repair you, bring you back to your optimum state." For all this to happen would require quite a bit of biochemistry, molecular biology, and cell biology.

A "molecular protein machine," as explained, already exists. Therefore, the fundamental principles of this technology have been described, and it will now be an engineering problem to make this more practical. In conjunction with gene therapy, where new DNA is introduced into cells, molecular machines may make it possible to truly "repair and reshape the body." If and when this does occur, it will be done "cell by cell."

To repair a club foot would entail both tissue and bone repair. Of the two, tissue repair would be the easiest. Bone repair would be a lot harder because of the biochemical nature of bone and the minerals, primarily calcium, which would have to have its very strong chemical bonds broken and realigned. To restructure bone properly would get into the area of "shape shifting," and this is discussed in more detail under the *Moonchild* entry, page 80.

Cerebral palsy is a defect of motor power and coordination related to damage of the brain. The repairing of the damage would correct the problem, and this is certainly possible with nanotechnology, though multiple factors would be involved (depending upon the severity of brain damage and whether it is caused by congenital deformities or some sort of trauma).

Could It Actually Happen: In a word, yes. The revolution in human health as a result of nanotechnology will happen within our lifetimes. Scientists understand what proteins and enzymes can do; and with the human genome project completed (and understood!), the combination of the two will make for healthier and stronger bodies. How well this all will be accepted will ultimately depend upon society. As you can imagine, there will be those elements of society that will be violently opposed to this, and those who will accept it all with open arms. (As you should easily guess, I belong to the latter group.)

Zombie 6: Monster Hunter (1995)

Synopsis: A zombie named Nikolaus escapes and is chased by a priest. The zombie accidentally rips open his belly while going over a spiked iron fence and is subsequently taken to a hospital for treatment. Shortly after the operation the zombie escapes again, kills a few people, and is eventually caught and decapitated.

Screenplay: John Cart.

Biological Science Principles Involved: Hematology. Cell Biology. Biochemistry. Infectious Diseases.

What Is Right with the Biological Science Presented: During the surgery on the zombie, he is given adrenaline to start his heart again. This is a routine procedure to keep a heart muscle pumping. Basically, that's it with this film.

The scientist/priest says that Nik the zombie "escaped from the laboratory after the contamination," which would suggest some sort of biological basis to the zombie disease. Also, he says, "It is his brain that is his weak point," giving an indication of how to destroy him, and that, like with normal humans, the brain is everything.

What Is Wrong with the Biological Science Presented: Zombies being zombies, different laws of biology apply. This one (and we only see one during the entire movie) has his belly ripped open (with his guts hanging out) apparently with no problem. He did not seem to be in any undue pain, nor did it seem to bother him. However, humans being humans (i.e., non-zombies or normal people), upon seeing someone with his guts hanging out (and not knowing he is a zombie), they want to immediately operate to fix his condition. During surgery, the zombie opened his eyes, which is more common than you may think. After surgery, one of the surgeons says, "…recuperative powers like that simply don't exist. What I remember was how quickly his blood coagulated while I was operating on him. That is simply nothing I have never seen before in my life." (Yes, a physician, a highly educated person, did indeed use a double negative!) An attending nurse responds with, "Could

it be an anomaly of the lymphatic system?" The doctor says, "It's possible." Well, if true, then anything is possible.

Humans all get various cuts on their skin (and internally; they're just not seen), and unless they heal properly a person would bleed to death. Our bodies have a self healing mechanism called blood clot formation which seals these cuts. Blood coagulation, or clotting, is a reasonably understood phenomena and is the process of changing liquid blood into solid blood. There are a series of proteins and enzymes which are activated in a cascade. Like a series of dominoes, knock down the first one and many subsequently fall down as a result. Blood coagulation is just like that — a result of cascade regulation. When a cut occurs, some cells are broken, especially the endothelial cells lining the walls of our blood vessels, releasing certain chemicals or signals to begin blood coagulation. Platelets already in the blood then adhere to the damaged areas and release chemicals that makes them sticky, making even more cells adhere and eventually forming a plug large enough to seal the injury. The clumped platelets then release certain chemicals that convert an inactive protein called prothrombin into thrombin; both calcium and vitamin K are necessary for this step (as you can imagine, those deficient in vitamin K have a difficult time healing various wounds). It is thrombin, an enzyme, which catalyzes the conversion of another clotting protein, fibrinogen, into fibrin. It is the fibrin protein which gets woven into a patch-like structure that seals the injury. In addition, other cells and proteins become involved, which finally seals the damaged vessel. All in all, more than a dozen clotting factor proteins and enzymes have been discovered, and they all are important to maintain proper blood homeostasis. As you can see, coagulation is a complicated process, and complicated processes take time to work effectively.

The doctors who perform the operation on the zombie take x-rays of the head (or cranium) before and after the operation. These x-rays show the zombie's brain has actually gotten bigger after the operation! Needless to say, for the brain to significantly increase its size enough to be easily seen by x-ray would require some significant swelling of the brain tissues, and good ol' Nik the zombie would have one hellacious headache. Maybe that is why he is so angry and why he takes out his aggressions on some unfortunate souls by brutally killing them. (As soon as Nik wakes up after the operation, his brain must have been screaming in pain, because he takes a nearby drill and pushes it right through the head of an attending nurse.)

The scientist/priest makes a few interesting comments about the zombie to the surgeons after the operation, saying, "His body can regenerate dead cells ... he does not regenerate cells perfectly ... his blood coagulates and his cell memory reconstitutes any organ that is injured." Unfortunately, once a cell is dead, it is dead. To replace dead cells, already living cells must replicate themselves through natural cell division. The biological processes which keep an individual cell alive must be actively maintained. The cell can "hibernate," but even then there are rudimentary metabolic processes which still occur, albeit at a much slower pace. The only cells in the body which have "memory" are a certain class of lymphocytes, a cell type active in the immune response. These memory cells freely circulate in the blood stream and are unable to "reconstitute any organ."

Finally, the scientist/priest has this to say about Nik the zombie: "His brain — once the cellular cells are destroyed, they cannot regenerate." It is unknown what a "cellular cell" is, though it sounds fascinating. Aren't all cells "cellular" cells? If there are such things then shouldn't there also be, say, molecular cells, physical cells, mini cells, etc.? As discussed earlier, research has shown that normal brain cells can regenerate, though perhaps zombie brain cells are a bit different and may not follow the normal rules.

What Biological Science Is Necessary to Actually Achieve the Results in the Film: For the zombie to have his remarkable "recuperative powers" would require the presence of abundant cell growth factors, so damaged or destroyed cells could be quickly repaired. Normal cell division, where one cell becomes two, takes about 20 to 24 hours and is composed of four distinct phases. The first is called growth phase one (G1), which typically takes about six to eight hours for actively growing cells. The second phase is the DNA synthesis phase (S), which takes about another six to eight hours. The third phase is called growth phase two (G2), which takes about four to five hours, and finally, the last phase, called cell mitosis (M), typically takes about one to two hours. For all cells in the body, from fibroblasts to epithelial to blood cells, the S, G2, and M phases are all about the same, so they account for about 11 to 15 hours of time for one cell to split into two daughter cells. The G1 phase is the most variable and can take literally zero time to decades, depending upon the cell type. For Nik the zombie to have his remarkable "recuperative powers" would mean that his cells would not have a G1 phase. All in all, this is acceptable. If he has significantly increased levels of growth factors and hormones in his body, then this can certainly happen, it's an interesting angle on "zombie biology."

Also, for Nik the zombie to have "quick blood coagulation" would imply that he is loaded with high concentrations of platelets, thrombinogen, fibrinogen, vitamin K, calcium, etc., for rapid blood clotting. Nik the zombie is shot several times during the film and these wounds are quickly healed, so tissue growth and blood coagulation are fast enough that he did not miss a step in his activities. Furthermore, what blood loss he did experience from his numerous wounds is quickly replaced by new blood cells, implying that his blood cell differentiation and proliferation cascades are also rapid enough that his physiology did not suffer in the least.

Could It Actually Happen: Blood coagulation does vary considerably from person to person, suggesting that there are individuals who do have high enough levels of the necessary circulating components to minimize blood loss from any wound. Obviously, some diabetics and hemophiliacs have a major problem here because of their inability to form blood clots. It would be interesting if Nik the zombie was a hemophiliac. Would he have the same recuperative powers? If he did, then the "contamination" he was exposed to was such that it significantly altered his DNA regions that coded for blood coagulation and repair.

And speaking of "contamination," whatever infectious agent Nik the zombie is exposed to is either a virus (most likely), a bacteria (doubtful), or some type of mold or fungus (even more doubtful). Speculating that viral DNA is the most probable culprit here, it must have some very interesting controlling sequences to be able to alter so much of his biochemistry. Not only all the clotting factors would have to be produced in excess, but other growth factors and hormones would also have to be overproduced to make cell growth fast enough that the G1 phases are eliminated.

2 MOLECULAR BIOLOGY

How do you spell DNA? I spell DNA (deoxyribonucleic acid) M-O-L-E-C-U-L-A-R B-I-O-L-O-G-Y. You better get used to it because DNA is here to stay. DNA is *the* code of life, the blueprint, that which makes each of us who we are. In the not too distant future everyone will have their DNA sequences known, with the information, perhaps used for both good and (unfortunately) bad. Individuals could have their DNA sequences coded onto a magnetic-like strip on the backs of credit cards or driver's licenses. In the future the examining physician (or, more likely, the health insurance agency) will simply say, "give me a drop of your blood" and they will be able to tell everything about you.

Genes were initially characterized as mathematical units of inheritance. It is now know that genes are made up of sequences of DNA. By virtue of their ability to store information in the form of nucleotide sequences, to transmit this information by conservative replication to daughter cells during mitosis and meiosis, and to express it by directing the incorporation of amino acids into proteins, DNA molecules are the chemical transducers of genetic information flow.

Recombinant DNA technology has provided the means to isolate, characterize, synthesize, and manipulate individual genes controlling proteins, and therefore biology. As a result of all this our lives will change and will improve.

The Monster That Challenged the World (1957)

Synopsis: Scientists at the Salton Sea in Southeastern California discover some unusual radioactivity following an earthquake. After investigating, they find large mollusk eggs. The eggs hatch and giant caterpillar-like creatures go on a rampage and kill several people. The Navy eventually destroys all the creatures.

Screenplay: Pat Fielder, from a story by David Duncan.

Biological Science Principles Involved: Molecular Biology. Biochemistry. Marine Biology.

The Monster That Challenged the World (1957): The giant mollusk on the loose in the nicely equipped lab of Dr. Rogers.

What Is Right with the Biological Science Presented: The effects of radiation on biological life, DNA, cell and tissue growth, etc., have been extensively dealt with elsewhere in this book. Suffice it to say that radiation does cause mutations in the DNA and therefore whatever proteins the DNA makes could also be mutated.

While investigating the remains of an attacked boat floating on the Salton Sea, one of the Navy men finds a milky white substance on the boat and a sample is taken for analysis. Mollusks do generate secretions, so this is certainly plausible.

To explain where the mollusks come from to the Navy brass, Dr. Rogers refers to an article in a "recent" issue of *Life* magazine about dehydrated eggs of shrimp which are subsequently rehydrated and live. Rogers speculates that the "creature's eggs lay dormant at the bottom of the sea, and the earthquake caused a fissure or

opening, allowing water to seep down. Because the water is slightly radioactive and the eggs have a capacity to absorb this radioactivity, they find an environment which is perfect to hatch and grow." Again, all this is certainly plausible.

While examining a (young) Navy man who dies as a result of an encounter with one of the mollusks, the doctor concludes that he died of a stroke and says, "In that age group, only two things could cause a stroke. Violent anger or fear. In my opinion, the man you found on that boat was literally scared to death." These kinds of facts can easily be discovered at autopsy. Contrary to the popular phrase that "dead men tell no tales," in the hands of a competent pathologist, dead men have many, many tales to tell (such as the time, cause, degree, and circumstances of death). Like a puzzle, much can be pieced together during an autopsy. However, the doctor's later statements makes one wonder about his particular competency (see below).

At the climax, a little girl accidentally turns up the temperature to the large vat in the lab that holds one of the mollusk eggs, and the increased temperature makes the egg hatch. It is known that warmth does lessen the time it takes for some eggs to hatch, so, in principle, they got this right (though hatching generally does not occur as fast as shown in the film).

What Is Wrong with the Biological Science Presented: Two dead Navy crewmen are autopsied and found to be completely drained of all blood and water! This would have to be an extraordinary feat. An adult male contains about 8 liters of blood, and since no blood is found at the site where the bodies are recovered, this would imply that the creatures consumed all of it without any spillage. The Navy men's bodies have some puncture wounds, but nowhere near enough to account for complete exsanguination, not to mention dehydration.

While analyzing a piece of skin from a Navy man, the doctor (pathologist?) says, "Usually, when a body is submerged in water the epidermal tissue becomes swollen, but this is like leather. It doesn't even resemble human skin anymore. Why, skin on a man over 100 would have three times the amount of moisture." Even Egyptian mummies, dead and desiccated for thousands of years, have some moisture. And don't forget, this was a "desiccated" body found *submerged* in water!

At the Navy lab, Dr. Rogers discovers that the mollusk secretion sample is radioactive. No mention of the type or nature of the radioactivity is mentioned. Is it radioactive carbon, as would be found in organic matter (like secretions), or is it of another compound, such as an iodine or a metal ion (like lead, uranium, or plutonium)? While not meaning to quibble, this difference is critical. If the radioactivity is

organic based, then it would have been very difficult to explain away the mutations which give rise to the giant mollusks. If the radioactivity is uranium, then other species would also have been affected and we should have seen more than just giant mollusks. What about plant life? How about other organisms who were near the radioactivity and/or consumed it in their food?

Speaking of radioactivity, the Navy sends out two scuba divers equipped with Geiger counters to the sea to investigate. At depths of around 60 feet they report normal readings. Note that the Salton Sea, at its deepest, is around 65 feet deep. However, the divers go to about 125 feet(!) and locate a cavern/fissure which must have opened up from the earthquake. At that depth the divers find "radioactive marine growth," including several large mollusk eggs, and they bring one back to the lab and place it in the convenient vat stored there. (Later they go back to the sea and destroy the other eggs.)

After the egg is safely in the lab vat, Dr. Rogers explains, "What you see here is the formation inside the egg sack we found near the creature's lair. You'll notice the shell is already beginning to harden [why?]. There's quite a bit of definition in the head. Until our studies are completed, we are keeping it alive by controlled water temperature. You'll notice the thermostat reads 38 degrees [Fahrenheit?]. The temperature is just low enough to keep it from hatching. We believe this creature is of the same family as the historically documented Kraken, the giant sea beast which was the direct ancestor of the modern water mollusk." Well, if true, then how did these creatures get there in the first place? Before that, a description of the factual history of the Salton Sea is necessary.

The Salton Sea was formed during 1905–1906 when the Colorado river broke through an embankment near Yuma,

Arizona, and overflowed into California. The "sea" first covered an area of about 1165 square kilometers (about 450 sq. mi.) but has since decreased about one-third due to evaporation. The area was originally a salt marsh about 200 feet below sea level, which was why it filled so easily and why it is now a salty "sea." At the time of the film (1957) the sea was only about 50 years old, so how could it have developed such interesting and diverse marine life in such a short time span? Whatever the level of radioactivity that was supposedly present must have been very potent to achieve the level of mutations observed.

Finally, during the climax when the egg in the lab vat hatches and the giant mollusk escapes, we hear the creature make growling sounds. This vocal noise would require a lot more anatomy than what the mollusk had. Other than members of the order Cetacea, which are whales and dolphins (all mammals), no other underwater life forms make conscious sounds, so for our mollusks to suddenly "growl" does stretch things more than what should be biologically possible, and represents reel science.

What Biological Science Is Necessary to Actually Achieve the Results in the Film: The fundamental cause of the birth of the giant mollusks is radioactivity. Whatever radioactive samples were placed into the Salton Sea had specifically interacted with (normal) mollusks, causing them to mutate. Whether the earthquake had anything to truly do with the results is open for debate. In any event, for the mollusks to grow to such gigantic proportions, the radioactivity had to have caused several mutations in their DNA. As a result, their growth metabolism kicked into high gear, with all the required mechanisms in place. For example, to grow to that size would require an adequate food source for support, and the Salton Sea just simply does not have this.

Another interpretation is that the excessive salt (sodium chloride) in the sea enhanced the growth of the giant mollusks. Sodium does have many interesting properties, primarily as an electrolyte which keeps the osmolarity a constant value in cells and tissues, but enhancing growth is not one of them.

Could It Actually Happen: DNA mutations resulting from radioactivity have been documented in a number of labs throughout the world since World War II. However, can such mutations give rise to such super giant creatures as these mollusks? It would certainly be an interesting world if true, but, fortunately, such occurrences are still the figments of writers' imaginations. Since the vast majority of mutations caused by excessive exposure to radioactivity would affect chromosomes (and, therefore, DNA) nonspecifically, then these genetic alterations would most likely be lethal. The DNA coding for growth, as well as that coding for, say, respiration, would be equally affected, ultimately causing the death of the organism.

"Help Me ... Help Meeeee"

The two "fly" films discussed in this book are based on the extraordinary story by George Langelaan called simply "The Fly." This is one of those rare films that is so famous that it has actually become an icon. Whenever anyone says in a high pitched voice, "Help me ... help me," you immediately know what film it came from. We are fortunate to have a series of films based on Mr. Langelaan's story. Of the five made (so far), two will be discussed, the original made in 1958 and the 1986 remake by David Cronenberg. A gap of almost 30 years separates these two films, and the entire fabric of biological science has changed during this time. This is one of those very rare occurrences where the remake is, on many levels, stronger than the original.

This is attributable not only to the advances made in molecular biology during the last 30 years or so, but also to the participation of someone of Cronenberg's ability. The molecular biology advances in the intervening 30 years are quite visible in the updated script. Though the 1958 version does hold a special place in the hearts of many, I prefer the 1986 version. The reason is simple. The latter version has a more credible story, with intriguing "cinema-science facts." In the context of this book, the 1986 version has better biological science.

The 1959 *Return of the Fly*, the 1964 *Curse of the Fly*, and *The Fly II* (1989) by Chris Walas are somewhat derivative and, though interesting in their own right, add very little new material to the biological science angle, so they are not included here.

The Fly (1958)

Synopsis: In the electronics lab in the basement of his home, Andre Delambre develops a disintegrator/integrator "teleportation" device. While teleporting himself, a fly accidentally enters the device and their genes mix together, with tragic results. In the end, Delambre's wife helps destroy the bug-eyed monster he's become.

Screenplay: James Clavell (soon to be famous), based on the story by George Langelaan.

Biological Science Principles Involved: Molecular Biology. Entomology.

What Is Right with the Biological Science Presented: Taxonomically, flies are classified as belonging to the order Diptera. Though there is some dispute among entomologists, they seem to agree that there are about 150,000 species of flies world wide and about 20,000 species in North America. Since this film took place in Canada, near Toronto, then we will limit ourselves to only those in North America. Later in the film, a Delambre house maid refers to the fly as being a "blue bottle," which is classified as Nematocera in the suborder Brachycera. That being said, this gives us much insight as to the behavior of the fly. These flies primarily have omnivorous diets and are considered saprophytic, meaning they feed on decaying organic matter, such as decaying vegetation and decomposing animal products including bacteria, yeasts, fungi, algae, and other small creatures. After Delambre has turned into the fly, all he requests for food is a bowl of milk laced with rum. This type of meal is very telling with regards to the type of fly which fused with Delambre. This milk/rum diet represents a mix of simple organic foodstuffs with the "energy" of metabolically digestible alcohol. Though there would be plenty of protein, vitamin D, and calcium in the milk, many of the other necessary vitamins, such as the C and B vitamins (not to mention the fat soluble vitamins such as E and K), would be sorely lacking. Since the majority of the Delambre/fly body is still visibly human, the organic matter from those simple meals would not have been enough. However, we do not see any internal organs, and who knows which of those were fly, human, or a mixture of the two. The biggest unknown would be the liver (and some muscle), which is where the bulk of the body's metabolism occurs. True flies really do not have a mammalian liver, so perhaps the Delambre/fly liver has different metabolic requirements, and milk plus rum may well have been all he needed.

Adult (Diptera) flies characteristically have rather short life spans, anywhere from a few days to a few weeks. This does not give the Delambre/fly much time to do anything, which is probably why he is so frantic to revert back to his normal self. In simple terms, aging is a major concern. As

The Fly (1958) — half fly, half human. The left half, including the leg, is fly-like. The structure and nature of internal organs is unknown. The compound eyes and proboscis are prominent.

each day comes he is that much closer to some serious problems. His frantic personality changes are therefore understandable.

As the fly genes slowly take over Delambre's functions, he loses the ability to think clearly and begins to degenerate. This is best shown when he can no longer type as efficiently as he had and can no longer coherently write on the blackboard. In essence, his "disease" is progressive. This is also true in real life, so I thought this was well done, correctly representing the "slow" nature of how many DNA related problems present themselves.

What Is Wrong with the Biological Science Presented: The metabolic comments above equally apply here too. Is a milk and rum meal sufficient to give him all the nutrients and sustenance he needs?

This is seriously doubtful. Flies also have sensory chemoreceptors (hairs) on their feet, called gustatory sensillae, for analyzing whatever "meal" they are standing on. Flies can actually distinguish a great variety of tastes. Delambre/fly has an arm and leg of a fly, so there should also be fly receptors present. He is never seen dipping his fly "claw" into the milk/rum to sample it before consuming it. Also, some sucking noises are heard, so he must have taken in the liquid through his proboscis. Flies of the Nematocera and Brachycera groups have sponge-type mouth parts. Soluble elements of solid foods are dissolved in saliva or regurgitated gut contents before being swallowed. Most Diptera have one or sometimes three diverticula (a pouch or sac opening) in their foregut which functions as a crop. Large liquid meals may be temporarily held in their pouches or sacs to be gradually released into the intestine for consumption. None of this is seen with Delambre/fly. (However, this IS seen with Brundle/fly; see the 1986 remake analysis below.)

The sensory input of the Delambre/fly is also troublesome. It is demonstrated that though he could not speak he could hear, because his wife talks to him and he appears to understand. He communicates back to her by both physical gestures (arm movement and body language), and through a typewriter and the use of a chalk board. This implies that he can hear, process the information, and respond in some sort of cogent way. To do this would require thinking and reasoning. All of these are problematical. Delambre/fly clearly has the head of a fly. Flies (Diptera) "hear" via tympanic membranes on their head. Tympanic membranes have a completely different anatomy and are unable to process the vibratory wavelengths as do mammals. Furthermore, his wife Elaine says he has "intelligence and a soul," so the ability to communicate is not lost. However, as the film progresses, Delambre/fly's ability to function as a "human" is being eroded. He types, "can't think easy since morning … brain says strange things now." Later he types, "feel my will going … already strain very difficult think straight." His fly genes are beginning to dominate him.

In addition to hearing, flies have compound eyes, and for Delambre/fly to see the keys of a typewriter well enough to spell is also not likely to happen. Furthermore, both hearing and sight are sensory related and processed through nerves, so it is interesting how this all would be integrated by the brain, which is another problem. Does Delambre/fly have a human brain, fly brain, or a combination? The head of Delambre/fly is larger, so what kind of tissue matter is inside the head?

Finally, there is the infamous "help me, help me" fly which is caught in a spider's web at the end of the film. This particular fly is human from the collar bone to the head, including one complete arm. The biggest problem here is a size problem, since the human portions are miniaturized. These aspects will be discussed more fully in the "shrinkology" section of this book. Suffice it to say that articulate speech would most likely not happen because of the miniaturized internal body parts. Furthermore, to talk requires lungs to push air over vocal cords, and flies do not have lungs. Perhaps some vestigial lung capacity of Delambre is transferred to the fly.

Since this fly can talk, it must have had some of Delambre's thoughts and, therefore, mental functions. If Delambre's brain (mind) is in this fly, then what is in the Delambre/fly? It is difficult to accept Delambre's mind being functionally present in both creatures.

What Biological Science Is Necessary to Actually Achieve the Results in the Film: On one level, DNA is DNA, no matter what species it comes from, and can be thought of like the letters of a language. The actual letters of western languages are essentially the same and it is the sequence and order of these letters which determine the specific language. The same is true for DNA. Though there are only four letters, C, G, T, and A (there are others but for simplicity sake these will be ignored), it is the sequence of those and what combination they take which means all the difference in the world. Only one letter change in the DNA sequence is all it takes to have something radically different. Not only that, it is the "syntax" and punctuation of DNA which regulates how individual genes are expressed. Mother Nature designed this so the various species of DNA would not be mixed together and therefore, keep species genetically "pure."

With that being said, in principle you

can mix DNA and have, say, human enzymes read and translate fly DNA. This certainly can be done on the individual gene level, but on more complex systems, like organs (not to mention complete organisms), it would be too difficult. In essence, whatever you created would have too many lethal changes for a viable species to exist.

The most described and understood fly is *Drosophila*, the fruit fly. This species is one of the few well studied and described species, like the bacteria *E. coli* or the Balb/c mouse (or even humans), which developmental biologists have used as a research model. Most of the genes of the *Drosophila* fly have been characterized, primarily by generating mutations and then seeing what results. Very weird species have been generated in this way, the oddest perhaps being those with eyes at the ends of antennae, an extra set of wings, or those with legs in place of antennae! By moving certain genes around, *Drosophila* scientists have learned much about the structure, organization, and function of genes. Certain anatomical sections, such as the wings, head, legs, etc., develop from appropriate gene segments. These genetic segments, which regulate the entire body plan of the fly (or other complex organisms, for that matter), are under the control of a set of regulatory genes called homeotic genes, or "hox genes" for short. Basically, hox genes are those which control the overall body plan of organisms by controlling the developmental fate of groups of cells. And hox box mutations are mutations in the genes which result in the abnormal substitution of one type of body part for another. These mutations replace structures from one body region or part with structures normally found at some other location. The products of hox box genes are regulatory proteins that bind to certain regions of DNA. Genetically, for the Delambre/fly to form would require a

mixing of fly and human hox box gene regulatory segments. Basically, regulatory hox gene mixing would say "fly leg goes here" and "fly head goes there." This could work because the 180 nucleotide-long hox gene region in flies is surprisingly almost the same as found in humans!

Could It Actually Happen: As gene therapy technology becomes more reproducible then perhaps certain evolutionary advantageous genes will be introduced in man, such as the ability to handle certain food stuffs like cellulose, the most abundant source of carbon on the planet. As stated before, DNA is DNA, and in principle the mixing of genes is possible. This will be more of a practical reality when the individual regulatory elements of certain genes are understood. Stay tuned, gentle readers, it could happen.

The Fly (1986)

Synopsis: Scientist Seth Brundle develops a teleportation device and, after some failed attempts, successfully sends matter through. When he sends himself, a fly gets mixed up with him. Over time, Brundle gradually changes into "Brundlefly" and, in the end, is killed.

Screenplay: Charles Edward Pogue and David Cronenberg, based on the story by George Langelaan.

Biological Science Principles Involved: Molecular Biology. Entomology. Endocrinology.

What Is Right with the Biological Science Presented: Though the central plot of this film is similar to that of the 1958 version, it is quite evident the screenwriters of this remake knew how to spell DNA! The scientific verisimilitude shown is refreshing, in particular the gradual changes which occur as Brundle turns into a fly — which, if possible, is exactly what would happen.

At first a few stiff, coarse hairs are seen growing out of Brundle's back. His girlfriend has these analyzed and the results are: "…not human … very likely insect hairs." It is certainly possible to identify a few hairs and determine what type of organism they originated from but whether enough hair material was obtained to do the necessary tests is unknown.

As time goes by we see a gradual change in both the physical and mental makeup of Brundle. He does not know why, but his energy and activity level begin to dramatically increase. The easiest way to explain this would be alterations in hormone levels. Brundle, at first, thought the teleportation caused some sort of physiological "improvement." Brundle explains, "…the sheer process of being taken apart atom by atom and put back together again … why it's like coffee being put through a filter. It's somehow a purifying process. It's purified me, it's cleansed me, and I'll tell you, it's allowed me to realize the personal potential I've been ignoring all these years … human teleportation, molecular decimation, breakdown, reformation is inherently purging. Makes a man a king." The process also affects his mental acuity.

Brundle's athletic prowess has also dramatically increased, as well as his hand to eye coordination. He is seen effortlessly tracking and grabbing a buzzing fly out of the air. Eventually, body parts, such as fingernails, teeth, ears, etc., begin to fall off (he keeps his former body parts in a bathroom medicine cabinet and refers to this as the "Brundle museum of natural history"). After several weeks he realizes that something serious has gone wrong and queries his computer about this. The computer acknowledges that two life forms have been teleported during the experiment, one of which is himself and the other is a fly, by responding with the following printed statement: "fusion of Brundle and fly at molecular-genetic level." Brundle then says to himself, "a fly got into the transmitter pod with me the first time I was alone. The computer got confused over what was supposed to be two separate genetic patterns, and it decided to splice us together. It made us, me and fly. The telepod turned into a gene splicer."

To eat, the Brundle-fly creature takes a donut in hand and regurgitates viscous fluid over it, then sucks in the liquefied meal. This is essentially the feeding method some types of flies utilize, and provides insight into what family the fused fly belongs to. As Brundle-fly himself (itself?) explains, "How does Brundle-fly eat? Very much the way a fly eats. His teeth are now useless because although he can chew up solid food, he can't digest it. Solid food hurts, so like a fly, Brundle-fly breaks down solids with a corrosive enzyme, pleasantly called 'vomit drop' [a wonderfully descriptive name]. He regurgitated on his food, it liquefied, and he sucked it back up." All in all, this is an accurate and elegant description. Flies that do this belong to the Brachycera and Nematocera groups.

To demonstrate the effectiveness of teleportation, Brundle takes a steak (on a plate), teleports it, cooks it up, and then serves it to his girlfriend. She responds by saying, "…tastes funny … synthetic." This "experiment" is a nice addition and serves as a positive control so Brundle's girlfriend can compare non-teleported steak with teleported steak. Very, very few cinema-scientists are seen doing control tests of any type or nature. Controls establish baselines, and deviations from those baselines give you meaningful and interpretative data.

One additional conversation between Brundle and his girlfriend deserves comment. She notices that throughout the film

Brundle wears the same clothes, the same pants, same shirt, same tie, same sport coat, same shoes, etc. She comments, "Do you ever change your clothes?" Brundle responds with, "Every day." She then looks in his clothes closet and says, "Five sets of exactly the same clothes." Brundle then says, "I learned it from Einstein. This way I don't have to expend any thought on what I'm going to wear. I just grab the next set on the rack." The reason I bring this up, for what it is worth, is because I too do the same thing. I do not have "five sets of exactly the same clothes," but I do not think about clothes at all, thereby saving valuable mental energy to expend on other (more important) matters. (To be honest, this drives my wife nuts, and she constantly berates me for what I wear and is convinced I am "color blind" [I'm not, thank you very much], since nothing matches. Quite frankly, I simply do not care. This "dress code" with scientists unfortunately adds to our [undeserved] reputation for being absent-minded.)

What Is Wrong with the Biological Science Presented: The key item in the genetic fusion of the fly's genes with those of Brundle's is his computer. Well, actually, more the software that is used than the computer hardware itself. And this is the biggest problem with this film. No software (nor computer, for that matter) can do all the gene splicing necessary. Getting all the myriad genes aligned and integrated into the correct chromosomal locations is beyond current hardware technology. This can be done, but you need several enzymes and other DNA reagents to accomplish this task, not to mention the weeks of work involved. Gene splicing at the individual cell level is certainly possible, and integrating some fly genes into a human cell can be achieved. Getting the entire fly genome integrated in a non-random manner into appropriate places within the human genome, in short, cannot happen.

Whenever a sample is placed in one of the teleportation pods (Brundle's girlfriend calls them "designer phone booths") the computer gives a readout of the chemical and/or biological makeup of the item. For example, after Brundle puts a nylon stocking in the pod, the computer screen shows the presence of "polyamino nylon, silicon, miscellaneous fibers, organic matter, ultra fine weave, etc." Later, Brundle places a baboon (!) in a pod and the computer screen shows the following information: "carbon based organic life form; elements: potassium, iodine, nitrogen, carbon, hydrogen, oxygen, iron; plasma volume 2032 ml; RBC volume 1678 ml; skeletal weight 3.2 kg; fat 9.7 kg; fat free body 36.98 kg." A fly gives the following computer readout: "plasma volume 0.00001 ml; RBC volume 0.000007 ml; structural weight: 0.0003 kg; fat N/A; fat free body 0.002 kg." Needless to say, all this data is obtained in a matter of seconds, which is unbelievable.

Near the end of the film we see Brundle-fly crawling, on all fours, on the ceiling of his lab/home. He explains, "...it's almost second nature [walking on the ceiling]. I seem to be ... turned into a 185 pound fly." The Brundle-fly creature still has mostly human feet and hands, and for these appendages to have the ability to easily attach to, then release, the contours of a ceiling stretches credibility too far. However, it looks cool and is a wonderful effect.

What Biological Science Is Necessary to Actually Achieve the Results in the Film: The physics of teleportation, integration and reintegration, are beyond the scope of this book. (The physical aspects of this effect were covered in sufficient detail in Lawrence Krause's book *The Physics of Star Trek*. Nothing new can be added here, so I highly recommend to all of you to get a copy and enjoy the read.)

All of the above comments for the 1958 version of this film on gene integration between two species apply here as well. Hox gene control, gene splicing, and gene control elements are also necessary for the 1986 version to "work."

Though no specific mention is made of the actual fly that enters the telepod with Brundle, a brief glimpse of it is provided, and it appears to be a common house fly. As such, all of the comments on fly species made for the 1958 original also apply here.

Could It Actually Happen: There is no need to repeat myself here, so please see the comments under this heading for the 1958 original version. Bottom line, DNA is DNA, and with the right enzymes and gene controlling elements it can all be blurred together. If you could do this, the resulting phenotype would be of interest.

Humanoids from the Deep (1980)

Synopsis: Dr. Susan Drake has been doing research to increase the size and numbers of Pacific Northwest salmon. Some of these DNA-treated fish are accidentally released into the ocean. More primitive coelacanth fish eat the salmon, causing DNA mutations that result in "Humanoids." These creatures come ashore, try to mate with women, and are eventually destroyed in a spectacular climax.

Screenplay: Frederick James from a story by Frank Arnold and Martin B. Cohen.

Biological Science Principles Involved: Molecular Biology. Ichthyology.

What Is Right with the Biological Science Presented: Salmon are one of the few species that are capable of freely migrating between fresh water and salt water environments. Those fish capable of doing this are scientifically referred to as being euryhaline, meaning they can easily handle the salt in ocean waters even though they

were spawned and bred in fresh water. They have specialized cells which are able to remove the excess sodium salt present in sea water.

Man has been doing selective breeding for centuries. One of the better examples is maize or corn. When Europeans settled in the Americas they took the smallish corn husks available and created much larger and robust versions by selective, domesticated breeding, transforming it into a major food stuff. Furthermore, natural horse and dog breeding has significantly increased breed health. Darwin was indeed right, only the fittest do survive. In simplistic terms, selective breeding does indeed change an organism's phenotype. (Please note that this was all done way before anyone heard of modern "gene cloning" with enzymes and PCR machines.) Dr. Drake's original intent in working with salmon DNA is "to make salmon grow bigger, faster, and twice as plentiful." True music to the ears of fishermen whose livelihood depends upon their day's catch. Though well intended, Drake's actions certainly did backfire. However, we all know that the path to Hell is paved with good intentions, and such is the plight of cinemascientists!

What Is Wrong with the Biological Science Presented: Though not explicitly stated, the biggest problem with the events in the film are those of time. Too little time is given for the creatures to have evolved into the viable and robust species seen. As Drake says, "This species only just appeared, so there has to be a reason that a humanoid creature evolved so quickly." The reason is called "special effects budget."

The humanoids are shown to easily walk on land, suggesting they have lungs—even though they clearly have gills on the sides of their heads. Though there are true amphibians who can do this, they cannot stay underwater for extended periods of time and need to surface for air. These humanoids must have both lungs and gills. If they are derived from coelacanths, as suggested by Drake, then the lung aspect is really hard to accept. Both salmon and coelacanths have gills so where did the lungs come from? Perhaps the fish that ate Salmon were not coelacanths. (Please note that coelecanths [*Latimeria chalumnae*] have been found off the coasts of Madagascar and Indonesia, which is a very long way from the Pacific Northwest.)

Drake says, "It's my theory that feeding on the DNA-treated salmon may have brought about evolution in more primitive fish, like the coelacanth." For the moment, let us say that is true. Then any other fish that ate the same salmon should also have evolved into something else. After all, coelacanths are neither the only primitive fish in the ocean nor the only species who feeds on salmon. So, are there other humanoid-like species lurking out there in the sea? (Perhaps a sequel could resolve this.)

Just about all species have natural defense mechanisms that prevent unwanted chemicals from harming them. Since all organisms must consume some sort of food for energy, their bodies must be able to prevent some of these ingested molecules from harming them. In vertebrate organisms (this includes man and fishes) there are natural digestive processes which degrade just about anything (though, to be sure, there are plenty of poisons which escape this natural degradative process!). DNA is one of those organic molecules which our natural digestive processes can easily handle. There are enzymes, collectively called DNAses, that break down DNA into harmless and metabolizable nucleic acids (not to mention the acidic environment of our guts that hydrolyze many of the chemical bonds of DNA, also causing degradation into individual nucleic acids). Our cells have natural salvage

metabolic pathways which reuse these nucleic acids and make new DNA, similar to reusing bricks from a wall to make a new wall. One of the safest ways to get DNA into our bodies is by oral ingestion. Even when consumed in quantities, ingested DNA just does no harm. Therefore, for the coelacanth, or any other species of fish for that matter, to consume the mutated salmon DNA and be mutated in turn just could not happen.

What Biological Science Is Necessary to Actually Achieve the Results in the Film: For the moment, let us assume that the mutated salmon DNA did make it past the digestive processes intact (or intact enough to cause significant changes) and mutated the coelacanth. The ingested DNA would have to be extensive enough to code for legs, arms, a thinking brain, and lungs. That is some serious DNA! (Let us not forget that fish did indeed crawl out of the oceans and acquire arms, legs, and lungs, but it took eons of evolutionary time for all this to occur.) Also, there could be mutated controlling elements in the DNA genes, so that somehow only primitive fish (such as the coelacanth) could be affected by it. That is a stretch, but it is plausible.

During the film Drake shows that her DNA experiments accelerate frog development, causing tadpole eggs to mature into adult frogs in a matter of days instead of the usual 12 weeks gestation period. For this to actually occur would require an enormous amount of DNA metabolism. An average cell may take about 24 hours to divide, producing two daughter cells. During this 24 hour period, about eight hours are devoted to duplicating all of the cell's DNA. To significantly shorten this time interval would require a quantitative change in all the DNA metabolic machinery; no easy task there. There *have* been individual cell mutants in which this has been done, but to do this for an entire organism is a Herculean task of the first order! As stated before, invoking some of these events to occur really is not a problem, and some can be actually achieved. It is the amount of time required to do them that is difficult to accept. If these cinemascientists worked within a more realistic time frame, then much of what they did is plausible.

Could It Actually Happen: Mutations in species are more common that thought. However, most of these mutations are due to environmental conditions, such as excessive ultraviolet radiation (which would not affect fish because water absorbs most of the UV light, rendering it harmless), polluting chemicals, and perhaps atomic radiation. Furthermore, mutations in the DNA as a result of these causes are by and large fatal because the mutations are not selective to certain regions of DNA but rather to all DNA, including the critical controlling regions that are absolute for life. The reality is that the "humanoids from the deep" mutations just would not happen.

The Thing (1982)

Synopsis: A military base in the Arctic Circle is invaded by an alien that can assimilate and duplicate any life form. Those at the base realize that any one of them could have been taken over, so they develop a method to test for the alien and see who can easily move from body to body. The alien is eventually discovered and destroyed.

(Note: There is, of course, the 1952 original version of this film, which in some respects, particularly the characterizations of those stationed at the base, is far superior to this 1982 version, whose characters are primarily one-dimensional. I chose the 1982 film because it had more interesting biological science to discuss, which is the whole point of this book.)

Screenplay: Bill Lancaster, based on the story "Who Goes There," by Don A. Stuart (aka: John W. Campbell, Jr.).

Biological Science Principles Involved: Molecular Biology. Cell Biology. Infectious Diseases.

What Is Right with the Biological Science Presented: The autopsy performed on one of the victims is well staged. The pathologist did what he should have done and asks the right questions. During one autopsy the doctor says, "What we have here appears to be a normal set of internal organs. Heart, lungs, kidneys, liver, intestines seem to be normal." However, the "body" is a biological mess, with multiple arms, legs, hands, heads(!), torsos, etc. One hand has more than 5 fingers and another has less. The doctor comments that the physiology of the body is "normal," but its shape is anything but. This is very interesting and says a lot about how the alien views human biology (and by implication, how to use human DNA). As long as the physiology and function of the internal components is sound, the outer appearance could literally be anything. For example, bodies as diverse as those with multiple or altered appendages (caused by birth defects), war casualties with missing limbs, cancer victims, such calamities as the "Elephant Man," and those afflicted with acromegaly — though their bodies are different, all of them have normal organ and organ functions.

Once the staff of the military base realizes the nature of the alien among them, they then take the necessary precautions to prevent further "infections." One member soberly states, "If a small particle is all that is necessary to take over anyone, then I suggest we all prepare our own meals. And eat out of cans." It is the "eating out of cans" part which indicates the level of natural paranoia this situation brought forth.

What Is Wrong with the Biological

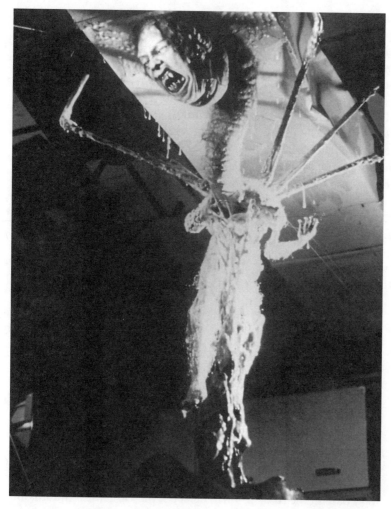

DNA would have some generic controlling elements that would allow it to assimilate, handle, and translate any DNA from any species.

A comment is made that "there is still cellular activity in these [human] remains; they're not dead yet." After death there is indeed some cellular activity which still occurs, and depending upon how long after death, the host can be revived. But in the case referred to here, the host has been dead for some time, making it near impossible to completely revive a "thinking" human.

One of the many forms of *The Thing* seen in the 1982 remake. This particular version had a variety of different species' DNA expressed as unique anatomical structures, such as crab/spider-like claws, dog/cat torso, human-like head.

Science Presented: The primary difficulty with this film is the time it takes for the mutations to occur. DNA just does not work that fast. For the alien DNA to be integrated, transcribed, and translated so readily is difficult to accept.

For the alien DNA to work in the manner shown in the film, it would have to be highly infectious. This would limit the type and nature of the alien DNA, since contact appears to be its method of horizontal transfer from host to host. The alien

The staff at the Arctic base speculate that the spaceship carrying the alien arrived on earth about 100,000 years ago, based on the geology of the area in which the ship is embedded. The ship's "pilot" was apparently thrown some distance from the craft, since its body is found encased in ice many meters away from the ship. Finding intact tissue frozen in ice is acceptable, since, after all, many ice age mammals (like the woolly mammoth) have been found well preserved in ice. However, an intact, thinking, and fully cognitive life form successfully revived after being frozen for millennia is hard to accept.

One of the base staff uses a computer to do some simple calculations of the "intruder's" ability to infect others and says, "Probability that one or more team members may be infected by intruder organism is 75 percent." Then, "If intruder organism reaches civilized areas ... entire world wide population infected 27,000 hours from first contact." That 27,000 hours represents a little over 3 years and is too long a time necessary to infect the entire world.

What Biological Science Is Necessary to Actually Achieve the Results in the Film: The main scientific thesis of this movie is that DNA is universal. As MacReady reads from Blair's notebook, "It could have imitated a million life forms on a million planets. It could change into any one of them at any time. It needs to be alone and in close proximity with life form to be absorbed."

In principle, the alien DNA could work like a virus. It does not need all of the genetic code to make a complete organism, and would rely on the respective hosts to provide those necessary components. Rather, like a virus, it only needs to use whatever genes necessary to control and dominate the will of the host. Part of the alien gene library would be the instructions to control tissue and bone growth. Perhaps the alien DNA has genes that are capable of super-amplifying what the respective hosts provide, such as an immune system, communication skills, cognitive powers, various body movements, etc.

Since the alien can change its form to whatever suits its purpose, then it must have some sort of "genetic memory"—in that it remembers what DNA it has taken from previous hosts and is capable of using what it wants, depending upon the circumstances. For example, during one particularly graphic (and effective) scene, the head of a human came off, grew crab-like legs, and scurried off. Nowhere in the human genome are there DNA segments which code for such appendages. The alien must have genetically "remembered" this from a previous host and used it as an escape mechanism. If true, then the mind of the alien can significantly influence which genes are used at which time. Fascinating adaptability.

One more word on physical adaptability. To better explain the different morphological forms seen of the alien, one can think of the creature as having the ability to morph, meaning the ability to rapidly change its appearance. Many of the morphs seen look quite painful. Pain is pain, and since the alien has such sophisticated DNA mutability, he also must have some way to biologically minimize pain. Mammals have natural analgesics called endorphins, which are morphine-like in their actions and deaden pain. Pain is caused by electrical misfirings between the junctions where nerve fibers attach to cells and tissues. The alien most likely has the ability to synthesize some sort of small molecules, probably peptides, which fold in ways that mimic the pain-suppressing effects of morphine. The alien would have these molecules coursing throughout the bodies of its hosts to minimize whatever pain was experienced due to the physical morphing it does.

Could It Actually Happen: If we assume that DNA is the basis of all life forms (or at least some outside our own solar system), there is the possibility that the respective DNA of us and them could intermingle, resulting in something truly bizarre. Would this new hybrid form be viable and functional? Possibly. Could it infect, mutate, and change physical appearances as often as seen in this movie? Possibly. Could it do it as fast as shown? Highly doubtful.

Watchers II (1990)

Synopsis: A super intelligent golden retriever dog named Einstein is psychically linked to a genetically engineered creature designed for assassinations. As expected, the creature escapes and goes on a killing rampage, and the dog is then used to locate it. The creature is eventually destroyed by electrocution.

Screenplay: Henry Dominic, based on the novel *Watchers* by Dean R. Koontz.

Biological Science Principles Involved: Molecular Biology.

What Is Right with the Biological Science Presented: In my own research I have worked with a number of small animals, in particular, rabbits and mice. As stated by Dr. Xavier (in film *Doctor X*), these animals are "mankind's benefactors." I would guesstimate that I have used thousands of mice over the years in my various experiments. Consequently, I am quite aware of the animal rights activists and their agenda. In their hearts they believe they are doing the right thing, though their energy is, in my opinion, definitely misplaced. Much of the success of the health care industry is due to the research done with small animals. If you take some type of medication for whatever ails you and you recover, you can thank some mouse or other small animal somewhere, because they were used to verify, monitor, and confirm the efficacy of what you used. Dr. Steve, the one who created the titular creature of this film, when informed that his project will be terminated, notifies some animal rights activists and lets them break into the lab and free all the animals. Here in San Diego, where I work and live, there is a large biomedical research community; unfortunately, from time to time, there are break-ins at labs and the housed animals are released. All in all, this represents a horrendous waste of time and resources. Unfortunately, lab break-ins by animal rights activists are an all too true and real occurrence.

In the film, the main focus of the "Anodyne" company is the "Aesop Project," a program to breed super-intelligent animals. This kind of work does indeed go on at a number of levels. However, in this film, the motivation for generating super intelligent animals is military in nature. This is all explained by Anodyne's chief scientist, Dr. Steve, when he says, "There is a 'psychic bond' between AE73 [the dog, Einstein] and AE74 [the creature]. We utilize human DNA. AE73 and AE74 are Anodyne's first steps towards biomedical means of infiltration and elimination. The canine 73s will perform efficient, undetected espionage, discovering enemy command posts. The 74s, non-human assassins, will be capable of tracking the 73s empathically, moving in, and neutralizing enemy command personnel. It may sound like science fiction, but the age of selective genetic breeding has arrived. The future looks bright." (Well, gentle readers, the "age of selective breeding" has been with us for centuries.) Time and time again we hear of dogs who seem to go to extraordinary lengths and endurance to be with their "masters." While difficult to put in molecular terms, some type of "psychic bond" does indeed exist between man and animals, so the filmmakers got this right.

The creature's appearance is interesting. It appears humanoid, has claws with webs between its fingers, rough skin, long drooping jaws, hair all over its body (though not as much as a monkey), is very muscular, has three spines visible running down the length of its back, has exoskeletal ribs (similar to the main creature in the movie *Alien* as created by H.R. Geiger), and a small tail. With all this you would think that it could withstand just about any environment. However, Dr. Glatman, a colleague of Dr. Steve, says the creature has "been a problem from the start. Its eyes can't handle normal light. Its metabolism is so delicate that is has to be kept in a sauna." These imperfections are interesting, because any genetically engineered life form (especially something as complex as this creature) would have a few flaws, and these make sense. For military purposes they would want the creature to only go out at night, so they make its eyes sensitive to light, forcing it to avoid the sun and carry out its clandestine operations under the cover of darkness. A nice touch. A delicate metabolism is also another effective means of controlling the creature. The room the creature is housed in is kept at 120 degrees Fahrenheit!

While out in the countryside the creature kills a cow for food. At least we know AE74 is not a vegetarian.

What Is Wrong with the Biological Science Presented: Dr. Steve, the creator of the creature, is seen surgically inserting a computer chip (which is a tracking device) into the creature. While doing this, Steve does not wear any surgical or sterile attire, just street clothes and a pair of rubber gloves. The risk of contamination is a real problem here, and he should have dressed appropriately. After putting in all the hard work to create AE74 in the first place, he should have taken every precaution to insure the proper care and maintenance of his "baby." Also, even if Dr. Steve engineered a super immune system in the creature to combat any and all germs and diseases in the environment, he still should have taken the necessary precautions. No need to tempt fate, and there is no excuse for sloppy technique.

The main hero of the movie, Paul, is thought to have committed one of the murders actually done by the creature. The dog, Einstein, knows better and actually types(!) on Dr. White's computer (by holding a pencil in its mouth, no less, and using the eraser end to hit the keys), "paul nokilr." Then, Paul asks, "That thing [the creature] in the desert, what was it?" The dog types, "outsidr kilr." Paul then asks, "Why's it following me?" The dog types, "not u hate me." Dr. White, also present during this exchange, exclaims, "This is a miracle! [A major understatement.] They were trying to breed super intelligent animals. To genetically engineer them, actually... Anodyne — we all thought Einstein was ordinary." There is no way a dog could respond in this manner. If we can accept a genetically engineered military assassin with psychic ability, then we can also accept a golden retriever that types.

Speaking of psychic talents, mention is made of the creature's ability to pick up the psychic bond with the dog over long distances (miles). It is unclear how this is done, but it is hard to accept that DNA is responsible for that.

What Biological Science Is Necessary to Actually Achieve the Results in the Film: The creature needs a warm environment to survive. In real world science, temperature sensitive mutants, those who survive better at around 116 degrees Fahrenheit (42°C), are generated all the time to analyze metabolic pathways and the functions of certain enzymes. After all, there are forms of bacteria on earth that readily survive in hot springs, where the temperature is even higher. At these higher temperatures some enzymes, and therefore an organism's metabolism in general, functions more efficiently. When the temperature is reduced to ambient levels, these organisms are sluggish and their growth is severely limited. A rather neat way to control metabolic growth. The concern in all this is that if the creature were put in cold environments would it be able to function at all? Since they were able to genetically engineer one to function in warm conditions, then they should be able to engineer another one that could adequately function in colder climates.

Could It Actually Happen: All the

previous comments on genetic engineering in specific abilities and traits apply here too. Even genetically creating whole organisms is certainly plausible. Dolly the cloned sheep is a real world example of this. However, we still have a long way to go to have dogs develop extensive communicative and cognitive skills on the level seen in this film.

Carnosaur (1993)

Synopsis: Scientist Dr. Jane Tiptree infects chicken eggs with dinosaur DNA in an attempt to let dinosaurs repopulate the earth. Human females who eat the chicken eggs give birth to melon-sized dino eggs and die during the process. The motivation here is that Dr. Tiptree wants to replace mankind with dinosaurs; after all, they were here first. In the end, Dr. Tiptree spawns her own dino egg and dies from the experience.

Screenplay: Adam Simon, based on the novel by Harry Adam Knight.

Biological Science Principles Involved: Molecular Biology. Biochemistry.

What Is Right with the Biological Science Presented: Tiptree. This is an homage to the award winning science fiction writer James Tiptree, Jr., which itself is a pen name for Alice Sheldon. For years Sheldon wrote under the Tiptree name and everyone thought the author was male. This subterfuge went on for some time, and included hardback books with a dust jacket profile photo of a cigarette smoking Sheldon/Tiptree that actually looked male! Everyone in the SF community was surprised when Tiptree was eventually revealed to be Sheldon.

In the film, a research institution/think tank located in Washington, D.C., goes by the name "Advanced Research Projects Administration" or ARPA. On the entrance walls of the ARPA facility are several representations of DNA and protein structures. All of them are quite authentic, indicating a keen attention to background detail. Usually the creators of SF films forgo these sorts of set trappings, and if they do use them they invariably get them wrong. The makers of *Carnosaur* got all of these right and should be congratulated.

During one scene a truck driver is killed by a freshly hatched dinosaur. A local physician, Dr. Raven, examines the body and removes a wound sample for analysis. He tests for rabies and other animal diseases, which are, of course, all negative. Raven thought the mutilated body of the truck driver is naturally caused by some wild animal, and he performs the standard tests to learn which one did it. This represents good, careful, and systematic thinking. (Not every experiment will yield the results you are seeking. However, if it is carefully planned and performed you will get some data or information that will help you reformulate your question for the next experiment, which could then possibly give you the results you want. This is what Raven did.)

An interesting comment by Tiptree is, "All of the potential for greatness is in the DNA. And just a pinch of it goes very far in the mix. GOD is an acronym, Generator of Diversity. That ever elusive inner drive of evolution." Immunologists have used "GOD" as an acronym for the "generation of diversity" for some time, long before it was mentioned in this film. Immunologically speaking, generation of diversity is in reference to the enormous number of antibody molecules (as many as 10^{15} different versions!), from only a few genes, made in humans to combat and neutralize antigens.

What Is Wrong with the Biological Science Presented: During the opening credits several DNA sequences are shown. Superimposed over these are such phrases as "sample species: ostrich, target: chicken," and "sample species: iguana, target: chicken," and "sample species: vulture, target: chicken." Other species listed in the same format are "albatross," "crocodile," and "turkey." It is difficult to understand why someone would be trying to insert ostrich, vulture, or crocodile genes into those of a chicken! This just does not make sense. (But then again, cinemascientists usually do not need reasons.)

The intellectual wizards at ARPA say that the research Dr. Tiptree did to earn her Ph.D. was developing genetic alternatives to pesticides. One of the ARPA mental giants then says, while holding up an insect (a moth?): "For her Ph.D. she bred this ugly color right out of existence, eliminating an entire subspecies from the face of the earth. She instantly became a hero to some and public enemy number one to others." In spite of all the efforts of mankind and our various pesticides and poisons, we have yet to eradicate any single species of insect from the face of the earth. Ants, flies, bees, mosquitoes are, unfortunately, here to stay. You may be able to control them but you will not "eliminate an entire subspecies" through genetic breeding.

At a company called Eunice, located in Climax, Nevada, Tiptree is the chief scientist in their food division. A division of Eunice, called "Purex Poultry Plant," is a chicken ranch and during one scene we see a freshly laid giant egg which splits the chicken apart while coming out, leaving a bloody carcass. Such a large egg, bigger that an ostrich egg, would never have developed to the size it did under normal circumstances. A dinosaur, a *T. rex* to be precise, hatches from this egg and grows into the main character of the film.

The reason Dr. Tiptree goes to Climax, Nevada, is because apparently the area used to be "dinosaur highway ... a migration route about 60 million years ago." Well, a large meteor hit earth near the Yucatan peninsula in Central America around 65 million years ago—what is called the Cretaceous/Triassic boundary (or K/T boundary for short)—and the cataclysm eliminated about 95 percent of all species on the planet. The dinosaurs were all wiped out thereby giving rise to the age of mammals. This was all common knowledge during 1993 when this film was done. Since dinosaurs were all gone 65 million years ago, then how could they have made a "dinosaur highway ... 60 million years ago?" All it would have taken to make this believable was to say the highway migration route was in operation 70 million years ago. This cinema blunder should not have happened.

While analyzing a tissue sample from a human dino victim, a scientist says, "DNA tests [most likely a PCR test] showed a genetic marker for a neutral sequence. The marker is registered to Eunice. It's supposed to be in chickens." A technician responds by saying, "Couldn't the animal have absorbed the marker by eating the chickens?" (For details on the problems of ingesting DNA and having it expressed intact, please see the description of this under the entry on *Humanoids from the Deep*.) The scientist then says, "Either that or the animal that attacked him was a chicken," implying a giant killer chicken is on the loose. If these "scientists" (using that term loosely) were able to locate and sequence DNA that typed as chicken, then they certainly should have been able to find lengthy sequences that would have come up as completely foreign; these would be from the dinosaur. Their conversation should have been something like this: Scientist: "Hey, all these DNA sequences we discovered from the wounds were not matched with any species we have in our extensive data banks." Technician: "Where do you think they came from?" Scientist: "I don't know, but this tiny little piece of DNA here marked as coming from a chicken. How do you suppose that got in there?"

To add insult to injury here, the above mentioned "neutral sequence" is actually shown, which is: "-DLVDRN-RQAEQQARR-." These single letters are code for individual amino acids, the building blocks of proteins. This sequence translates as: Asp-Leu-Val-Asp-Arg-Asn-Arg-Gln-Ala-Glu-Gln-Gln-Ala-Arg-Arg-. Four of these amino acids are positively charged, three are negatively charged; and at physiological pH conditions, there would be one more positive charge and three more negatively charged amino acids, resulting in a total of five positive charges and six negative charges—anything *but* a "neutral sequence." They got this piece of biological science completely wrong.

The dinosaurs that hatched from the chicken eggs grew very fast. One local sheriff cracks open some eggs for breakfast and one of the eggs has a "lizard embryo" in it. The sheriff, after taking this to Dr. Raven for analysis, says, "…it's grown three times since morning." The developed embryo is removed from the egg fluid (and nutrient source) by the sheriff, so there are no nutrients available for the dino to ingest for growth. As such, it is unclear what the dino ate to "grow three times since morning." Let's be generous and say that even if the dino was able to assimilate half of the ingested foodstuffs, this would mean the dino had to consume at least six times its size in food! No way.

As mentioned above, Tiptree's receptionist becomes pregnant with a dino egg, just before delivery she has a body temperature of 113°! This is incredible. For an adult, anything above 105 is severely debilitating, and above 108 is just about fatal; she would have been unconscious way before she reached 113! Imagine someone in labor with a temperature of 113 listening to Tiptree mouth gobbledygook on "genetic

text … soul … fire of creation." No wonder the woman died while giving birth!

Those women who did give birth to dinosaurs did so not via the traditional birth canal but by the dinos bursting *Alien*-like through the abdomen. As engineered by Tiptree, this traumatic birth scenario causes the death of the mother. This is a very effective and efficient way to eliminate women — and therefore mankind — from the planet, thereby giving it back to the dinosaurs, Tiptree's original agenda. To reiterate, Tiptree says, "The earth was not made for us. She was made for the dinosaurs."

Once the always-on-their-toes military figures out Tiptree's plan to eliminate women, the following conversation takes place. Military genius #1: "Worst case scenario?" Military genius #2: "At this rate, in 10 days, we could lose 34 percent of the female population. Barring the discovery of a serum, we could lose half of the species in six months." Given a total earth population of six billion, three billion of which are women (with about two billion able to bear children), then 34 percent represents about 680 million women. That many women dead in 10 days would be 68 million a day! It boggles the mind. With these same statistics, why would it take another 5.7 months to lose the remaining 66 percent of the women? (Only the crack military could come up with math like that. After all, they are the ones who budget for $500 hammers and $1,000 ashtrays!)

In answer to all this military posturing on the amount of female casualties, the CEO of Eunice offers this solution: "We've been working on artificial wombs for years … we have the technology. It would take some time but we could breed a new generation of females." In response, the always sympathetic military brass says, "That would call for some drastic social engineering. With firm leadership, prudent organization, and aggressive fertilization programs, I think the species could survive. Who knows, a strong federal scientific fertilization plan might even build a new, stronger breed."

Finally, we have the issue of the serum Tiptree makes that can counteract the effects of the infecting dino virus. Yes, there are antiserums that do indeed neutralize viruses, but none that look like translucent green antifreeze, which is what the anti-dino virus appears to be. True serums would be a clear liquid. The bottle of Day-Glo green serum we see has about 200 milliliters (a few ounces) of fluid in it. The main hero of the film gives an injection of this (about 3 milliliters volume — a teaspoon full) to his girlfriend in hope that it would prevent her pregnancy; it did not and she died. The problem here is that not only was the volume and dose wrong, but he gave her the injection behind her neck, in the upper shoulder area! A most unusual (and ineffective) spot for an injection.

What Biological Science Is Necessary to Actually Achieve the Results in the Film: The most likely source of obtaining dinosaur DNA is from an insect (mosquito?) that has dino blood inside its body. (This is the basis for the book — and subsequent film — *Jurassic Park*.) This does not mean dinosaur red blood cells (since these, most likely, do not have DNA inside them) but some other cell type, either a lymphocyte (a white blood cell) — assuming, of course, that dinosaurs even had the equivalent of a lymphocyte (they may not have) — or, more likely, a skin cell, which would have DNA. This DNA would have to remain completely intact, with all the necessary genetic controlling sequences and regulatory elements in the proper reading frame. (To help understand this, think of a typeset page of a newspaper. If the set type is intact and in proper sequence, then you could read the words. However, if the punctuation, a few of the letters, or whole columns of type were missing or destroyed — or if headlines were rearranged — then you could not read the entire page as intended. DNA is the same way, but instead of a single page of type, imagine thousands and thousands of pages of type. Then think of the odds of all of the pages remaining intact and in complete reading sequence and surviving for more than 65 million years. The odds of this happening are astronomical.)

For the sake of argument, let us assume we have found intact dino DNA. The next step of placing this DNA into chicken embryos is a relatively easy step. However, the chicken enzymatic machinery necessary to convert the DNA sequences into real and viable cells and tissues may not be compatible with dino DNA. It'd be like trying to read Apple software on an IBM computer. Without the necessary translation codes, what you get is garbled machine language. So, in order to work, the chicken DNA translation and transcription instructions would have to work on dino DNA. Quite frankly, that may be so, because even bacterial DNA enzymes can "read" human DNA with complete fidelity. Essentially, DNA is DNA, regardless of what species it is. Since dinosaurs were derived from the same source material as all life on earth, their DNA should be readable by chicken DNA enzymes too. The problem with this is in the control elements (essentially, the genetic punctuation) that regulate how DNA is translated. Many of these control elements are species specific.

Could It Actually Happen: A wealth of interesting cinemascience is dealt with in this film, and all of it is interesting. To locate complete sequences of dinosaur DNA is a major problem; and the biggest difficulty with this is recognizing the DNA for what it is, since we have no reference material upon which to base the data. Some real scientists have indeed tried just that, but they do not know if they sequenced contaminating bits of DNA (from, say, bacteria or mold) that grew on the samples or real dinosaur DNA. As stated, there are no reference samples from which to compare. Furthermore, the DNA sequences that have been obtained are fragments and not the complete genome of a dinosaur. You see, DNA is organic matter, and it is highly unlikely that intact and complete sequences (with all the appropriate regulatory and controlling elements) would be functional after more than 65 million years. You would need all of this for a viable and living dinosaur to be cloned.

The ability to take this dino DNA and, with the aid of an appropriate virus vector, infect chicken eggs with it is not that far fetched. In principle, this has been successfully done in many virus laboratories throughout the world; these scientists typically *do* use chicken eggs to incubate virus stocks for study and analysis. However, to ingest this DNA from a cooked egg(!)—resulting in a woman becoming pregnant—is ludicrous and quite impossible.

Jurassic Park (1993)

Synopsis: Dinosaur DNA is discovered inside an amber (tree sap)–preserved mosquito. Scientists remove the dino DNA, insert it into a frog embryo, and get it to grow and mature into a complete and functional dinosaur. A theme park is constructed on an island for these genetically engineered dinosaurs. The dinosaurs escape and kill a few people.

Screenplay: Michael Crichton and David Koepp, based on Crichton's novel *Jurassic Park.*

Biological Principles Involved: Molecular Biology. Biochemistry.

What Is Right with the Biological Science Presented: Yes, insects have been found preserved in amber or tree sap that is millions of years old, and yes, scientists have attempted to analyze the DNA contained therein. The results are, unfortunately, ambiguous; they are unable to determine the actual source of the DNA—a contaminating bacteria, yeast, mold, fungus, virus, or actual dinosaur (or a combination of the above)—because there is no reference DNA sequence to which it can be compared. Any one of these organisms could be present, either as natural flora or as a contaminant (either obtained in ancient times or introduced during the discovery and cloning stage).

The lengthy description in the film of "the miracle of cloning" hosted by the animated "Mr. DNA" is well done and probably serves as the first exposure to genetic engineering for many who see this film. This segment starts (correctly) with obtaining a drop of blood. As Mr. DNA says, "Just one drop of your blood contains billions of strands of DNA, the building blocks of life. A DNA strand like me is a blueprint for building a living thing. And sometimes animals that went extinct millions of years ago, like dinosaurs, left their blueprints behind for us to find. We just had to know where to look. A hundred million years ago there were mosquitoes just like today ... they fed on the blood of dinosaurs ... landed on a tree and got stuck in the sap ... fossilized ... preserved mosquito ... in amber.... Using sophisticated techniques they extract the preserved blood from the mosquito and ... dino DNA. A full DNA strand contains three billion genetic codes. If we looked at screens like these once a second [here many segments of actual DNA nucleotide sequences flash by as background, and each "screen" shows approximately 4000 nucleotides] for eight hours a day, it'd take two years to look at the entire DNA strand. It's that long ... it's full of holes. Now that's where our geneticists take over ... gene sequencers break

The principal (human) characters look at a velociraptor egg just as it is about to hatch in *Jurassic Park* (1993). In the case of the genetically engineered dinosaurs at Jurassic Park, the dinosaur came before the egg.

down the strand in minutes and virtual reality displays show our geneticists the gaps in the DNA sequence. We use the complete DNA of a frog to fill in the holes and complete the code ... make a baby dinosaur." In a nutshell, this is a wonderful introduction to the world of genetic engineering and recombinant DNA.

The comment, "it's full of holes," is in reference to the incomplete nature of the dinosaur DNA. The degree of incompleteness is critical. If perhaps just a few key genes were missing or inactive, then those from the frog could compensate for this deficiency. In this case, the resulting organism would indeed resemble a dinosaur. However, if many genes were missing or inactive, and the frog would have to provide many genes to compensate, then the resulting organism could be more frog-like than dinosaur.

Population control through the control of an organism's sex is common, and this as-

pect is engineered into the dinosaurs. Henry, one of the Jurassic Park scientists says, "They can't breed in the wild. Population control is one of our security precautions ... all the animals in Jurassic Park are female ... we've engineered them that way ... we control their chromosomes.... All vertebrate embryos are inherently female anyway; they just require an extra hormone given at the right developmental stage to make them male. We simply deny them that."

Many scientists do ponder the long-term implications of their work and the potential impacts on life and society. Malcolm, the mathematician, says, "Genetic power is the most awesome force the planet's ever seen.... I'll tell you the problem with the scientific power that you're using here. It didn't require any discipline to attain it.... Your scientists were so preoccupied with whether or not they could, they didn't stop to think if they should." Yes indeed, DNA is an "awesome force."

Grant, a paleontologist, notices some broken egg shells in the wild, indicating breeding has taken place — even though all the animals are female. To explain this, Grant says, "Amphibian DNA — on the film tour they said they used frog DNA to fill in the gene sequence gaps. They mutated the dinosaur genetic code and blended it with that of frogs. Some West African frogs have been known to spontaneously change sex from male to female in a single sex environment."

The amino acid, lysine, one of the building blocks of proteins, is an essential amino acid, meaning it must be obtained from dietary sources since it cannot be manufactured by many animals. Humans typically get lysine from plant sources. A chronic diet deficient in lysine will ultimately cause disease and death, and this "lysine contingency" is engineered into the dinosaurs. A Jurassic Park employee explains, "Lysine contingency is intended to prevent the spread of the animals in case they ever got off the island. Doctor Wu inserted a gene that creates a single faulty enzyme in protein metabolism. The animals can't manufacture the amino acid lysine. Unless they are completely supplied with lysine by us they slip into a coma and die."

During the credits, acknowledgment is given to "Genetic Engineering News, Mary Ann Liebert, Inc. Publishers" and to "Carl Zeiss, Inc." *GEN* is a bimonthly free publication to all in the biotechnology industry. It is an excellent newsletter that keeps those in the industry well informed and up to date on all biomedical and biotechnology developments. Carl Zeiss, Inc., is the Rolls Royce of microscope makers, and there are none better.

What Is Wrong with the Biological Science Presented: During the segment where Mr. DNA gives the description of the "miracle of cloning," the extraction of fluids from an amber-bound mosquito is seen. The needle seen going into the drilled hole in the piece of amber is covered with all sorts of particulates that could introduce a myriad of contaminations. This needle should have been completely clean. With a contamination much time could be wasted cloning the wrong DNA. Just after this extraction scene a pink fluorescent liquid is withdrawn into a syringe. The audience is led to believe this is DNA when it is just a pink fluorescent dye with an ultraviolet light shining on it. DNA itself has no color.

During the animated "miracle of cloning" segment a very odd cartoon of a DNA molecule is seen — and it's unclear why it is presented this way. The helical double strand structure, though correct, has sections of the DNA strand with the nucleotide sequence CGAGTAG interrupted with nondescript box-like structures. The inclusion of these box structures is not only wrong, but pointless and serves no purpose.

Also, toward the end of the "miracle of cloning" segment Mr. DNA says "…virtual reality displays…" in reference to the analysis of complete sequences of dinosaur DNA. The *Jurassic Park* "virtual reality displays" show DNA in real time, and how they can spot gaps or holes in the sequence while analyzing the strand and make the appropriate repair. None of this is currently possible and is highly improbable in the future.

The scene of the theft of the dinosaur embryo eggs deserves comment. Two liquid nitrogen storage containers are opened and a copious amount of condensation is seen coming out. Liquid nitrogen is about −180°C (very cold), and when this contacts normal air — with a temperature of around 20–25°C (a two hundred degree difference!) — normal air essentially freezes and the heat evaporates the nitrogen liquid into a gas. Way too much evaporating liquid nitrogen is seen coming out of the tanks. The ampules containing the dinosaur embryos should have been frozen solid (at liquid nitrogen temperatures), but when they are being removed from their aluminum rod holders they are clearly thawed. Also, condensation comes off ampules freshly removed from liquid nitrogen, and nothing like this is seen, indicating they are at room temperature.

Part of the confusion of what is wrong with the biological science presented in *Jurassic Park* is the blurring of gene engineering with that of cloning, both of which are two separate procedures that accomplish different goals. In one respect the difference is that of scale. Gene engineering (or gene cloning) is working at the molecular level with an individual or a family of genes, whereas cloning is dealing with an entire organism. Furthermore, cloning requires the use of germ line cells, while gene engineering can use either germ line or somatic (body) cells. This difference between gene engineering and cloning in this film is significant. Cloning a few dinosaur genes is certainly possible, and some actual ancient samples may have provided such information. The cloning of an intact dinosaur would require a completely functioning dinosaur genome, which would not have survived since the time before the Cretaceous Period.

Assuming that some dinosaur genes were successfully cloned and expressed in frog eggs (see below), then the resulting organism would certainly have been a hybrid between frog and dinosaur. The dinosaur species we see look exactly like dinosaurs rather than some interesting combination of frog and dinosaur.

What Biological Science Is Necessary to Actually Achieve the Results in the Film: What comes first, the dinosaur or the dinosaur egg? Dinosaur DNA would have to survive completely intact in the abdomen of a mosquito preserved in fossilized amber. (The odds against this happening are discussed in the entry on *Carnosaur.*) With the sophisticated techniques available (such as PCR technology), then as little as one dinosaur cell need survive to be able to clone the DNA. Within each cell is the entire DNA of the species, and only those genes specific to each cell type are expressed. To develop an entirely new organism from cloned DNA would require the ability to turn on and turn off genes in such a way that embryogenesis (the growth of a fetus), development, differentiation, and coordinated growth occur in a non-lethal way, resulting in a healthy, viable dinosaur. Yes, frog embryos are capable of doing this. A complete copy of cloned dinosaur DNA (the species of your choice) is inserted into an unfertilized frog embryo. The embryo is allowed to grow and develop until it hatches. Land dinosaurs had lungs, so once the frog/dinosaur hatched from its frog embryo, it would have to get out of its water environment right away or risk drowning. However, this would only apply to the first dinosaur created in each species, because subsequent ones are hatched from laid dinosaur eggs. To answer the question posed at the top of this paragraph — which came first, the dinosaur or the egg — at Jurassic Park the answer is the dinosaur.

To actually create a dinosaur at Jurassic Park, a complete (or near complete) dinosaur genome would have to be obtained. The question here is how would the scientists know whether they had an intact genome or not, since there is nothing with which to compare it. A partial genome could have critical genes missing or expressed as an inactive form, which would not have resulted in a viable dinosaur. The worldwide Hugo program to completely sequence the human genome has consumed hundred of thousands of man hours over several years. To completely sequence a dinosaur genome would require an equally Herculean task. With enough gene sequencers working around the clock, perhaps the work could be done within several years. The dinosaur genes would then be inserted into a frog embryo using a micromanipulator machine (see the film *Species* for an example of its use). The frog embryo, composed of gene regulatory and gene activation components, would coordinate the activation and inactivation of the various cell's genes undergoing embryogenesis. The fertilized egg would then be induced to grow and mature by the frog embryo proteins and enzymes until it hatches. As stated, the baby dinosaur would need air for breathing with its lungs, so it would have to be removed from the water immediately after hatching. This means it would have to be carefully watched, possibly with robotic instruments. The dinosaur hatchling would be fed and nurtured into adulthood.

Since we see a liquid nitrogen storage depository containing dozens of "frozen" dinosaur embryos (i.e., fertilized and ready to grow fetal dinosaurs), then a series of fertilized frog eggs had been generated by the Jurassic Park scientists, developed individually, then cryopreserved and stored for future study or hatching.

Could It Actually Happen: Not right now, but someday, when genetic engineering technology has advanced enough, perhaps some of this would be possible with ancient DNA — and certainly possible with completely intact DNA from more recent species. Perhaps the Dodo bird can be cloned from surviving tissue samples and literally brought back alive.

Moonchild (1994)

Synopsis: Jacob Stryker, a genetically enhanced hybrid human, escapes from the "Moonchild Project," a prison complex called "Sodality," to save his missing son, Caleb. Stryker has the engineered ability to shapeshift and turn into a werewolf. For the climactic battle, Stryker turns into a werewolf to fight the mutant dictator of the bad guys and kills him, thereby saving his son.

Screenplay: Todd Sheets, "inspired by," according to the opening credits, "the Book of Mark, Chapter 13, of the King James Bible and the song "Moon Child" by Iron Maiden.

(Note: Todd Sheets' movies are made on what you would call "bottom of the barrel" budgets. Consequently, there are virtually no extraneous trappings or set designs. The actors are all local citizens of "Todd Sheets county" and not recognizable names. Even though the budgets are typically less than zero, the films are usually high on creativity and ideas; the basis of this film was most creative. It is included because of its biological science idea of making a hybrid of human and wolf cells.)

Biological Science Principles Involved: Molecular Biology. Cell Biology.

What Is Right with the Biological Science Presented: On a personal note, one of the areas of my scientific research has been the creation of various mouse-human hybrids with individual cells. I do in no way suggest that I created actual living beings that resembled something like Mickey Mouse and that talked and had other anthropomorphic features. The mouse-human cell lines I created were of individual cells for the mapping of certain genes and to determine in which chromosomes these genes were located; this is a very efficient and neat way to do that type of work. This research could give you answers, for example, about how one gene on, say, chromosome 6 influenced another gene on chromosome 14. To describe the creation of these hybrids in simple terms, I took individual human cells (usually tumor cells like melanoma, a skin cancer, or human lymphocytes, a type of white blood cell) and, using certain chemicals like polyethylene glycol (this is a polymer of ethylene glycol — which is radiator antifreeze! — that helps "glue" cells together), I fused them with mouse cells. These human × mouse cells were true hybrids. The interesting aspect about this is that by using certain selection techniques you can completely rearrange the chromosomal makeup of the hybrids. To help conceptualize this further, think of an incident dog breeding in which a collie is crossed with a beagle, the result being a collie x beagle hybrid combination. In principle, I did the same thing, but instead I worked with individual cells and not living animals. The reason the mouse-human hybrids I made stayed as individual cells was because the cells I used were called somatic cells, meaning they were derived from already existing body tissues. (This is the main misunderstanding non-scientists have about the field of cloning. To actually create a living being, like Dolly the sheep, you need germ line cells, those cells which are capable of reproducing and developing into an embryo. Another misconception is that non-scientists think the cloned animal — or human — will think, act, and behave *exactly* as its parent. This simply is not true. You can only clone physical appearance and not the thoughts and collective experiences of the parent.) The same technology used by (real) scientists to create mouse × human hybrids was also used in this film to create the wolf × human life form of Jacob Stryker.

The highly imaginative biological science angle in this film, in which the "Moonchild Project" is a gene splicing program that mixes animal and human cells to create a new species (albeit for military purposes), is interesting. When gene therapy becomes more routine, this indeed is what will happen. Scientists will be taking the genes from certain species and inserting them into humans who are deficient in that gene. The demarcations between species will truly begin to blur as this technology becomes more and more accepted by society in the future. There will be a time when you will be able to genetically engineer (genengineer) just about any physical feature you want. This may scare some of you gentle readers, but the dawning of the DNAge is at hand, so be prepared.

What Is Wrong with the Biological Science Presented: A bounty hunter asks, "What's so important about the escaped prisoner [Jacob Stryker]?" The commander responds, "The prisoner was an experiment. We began gene splicing, mixing animal and human cells together. Jacob Stryker was our first experiment. He was put through a series of treatments, but before we could erase his memory, he escaped. He's extremely dangerous for us. He was put on a computer that caused accelerated learning." The bounty hunter then asks, "What exactly were you splicing into his cells? What other mammal?" The commander responds with, "A wolf. We were creating the ultimate warrior…. [The gene splicing] has given him superhuman strength and the ability to shapeshift." The bounty hunter says, "Like a werewolf?" Commander: "Exactly." Later another person comments to Stryker, "You're a hybrid being. There is no such thing as a werewolf. You're a hybrid. They've combined your cells with those of a wolf. My guess is they're creating a whole army of hybrids such as yourself…" If I were going to pick a warrior animal to "gene splice" with a human, I would not have picked a wolf. I think a tiger or lion would be more appropriate. Imagine the ferociousness of a weretiger or a werelion.

After receiving the gene splicing treatments Stryker fathers a son who "didn't look completely human when he was born — looked almost like an animal, a wolf or something." Someone then asks,

"Radiation?" The answer: "No." If you are doing gene splicing experiments, the last thing you want is have it interfered with by uncontrollable radiation!

When talking about his son, Stryker says, "...his blood can combat and overcome all known diseases. He can heal himself at an accelerated rate, he can withstand the highest radiation they gave him. He was strong too. Doctors said they could use his blood as a starting point to give the human race a new chance, a new lease on life." Later someone else comments, "His son has special blood that can cure ... plagues ... and help regenerate lost and twisted cells." It is very difficult to imagine someone's blood having enough of an "immune punch" to "combat and overcome all known diseases!"Also, excessive radiation exposure destroys DNA, making it virtually impossible for cells to successfully divide and replicate. Moderate amounts of radiation are tolerable because we have within our bodies certain DNA repair enzymes that can fix some minor damage, particularly that caused by ultraviolet radiation from the sun. It is unlikely this boy could withstand the "highest radiation," since some radiation, like an alpha emitting particle, is very nasty and can easily destroy any biological cell.

During the transformation sequences in which Stryker turns into a werewolf, certain shape-shifting body alterations occur. Shape-shifting would require the alteration of bone and muscle structure, which in turn would require very complicated biology and biochemistry to achieve this. Also, there would be much pain involved because of the disruption of all the neuromuscular connections. Bone would have to solubilize itself and then reform with the same tensile strength (see *The Incredible Shrinking Man* entry for a further discussion of bone). When Stryker changes into a partial wolf his forehead over his eyebrows bulges out, his teeth lengthen

and sharpen, his cheekbones become bigger, and he has super strength. After reverting back to his human shape he asks, "What happened ... I must have blacked out," suggesting that when he does shape change he loses all memory of the event. Massive endorphin release to counteract the pain of shape-shifting could have contributed to this. The implication here is that after changing, his "wolf instincts" took over and his human side lost all contact with reality. There are actual documented psychiatric cases of lycanthropy where the patient does indeed lose contact with reality. The mind can play tricks and can convince you of just about *any* reality.

What Biological Science Is Necessary to Actually Achieve the Results in the Film: The generation of a true human hybrid (or clone) requires a fertilization stage without the union of a sperm and an egg. The genetic material would have to come from cultured cells, most likely a few-days-old embryo, originally derived from both prospective parents. This embryo would then have to be implanted in a human uterus (the surrogate mother) for proper growth and development until time for birth. You need not wait a full nine months for this to happen. In humans, the nine month time is necessary primarily to allow the lungs to fully mature for breathing outside the womb. Premature births at even as few as 25 weeks after fertilization have successfully recovered, even though extensive care is necessary. For a cloned human, perhaps only about 30 weeks in the uterus would be necessary before (cesarean?) delivery. Technology will soon be advanced enough so that this can be bypassed and the embryo can be grown in suitable organ culture systems. As you can imagine, this will be something society will hotly debate for some time.

In simple terms, cloning is based on transfer of cell nuclear material (where the DNA is located), and involves the use of two cells. The recipient cell is typically an unfertilized egg taken from an animal right after ovulation. The donor cell is the one to be copied. It is critical that these cells contain all their genetic information. Since we see more of Stryker than wolf, the donor cell was probably Stryker and the recipient cell was wolf.

There was the statement made that Caleb's "blood can combat and overcome all known diseases." They use the term "blood" here essentially to mean the immune system, which is composed of both a diverse array of cell types (collectively grouped as white blood cells or lymphocytes) and two large families of proteins (one collectively called antibodies and the other "complement"). To avoid a lot of technical jargon and detail, it would be best to think of the lymphocytes as those whose primary job is to destroy other cells and tissues, the antibodies as the proteins that seek out and eliminate (or inactivate) antigens, and complement proteins as those that can literally break apart the membranes of cells, thereby destroying them. Another class of white blood lymphocyte, called cytotoxic lymphocytes, can literally destroy an entire cell. When all the components of the immune system, cellular and molecular, work in unison, there is not much that can survive. However, because animals do indeed suffer from a variety of diseases, at times our immune systems are not adequate. To be sure, not everyone's immune system behaves or operates with the same efficiency. Those individuals who seem to go through life with a minimum of diseases or problems do indeed have a well functioning immune system, and those who suffer from one disease after another do not. (One of my personal research goals is to understand this difference and be able to correct the immune system in those individuals who need the help. Cancer progression is a big part of our malfunctioning immune system. If cancer cannot be outright cured, then at least it can be effectively controlled—much like a diabetic's problems—with periodic immune system "cleansing.") The immune system of Caleb must be "super charged" to behave as it did. And if that is indeed true, then his blood would be very valuable to the future of mankind (or at least the cinemankind in *Moonchild*). Caleb's overall immune system would be quite active in eliminating all pathogens and other disease related causes.

Could It Actually Happen: As explained, the ability to generate somatic cell hybrids and the cloning of animals is here now. It is the development of a complete and functioning human that is a long way off, but that day will arrive sometime during the 21st Century, perhaps within our lifetimes.

Of all the cinemacomments and cinemaideas discussed in this book, the one that I most wish to happen is to have blood that "can combat and overcome all known diseases." That is the best biological science there is and a goal worth achieving. Yes, it could actually happen! Kudos to Todd Sheets for coming up with such wonderful ideas and goals.

Proteus (1995)

Synopsis: An off-shore oil rig is converted into a genetics lab. The oil rig scientists create synthetic DNA called "Proteus," that hijacks the DNA of its victims and can assume their identity. A boat of drug smuggling young adults come on board the oil rig just after the main mutant creature escapes and kills just about everyone present. Eventually, the creature is destroyed by fire.

Screenplay: John Brosnan, from the novel *Slimer* by Harry Adam Knight.

Biological Science Principles Involved: Molecular Biology. Pharmacology.

What Is Right with the Biological Science Presented: Though nothing specific is said which indicates accurate biology, what is convincing are all the particular sets (or labs). They were accurate and immediately generate an air of verisimilitude. There is no doubt that some sort of DNA work is going on in this facility. Legal or illegal, moral or immoral, it does not matter — it is accurate. It is quite clear that the DNAge has arrived on that oil platform.

One of the oil rig scientists, Dr. Shelly, states, "95 percent of all living tissue is made up of water," which is correct. Living, sessile organisms of earth are essentially moving bags of water.

As previously stated, though DNA is DNA, it is species specific. Like the individual letters of the alphabet, it is the sequence of the letters that depends upon which language it is. DNA in principle is the same, its sequence determines which species it comes from. The reason this is mentioned is because Dr. Shelly states that of all the different animals given the synthetic DNA they develop only one species — a shark (*Car caradon*; i.e., great white) — that accepts it. This would suggest that the developed DNA is species specific, which is quite accurate. It would have been too easy to say that every species accepts the DNA, so the creators of the film knew that DNA does have some limitations, which is certainly correct.

When the yuppie-like, upscale drug smugglers enter the oil platform (their small boat exploded and they were afloat at sea until they drifted to the rig) they go through a chamber that is some sort of sterilization unit. As soon as they enter a soft blue light comes on, which is characteristic of an ultraviolet light used for many low level sterilization procedures in biology. This makes sense. The workers on the rig would want some sort of biohazard control protection, and ultraviolet light is simple to use, inexpensive, and is the method of choice.

What Is Wrong with the Biological Science Presented: Shortly after the drug smugglers enter one of the labs and see the DNA nucleotide sequence profiles on the wall, one of them says, "That's human DNA." Even the most seasoned molecular biologist could in no way determine what species a sequence profile came from. Using the alphabet letter analogy mentioned above, this would be like seeing individual letters in a different sequence and saying "that's Spanish." After this, the same person then goes on to say (while still looking at each DNA gel nucleotide sequence film) that a "chemical breakdown is next to each." DNA sequences provide no information regarding a "chemical breakdown," so it is not clear what was meant or implied here.

One of the labs has something that looks to be a model of DNA. This makes sense since, after all, the action does take place in a genetic engineering lab. However, that model, though it looks like DNA (in that there is a hint of a double helix structure connected by different colored balls), is not DNA. DNA is a helical structure, much like a circular stairway. The actual stairway steps would correspond to the nucleic acid base pairs, and the handrail would correspond to the ribose sugar backbone that holds the whole thing together. The DNA base pairs come apart (and together) much like a zipper. You undo it and each side has the complimentary part of the other side. It's elegantly simple, yet they got it wrong. What is puzzling is that the creators of the film went to such great lengths to make the labs look real (even including a radioactive waste disposal box!) that they should have been able to get a simple model of DNA right.

In explaining how the main creature was created, Dr. Shelly states, "We succeeded in making a package of synthetic

DNA [called Proteus] capable of instant evolution. Test animals were given Proteus. Other animals receiving Proteus failed to accept Proteus, except shark. We thought we killed the shark [they nicknamed it "Charlie"] when it ran out of adaptive changes. We were wrong. Proteus had moved on to a new level. It had converted shark tissue to a new form. Amorphous. At night it crawled out of the tank and consumed every other specimen in the aquarium. We were overjoyed ... we were idiots. Our own success in creating something unkillable finished us. In the end it got us all. Changing, mutating, becoming more powerful. Proteus DNA has succeeded in creating an ultimate survival mechanism. Charlie hijacks DNA of his victims along with other potentially valuable survival characteristics ... and our knowledge and memories." What a mouthful. First of all, the two reel biological science phrases "instant evolution" and "hijacks DNA," though interesting and descriptive, have no foundation in real biology. Making "synthetic DNA" is no problem and is done all the time in many labs throughout the world. The BIG problem is getting that DNA expressed and functional in any species (this has been described in detail in other films). Once the Proteus synthetic DNA gets into a shark it mutates "instantly." Most mutations are lethal, and only over millennia do improvements take place. This is what is called evolution, and it takes millions of years for major changes to occur. The "changing, mutating, becoming more powerful" could occur — but not instantly.

As stated, "hijacking DNA" is a powerful concept and the most appealing from this film. It would be interesting indeed to give an organism that ability. If true, then only those sequences of DNA that enhance itself would be acquired, such as intelligence, strength, ability to handle extremes of the environment, etc., much like the main character in *The Thing* or the *Alien* series.

During one particular scene Shelly states, "Heroin has a strange affect on the creature. It confuses it. A very large dose of heroin will knock Charlie out." Heroin is an alkaloid prepared from morphine by acetylation, and morphine is derived from opium. Heroin produces a combination of depression and excitation in the central nervous system and some peripheral tissues. Whether its major effects are in central stimulation or depression depends upon the species and dose. If Charlie "hijacked DNA" from multiple species, then it is anyone's guess what effects heroin would have on it. "Confusion" is probably correct. How they found out that heroin does affect Charlie is unknown. In the end, heroin is used to slow down Charlie, with the amounts used large enough to turn a Colombian drug lord green with envy.

Finally, we get to the creature itself, Charlie. The biggest problem with Charlie is his ability to shape change or morph. This has been discussed elsewhere, and those comments apply here too. However, it is known that sharks do not have bones; rather, they have cartilage, which is much softer and more pliable. It is tempting to speculate that cartilage would be easier to morph or alter than traditional bone. Morphing requires invoking too much biology to make it seem acceptable and seeing Charlie morphing into several different people on the oil rig is excessive. In appearance Charlie is humanoid, has many multi-layered teeth (much like a shark), and has a flattened face and small eyes. Several times we get a "point of view" shot (as if looking through Charlie's eyes), and these POV shots are like looking through a "fish eye lens." After Charlie takes over a female victim we see that her (its?) heart rhythm becomes immediately erratic (shown as an unusual EKG profile). Her EKG then becomes flat, though she talks coherently and then walks away. This could not happen.

In the end Charlie morphs into a large shark-like creature with a huge shark head (and big teeth to match) and tentacles with claws (perhaps "hijacked" from an octopus and crab?). After giving Charlie several doses of heroin, which does indeed slow him down, he apparently develops a drug habit, because he wants more. Just before Charlie's demise (he is set on fire), one of the survivors reaches for a large load of heroin and says, "You're a fuckin' fish with a drug habit!" Interesting biology.

What Biological Science Is Necessary to Actually Achieve the Results in the Film: To have Proteus, the synthetic DNA, be correctly integrated into the shark DNA genome would require it to be introduced into a developing embryo. That is easier than you may think. An already formed adult shark would not have been able to have all of the cells in its body altered at the same time, as suggested in the film. Even with "instant evolution" there still would not have been enough of an effect for Charlie to have all the physical properties attributable to him.

For Charlie to absorb and integrate other species' DNA, thereby bringing about significant changes and mutations, would require him to have the ability to correctly read and translate the DNA into proteins and enzymes. To suddenly grow tentacles and claws would involve the expression of tissue growth factors to allow these cells to grow and differentiate. Furthermore, to form claws would require completely different biochemical reactions to occur that would give rise to hard, shell-like tissues, much like chitin, the carbohydrate derived molecules that make up the protective shells of crustaceans.

Heroin is classified as an analgesic, which means it is capable of moderating painful stimuli so much that, though the stimulus is still there, there is no perceived pain. In essence, it reduces the response to pain. Since Charlie does morph, this could cause a lot of pain (nerve and muscle connections are significantly altered, which is indeed painful); perhaps this is why he develops such an instantaneous addiction to heroin. The heroin dampens the pain experienced while morphing.

Could It Actually Happen: DNA has too many stopgap-like measures in it to radically affect organisms in the manner suggested in this film. Even viruses, which can easily get into cells and tissues to cause havoc, are mostly limited to certain species. Scientists refer to the limited infectivity of viruses as unable to cross species barriers. They can hop from organism to organism within the same species but cannot go from species to species. Even species as close as chimpanzees and humans, whose DNA is at least 98.5 percent identical, have specific viruses that do not affect each other. This is a good thing, otherwise humans could be infected with, say, shark viruses!

Species (1995)

Synopsis: The "Search for Extraterrestrial Intelligence" (SETI) program at Arecibo, Puerto Rico, receives a message from outer space with a sequence of DNA and "friendly" instructions on how to use it. As a result, a female creature named "Sil" is developed who subsequently escapes and leaves a path of death and destruction. After Sil quickly evolves and matures, she looks for a human male to impregnate her. In the end she is found and is killed, though she gives birth to a baby boy.

Screenplay: Dennis Feldman.

Biological Sciences Principles Involved: Molecular Biology. Biochemistry. Developmental Biology.

What Is Right with the Biological

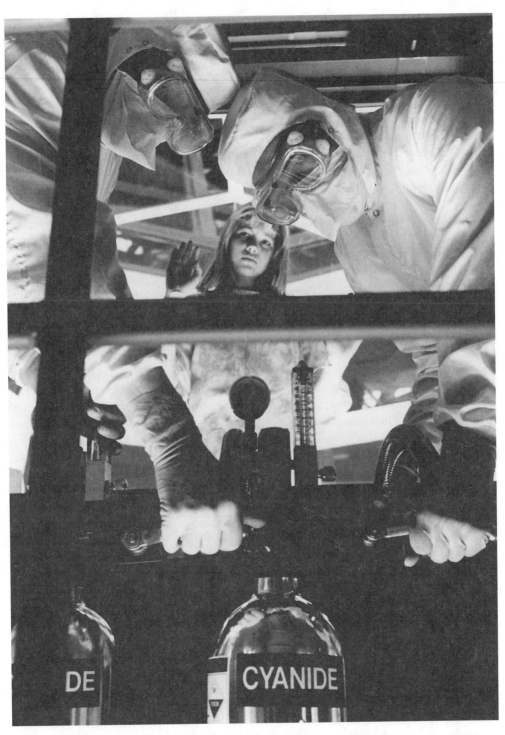

The "12-year-old" Sil, of *Species* (1995) (actually just a few weeks old) in her glass chamber, about to be given a lethal dose of cyanide. Cyanide inhibits the last step in oxygen respiration by inactivating the cytochrome oxidase protein complex found in the mitochondria within our cells. The result is death by suffocation.

Science Presented: On November 16, 1974, NASA did indeed send out a radio message from the SETI unit at Arecibo, Puerto Rico, consisting of about a quarter of a kilobyte of information containing a variety of data on Earth, including a DNA sequence. This sequence had 1679 characters and included the atomic masses of carbon, hydrogen, oxygen, nitrogen (CHON), and phosphate—all the components that biochemically comprise DNA. All of this is real. The fictitious response SETI receives back in the film is, of course, reel.

The micromanipulation scenes in which Laura tries to reproduce the conditions that result in Sil are accurate and similar to those usually shown on the nightly news when someone talks about cloning. The micromanipulation device consists of a very precisely controlled, extremely small (about a micrometer in diameter) glass needle that enters the nuclear region of a single cell, such as an unfertilized egg, and injects genetic material in the form of DNA. Fitch generates the DNA sequence provided by the "friendly" aliens, and through the use of micromanipulation inserts this DNA into human eggs, one of which eventually results in Sil.

During the film it is made clear that Sil has special sensory capabilities. For example, to get pregnant she goes to a bar and has a man take her to his house. She eventually turns this man down (which results in his gruesome death) because she "sensed" he is a diabetic. Apparently, she wants "non-diseased" DNA to mate with. The molecular biologist, Laura, explains, "Sil has some special kind of senses. Rats can sense disease or genetic damage in their potential mate." This is true and Sil apparently has the same ability. Perhaps she is able to "smell" the bad DNA.

In one particularly interesting sequence the 12-year-old Sil transforms into a mature adult woman. To accomplish this requires some interesting biological science. The 12-year-old Sil gets on a train and obtains a large quantity of high calorie food, like Twinkies, candy bars, milk, etc., and consumes it all. Most of this food consists of processed carbohydrates (sugar) which, as stated, are very high in calories. She is storing up caloric energy needed for her transformation. After gorging herself she forms a chrysalis-like cocoon, where in a brief matter of time she completely transforms into an adult woman. This entire process is similar to what a caterpillar does just before forming a cocoon to transform into a butterfly. It is visually very appealing.

The physical appearance of Sil, as conceived by designer H.R. Geiger, is also interesting. As Dan (the empath hired to help locate Sil after she escapes) says, "She's a predator. Her eyes are in front so she can judge the distance to her prey." That is a chillingly accurate statement. Later, Sil is shown to menstruate, a clear indication she is capable of reproduction. We are shown a microscope point of view shot of a Sil blood smear (menstruation blood?) that shows normal red blood cells. Also present in the view is a single white blood cell called a polymorphonuclear leukocyte, or PMN for short. This PMN appears to be fused with two red blood cells, which is certainly an odd combination and one not found in nature.

What Is Wrong with the Biological Science Presented: The biggest biological science mistakes made in this film are those of time. Everything happens way too fast. Fitch explains the work which results in Sil by saying, "The new combined DNA sequence was [micromanipulation] injected into 100 human ova [which women volunteered their eggs?]. We got seven to divide, four petered out.—Two were stored in liquid nitrogen and we allowed one to grow. 'Sil' stands for 'S1L,'—plate S, column 1, row L. After two hours, the egg was at the four cell stage. One day, there was a visible fetus with eyes, head, arms. Two days, the fetus looked about one month old. At one week the fetus looked about three months old. One month after birth, Sil looked like a five year old. Three months after birth, Sil looked like a 12-year-old girl." What an incredible sequence. The fastest growing animal on earth is the blue whale, and Sil's development made that look like it happened on a geological time scale instead of a biological one. The sequence of events happened too quickly.

The first time Sil is seen is as a 12-year-old girl, and Fitch knows that she is a biological threat. He can not let her live, so he decides to terminate her using cyanide gas. The 12-year-old Sil is housed inside a "nonbreakable" glass isolation unit, so the gas idea is a good one. Unfortunately, Sil has developed superior strength, and after the gas is released into the chamber she breaks through the glass and escapes. Those in the room die when the cyanide gas leaks out. (The comments made for the film *The Indestructible Man* and his death from cyanide in a gas chamber apply here.) To refresh your memory, cyanide is a chemical that inactivates a key enzyme in respiration called cytochrome oxidase, which is necessary for oxygen utilization and consumption. The cytochromes are electron-transferring proteins containing iron-porphyrin or heme groups. The cyanide tightly binds to the iron molecules, preventing electron transfer from oxygen. Without these enzymes you will quickly die of suffocation-like symptoms. Since the gas has no apparent effect on Sil, then she must have some alternative biochemistry to bypass the poisonous effects of cyanide.

Her transformation on the train from a 12-year-old girl into an adult requires an enormous amount of energy, far more than she gets from eating candy bars, chips, and milk. Such an increase in body mass—her size plus all the tissue of the actual cocoon (which appears greater than her weight)—would require a tremendous amount of foodstuffs. Way too much organic mass is created from the foodstuffs to be believable.

Fitch explains how the DNA sequence that gives rise to Sil was received at Aricebo. "The ... message turned out to be a new sequence of DNA with rather friendly instructions in how to combine it with ours." This is OK by itself. However, Fitch then goes on to state that the DNA sequence contains about 936 bases, which could translate to a single protein of about 312 amino acids (three base pairs code for one amino acid). A protein of 312 amino acids would "weigh" about 57,000 Daltons, making this about the size of a single chain of hemoglobin (about the size of an average protein). There is simply no way one protein with a molecular weight of 57 kiloDaltons could have developed into Sil. This is disappointing. The creators of the film should have made the DNA sequence at least a million base pairs long to make this at all believable. DNA of this size could then give rise to a series of proteins and enzymes that could have done the developmental work necessary to create Sil.

Laura suggests the team go back to the lab and try to create Sil from her own DNA to study what weaknesses she might have and develop a method to combat her. In principle, a nice idea. In the lab, Laura injects the outer space DNA sequence into another egg via micromanipulation. (Whose egg is it and what species? The assumption is that it is human, but it could have been any species, like a frog, pig, chimp, etc.) If they want to create her from her own DNA, then why inject it into an egg, thereby mixing her DNA with some from earth and getting essentially what they got the first time? This does not make cinemasense. Anyway, the injected DNA shows immediate, rapid, and enormous growth as soon as it enters the egg. A huge bubbly mass of tissues and cells results, prompting the question of where the energy and cell mass to do this comes from. Does this creature also use photosynthesis to obtain carbon dioxide from the atmosphere to create mass? In about one minute the growth goes from a single cell to an organism about one foot long! Within three minutes it is about three feet long, with tentacles and muscle movement, suggesting coordinated cellular development. Then a long tentacle with a suction apparatus shoots out to about eight feet long and hits the glass wall of the incubation unit. As such, the creature must have developed sensory organs and the ability to control them. The creature is eventually killed by fire, but because of its relatively large body mass it is difficult to rationalize how it gets that big without an appropriate carbon and energy source.

Sil is seen to have incredible regenerative powers. Part of this is the ability to morph between her human appearance and her alien appearance. This morphing ability happens very fast. Part of this regenerative power is manifested in her ability to regrow a finger. During one scene she deliberately cuts off a thumb, and it rapidly regenerates itself. The thumb tissue fibrils, bone, and tendons form first, then the skin forms around this. In a matter of seconds she has a perfectly working thumb again. Amazing. All of these abilities from only 936 base pairs of DNA! It must be the quality of DNA instead of quantity.

Later in the film the adult Sil is hit by a car resulting in a severe scapula bone fracture. She is taken to a nearby hospital, and while lying on a bed she is able to repair her own fracture. The attending physician sees this and exclaims, "This girl literally re-formed her bone structure." Again, more morphing.

Sil eventually has sex with a healthy man (a Harvard anthropologist no less!); she immediately becomes pregnant, and the baby grows very rapidly. She delivers the "baby" through her stomach instead of the usual birth canal route.

What Biological Science Is Necessary to Achieve the Results in the Film: For Sil to have survived the cyanide gas poisoning would require her to have some biochemical mechanism(s) to bypass the effects of cyanide binding to cytochrome oxidase. One possible solution would be to have some sort of chelation complex, which could be a type of "super heme," that could efficiently absorb cyanide. Either that or she could have some alternate respiration mechanism that did not require cytochromes to transfer electrons to oxygen to generate carbon dioxide. Both ways would involve some interesting biochemistry.

Sil has super strength, and this would mean her muscle fibers (though not dense — as in very muscular, because she wasn't) would be more efficient in being able to stretch and pull better. She is seen to jump higher and break through "nonbreakable glass" and steel doors, so her muscle tensile strength would have to have been very high. In simple terms, muscle is essentially actin and myosin filaments, types of proteins, that contract and relax. The more they contract the more strength you have. And, of course, the more you have of them the easier it is to do the required work. Since Sil had great strength, she must have had very efficient contraction and relaxation processes. This also makes for interesting biochemistry.

During Sil's transformation on the train, when she forms the cocoon and changes into an adult female, a lot of tissue mass is seen. The question is where does this organic mass come from? It is too easy to evoke the fixation of carbon dioxide from the atmosphere using photosynthesis. (Also, there is a similar scene later in the film where Laura and her team try to recreate Sil inside an incubation chamber. After fertilization with the space DNA the organism rapidly grows—representing another instance of "where did all that tissue mass come from?") Here is a plausible explanation. There are certain chemicals, such as polymeric diisocyanate, polyether triol, chlorodifluoroethane, and chlorodifluoromethane, which, when exposed to air (oxygen) rapidly expand. At your local hardware store or home fix-it center you can get metal spray cans that contain pressurized insulating polycel urethane foam (containing the above chemicals) that rapidly expand when sprayed out. The main function of this foam is to serve as some sort of sealant for cracks and various holes. Their expansive properties are quite impressive. It is possible that Sil has these chemicals in her body (they would be relatively easy to biochemically make and store, using simple enzymatic reactions), and upon their release to the air they rapidly expand thereby creating the cocoon and other appendages she needs. This rapid expansion creates size and not mass. This is plausible. Also, Sil could easily have metabolically made the polymeric diisocyanate from the cyanide gas she was exposed to earlier.

What is not plausible is how a protein with a molecular weight of only 57,000 Daltons (coming from the 936 base pairs of DNA) can do all the things Sil is seen doing. To be real, this "super" protein would have to not only be able to transcribe and translate DNA into a self replicating mode, but would also have to be able to withstand cyanide, provide super muscle strength, be able to allow her to shape change from human to "creature," provide the ability to heal cracked bones, endow her with the ability to get pregnant, and let her survive multiple gunshot wounds. Admittedly, this may seem impossible, but there may be a way around

this. The smallest protein we have in our bodies is insulin, which has a molecular weight of 5,700 Daltons. Perhaps the 936 base pair space DNA codes for 10 different proteins with molecular weights of 5,700 each, giving rise to a total mass of 57,000. This way, the 10 different enzymes could possibly do all that was shown. Furthermore, there is the possibility of peptides. To describe this in simple terms, think of a wall of bricks. The individual bricks would correspond to individual amino acids. You connect the bricks (or amino acids) and you have a wall (or a protein). To take this one step further, a peptide is sort of like one wall, and a protein would be a complete building of four walls. The difference is in degree. A peptide is not big enough to be called a protein, just as a wall is not complete enough to be called a building. Both walls and buildings are all made of the same unit—the brick, or, for this analogy, amino acids. Therefore, various peptides could have been generated from this DNA sequence, and these peptides could have powerful effects. What is interesting here is that there are examples of this in nature. Previously mentioned endorphins are small peptides that exert very powerful analgesic effects on animal cells and tissues. By invoking the existence of several regulatory peptides, then perhaps the 936 base pairs of space DNA could have been enough to do the job.

Also, the 936 base pairs of DNA could code for certain gene promoters and gene regulators that turn on (technically called gene derepression) other genes, active, silent, or otherwise. This possibility is intriguing because humans have an enormous amount of what is called "junk DNA" or "selfish DNA," meaning endless sequences of DNA that do not code for any known protein; the Sil DNA could activate some of this junk DNA, giving rise to an entirely novel set of proteins, which in turn gives Sil her characteristics. In other words, the Sil DNA could contain the translators of this junk DNA and cause it to be either misread or realigned, resulting in novel proteins. The amount of junk DNA far surpasses what is actually translated (about 100,000 genes), so there is plenty of actual DNA sequences to work with. (Much speculation has been published in the scientific literature on the nature of selfish DNA, and we may never actually know what it is, why it is there, or what it does, if anything.)

Finally, the Sil 936 base pair DNA could be some sort of retrovirus, like HIV, that wreaks all sorts of havoc with both normal DNA and junk DNA (a "riot in its DNA"; see the entry for *The Relic*), mixing and matching the genes that eventually results in Sil.

Mention is made by Laura, the molecular biologist, that Sil has the ability to "sense" that a man is a diabetic. Diabetics utilize relatively little glucose as fuel (except by the brain), so their tissues (especially the liver) burn a large amount of fat or lipid. A byproduct of excessive fat metabolism is a higher than normal production of a class of lipids called "ketone bodies," which have a characteristic odor. These ketone bodies, being lipids, are volatile and are readily exhaled from the breath. When I smell ketones on people's breath I immediately know they are diabetic. Sil did not negatively react to this man until she got within kissing range. At this short distance she could easily have detected the smell of ketones on his breath. Her heightened olfactory senses picked this up and told her this guy has "bad DNA," and therefore should not be the father of her child.

A process called "allometric growth" refers to the non-random way in which certain cells and tissues grow in relation to their surrounding neighbors. The most obvious example of this is the case of acromegaly, where certain bone structures,

because of the presence of excessive growth hormones, grow out of proportion. As a result of being hit by a car, Sil's scapula bone (shoulder blade) was fractured. This is one of the bones that continues to grow in those with acromegaly. For Sil to heal her fractured scapula, the damaged tissue released bone growth hormones that caused allometric growth of her scapula, thereby healing the fracture. This, in principle, is acceptable; however, the few seconds in which the healing took place was way too short a time to be believable.

Finally, we have the scene where Sil cuts off her thumb (she needs a body part to help make a staged accident look real) and it is seen to rapidly grow back. When she cuts the thumb off there is no cry of pain, so she must have some natural pain killing peptides flowing through her system, probably an excessive amount of endorphins, the pain killing analgesics in humans. Furthermore, there is no excessive spilling of blood, so she must have immediate clotting mechanisms that stop blood loss. All in all, Sil has some very interesting body biochemistry and fantastic survival mechanisms. Laura, the molecular biologist, best sums it up by saying, "[Sil] would make an excellent biological weapon."

Could It Actually Happen: Quite a number of hard working scientists (and volunteer amateurs) are listening with radio telescopes in the hopes of receiving a signal from outer space. Those who spend their lives on the SETI project are to be commended. I am one of the many who hope that someday we actually get a bona fide message. However, it is doubtful if the first message we get is a sequence of DNA with "friendly instructions."

The Relic (1996)

Synopsis: A South American archaeological artifact is sent to the Chicago Natural

History Museum. Within the shipping crate is a mutant creature who escapes and begins ripping people's heads off to consume their brain hormones. The creature's name is Kathoga, a South American name that means "great devil god." Kathoga goes through the museum, killing and destroying. He is eventually set on fire and is killed.

Screenplay: Amy Holden Jones, John Raffo, Rick Jaffa, and Amanda Silver, based upon the novel by Douglas Preston and Lincoln Child.

Biological Science Principles Involved: Molecular Biology. Endocrinology. Biochemistry.

What Is Right with the Biological Science Presented: Most of the interesting biological science in this film is in the details. For example, the packing crate containing Kathoga also contains some carved antiquities that were packed with large frond leaves. (Not everyone has access to Styrofoam "packing peanuts.") Green inspects these leaves and notices some small, round, translucent spheres on the underside of the leaves. (Most likely those in South America who packed the crate could have used such large leaves and would not have noticed nor cared if these "spheres" were present.) Green says to Whitney, "Do you think they are eggs?" Whitney responds with, "More like fungus, probably parasitical. Best not to take any chances." Then Cuthbert says, "Best to have leaves and crate incinerated." Green, the ever curious scientist, takes a sample of the leaves, places them in a Styrofoam container, and puts it into a refrigerator for future analysis.

The procedures Green uses to analyze the eggs are also interesting. She places one of the leaf eggs in a small Eppendorf tube, mixes it around, and places a sample in a computer controlled PCR machine. (Eppendorf tubes are small centrifuge tubes used by the thousands [a week!] in mole-

cular biology labs throughout the world. They are so prevalent they even come in a variety of colors for easy grouping.) PCR machines (PCR stands for polymerase chain reaction) are found in just about every lab in the world and are as common these days as microscopes, centrifuges, and refrigerators. These machines are used for analyzing DNA. All you need is just a single strand of DNA and these machines will make millions of identical copies for sequencing procedures. PCR machines are elegantly simple, easy to operate, and very powerful in providing the data you need. PCR technology has so completely revolutionized the field of molecular biology that its inventor, Dr. Cary Mullis, received the Nobel Prize for its discovery.

During another "PCR moment" Green explains a procedure by saying, "First I liquefy my sample [correct]. Then this [PCR] machine will amplify the DNA strand. Then, finally scanned and create a gel image and matched against a huge data base we have compiled the last few years." There are a number of DNA data bases available, and just about any sequence can be entered for comparison. This is the way you can identify which species the DNA came from. The results are usually given in percent homology, meaning how much of your sequence matched those species already in the data base.

One of the favorite items to display in natural history museums are bones. For contemporary animals it is necessary to remove all skin and tissues from the bones, and this is accurately described in this film. Bones with flesh still attached are placed in a maceration tank. As Green explains, they "...skin 'em and toss 'em in warm water, wait until the meat and flesh fall off, and then give them to the beetles." Domestic beetles eat the flesh off almost anything and they pick the bones clean. The beetles will take care of what does not come off in the maceration tank.

Green states that there are about three million specimens in the museum and only about two percent were on display, which comes out to be about 60,000 specimens, and most of these are probably insects. Unfortunately, this is true of most large museums, in that they only have a very small percentage of their holdings on display. Most of the paying public who visit museums see very little of what they actually have.

One of Kathoga's first victims is a museum security guard (he is sitting on a toilet smoking a joint when he has his head chopped off), and the subsequent autopsy is authentic. The pathologist says the following during the autopsy: "...undetermined number of lacerations ... entire brain missing. Fell out or extracted in large hole in head. Brain doesn't weigh as much as it should, so something is missing. Thalamic region missing, pituitary missing. Brain is severed at medulla oblongata. Cerebrum completely severed from mesencephalon." All realistic. The morgue where the autopsy is performed is also authentic. The thalamus and hypothalamus, among other things, secrete hormones that regulate heart beat, blood pressure, body temperature, and regulate the presence of hundreds of other hormones in the blood stream. Needless to say, the thalamus and hypothalamus make most of an animal's interesting hormones.

A subplot of this movie concerns two scientists, Green and her colleague Dr. Greg Lee, applying for the same grant. Grant applications are a way of life for academic scientists, and they can spend over 50 percent of their time dealing with them. This time involves not only the actual mechanical writing of the grant but the researching of background and supplementary material (the actual research necessary to justify the proposed expenses and budget) and the physical management and report writing after you are lucky enough to get the grant. The up side of all this is that once you do get one your time is completely your own; however, that time is only the other 50 percent. This up side is so significant that academicians will sacrifice to no end to get grants. The "friendly" rivalry between Green and Lee for the same grant also has its own subterfuge. In the real world there are thousands of dedicated, hard-working scientists competing for a very small pot of grant money. Fortunately, these rivalries are not deadly. Lee is the selfish bad guy here and is seen doing all sorts of groveling while in the presence of the wealthy patron who will be funding the grant. Since the "evil" scientist always gets his just desserts in cinemascience, Lee does, literally, get his head handed to him when Kathoga eventually kills him.

Drs. Frock and Green make the discovery that Kathoga consumes hormones that help to catalyze its subsequent genetic mutations. As Frock says, the interactions of excessive hormones, coupled with mutations, "caused a riot in its DNA." An accurate and apt description of mutated DNA.

What Is Wrong with the Biological Science Presented: What is wrong with the biological science in this film is far more interesting than what is right with it. The wrong stuff gets you to thinking about what would be necessary to make it right.

One of the domestic beetles they use to pick bones clean of flesh ends up eating some of the eggs that come with the leaves in the crate from South America. Later, when Green takes the Styrofoam cooler out of the refrigerator to analyze the eggs, a very large beetle, about 20 centimeters in size, comes crawling out. The hormones in those eggs must have been quite potent. Beetles from South America do get to be big, but this one was stretching it a bit, though not outside the realm of possibility. Green then squashes the beetle by slamming a biochemistry textbook on it! (Personally, I love this scene! While getting my Ph.D. in biochemistry I went through a lot of textbooks, and I thought of all sorts of uses for them — but squashing giant bugs was not one of them.) Later Green dissects the remains of this squashed beetle and does a PCR test on some of the tissue to determine its genetic (DNA) origin. The results from her computer indicate the species is *Domesticus volpinus* (a domestic beetle) and its DNA matches 33 percent with the species, *Termadactylus tersicus*, which is a Turkish gecko. Green says, "reptilian and beetle DNA on the same strand!" Incredible. At first she doesn't believe this bit of cinema-science (who would?) and actually repeats the experiment three times, getting the same results. (All good scientists, both real and reel, should make sure their results are reproducible.)

Though the mechanics of the PCR work Green did to analyze the various DNA samples is accurate, the presented computer results are anything but. Green's "specimen identification" work appears to be completely automated. All she did was place a sample to be analyzed in the PCR machine and a computer did all the rest. By "rest" I mean amplify the DNA, separate the components on a special type of acrylamide gel (like a refined, clear gelatin), "read" and sequence the DNA strands, and then make the necessary interpretations as to what species the DNA belongs to. Needless to say, it would be absolutely wonderful to have automated machinery that actually did work like that, and someday it may actually happen. What a time saver that would be. In reality, there are several separate pieces of equipment required to obtain this data, and many days between each step. For the sake of simplicity, let us assume this all was possible. The final interpretations from the computer (this is a simple desktop model

and not some fancy Cray super computer or mainframe) were interesting. The readouts are "glycotetraline collagenoid" (a fabricated name, though it certainly sounds authentic!), "Hawaiian side cytotropic hormone" (also fabricated), oxytocin (a real neurohypophysial hormone that causes labor contractions at term and promotes milk release during lactation), and "minoxytocin suppressant" (another fabrication). All in all, the computer lists a staggering 28 different hormones that come from these leaf eggs! All told, these are animal hormones, a combination of proteins, peptides, and organic configurations, all analyzed by the same computer program and coming from what they called a fungus! Green says, "Parasitic fungus was loaded with animal hormones produced in the thalamoid region of the human brain. Animal maybe started out as something else — lizard, dog — and ate the leaves and changed."

This automated PCR machine/DNA sequenator/computer performs even more amazing experiments. After some more data is generated, Dr. Frock reads the results, saying, "gamma globulin a, x, and y, left positive, reverse transcriptase[!]. Supposed to be hormones. Reverse transcriptase is always seen with viruses." Though animals, humans in particular, do have gamma globulins in their serum, and the "a" type is one of them, they do not have any called "x, and y." It is unclear what "left positive" is. Reverse transcriptase refers to a family of enzymes, technically called RNA-directed DNA polymerases, that essentially make DNA strands from RNA. Reverse transcriptase enzymes have been found in many species, including humans, so why Dr. Frock says they are always seen with viruses is a mystery. To be sure, these enzymes were first found in viruses during the late 1960s and early 1970s, so maybe Frock is "stuck in time" (much like Billy Pilgrim in Kurt Vonnegut's *Slaughterhouse*

Five). In addition to this, Frock also says, "One milligram of this material is equal to more than 100 milligrams of the hormone produced by the hypothalamus." This would be an astonishingly potent biomolecule. Finally, Frock does get it right when he says, "…supposed to be hormones," because none of these putative proteins are hormones.

After the verbal exchange in the above paragraph by Green and Frock, Green then says, "Why would a virus code for animal proteins? We know these hormones [referring to the computer-listed 28 discussed earlier] are responsible for growth, bone structure, exoskeletal physiology, and skin maintenance. A huge influx of these could easily cause it to change." How does "exoskeletal physiology" figure into a list of animal hormones?

Still using her amazing computer, Green is able to list a series of hormones from a web site called the "biochemistry encyclopedia site." Listed are the following:

1) "glycotetraline collagenoid" [see above].

2) "Weinstein's thyrotropic hormone: N-Terminal tripeptide (from hypothalamus). Composition: catacholamine. Controls deamination of adenosine nucleotides in the processing of foodstuffs and absorption of phosphorylase nutrients" [incorrect].

3) "oxytocin-4 monoxytocin suppressin: somatomedin from hypothalamus. Inhibits metabolic polymorphism by catalyzing preprogrammed eukaryotic gene expression in new cells and vascular tissue" [incorrect].

4) "gamma globulin A: protein from hypothalamus[!]. Controls biosynthesis of cerebrosides and dermal and epidermal formation and modification to specific morphological thresholds." [incorrect; please note that gamma globulins are *not*

made in the hypothalamus!! There are three major classes of gamma globulins. The "alpha" and "beta" type globulins are composed of liproproteins, mucoproteins (such as orosomucoid and haptoglobulin), and metal-binding and metal-transporting proteins (such as transferrin, siderophilin, and ceruloplasmin). The third class, the "gamma," are immunoglobulins (i.e., antibodies). None of them are from the hypothalamus.]

5) "hypothalamic corticotropic hormone: polypeptide from hypothalamus. Stimulates the release of adrenocorticotropic steroids to increase muscle development and structure as well as maintaining salt and water balance" [all of this is correct].

Green obtains a tissue sample from Kathoga and submits it for analysis by her computer. The gene bank sequence data stored in the software of this computer then sifts through the data and comes up with an interesting answer. The printout from the PCR analysis lists five more matches, and for each gives a reference, a citation, sequence tags, expression matches, and protein matches for kingdom, phylum, subphylum, class, order, and family. The five listed matches and their classification names are:

1) "Gonocephalus boydii—11 percent match
Animalia, Chordata, Vertebrata, Reptilia, Sauria, Agamidae"

2) "Panthera tigris braziliae—4 percent match
Animalia, Chordata, Vertebrata, Mammalia, Carnivoria, Feliadae"

3) "Lucanus cervus—2 percent match
Animalia, Arthropoda, Uniramia, Insecta, Coleopter, Lucanidae"

4) "Hemidactylus tersicus—45 percent match

Animalia, Chordata, Vertebrata, Reptilia, Sauria, Geckoridae"

5) "Homo sapiens— 33 percent match Animalia, Chordata, Vertebrata, Mammalia, Primates, Hominoidea"

The total match comes to 95 percent, with the remaining five percent being unknown. Interestingly enough, the 33 percent match with human DNA turns out be identical to the DNA of Dr. John Whitney, the museum scientist who went to South America and shipped the artifacts back. Shortly after doing this he disappears and ends up being transformed into Kathoga. So, in summary, Kathoga is composed of part reptile, part insect, part panther, and part human. All in all, a pretty nasty combination, and this explains why Frock calls the creature a "riot in its DNA!" Green says, "According to the data, that thing [Kathoga] started out as a human [Dr. Whitney] and is rapidly evolving into something reptilian." The key word here is "is," meaning the creature is still changing or evolving into something else.

To kill the creature, Green says that the beast is, "part reptilian, probably ectothermic. Can't handle extremes of hot and cold, so if we change its temperature by 30 to 40 degrees, maybe we can freeze the son of a bitch." Ultimately, they end up killing the creature by fire.

One final comment about Kathoga. We see it climbing walls with the ease of a fly. Anything that big would not be able to hang on a wall that easily nor move with the speed it did. Also, if a couple of tons of flesh and bone are hanging on a plaster wall, a fair amount of the plaster would come off, but none of this is seen.

What Biological Science Is Necessary to Achieve the Results in the Film: This whole adventure starts out with the arrival of the eggs and/or fungus from the packing leaves from South America. The DNA from this organism(s) would have to have all sorts of abilities that could completely change all the regulatory elements of animal and insect DNA, be infectious and be able to cross species barriers, and be able to reproduce a cornucopia of hormones that can alter both form and function of a variety of cells and tissues. This is what happens during embryogenesis growth, so this fungus has the ability to radically alter DNA.

The genetic DNA sequence data base and assay development necessary to give the results shown in this film would take up an enormous amount of memory space, far more than that possessed by the computer shown. Such data bases are available and are used all the time in labs throughout the world for the same purpose as in this film (searching for suitable and closely related matches). However, most of these data bases are grouped into such categories as prokaryote, eukaryote, virus, etc., and are not as all-encompassing as implied in this film.

Not specifically described in any detail in this film is the reason Kathoga rips off the heads of its victims. Implied, though not stated, is access to hypothalamus and pituitary hormones. This would have been an interesting plot line to develop. Like a drug addiction, Kathoga needs more and more hormones to feed its habit. Its "habit" being the need for hormones to help along its evolution from human to whatever it was going to end up as. When we finally get a good look at the creature, it is about the size of a rhinoceros.

Could It Actually Happen: No. First we have this magical lab computer that can do so much and yet produce data so full of biological science mistakes. Then to have DNA that could actually do all the things seen would literally wipe out life on earth because all the species would be warring with each other for food, shelter, and survival.

3 PHARMACOLOGY

Drugs—where would we be without them? To be clear, this is not in reference to recreational drugs, but rather the pharmaceutical kind, such as aspirin or human MAbs (monoclonal antibodies). The FDA uses a very broad definition in its classification of what constitutes a drug. A drug is *anything* chemical that is used for humans. Believe me, *everything* is chemical!

Make no mistake about it, the pharmaceutical industry is *huge*, about $300 billion a year — and is here to stay. As time goes on, even more and more pharmaceutical choices will be made available to us to make our lives less painful and more enjoyable. Most of these new drugs will actually be beneficial.

ZOMBIES

Interestingly, there may actually be a scientific basis for the identification of the causative agent that produces "zombies." A pharmaceutical basis for zombies? Yes, let me explain.

Tetrodotoxin, a neurotoxin drug, is a chemical compound found in high concentration in the puffer fish, and it works by blocking critical sodium ion gates in nerve fibers. With these ion gates blocked, the neuromuscular action potential and transmission of impulses is inhibited, resulting in sluggish motor control; excessive exposure could be life threatening. For tetrodotoxin to work it must get into the body, and the usual means to do this are injection directly into the blood system, absorption through the skin, or ingestion. Each of these routes has pluses and minuses. To get the drug directly into the blood stream you must physically be present to do this, oftentimes without the help of your intended victim. Absorption through the skin is easier, though there may be some irritation and the victim may not want to "cooperate." The easiest route is, of course, by ingestion. The problem here is that the natural digestive and salivary processes could be very damaging to the drug of choice. The enzymes and/or harsh acidic environment of the stomach and gut may inactivate the drug. Puffer fish powder, a source of tetrodotoxin, is an ingredient in zombie rituals. The use of proper amounts of tetrodotoxin could severely interfere with normal body movements and could result in a catatonic, zombie-like state.

VENOM

It is common knowledge that certain

99

snakes have toxic poisons in their venoms. The cobra snake is one of those with a highly toxic venom which contains cobra venom factor (CVF). The molecular structure of this protein has been established, and how it works is also fairly well understood. CVF is a protein drug composed of two chains folded in a sort of globular fashion. One of the chains is used to bind to the surface of cells, and the other chain is the actual poison that inhibits cell metabolism. Like one hand knocks on your door and the other hand chokes you once it's in your house. The problem here is that the "choking hand" portion of CVF can do quite a lot of damage, so much so that in some cases it can cause your death. Knowing this, scientists (including myself) have attached a form of CVF to antibodies to serve as a "guided-missile-plus-warhead" method of destroying cancer cells. All in all, a pretty neat trick and a pharmaceutical protocol approved by the FDA. The antibody targets (like a guided missile) the antigens found only on cancer cells and, through its natural biology, gets into the tumor cell. Once inside it releases its "payload," the CVF, which then stops the cancer cell's metabolic machinery, thereby causing its death. In principle this sounds great, and it really is, but the drawback can be the dosage delivered. You have to be very careful, in that too much CVF could then start to kill normal cells that surround the tumor clump. Antibody-CVF conjugates are classed as experimental cancer therapy. (Just so you know, there are other compounds that work like CVF but are less toxic, which are currently being used on cancer patients in the same manner as these immunoconjugates.) Since CVF is used in clinical settings to treat cancer the FDA has classified it as a drug, which is why it is included in this section. CVF plays a key role in the film *The Undying Monster* (see page 103).

ENDORPHINS

Another set of "drugs" that act on the brain are, in one respect, not drugs at all. Rather, they are natural compounds already existing in our bodies— endorphins. The reason they are classed as drugs is because they are removed from the body and then returned as medication. These endorphins are small brain peptides (fragments of larger proteins) that have opiate-like activity and make you feel good by giving you a natural sense of well being. When athletes get their "endorphin high" they have a burst of endorphin production that was generated in response to their intense physical activity. It is interesting that nature created these substances to more or less let animals deal with pain and hardships in life, both physical and emotional. Like any drug, once the natural endorphins are better characterized and become more widely available, then they will be used (and abused) like other recreational drugs. Everyone wants to feel good, and if nature has a natural drug that can do this, then it will be a safe bet that everyone will want it. Users will also develop addictions to them, which will bring about a completely different set of problems.

Endorphins bind to their individual receptors on nerve endings, which causes the release of certain neurotransmitters that not only help to block pain or the sensation of pain but also provide a sense of euphoria.

LYCANTHROPY

Believe it or not, drugs are also considered to be the basis of lycanthropy, which is the study of werewolves. Yes, the basis for the actual appearance of werewolves may be due to pharmacology. The film *The Undying Monster*, though it deals with cobra venom factor, also deals with lycanthropy or werewolves, so this is as good a time as any to discuss how pharmacology plays a role in their creation.

Lycanthropy has its origins primarily in 16th century Europe, though it can be dated as far back as the ancient Romans. According to Roman mythology, Jupiter transformed the cruel, cannibalistic King Lycaon of Arcadia into a wolf. (Lycos is Greek for wolf—and where we get the word lycanthropy from—and lycorexia means a craving for raw meat.) Much has been written about werewolf folklore and need not be repeated. However, there is an interesting scientific explanation behind the legend. Here are the facts. During the 16th Century all the reported cases of lycanthropy occurred primarily within the peasant class in low lying areas in Europe that were under 500 feet above sea level. Interestingly, regions above 500 feet have no reported cases.

As a rule, peasants could not afford wheat bread, which was saved for the upper class, and therefore had to eat cheaper rye-based bread. Unfortunately, rye grains were contaminated with ergot fungus, and when the peasants harvested the grain the ergot fungus came along with it. (Ergot does not contaminate wheat, so the upper class was never exposed to it.) Ergot contains natural hallucinogens (drugs like LSD) that, when consumed in quantity with bread, induce psychotic episodes. The peasants who had a lot of the ergot fungus in their system were subsequently very susceptible to outside influences. And since werewolves were popular at the time, the power of suggestion convinced many of the peasants that their communities were rampant with werewolves. So, much of our werewolf lore originated through the use of mind-altering drugs.

In addition to the basis for a drug induced "birth" of werewolves, there is also a clinical basis. There are documented cases of hypertrichosis, which is excessive hair growth all over the body, primarily on the face. In severe cases, hair actually grows on the eyelids! The existence of such individuals, in combination with werewolf lore, has added credibility to their existence.

White Zombie (1932)

Synopsis: Mr. Beaumont, who lives in Haiti, wants to marry a woman, Madeline, who is engaged to another man. Beaumont asks Murder Legendre (Bela Lugosi) to help him. Legendre makes Madeline a zombie who then obeys the will of Beaumont. In the end, Beaumont and Legendre are killed, thereby releasing Madeline from her zombie spell.

Screenplay: Garnett Wilson.

Biological Science Principles Involved: Pharmacology.

What Is Right with the Biological Science Presented: Zombification, the application of certain drugs to take over the "will" of a human, is a very interesting phenomenon when considered in light of pharmacology. As with hypnosis, some people would be more susceptible to suggestion than others, and therefore more easily "zombified."

But why have only the Haitians developed the concept of zombies? Others have written books on this subject (mostly from a religious and anthropological point of view), which is beyond the scope of this book. Our interests are in the biological science basis of zombies. Suffice it to say that poisonous extracts of puffer fish, which contains the toxin tetrodotoxin (see the entry for *The Serpent and the Rainbow* discussed on page 106), have been available to many other cultures, so why didn't they use them to affect other humans?

What Is Wrong with the Biological Science Presented: The instructions Legendre gives to use his "zombie powder" are: "...put only a pinpoint in a glass of wine," an interesting statement that deserves

Murder Legendre (Bela Lugosi, left) has used "only a pinpoint" of zombie powder on the girl making her into the *White Zombie* (1932). Most likely the powder is a neurotoxin drug known as tetrodotoxin, obtained from the puffer fish.

analysis. First of all, for any drug to work it must get into the body, and Legendre decides that ingestion is the easiest. Also, the liquid environment of wine will not only solubilize the zombie powder but will somehow "strengthen" its method of action. Alcohol can act as a catalyst and enhance the absorption of the drug, more effectively turning the intended victims into zombies. The small amounts used ("only a pinpoint") are hard to believe. However, snake venom is used in very small quantities because it acts in a catalytic manner, and perhaps Legendre's zombie powder acts in the same way. In other words, a little goes a long way.

What Biological Science Is Necessary to Actually Achieve the Results in the Film: Legendre's zombie powder has to affect certain neuromuscular parts of our body for it to work. The chemical communication between a nerve ending and a muscle cell would have to be disrupted. By itself this is a relatively easy thing to do. There exists many such drugs that interfere with neuromuscular junctions. In addition, the powder must be somehow either very long acting or semi-permanent, since only one treatment was given to the victims. We do not see multiple doses given to keep the people as zombies. Also, zombies will need some source of food and water to sustain themselves.

Could It Actually Happen: Based on the real work of Dr. Wade Davis, an ethnobotanist who discovered tetrodotoxin in Haitian zombie powder, some say that indeed zombification does actually happen. Most folklore is based on some semblance of fact, and it is very interesting that tetrodotoxin has been suggested as the basis of zombie lore. This is a case where science fact does indeed make science fiction.

The Undying Monster (1942)

Synopsis: The "Hammond Legend" is a curse that has plagued the Hammond family for generations. A male member of the family is a victim of lycanthropy; that is, he becomes a werewolf. The Hammond family knows what the problem is and they hide the "curse" from others. Robert Curtis, a Scotland Yard scientist, discovers that one of the werewolf's victims has cobra venom extract in her blood. A Hammond family doctor is using cobra venom in an attempt to "cure" Mr. Hammond of the curse.

Screenplay: Lillie Hayward and Michael Jacoby, from the novel by Jessie Douglas Kerruish.

Biological Science Principles Involved: Pharmacology. Biochemistry. Hypertrichosis.

What Is Right with the Biological Science Presented: Those Scotland yard scientists must receive excellent training, because Mr. Curtis uses a wonderful piece of equipment and technique to help him solve some riddles and uncover some clues. Flame photometry is a procedure used to analyze the chemical spectrums of certain materials. Each chemical has a unique spectrum, very much like a fingerprint (since no two are alike). Curtis uses flame photometry to analyze both a thread sample and a hair sample. To describe the technique, Curtis himself says, "First we take a sample of thread, then we incinerate it thus [while saying this he holds a thread over a Bunsen burner flame with tweezers]. Place it in this tube ... withdraw

the air because the nitrogen and oxygen in there interferes with the desired light bands of the spectrum." All in all, it's an accurate and authentic explanation of flame photometry.

Curtis then repeats the procedure with a hair sample from a crime scene and is surprised to learn that it is identical to wolf's hair! (Nothing gets by those Scotland Yarders.) Curtis must have had a photographic memory, because he knew that the resulting spectrum came from a wolf! Implied in this discovery is the notion that wolf hair is identical to werewolf hair and not some possible new hybrid combination of a human and a wolf.

During a flame photometry procedure, Curtis says, "Science doesn't recognize total destruction. You can change the form of matter but you can't actually destroy it." Correct.

What Is Wrong with the Biological Science Presented: Though the authenticity of the described scientific procedures used is accurate (flame photometry and cobra venom to affect nerve tissue), they are also disturbing. CVF works on all cells of the body, not just nerve cells. The concentrations used by the Hammond physician would have quickly killed the intended individual.

Also, even in the most severe case of hypertrichosis and hirsutism, the hair is still human. It would be some remarkable biochemistry to be able to transform human hair into wolf hair! The amino acid sequence of the hair protein would have to dramatically change, and this would mean new DNA coding for new enzymes to accomplish this. If true, then lycanthropy must also cause human hair to change in both quantity and quality.

What Biological Science Is Necessary to Actually Achieve the Results in the Film: As mentioned above, the CVF used must be able to target specific brain tissues for it to work. Unless there is an antibody

Scotland Yard Inspector Curtis (John Howard, right) at his impressive and well equipped home lab in *The Undying Monster* (1942). The various apparatus shown are typically used in organic chemistry, just the tools a chemical detective would need. The current world of forensic chemistry has completely changed since these days at Scotland Yard; most of the elaborate glassware has been replaced with sophisticated machinery and computers.

attached to the CVF to help target it to nerve tissues, there's no way this could happen. By itself the CVF is not specific enough. The Hammond family doctor says, "I've been working on the theory that the shock of the cobra venom would eventually straighten out the dreadful kink in his brain." The assumptions here are that the CVF will only go to the brain in the concentrations necessary (and be able to effectively bypass the blood brain barrier), and that a drug can cure a complex psychiatric disorder.

Also, the fundamental nature of hair follicles would have to change by making human hair appear to resemble, it not actually become, wolf hair.

Could It Actually Happen: A family "curse" can be thought of as some sort of inherited trait, like baldness; so yes, certain genetic traits (or, if you wish, a "curse") can be passed from one generation to the next. Being able to pass on hypertrichosis to subsequent generations has also been shown to occur, primarily through the X-chromosome (where the gene for excessive hair growth is located). However, hypertrichosis does not come and go, subject to the whims of a full moon or the autumn season ("even a man who is pure in heart and says his prayers at night may become a wolf when the wolfbane blooms and the autumn moon is bright…"), so this is highly unlikely. Psychoses that are either drug induced, caused by brain abnormalities, or trauma induced are real and could give rise to a plethora of mental states, lycanthropy being one of them.

Zombie (1980)

Synopsis: A sailboat comes into New York harbor with a zombie on board. The daughter of the boat owner goes to the Caribbean to investigate and look for her father. Dr. Menard, a physician on the Caribbean island of Matule, is conducting research into why the zombies exist. The only way to kill a zombie is by destroying its head. Zombies overtake the island and kill all the inhabitants. Two humans escape on a boat.

Screenplay: Elisa Briganti.

Biological Science Principles Involved: Infectious Diseases. Microbiology. Pharmacology.

What Is Right with the Biological Science Presented: Dr. Menard uses the scientific method and principles to investigate the cause or causes that result in the dead becoming zombies. Scientists are trained to keep asking questions until they get answers. In one scene Menard says, out of frustration, "I'm sure there's a natural explanation and I'm determined to find it!" Only a true hard-core scientist would not stop no matter what the adversity.

One of Menard's statements says it all: "I don't believe in voodooism, but the phenomenon defies logical explanation. I've attempted to apply the disciplines of bacteriology, virology, even radiology. We've performed tests. Epilepsy and for catalepsy. Nothing fits." If only Menard had also included pharmacology. Since the plot already established that the "zombie disease" is infectious, then it is unclear why Menard references epilepsy and catalepsy, which are not infectious diseases. Perhaps these comments were aimed at the phenomenon of the dead getting up and walking, albeit slowly and very methodically, which could have been epileptic-like effects.

None of the zombies carry on articulate speech, so perhaps they do not need a fully functioning brain. There is also a general lack of mental acuity to these zombies, also indicative of damaged or non-functioning brain parts. An oxygen starved brain is damaged, similar to a stroke, resulting in problems in body motor movement, and since these zombies are the revived dead, then each of them would have some associated brain damage.

What Is Wrong with the Biological Science Presented: The general lack of sterility is the biggest problem, and Menard should have known better. In one scene Menard takes about 5cc of his own blood, enough to fill a large tablespoon, and then puts only a few drops onto a slide for examination. (Why take so much to begin with if he is only going to use a small amount?) The needle he uses on his syringe is left open, thereby possibly introducing unwanted contamination. Also, the manner in which he obtains the blood from his own arm is completely unscientific.

(On a personal note, in my own research I have often needed blood samples and have looked no farther than my own arm. Taking a sample of one's own blood is a relatively easy thing to do with the proper technique and mind set — it helps if the sight of blood, especially your own, does not bother you. Over the years I have removed quite a bit of blood from my own arm without any problems.)

One puzzling thing about so-called post *Night of the Living Dead* zombie films is the idea that zombies need to feed on human flesh. In the strictest sense, zombies are not cannibals. There must be something that, like a drug addict, they crave, and only human flesh will satisfy that addiction. Is it hemoglobin, or certain proteins and/or vitamins that humans possess that other species lack? Since only the destruction of zombie heads, preferably by a bullet to the brain, "kills" them for good, then their need for human flesh must have some sort of neurological basis.

Do they need brain hormones only provided by the hypothalamus or pituitary or perhaps brain neurotransmitters to keep their bodies functioning? Maybe they need the tissues located in the cerebral cortex or the cerebellum to satisfy their needs.

In one scene a human is scuba diving and takes photos of the underwater environment. While underwater she is attacked by a zombie. A submerged zombie begs the question of how does a zombie "live" underwater? Apparently, zombies do not need atmospheric oxygen, and the small amounts found dissolved in water, if even necessary, are apparently sufficient. Though it did not appear so, perhaps this zombie had gills. Also, what does an underwater zombie feed on? Sushi?

Finally, in several scenes it is shown that zombie skin is loosely attached and can easily fall off. In addition, zombie fingers also readily fall off. Their connective tissue must be missing several key components, such as junctional connections (tight junctions and gap junctions) that contribute to the tensile strength of holding normal skin cells together.

What Biological Science Is Necessary to Actually Achieve the Results in the Film: It is made clear that one zombie can pass on the "zombie disease" to another human only by direct blood to blood contact, very similar to many infectious diseases (such as HIV and AIDS). That being said, then the basis of zombie disease must be an infectious particle(s). Whether this infectious agent is a virus, bacteria, or perhaps a prion (an infectious protein) is only speculation. However, it could happen. And *that* being said, then can these victims truly be called zombies? The answer is no, at least not in the classical sense — in that a true zombie is someone who can be controlled by another's will. These zombies do not listen to anything and, like a shark smelling blood, have a one-track mind, lusting only for human flesh.

The zombie body motor movements are slow, sluggish, and methodical, indicative of inefficient neuromuscular control. The dominant sensory input of these zombies is olfactory, and their sense of smell (of human flesh) plays a larger role in their behavior than does hearing or sight. Therefore, whatever infectious agent is involved in creating zombies, it results in a heightened sense of smell, suggesting this is a key survival trait.

Could It Actually Happen: To revive the dead is difficult to accept and is discussed elsewhere in this book. However, there are documented instances where patients on the operating table have been "clinically dead" and have been revived. Many of these patients have commented on seeing the so-called "tunnel of light" after being revived, and perhaps zombies have seen this too.

The Serpent and the Rainbow (1987)

Synopsis: Boston Biocorp, a biotechnology company, hires Dr. Allen, an anthropologist/ethnobiologist, to find a "powder" that transforms humans into zombies. Allen goes to Haiti, gets some of the powder, and brings it back to his lab for analysis. Allen shows that the powder works by acting on certain areas of the brain.

Screenplay: Richard Maxwell and A.R. Simoun, inspired by the book *The Serpent and the Rainbow* by Wade Davis.

Biological Science Principles Involved: Pharmacology. Neurology.

What Is Right with the Biological Science Presented: Boston Biocorp's (BB) desire to develop a new anesthetic that would not be as harmful to surgery patients is commendable. As a BB scientist in the film says, "Approximately 40,000 to

50,000 patients a year are lost on the operating table — not because of surgery but because of anesthetic shock." Anesthetic shock is a real problem, and if a less toxic and life threatening alternative could be found, then this would be genuinely helpful.

Allen is a careful scientist. Back at his lab he tests the zombie powder on baboons, a nice experimental animal for these kinds of tests. The powder is shown to work simply by being put on the intended victim's skin. A nice touch is that those in the film who use the powder on someone else are seen wearing gloves on their hands while holding the powder, indicating that they want to protect themselves from having the powder absorbed into their skin. To test the effects of the powder in his lab, Allen puts some of the powder on the palms of some baboons and says, "10 to 20 minutes later the baboons were dead. They looked dead. It's [the powder] very focused and targets only certain areas of the brain." Allen then monitored baboon respiration, pulse, blood pressure — the key indicators of "death" — and noted the responses were "flat lined." Allen then analyzes brain scans of the limbic, sensory, autonomic, and motor functions of the baboons and comments, "vital functions ... it looks like somebody turned them off with a switch. But here, in the areas of the brain controlling sensory awareness, thoughts, and emotions ... the animals know what's happening the entire time ... but are unable to do anything about it." If zombie powder did work as suggested in the film, this is exactly the response one would see. It's a nice sequence indicating a careful scientist.

One other element of interest is that the effects of the zombie powder "wore off after 12 hours or so, leaving the victim completely normal again." This is just the opposite of the results seen in the film *White Zombie* where the zombification

effects appear to be much longer lasting. "Wore off after 12 hours or so" would be a result of the dose administered. Since Allen just put a small amount on the palms of the baboons, little is actually absorbed into their system. If more is applied or another dose is given — say, after 10 hours — then perhaps the victim would stay a zombie longer.

The trade name that Boston Biocorp gives to the active ingredient in the zombie powder is "Zombinol." Personally, I love that name! Coming up with interesting, catchy, and "sexy" names for new drugs is a challenge. Major drug companies have teams of marketing people actively working on coming up with names they hope will stick in the minds of the buying public, and often times the names the drug companies come up with actually make or break the product. The fact that it works is beside the point; how much they can sell via its name recognition is everything. The next time you are at the drug store, count how many times you see the word "sine" in reference to nasal and cold medications.

What Is Wrong with the Biological Science Presented: On the surface there really isn't much wrong with what is presented from a scientific point of view, and the creators of the film are to be commended.

The main job of the US Food and Drug Administration (FDA) is to insure that products made for human use are manufactured in a consistent and reproducible manner. Based upon the method that one of the native Haitians used to make the zombie powder, the FDA would have a major heart attack. Here is a bit of dialogue that illustrates this: "The ingredients of the powder are terrifically varied [that statement alone would hemorrhage the FDA!]. There is the poisonous sea toad, *Bufo marinis*, the same animal Lucretia Borgia used. Made even more toxic by frightening it with a stinging sea worm. And the puffer fish, which produces one of nature's most powerful poisons, tetrodotoxin. Plus, a whole pharmacy of herbs, minerals, charred, then ground and mixed with a skill that's astonishing ... the process will take three days and nights.... [The Haitian preparing the powder] could give any Harvard Ph.D. a run for his money." (I seriously doubt that last statement.) If this procedure was presented to the FDA they would laugh you out of the building!

Finally, in the preparation of the powder the Haitian doing the formulation takes a female corpse (freshly dug up from a grave) and extracts matter from the skull (most likely her pituitary, hypothalamus, or other brain tissues) to add to the powder. The question is—why female? Are the estrogen based hormones necessary to make the future zombie victim (almost always male) more pliable to suggestion and control?

What Biological Science Is Necessary to Actually Achieve the Results in the Film: The active ingredients in the zombie powder must be active for some time after their preparation. This is referred to as "shelf life." The powder should be somewhat stable for its storage and transportation. The powder is shown to be applied on the skin, so it must be absorbed and enter the blood supply. If too much of the active ingredients are given, then there is the problem of the intended victim not waking up.

Also, "you cannot eat the powder in food. That would kill completely. The flesh would never rise and serve you." Perhaps the natural digestive processes in the stomach and intestines could alter the ingested powder into a form that is highly toxic and would cause death.

Could It Actually Happen: "Zombification," the process of making zombies, has been practiced in the Caribbean for quite some time, and it was a major piece of detective work done by Wade Davis to actually discover that tetrodotoxin is the main ingredient in the zombie powder. This gave zombies a real and, more importantly, credible basis in fact. Like many things in life, there are those who are more susceptible to certain elements than others, and there are some who, through whatever method—chemical or by the power of suggestion—believe themselves to be zombies when exposed to the "powder."

I Come in Peace (1997)

Synopsis: An alien comes to earth (in particular, Los Angeles) in search of "blarcy," an illegal recreational drug on his home planet that just happens to be in abundant supply in human bodies. Blarcy is the alien name for human endorphins. The alien injects his intended victims with a high dose of heroin, which causes a massive release of endorphins. The alien then extracts the endorphins from the victim's brains for his own use. Jack Caine, a cop, searches for the alien and, after a few encounters, eventually kills him.

Screenplay: Jonathan Tydor and Leonard Maas, Jr.

Biological Science Principles Involved: Endocrinology. Pharmacology. Biochemistry.

What Is Right with the Biological Science Presented: Endorphins are, as the coroner stated, "nature's ecstasy." The coroner also states that, "heroin stimulates the pituitary to make endorphins. Endorphins are hormones that create an incredible sense of well-being. Theoretically, you'd have your hands on a nearly perfect drug. One ounce [of endorphins] would be enough for 1000 doses ... at least for humans." An ounce is 28.35 grams, and dividing it by a thousand would make 28.35

milligrams per dose. A hefty amount for anyone! From what we see of the alien's actions, he gives himself a much heftier dose that that. He would definitely be "flying!"

What Is Wrong with the Biological Science Presented: Heroin does induce the production of endorphins, though not at the level dictated in the script. And a probe sent directly into the brain, most likely to target the pituitary and/or hypothalamus, is not the way to go to obtain the quantities the alien wants. If I were the alien, I would locate a synthetic chemist and have him make kilograms of synthetic endorphins, which would have been a lot easier to get. Better yet, the alien should have gone to chemical/biological supply companies that have endorphins listed for sale in their catalogs (true). This would have been a lot more clandestine, so the authorities would not have noticed. Furthermore, the alien could have made a deal with a chemist and traded some advanced technology in exchange for the endorphins. That way they both would have benefited from the arrangement.

The alien places an injection device directly into the hearts of the victims for the delivery of the massive amount of heroin, thereby using the immediate circulation of the victims' blood to deliver the drug throughout their bodies. This is what we call a "bolus," which is a direct, massive injection of any substance into the general circulation. Needless to say, the victims all die by heroin overdose, which is certainly an interesting way to go when you think about it. What a rush!

The alien uses both males and females as his victims. However, females do not make as many endorphins as males, so this raises the question as to why he would use suboptimal females when there were plenty of males available.

What Biological Science Is Necessary to Actually Achieve the Results in the Film: In a word, speed (and I don't mean amphetamines!). Just a few seconds lapse between the time the alien injects the heroin into his victims and when he extracts the brain's endorphins. This does not allow enough time for adequate production of the required endorphins. The heroin would enter the blood stream, course throughout the body within a few minutes, find its way to the pituitary, and stimulate the production of endorphins. Most likely this could take quite a few minutes or hours—and not the mere seconds shown in the film.

Could It Actually Happen: Assuming that there are other life forms out there and they are based on carbon, have DNA, etc., then, perhaps their metabolism is such that a natural biochemical from humans could be a "recreational drug" for them. In that case, there could be some type of alien rogue who comes to our planet and does his best to obtain as much "blarcy" as possible. In and of itself, that certainly could be possible. And the corollary could also be true. Humans could visit some alien civilization and find a native biochemical in their bodies that could serve the same purpose, such as, say, the active ingredient in marijuana or an analgesic like cocaine.

The real interesting question posed by the scriptwriters is whether a massive heroin overdose could give rise to significant endorphin release. This concept does make biochemical sense so it is certainly possible.

ENDOCRINOLOGY

In the biological world, no cell lives in isolation. In multi-celled organisms their survival depends heavily on the ability of each cell to communicate with the others and efficiently control all biological functions, such as growth and metabolism. This elaborate communication network is managed by a diverse class of chemical messengers known as hormones. Hormones are amazingly powerful biological modifiers that can alter both structure and activity within animal bodies. They help animals grow, enter puberty, digest food, produce energy, and respond to their environments. Quite frankly, much of what is presented in the biological sciences in SF cinema could actually happen under certain circumstances; the only real problem is that of time: days and months in real life and seconds and minutes in reel life. DNA controls everything, including hormones. How our hormones work is dictated by what is in our genes. This is readily apparent, since some of us are tall, short, skinny, fat, etc., all dictated by how genes regulate hormone production.

Most of the biological changes presented in the films in this section (or others for that matter, since hormones are at the basis of much biology) are possible with the use of the right amounts of particular hormones in specific ways. What is important to keep in mind is that hormones are released by specific cells, have specific responses, and work only on specific target cells. Hormones themselves come in all sorts of shapes, sizes, and chemical compositions, ranging from small molecules (acetylcholine and amino acids) to peptides (a few to up to about 30 amino acids in length) to proteins to lipids. (Lipid hormones are essentially all derivatives of cholesterol.) Also, in keeping with the concept of a hormone being a compound made by one cell and carried by the blood to another cell, there are intracellular "hormones," that are made in one part of a cell and transported to another part within the cell to cause an effect. Examples of intracellular hormones are cyclic AMP, diacylglycerol, and calcium ions. This could be called intracellular endocrinology.

There is another thing to keep in mind when thinking about hormones. Like throwing a pebble down a hill to start an avalanche, a hormone also initiates a series of cascade-like events that have long term outcomes. Hormones help keep everything in our bodies in order — what is called homeostasis, a constant internal environment. Deviations from this homeostasis can have detrimental effects on other parts of our bodies. Many of the creatures in SF cinema would have incredible hormonal swings from the way hormones were used on them. No wonder many of them were angry ... their hormones were out of balance!

THE ISLANDS OF DR. MOREAU

H.G. Wells (along with Jules Verne) is one of the two writers most responsible for making science fiction real. All those who followed the trails they blazed are forever indebted to these two pioneers. One of Wells' more interesting stories is *The Island of Dr. Moreau*, a tale of a single-minded scientist trying to make the world a better place by understanding the genetic principles and deeds that make man, man.

We are fortunate to have three different film versions of this story available to us, each done at different times—1933, 1977, and 1996—with different biological science principles known at each time. This provides us with a wonderful opportunity to compare and contrast what was known at the time and what the screenwriters did (or did not do) with this knowledge. Each of these films is unique, and a perfect example of the then-contemporary science of each respective era.

In 1933, scientists knew of nucleic acids, the stuff from which DNA is made, but were unaware that DNA is the basis for all that we are. Nucleic acids were thought of as just that—acids from inside cells. "Germ plasma" was still some poorly understood "vital humor."

By 1977 DNA was known to be the genetic basis of life. Proteins became well understood, and the majority of cellular structures, metabolism, and functions were clarified.

By 1996 the DNAge had arrived, and gene cloning had become so commonplace that high school students were doing these experiments in their lab courses. Successful gene therapy procedures were being performed all over the planet. Using very simple reagents, like cold alcohol and bits of fruit, anyone could extract DNA in their own kitchens.

The time periods of each of these films reflect what was known at the time they were done. Nowhere in the 1932 version (nor, surprisingly, in the 1977 version) do you hear the term DNA. The term gene cloning is also not uttered in the 1977 version, though the groundbreaking work in cloning DNA was already done by then. The writers wised up by 1996, and gene cloning was liberally used in the story. In fact, in the 1996 version the writers even went so far as to mention "DNA restriction fragments," "plasmid origin of replications," "gene signal sequence," and, surprisingly, the "pCANTAB 5" cloning vector, though there is serious doubt whether the writers had any clue as to what they were talking about.

Synopsis (applies to all three film versions): A survivor of an accident at sea arrives on an island inhabited by Dr. Moreau and his staff. Moreau is attempting to transform various animals into men, called "manimals," and vice versa. The lone boat survivor thinks all this is blasphemy and attempts to escape. Ultimately, the manimals mutiny and kill Moreau.

Island of Lost Souls (1933)

The first version, done in 1933, is called *Island of Lost Souls* and is the best of the three. The major star is Charles Laughton (Dr. Moreau), and he plays a wickedly cunning and vile protagonist.

Dr. Moreau (Charles Laughton) notices the "...stubborn beast flesh ... creeping back..." on Lota's (Kathleen Burke) fingers in *Island of Lost Souls* (1933). To maintain the level of cellular differentiation, finger joints, and keratin on fingernails, a constant source of hormones and growth factors would be needed. Without them the tissues would "revert" to their natural state.

Screenplay: Philip Wylie and Waldemar Young, based on the novel *The Island of Dr. Moreau* by H.G. Wells.

Biological Science Principles Involved: Genetics. Endocrinology. Surgery.

What Is Right with the Biological Science Presented: Many scientists start out in one field (in this film, Moreau starts out in botany) and at some point in their career end up switching fields. Their research takes them different directions, or perhaps they become intellectually bored with what they were doing and look for greener pastures that may be more stimulating. Moreau calls his island laboratory "...an experimental station of sorts for bioanthropological research." "Bioanthropology" is a bit removed from "starting in plant life!" Here is a case of the cinemascientist radically changing his field of scientific interest.

In addition to the visceral reactions Parker has towards the manimals, Moreau is also interested in the more subtle psychological reactions. To partially satisfy this interest, Moreau introduces Parker to Lota, the panther girl. In doing so, Moreau says, "Lota is my most nearly perfect creation. I wanted to prove how completely she was a woman. [She looked pretty good to me!] Whether she was capable of loving, mating, and having children." Since Lota is the only "woman" on the island, Parker did indeed show a sexual interest in her. Moreau's questions of whether he could convince a typical man (Parker) that Lota is something of interest is answered quite well; hormones win once again.

And speaking of hormones, they play a key role in this film. Depending upon the hormone, their effects are either permanent (like growth hormone) or transient (like insulin). During one scene with Lota, Parker sees her fingers begin to turn claw-like. The implication here is that whatever Moreau did to her is transient. This is closer to reality (if indeed manimals could be created). It would have been too easy to have the changes permanent; but since there are reversals (at one point Moreau exclaims, "It's the stubborn beast flesh which is creeping back. Day by day, it creeps back."), this is more reflective of reality and therefore biologically satisfying.

What Is Wrong with the Biological Science Presented: Let us start with a series of quotes by Laughton's Moreau; in these scenes, he is talking with Parker, the survivor who comes to the island. Moreau says, "I started in plant life in London 20 years ago. I took an orchid and performed a miracle. I stripped 100,000 years of slow evolution from it. And I had no longer an orchid. What orchids will be 100,000 years from now. A slight change in the single unit of the germ plasma. I let my imagination run fantastically ahead. Why not experiment with a more complex organism…. Man is the present climax of a long process of organic evolution. All animal life is tending toward the human form…. Plastic surgery, nutrient infusions, gland extracts, ray burns … look what I have discovered in my own work among the cellular organisms…. With these, I have wiped out hundreds of thousands of years of evolution. From the lower animals I have made … that was my first achievement, articulate speech controlled by the brain … with each experiment I improve upon the last. I get nearer and nearer, Mr. Parker. Do you know what it means to feel like God?" Wiping out "hundreds of thousands of years of evolution" just could not happen. Also, how could anyone know what an orchid would look like 100,000 years in the future; in terms of evolution, a mere 100,000 years is a drop in the ocean and not enough time to allow much of any-

thing significant to happen. Nor could he have given the manimals "articulate speech."

During one of the surgery scenes the only one not wearing a surgical face mask is Moreau, and this represents a lack of surgical technique. Perhaps the vanity of Laughton prevents him from hiding his face from the audience with a gauze mask.

What Biological Science Is Necessary to Actually Achieve the Results in the Film: You will read this again and again in this book: Everything is controlled by DNA. Even the amount of hormones necessary to cause all the changes seen in the manimals would ultimately have to be controlled by DNA. Such things as articulate speech (controlled by the brain), fingers and opposable thumbs, toes, jaws realigning, hair disappearing—whether caused by an alteration in genes or by hormone injections—can be attributable to the actions of DNA.

The manimals are seen walking on two legs instead of four. This would require some significant changes in leg femur and hip bone structure. And those changes would be painful. The manimals called Moreau's lab/surgery room the "house of pain," and the reason is that the nerves attached to bone and muscle would be stretched, pulled, and torn to accommodate the new tissue growth. The hormones would induce the effects and the manimals would simply scream in pain as a result.

Could It Actually Happen: Yes, some of the manimal changes could be done, but the more important thing to ask is why would anyone go to all the trouble and expense to do this? Perhaps there may be some military reasons for developing an army of beasts whose sole purpose is to follow orders, no matter how life threatening. However, this would be difficult, because the instinct for survival is so overpowering that to genetically extinguish this drive would be near impossible, even by very loose cinema standards.

The Island of Dr. Moreau (1977)

The second filmed version was made in 1977 and starred Burt Lancaster as Dr. Moreau and Michael York as Braddock, the shipwrecked survivor who landed on the island.

Screenplay: John Herman Shaner and Al Ramrus, based on the novel by H.G. Wells.

Biological Science Principles Involved: Genetics. Endocrinology. Surgery.

What Is Right with the Biological Science Presented: Over a dinner, Moreau and Braddock exchange philosophical ideas, and Moreau says, "[Man] may know exactly how and why an engine works, but a one celled organism is more complex, more mysterious that any sophisticated machine." Machines can easily be understood, but the details of a single cell are still being worked out.

All scientists have a view of themselves, and here is how Moreau describes himself. He said, "Moreau, Paul. Born April 12, 1851, Boston, Massachusetts. Doctor of chemistry, physiology, anatomy. Showed brilliant promise in his early monographs on cellular structure and growth. His most significant contributions were made before the age of 30. But his work was highly criticized by academicians as being highly speculative and insufficiently documented.... Too often men of

The first changes of Braddock (Michael York, right) to a manimal, as seen in *The Island of Dr. Moreau* (1977). The increased hair growth and facial musculature begin to take hold. All changes were brought about by hormones.

vision become outcasts." This is certainly an interesting comment on one's own career and a sad commentary that "men of vision" are certainly thought of as "outcasts."

Moreau considers himself a bibliophile, and he describes his personal library to Braddock by saying, "My books. The distillation of man's experience on earth. Immortality and the soul. The nature of good and evil. Physical universe. And here, eugenics and inheritance. Why is one flower red, another yellow? Why is one man tall, the next one short? Embryos. A dog, a mouse, a human. They look almost the same. They virtually start out the same. A bit of protoplasm, a nucleus, a chain of chromosomes. Yet we all know what they turn out to look like. Why? How does a cell become enslaved to a form, to a destiny it can never change? Can we change that destiny?" This is certainly heady stuff, and these are questions today's real scientists are asking. With more and more information being provided about human genes, man will certainly be able to control his own destiny. Stay tuned, gentle readers, the DNAge is just getting started. Like on the first step of a thousand mile journey, much adventure is ahead of us.

The action of this movie takes place during the early 20th Century. DNA was discovered to be the genetic determining material in 1944, so I do not expect Moreau to know what DNA is. During one verbal exchange between Moreau and Braddock, Moreau says, "I have proved — almost proved — the existence of a cell particle that controls the living organism. This cell, this particle, controls the shape of life." Today we call this "particle" DNA.

Near the end of the film, Moreau attempts to change Braddock into an animal. The reason, as explained by Moreau, is "...they [the manimals] can't tell me what's happening inside their bodies.... You will do that for me. You will explore a

new battlefield, that war of the cells and bring back the knowledge. Become an animal, to feel inside your body and brain what no man has ever known before. You will bring that back to me." After some changes occur to Braddock, Moreau then says, "Your mental processes are changing. The way you think is changing. You're beginning to think in images, concrete images. Hot, cold, light, dark, food, hunger, pain. Words are becoming meaningless to you, except for the most elementary command. You've lost control. You are becoming animal." This is certainly much to think about.

The changes Moreau makes in the manimals are transient and not permanent. As Moreau says, "I bring them to within a hair's breadth of being human. Almost give them human form, feeling, thought, speech. Always in the end — almost always — they revert to what they once were. Lions, bears, hyenas. I suffered many disappointments, but I've learned to wait, watch." Hormonal changes would indeed be transient, and after some time these changes would revert back to their original form and function.

What Is Wrong with the Biological Science Presented: When Braddock lands on Moreau's island he has been adrift on a small boat for 17 days. Anyone adrift on the open seas with no protection would have suffered from sunburns, heat stroke, exhaustion, etc., and would have had a difficult time functioning on land as well as Braddock does. After a significant period of recuperation, then perhaps Braddock's behavior would have seemed more reasonable.

During one scene Braddock enters Moreau's lab and sees a bear undergoing transformation into a human. While examining the manimal, Moreau says, "This serum [Moreau gives it to the creature as an intramuscular injection] contains the distillation of a biological code message, a new set of instructions erasing the natural instincts of this animal. Some surgery, implants of the various organs, he should grow to resemble any creature we please. In this case, a human being." No single injection of any serum, which is the fluid portion of blood obtained after removal of cells, would be able to cause the changes seen in the bear manimal, not to mention "erasing natural instincts." The implantation of organs is the biggest problem with this statement. Because of immunological problems of transplanting foreign tissues into any animal, no organ would be accepted and instead would be rejected. And besides, organs are not what distinguishes animal from animal, but rather bone (and muscle) structure, brain size, and skin (and instincts). All organs, like lungs, livers, kidneys, intestines, spleens, etc., are essentially the same in all animals.

What Biological Science Is Necessary to Actually Achieve the Results in the Film: The comments for the 1933 version of this film also apply here. DNA is the key to Moreau's success, as well as the use of functional hormones.

The surgical transplantation of various organs would require two things to be successful. The first is to make sure the tissue is histocompatible, which means immunologically similar (or identical), so the transplant would be accepted. Transplantation of organs between different species is called xenotransplantation, and rarely (if ever) is it successful. For this to be successful would require the use of significant quantities of immunosuppressive drugs, such as cyclophosphamide or cyclosporin. So much would be needed that the manimal's entire immune system would be suppressed to the point that many other infections would occur. To survive they would have to live in a bubble-like, sterile environment.

Could It Actually Happen: Some of the genetic experiments could happen, but

as discussed above for the 1933 version, why would anyone want to go to all the trouble and expense to do this? Even the most insane and maniacal of real scientists would not try to create such manimals. Therefore, this only leaves military applications, which to me would be very depressing.

The Island of Dr. Moreau (1996)

The third version, the weakest of the three, was made in 1996 and stars Marlon Brando as Dr. Moreau. This version is just downright bizarre, though it does have its moments.

Screenplay: Richard Stanley and Ron Hutchinson, based on the novel by Wells.

Biological Science Principles Involved: Molecular Biology. Endocrinology. Surgery.

What Is Right with the Biological Science Presented: The house Moreau lives in looks very much like a natural history museum, with the appropriate clutter one would expect of this. A large variety of flora and fauna is scattered about his home. On a wall is a diploma from the Stockholm Nobel Prize committee listing Moreau as the 1989 recipient for "gene manipulation." This is interesting because Moreau says that he had once been a "brilliant neurosurgeon," which is a far cry from gene manipulation!

Moreau states that he has been on the island for 17 years (therefore, he received his Nobel Prize while already living on the island; so much for hiding from the public's eye); he became obsessed with his animal research, and it was animal rights activists who drove him out of the USA. (The activities of animal rights activists are a real problem. Though I personally admire the dedication and fortitude of these activists, their energy is misguided and misspent. There is no excuse for the vandalism they perform. Just about all current medical knowledge has been obtained with the use of animals. If these activists take any sort of medications, they can thank some animal somewhere for making it possible.)

In this version the boat survivor's name is Douglas. While walking around Moreau's camp barrack buildings, he comes across one of the labs filled with exotic animals (llama, panther, monkeys, etc.). A newborn delivery of sorts is taking place, and a "crew" of five manimals is assisting a female through labor. The female has six "human" breasts on her chest, feet with hooves, "hands" with three fingers, and copious body hair. She delivers a "baby" with a cleft palate. This is interesting because if the genes of animals are altered in the way Moreau describes, then one would expect a variety of abnormalities to occur. A baby with a severe cleft palate would be a natural part of this process.

Brando's Moreau has very pale skin. He cannot tolerate the heat and sun and wears heavy makeup when he goes outside. He says he has an "allergy to the sun, which is why I put this medication on." There are many humans who indeed have skin sensitive to direct sunlight and as a result are susceptible to skin cancer, like melanoma. They too put adequate sunscreen lotions on their exposed skin when under direct sunlight.

Like too many real scientists, Moreau is also extremely arrogant. Later in the film Moreau says his dream is "to create a perfect human race." Perfect by his arrogant standards. Manipulating genes may make a perfect body, but trying to make a "perfect mind and intellect" are problems society will have to ultimately deal with. These problems are a whole different matter and beyond the realm of DNA.

Moreau gives his manimals injections with an air gun device, definitely a nice modern '90s approach. This takes care of the problems of dealing with sterile needles. The injected fluid is composed of "a combination of endorphins and hormones. It keeps them from retrogressing." Regarding the problems of retrogressing, Moreau says, "They are just a question of chemical imbalances." This is an odd way of saying this but, nevertheless, an accurate one. In this respect all diseases could be considered "chemical imbalances," in that some body biochemical(s) is/are out of "balance," resulting in a disease state.

And finally, there are the following words found in a notebook: "on site enzyme breakdown" (in reference to DNA restriction fragments); "plasmid origin of replication"; "E. Tag"; "Gene signal sequence"; "Gene 3 protein"; and "pCANTAB 5." All of these are in reference to various procedures, reagents, and mechanisms of manipulating DNA for gene cloning. Someone went to a lot of trouble to have these words of the real molecular biologist appear in this film.

What Is Wrong with the Biological Science Presented: Moreau describes the manimals to Douglas thus: "These people you have witnessed before are animals that have been fused with human genes. The Devil is nothing more than a tiresome collection of genes." The interesting concept here is that the Devil is just bad DNA! During the same conversation Moreau further elaborates by saying, "They [manimals] represent a stage in the process of the eradication of destructive elements found in the human psyche." "A stage in the process of the eradication" is an inaccurate way to think about DNA. Many of the "problems" he is referring to are learned behaviors and not a problem with DNA, so you cannot "eradicate" them through genetic manipulation.

During one of the scenes we see a

manimal reverting back to animal form, and the teeth become more pointed. The question is, How can teeth revert? The facial maxilla bone structure and surrounding teeth cannot change so rapidly.

The most obvious mistake is one I am still shaking my head over. With all the pains the producers took to make the lab setting so authentic looking, their *big* mistake is hard to understand. At the end of the film, the shipwreck survivor, Mr. Douglas, looks through a lab notebook and finds a section on him. Shown are his blood type (B negative) and a short sequence of some of his DNA. (Moreau intends to use Douglas' DNA to stop the regression of his "daughter," who is derived from a panther.) The Douglas DNA sequence is shown as: "MMA TTA MMA TAM TTT MMA AMM." As I have stated elsewhere, the alphabet of DNA is a four base code and comprised of C(ytosine), A(denosine), T(hymidine), and G(uanosine); CATG, in an endless combination or order. Though they got the triplet concept right (DNA sequences come in groups of three, such as CGA, ATC, AAG, TAT, etc.), there is no DNA code with an "M" in it — no "MMA," no "TAM," and no "AMM." Even grade school kids know this, so the producers (or writers) getting this wrong is unforgivable.

What Biological Science Is Necessary to Actually Achieve the Results in the Film: Again, Mr. DNA must be effectively and efficiently controlled. All the comments for the above two versions of this film also apply here.

Could It Actually Happen: Never say never to DNA! Moreau trying to make animals like humans is like trying to put the proverbial square peg in the proverbial round hole. Pointless.

Monkeying Around with Apes

In the film *The Planet of the Apes* (1968), the Dr. Zaius character states that

"The proper study of ape is ape." The character played by Charleton Heston, Taylor, is outraged at this comment, most likely because of the notion that man thinks of himself as the center of the universe in that he alone can communicate (write and talk), build, and contemplate his own existence; how dare the apes think they can do these things!

Man's fascination with the great apes has a long history, and being descended from common ancestors probably has a lot to do with it. Most people do not realize that the difference between the genes of man and those of the apes (the chimpanzee in particular) is amazingly small. At least 98.5 percent of man's genes are identical to those of the two species of chimps. Yes, you read that right, at least a whopping 98.5 percent similarity in genes between man and monkey! Furthermore, the average human protein is more than 99 percent identical to its chimpanzee equivalent. This then begs the question, which of our genes makes us human, and what does that 1.5 percent genetic difference look like? The human genome contains about 30,000 genes, and a 1.5 percent difference means there are only a maximum of 450 genes that differentiate man and ape! (For some humans I know, this difference is closer to only 50 genes or so!) What this minuscule difference means is that these few genes gives us the ability to write books (such as this one), create SF films, walk upright, design cancer treatments, talk, etc. Since man doesn't look nor act like apes, these few genes are everything.

With such a close genetic relationship, it is no wonder that Hollywood decided to make films that exploit these magical 1,500 genes. Changing, altering, and/or mutating only 1,500 genes is, on the surface, not that difficult a task. Here is something interesting to think about, especially in light of what the Hollywood ape is like: What would happen if scientists identify the genes that control the development of the larynx, our voice box, and, say, the cerebellum, and, through recombinant genetic technology, gives these genes to, say, a chimpanzee, thereby giving him the anatomy needed for speech? Shades of Dr. Moreau and *Planet of the Apes*!

Though there are several man/ape films, most are fantasy and are something the writers and producers wanted to do (probably to make a quick buck). The best example of these is the granddaddy of all ape films, *King Kong* (1933). Also, these films are certainly a sign of their times. Back in the 1930s, '40s, and '50s, apes were news. They were just being discovered and described, primarily through the exploits of famous adventurers like Frank "bring 'em back alive" Buck. After the apes became better known and less mysterious, they ceased being something Hollywood could exploit. Jane Goodall, the famous gorilla scientist, put the final nail in that coffin with the publication of her book *In the Shadow of Man* in 1974.

The Ape (1940)

Synopsis: Dr. Adrian (Boris Karloff) uses the spinal fluids of humans to help paralyzed people walk again. Adrian needs spinal fluids from freshly killed humans(!) for his paralysis cure and disguises himself as an ape to collect the samples. Adrian injects these fluids into paralyzed patients and they begin to show signs of being able to walk.

Screenplay: Kurt Siodmak and Richard Carroll, adaptation by Kurt Siodmak, suggested from the play by Adam Hull Shirk.

Biological Science Principles Involved: Endocrinology. Neurobiology.

What Is Right with the Biological Science Presented: During the era of this

film's production, and before the Jonas Salk vaccine, polio was considered a very devastating disease — and rightly so — as was paralysis and its various forms. Many paralyzed people spent most of their lives in either "iron lung" machines to assist their breathing or confined to wheelchairs. Fortunately, medicine has progressed enough that iron lungs are a thing of the past, though wheelchairs are still with us. Great progress has been made with the understanding of neuromuscular biology, in that these afflictions will soon be a "20th Century disease." As such, this film centered on a pre–World War II plot to deal with the horrors of polio or paralysis and the promise of a potential cure, which was welcomed by the paying public. After all, President Roosevelt was stricken with polio at the time, so it was on the minds of many.

What Is Wrong with the Biological Science Presented: Adrian writes the following in his lab notebook: "Death of patient [a zoo keeper attacked and killed by a gorilla] due to fractured cervical vertebrae caused by attack of ape. By means of lumbar puncture, 2cc spinal fluid removed from deceased circus trainer. With this human spinal fluid, will attempt to relieve paralytical condition of patient Francis Clifford [a patient Adrian treats like a daughter] by means of spinal injections." Spinal fluid is referred to as cerebrospinal fluid, and is a fluid secreted by the choroid plexus of the brain, filling the ventricles and the subarachnoid cavities of both the brain and spinal cord. In an average human there are about 150 milliliters (ml) of spinal fluid, which contains, per ml, about 2 milligrams (mg) of protein, five mg of glucose, and about 0.05 mg of cholesterol. Very little, if any, DNA is in spinal fluid. Therefore, whatever effects Adrian is hoping for must have been contained in the proteins present in the fluid. Since Adrian removes "2cc" of fluid, then he removes about 4 mg of protein. There is not very much you can do with only 4 mg of protein. It is doubtful if any of that protein had any hormonal effects; and most likely it is "structural" protein, which does not have any metabolic benefit.

Later Adrian writes the following into his notebook: "Two injections should have been enough [to cure Francis Clifford]." If all Adrian needed are two injections of the fluid, then it must have been very powerful stuff!

Regarding these spinal fluid samples, there is one thing not taken into consideration, and that is the variability of the samples from person to person. There could be a variety of reasons why one person's spinal fluid could be both quantitatively and qualitatively different from another's. No mention is made of how Adrian analyzes the samples he obtains. In modern medicine, the Food and Drug Administration would have had plenty to say regarding the practices of Adrian.

What Biological Science Is Necessary to Actually Achieve Results in the Film: Paralysis is the loss of power of voluntary movement in the muscle through injury or a disease of its nerve supply. This paralysis could be due to a variety of causes and could be temporary or permanent. If they are temporary in nature, then perhaps Adrian could have made Francis walk again. If her disease is simply a compression of the nerve trunk or lower spinal cord, then a spinal injection could have temporarily relieved her symptoms, thereby allowing her to reestablish sensations in her legs. If she has a lesion in her spinal cord, as seen with patients with myeloparalysis, then spinal injections would have done little to alleviate her symptoms. If her problem is with a motor neuron — which is a nerve cell in the spinal cord that, via an axon (a specialized nerve cell that conducts nerve impulses), establishes a functional connection to muscle cells — being disrupted, then no way could any number of spinal injections have helped her.

One possibility for which Adrian's spinal injections could have worked on Francis is that within the spinal fluids he obtained is present (highly unlikely, especially in the quantities he needed) a protein called nerve growth factor, or NGF. NGF controls the development of sympathetic postganglionic neurons, and possibly also sensory ganglion cells. With enough NGF, then perhaps she could have grown new nerve cells and tissues, giving her the ability to walk again. However, that is really stretching things beyond the comfort level. But you never know...

Could It Actually Happen: Medical science has made great strides to eradicate paralysis in all its forms. The most prominent examples of this in the public's mind are the "career ending" injuries of professional athletes. Not too long ago these injuries would definitely have been career ending. Now, with modern treatments (such as electrical stimulation of muscles, rapid bone healing, and appropriate physical therapy) these athletes (or anyone else with similar injuries; they just don't make the headlines) return to the playing field in record time. In light of 1940's *The Ape*, all of this would be considered a "cure!" As stated above, paralysis will soon be thought of as a "20th Century disease," since cures and treatments are making it a "thing of the past."

The Ape Man (1943)

Synopsis: Dr. James Brewster (Bela Lugosi; it's hard to picture Bela as a "James"!) has created a spinal fluid serum that transforms him into an ape-like creature. To revert back to human form, Brewster the ape kills others to obtain the necessary spinal fluid cocktail. In the end a gorilla attacks and kills Brewster.

This title lobby card shows Lugosi as *The Ape Man* (1943) preparing a "sample" for himself. The mortar and pestle seen in the foreground are for grinding and mixing solids. For the purposes of this film the mortar and pestle were most likely used to grind phosphate salts to be used as various buffers, such as the one in the syringe used to dissolve a glandular fluid extract.

Screenplay: Barney Sarecky, based on an original story by Karl Brown.

Biological Science Principles Involved: Endocrinology. Cell Biology. Genetics. Dermatology.

What Is Right with the Biological Science Presented: When Brewster appears as a pseudo-ape he tries to emulate the walk and mannerisms of an ape. His shoulders are hunched, giving the false impression of longer arms, his hands are bent at the knuckles, and the hair present on his face, chest, and hands resembles that of a chimpanzee. All in all it is a nice effort, though one-dimensional.

Brewster is also seen going about the mixing of various chemicals, and he looks like he knows exactly what he is doing.

Some probably have the wrong impression that mixing chemicals is all that scientists do!

What Is Wrong with the Biological Science Presented: To describe how Brewster is transformed into an ape in the first place, his colleague, Randall, explains, "Six months ago we made an astounding discovery. It was so far advanced from anything that's been done to date that Jim decided to be the guinea pig for this experiment himself. I tried to talk him out of it but you know how stubborn he is when he gets an idea in his head." Well, it is never explained what this "astounding discovery" is, so we are clueless about what it is designed for. What is most interesting about this "discovery" is that it involves "ape fluid injections." Apparently, Brewster injects himself with ape fluids. What fluids (or glands) does he use? Serum? Plasma? Spinal fluids? Seminal fluid extracts!? This could be a long list. Whatever source of ape fluid he uses, this stuff must have been very powerful to cause such dramatic changes.

The changes seen in Brewster are only those of an outer physical appearance, such as gait and hair. Brewster could still think and talk as a human, so the changes are partial and, in all probability, temporary.

During one scene, Brewster the ape tells his colleague, Dr. Randall, "I must have human spinal fluid injected into me. It's my only chance. It's the only way to counteract the ape fluid injections." (It is never stated whether these counteractions would be permanent or temporary.) After Brewster has his pet gorilla kill a man, the ape-scientist uses a syringe (with incredibly poor sterile technique) to remove some spinal fluid. Back in his lab Brewster mixes some chemicals, makes some culture solutions, and then prepares the spinal fluid for injection into himself. Randall injects the fluid preparation into Brewster's lower spine! Of all the places to inject, why the lower spine!? Right after the injection, Brewster begins to walk upright, with the mannerisms of a human. However, he does not lose his hairiness. Soon the injection wears off and Brewster reverts to his previous ape-like state. If the human spinal fluid is temporary, then why isn't the ape fluid also temporary?

What Biological Science is Necessary to Actually Achieve the Results in the Film: Mentioned above is the fact that the genes of man and ape are at least 98.5 percent similar. Therefore, whatever Brewster found in his "ape fluid" to cause him to become ape-like must have been within that 1.5 percent difference. Some combination of about 450 genes causes him to

acquire the walking mannerisms and hair of an ape; it could have been as few as a dozen or so genes. All in all, this is pretty wild stuff.

The only way these dramatic changes could occur would be through the use of DNA. Proteins such as enzymes, growth factors, hormones, etc., would not be able to accomplish the biological science seen on the screen all by themselves. For such changes to be permanent would require the interaction and intervention of DNA.

Could It Actually Happen: In a word, no.

Bride of the Gorilla (1951)

Synopsis: Barney Chavez (Raymond Burr) kills his boss after being fired by him. An old lady witnesses the event and concocts a potion to transform Barney into a gorilla to "get even." Barney marries the widow of his boss and eventually kills her when he is in gorilla form. The police commissioner (Lon Chaney, Jr.) shoots Barney/gorilla, killing him. After death, the gorilla reverts back to normal Barney.

Screenplay: Curt Siodmak.

Biological Science Principles Involved: Endocrinology. Pharmacology. Dermatology. Cell Biology.

What Is Right with the Biological Science Presented: The use of plant extracts is almost as old as man. The medicinal benefits of plants and their extracts is largely untapped. Many of the larger pharmaceutical companies have teams of specialists scouring the planet, looking for exotic plant species from which new and beneficial drugs can be identified and ultimately synthesized for the eventual control and eradication of diseases.

Also acknowledged in this film is the difference in the senses between man and animal. As Mr. Chavez explains to his wife, "I'm not happy here [in the house]. I'm happy out there [in the jungle]. Out there in the jungle, out there everything's different. I seemed changed. My hands, my eyes. I can see further than I've ever seen before. The smallest leaf on top of the highest tree. I can climb it as if I had wings. I can smell a thousand smells. Flowers, plants, the animals. I'm strong, powerful. The jungle is my house. It belongs to me. I can hear voices, miles away. The animals talk to me [shades of Dr. Dolittle!]. I understand them … they're afraid of me." Senses would indeed be heightened.

What Is Wrong with the Biological Sciences Presented: When the old lady, Pal Long, makes the plant poison from a "pied iguana" plant(?), that transforms Barney into a gorilla, she is seen squeezing the juices out of the plant's flowers using her bare, unprotected hands. Why didn't the poison seep through the pores in her skin and affect her? She puts the poison into a drink and gives it to Barney. Does the combination of the poison with water (or ethanol?) enhance its effects? Perhaps the poison only works when ingested. Either way, the old lady would certainly have gotten some of the poison absorbed into her skin, so it should have affected her. One other possibility is that she has handled so much of the poison over the years that she has developed an immunity to the stuff. This has been seen in handlers of poisonous snakes who have been bitten often enough that they make antibodies to the poison, so it no longer has potency for them.

What Biological Science Is Necessary to Actually Achieve the Results in the Film: What kind of plant extract could have transformed a man into an ape? That is difficult to answer. One obvious answer is that the poison wasn't a poison at all but some sort of hallucinogen. After taking it, along with some appropriate verbal "sug-gestions," then Chavez could indeed have envisioned himself to be an ape, with all the mental acuity that comes with it. With the aid of hallucinogens he could have psyched himself into a mental frenzy, so to speak, and thought he was a gorilla. The problem with this is that we, the audience, do indeed see Chavez become an ape.

The notion of a human becoming ape-like when actual ape genes have been successfully incorporated into human cells and tissues (though there would have to be a tremendous amount of genetic hand-waving necessary) is acceptable. To have genes in plant extracts that can transform human genes into gorilla genes is just too difficult to rationalize and accept. For this to actually happen would take this out of the realm of science and put it into the world of fantasy, which is beyond the scope of this book.

Could It Actually Happen: Plant extracts of all types do affect humans in many profound ways, from anti-cancer drugs to psychoactive drugs. However, there is not anything even remotely resembling the ability to bring about such physical transformations. The only way this could happen, as mentioned above, is by the plant poison generating powerful hallucinogenic activity, thereby causing some mental aberration that has Mr. Chavez thinking he is a gorilla.

THE NEVER ENDING SEARCH FOR THE FOUNTAIN OF YOUTH

Aging research is being conducted all over the world. The reasons are obvious—we all want to retain the mental acuity and physical skills of youth. As the world's population ages, the costs will be staggering to maintain health. What aging does to our bodies is fairly well understood. Our skin loses some of its durability, our muscles begin to atrophy, our brain loses its capacity to remember, think, and create, and bones become more brittle. Senility and Alzheimer's disease will become more prevalent as our population ages. Some of these things can be corrected by a variety of interventions, such as artificial bone replacements, medications ("better living through chemistry"), etc. (Quite frankly, it is a privilege to age because not everyone gets the chance.)

The major reason for hope is that within our population there are individuals who can enter their ninth decade of life with their body functions largely intact. They are mentally active, physically fit and mobile, and can do a number of things many of their contemporaries (not to mention those who are decades younger) cannot. Yes, healthy living (such as not smoking) is a significant part of this, but good genetics is essential for a prolonged, active life. As a result of the Human Genome Project, scientists and physicians will be better armed with the genetic basis of why some age better than others. With appropriate gene replacement therapy, corrections in our physiology will become routine, thereby allowing us to live longer. The medicines of the next millennium will make our lives amazingly better. Many of those born now will live into the 22nd century, and a life expectancy of 150 years is achievable.

However, there are still some hurdles yet to be overcome. The "Hayflick limit" is a finite biological limit on the number of times normal cells and tissues can reproduce themselves. Cancer cells, however, have shown that this can be overcome. These cells have lost the ability to stop growing. If this ability can be gently tweaked, then perhaps we can allow normal cells to continue to divide at a more controlled rate.

This may be possible with the use of an enzyme called telomerase. At the ends of our chromosomes is a region we call the telomere. As cells age, the telomeres shorten and become more difficult to deal with. With the presence of the enzyme telomerase, this problem may be correctable, thereby prolonging the life expectancy of cells. So there is hope. It is also possible that someone exists now who will be one of the first meaningfully immortal humans who could perhaps live well into the 22nd century or beyond. The real problem with this will be overpopulation—if death is postponed for some indefinite period. Our planet's natural resources can only get us so far. If this comes to pass, then perhaps new diseases will manifest themselves and act as a "weeding out" process to limit this. Only time will tell.

One of the easiest things we can do to help ensure a longer, higher quality of life is to live healthier. The lifestyle choices we make, such as smoking, pollution, etc., definitely have a detrimental effect on our health. With better living combined with better medicine, who knows what limits there will be?

The Wasp Woman (1959)

Synopsis: Janice Starlin runs a cosmetics firm and wants to stay perpetually young so she can boost sales of her products. She employs an entomologist, Dr. Zinthrop, to make some wasp royal jelly that will help keep her skin looking young. After several injections of the wasp extract, Starlin turns into "the wasp woman," sealing her fate and ultimately dying as a result.

Screenplay: Leo Gordon, from a story by Kinta Zertuche.

Biological Science Principles Involved: Endocrinology. Dermatology. Entomology.

What Is Right with the Biological

The visually interesting and graphic one sheet poster for *The Wasp Woman* (1959). The art of selling films with science.

Science Presented: Legitimate scientific experiments are typically done in stages, building upon what has been learned and improving for the next experiment. Zinthrop the scientist is cautious in his approach to his experiments and goes about reproducing what he has done. I thought this was excellent, and I congratulate the writers for incorporating this subtle, though important and very real, concept into the film. This element of real science is very often overlooked in reel science.

During a meeting between Zinthrop and Starlin he explains that no two people react to royal jelly in the same way, and the queen wasp behaves similarly to the black widow spider in that both are carnivorous, poisonous, and devour their mates. He got all this right.

Starlin tells Zinthrop that she is interested in "the possibility of using enzyme extracts from royal wasp jelly." This is amazingly prescient in knowledge about telomerase! (Every now and then screenwriters get lucky.)

Ever the careful chemist, Zinthrop tells Starlin that, "I've been experimenting with concentrated solutions of the enzymes. [Now his formula becomes enzymes instead of an "extract" he worked on earlier.] A great deal more powerful than the solutions I've been using in your injections." A Starlin executive further comments that, "[Zinthrop] claims he can stimulate the processes of rejuvenation through the use of enzymes extracted from wasps." Though enzymes would be necessary, wasps do not have telomerase (see next page) or anything like it in their systems because telomerase is an animal enzyme and not associated with insects.

What Is Wrong with the Biological Science Presented: During an early scene in this film one beekeeper says he collected "over 1000 pounds of orange blossom honey and 400 pounds of beeswax last month." For such a small bee "farm" as shown, that is in an incredible amount. Not only have those bees been amazingly busy, there must have been some very potent flowers nearby, oozing with gobs of honey.

During one discussion Zinthrop says, "Already I've learned to slow the process of aging. Soon I shall be able to reverse it entirely." Being able to slow down the process of aging is one thing, but being able to reverse it is another matter entirely. There may be a way to slow, if not altogether stop, aging (see next page), but royal jelly will not be the way to do it.

After some work at the Starlin lab, Zinthrop demonstrates the effectiveness of the wasp extracts he generates. He fills a syringe with about 3cc of liquid from a refrigerated vial and injects it into a guinea pig. The guinea pig then becomes smaller and eventually changes into a rat! Some may think that a rodent is a rodent, but no way is a guinea pig a rat. (However, Zinthrop then does something interesting. He repeats this experiment with a second guinea pig. Repeating experiments makes for good science! Unfortunately, he gets the same results—another rat!)

After three more months of experiments Zinthrop finally gives Starlin her first injection, an intravenous shot in her arm of about 3cc volume. The cosmetic changes are not fast enough for Starlin, so she decides to give herself her own injections—and the second one consists of about 20cc volume! The next day Starlin looks much younger and goes from about a 40-year-old woman to one in her early 20s. Later she gives herself a third injection of about 30cc volume. Meanwhile, Zinthrop notices that a cat he gave the formula to goes berserk, so he knows that his extract still needs some work.

During one exchange with Starlin, Zinthrop says, "I think it [the improved wasp extract] would be better for a lotion, an emollient lotion ... [you] can make creams and all such products." Enzymes are not used topically on the skin for affecting genetic or hormonal changes within the body.

As a result of her injections with wasp enzyme extracts, Starlin changes into the wasp woman, an interesting looking though somewhat silly makeup. As the wasp woman she has large bulging eyes, antennae, course hair, long fangs/incisors, and stingers on her index fingers! She stabs her victims in the neck and drinks their blood. Even after changing back into her human self Starlin inexplicably continues to give herself large volume injections of the concentrated enzyme extract. By now she has turned into a full blown needle junkie! The next time she transforms into the wasp woman she appears more wasp like, with pseudo-compound eyes, an even larger "stinger" on her index fingers, and even hairier hands. However, she still has her nose (something she could still "powder" should the need arise!).

The film ends with a big fight scene in the lab between Zinthrop and the wasp woman. Zinthrop throws a bottle of "carbolic acid" (what?!) at the wasp woman and hits her squarely in the head. The acid bottle breaks and smoky fumes go everywhere, searing her flesh. She is then pushed out a window and falls to her death. This is puzzling, since it is shown she has wings, so even though she is covered with "carbolic acid," she could still have flown away or at least softened the landing on the street below.

What Biological Science Is Necessary to Actually Achieve the Results in the Film: The cosmetics industry is *huge* and is a multi-billion-dollar-a-year business. To be sure, there are thousands of scientists actively working on ways and means to preserve youth. Some significant progress has been made, however, especially with an enzyme called telomerase. Some consider this the "Holy Grail" of

aging. Telomeres are the end regions of mammalian chromosomes that undergo dramatic changes during the aging process. In brief, during aging the telomeres shorten, thereby preventing chromosomes from functioning properly (as they do in younger animals). Telomerase is an enzyme that participates in the repair of the telomere regions of chromosomes. As humans age they make less and less telomerase and therefore lose the ability to repair the chromosomal damage caused by aging. Some scientists have shown that by restoring the levels of telomerase they have been able to keep tissue culture cells and lab animals living longer. When more is learned about this interesting enzyme then perhaps the one way street of aging can be neutralized, if not actually stopped. Actual reversal is another matter entirely, and that would imply a completely different set of genetic circumstances.

To change from human to wasp/human and then back to human would require the metamorphosis and the alteration of skin. Way too much biology would be required for all this to occur. Starlin would need massive tissue morphology changes and altered biological functions for all this to be real instead of reel — not to mention the development of wings.

Regarding the wasp enzyme extract, does the wasp royal jelly substance it is derived from have a short half life or a longer one? How long does it maintain its potency? What effect does our body's natural processes, such as enzymes, immune response, etc., have on the extract? With repeated extract injections, Starlin's immune response should have been able to somehow neutralize some of its effects by generating antibodies to the injected protein (i.e., enzymes). Starlin would have made human anti-wasp antibodies with repeated injections.

Could It Actually Happen: The

effects of insect hormones on human biology are largely unexplored and may have some benefit to human skin texture and tone. Also, a class of insect compounds called cecropins are small peptides that cause the killing of many cell types, so insects have interesting biology. Can insect hormones and enzymes actually and dramatically affect human genetics? This is doubtful. Furthermore, unless some dramatic results come from the research on telomerase, then actual reversal of aging is only something the cosmetics industry can promise and not actually do.

The Leech Woman (1959)

Synopsis: Dr. Paul Talbot, an endocrinologist, is conducting research on aging and wants to make women look younger. Talbot goes to the African jungle in search of a powder that restores youth. His wife uses the powder, has her youth restored, and dies as a consequence.

Screenplay: David Duncan, based on a story by Ben Pivar and Francis Rosenwald.

Biological Science Principles Involved: Endocrinology. Dermatology. Cell Biology.

What Is Right with the Biological Science Presented: In principle, hormones do much to alter our body's metabolism, and a potion that can slow aging may indeed be hormonal in nature.

Talbot makes a comment to his nurse regarding his research into the aging process by saying, "It's worth millions if I can ever find a way to make them [women] young again." The economic side of research is a

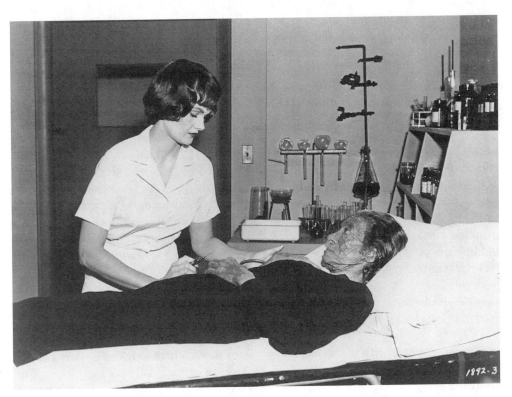

The old lady, Mala, about to receive an injection in *The Leech Woman* (1959). The reagent bottles, test tubes, and other glassware are out of place in an examination room.

major motivational factor for many scientists and should not be taken lightly. The end point in aging research will have a huge economic impact.

One of Talbot's patients, a very old lady named Mala, comes from the jungle(!) to see him. Talbot looks at her blood sample under his microscope and says, "It's remarkable. Corpuscle count, blood pressure, teeth all indicate extreme old age." He did not have to look at a blood smear to get that information. All he had to do is look at *her* and he could have seen that she is ancient.

Talbot has a conversation with the patient, Mala, about aging, and the doctor says, "Only to make them [women] look younger. Nothing can reverse the aging process." In this he is correct. Mala responds to Talbot's comments by showing him a "powder" and says, "Life giving Nipae [her name for the powder]. It has kept me alive many years beyond my time." She goes on to say the powder "slows the approach of death. Another potion makes one younger." She then puts four pinches of her powder in a glass of water, which turns dark, and drinks it. Many home or "folk remedies" are consumed in this simple manner.

What Is Wrong with the Biological Science Presented: Talbot obtains some of Mala's anti-aging powder (Nipae) and takes it home to show his wife, who is conveniently 10 years older than him (a very unsubtle plot device). Talbot says, while holding the powder in his hand, "You're looking at the most powerful concentrated hormone known. A hormone that retards aging. A similar hormone was first discovered in insects by a British biologist 20, 25 years ago. A common silk worm produces it. The only trouble with that hormone is it works only in insects. [Who cares about retarding aging in insects?] This [Nipae] works in humans. It kept a woman living more than twice her normal span of life.

She's 152 years old." Well, Mala looks old but not 152 years old. Needless to say, Talbot is hooked, so off to the jungle he and his wife go to see Mala and get some Nipae.

Mala obtains the Nipae, the powder that only slows the approach of death, from an orchid plant that only grows in the African jungle. The Nipae is made from the plant's pollen. Mala says, "It takes years to harvest even a few ounces of the pollen. Then it is aged five years more." Quite a lengthy and laborious process.

The reverse aging process is the most difficult to accept aspect of the presented biology. According to the film, the African tribe who makes Nipae is called the Nandos. They have a particular ceremony to make the reverse aging formula. A young man, between 20 and 30 years old, is drugged and made unconscious. A Nandos "priest" takes a finger ring that has a long (about 2mm) curved crystal and uses it to lance the back of the unconscious man's neck. While observing this ceremony, Talbot whispers to his wife, "He's lanced the pineal gland, deep in the cerebellum. He's adding the pineal hormone to the Nipae." Water is then added to this and Mala drinks it. This formula works almost instantly. In about 10 seconds Mala goes from "152" years old to a woman who appears to be in her early 20s. Talbot's wife also consumes the same stuff, and she too becomes much younger looking.

The pineal gland is a small, flattened body shaped somewhat like a pine cone (hence its name), and is attached at its front area to the brain commissures and lying in the depression between the two superior colliculi below the splenium of the corpus callosum. In layman's terms, it is in the middle of the brain, and no crystal less than an inch long can go deep enough to even get near it! Also, the pineal gland is composed of follicles containing epithelial cells, and lime concretions called brain sand. The pineal gland receives nerve fibers from the peripheral autonomic nervous system and primarily produces melatonin. Melatonin is N-acetyl-5-methoxytryptamine, a derivative of the amino acid tryptophan, and is involved in depressing gonadal function in mammals and causing contraction of amphibian melanophores, giving them rapid color changes. Melatonin is also involved in some physiological circadian rhythms, so its production fluctuates considerably. How all of this is related to a "reversal of the aging" process is difficult to understand.

Obtaining pineal glands does not need to result in the death of the individual. The actual device used to obtain the pineal gland, a small finger ring used to lance the back of a man's neck, is ludicrous. After drinking the potion, to have it enter our digestive system and then enter our bloodstream unaltered is stretching it too much. It would be best to introduce the anti-aging extract into our bodies with a syringe; get it directly into our bloodstream.

Finally, a comment about the misleading title of this film. During the opening credits, the following comes on the screen: "dictionary quote: Leech — 'a bloodsucking worm sometimes used medically to bleed patients.'" Well, that is fine but what does it have to do with a film whose plot centers on aging? The only application has to do with Talbot's wife. After she realizes she can actually reverse her aging and look younger, she tries to get more "pineal gland extract" from other men so she can maintain her youth. In using other men for her own means, then she could be a "leech," a bloodsucker in the figurative sense. With the title of *Leech Woman*, a plot about vampires would be more appropriate.

What Biological Science Is Necessary to Actually Achieve the Results in the Film: To effectively reverse the aging process, an extract that can rejuvenate skin, bone, and mental acuity would have to be available. A mixture of proteins, hormones, and good ol' Mr. DNA could take care of that, but there is nothing in the pineal gland that even comes close to accomplishing this. Use of the enzyme telomerase would be sufficient to retard or temporarily stop the aging process. Skin is another matter completely. The texture of fibers, filaments, tissues, and cells that make up the bulk of skin would have to be completely overhauled. Given enough time, then the proper application of, most likely, topical ointments or creams would be able to return the suppleness to skin. Bone degeneration would be another matter, and individual bone cells would have to be strengthened, which would require new bone growth; hormones could take care of this.

Could It Actually Happen: In a word, yes. However, you need not run out and locate exotic orchid plants and make your own powders! Research on aging is being conducted all over the world and is a high priority (for all the reasons discussed above). Advances will be made that will help us live longer; however, the quality of that life will be important — and *the* determining factor.

Dr. Jekyll and Sister Hyde (1971)

Synopsis: This is an interesting twist on the old Jekyll and Hyde theme, in that Dr. Jekyll, through the use of female hormones, transforms himself into a woman, his "sister," a Mrs. Hyde. After so many transformations, the female Hyde takes over Jekyll's personality, ultimately causing his/her death. The action takes place during the late 19th century.

Screenplay: Brian Clemens, based upon the story by Robert Louis Stevenson.

Biological Science Principles Involved: Endocrinology. Dermatology.

What Is Right with the Biological Science Presented: Jekyll is shown to be a driven man absolutely possessed to get his research done. During his most intense research activities Jekyll loses all sense of time and care for his well being and personal hygiene. This is a common trait of many "driven" men of science. What is interesting about this is that many real scientists do conduct literature searches in support of their ideas, and an intense Jekyll is seen going through many books to obtain background information on his research activities. (Personally, I would be hard pressed to say how many hours I have spent reading scientific and medical books and journals to find supplementary information for my research.)

When Professor Robertson, a colleague of Dr. Jekyll, asks what line of research Jekyll is following, Jekyll responds, "An elixir of life. Nature's elixir. Hormones. Female hormones." Female hormones can certainly be thought of as "an elixir of life." When Robertson asks Jekyll about his use of female hormones, Jekyll responds with, "Now, what is it that gives a woman's skin that silken texture? Why does she keep her hair when so many men lose theirs? Hormones. Female hormones." This is correct; hormones are the difference.

What Is Wrong with the Biological Science Presented: During the beginning of the film Robinson visits Jekyll and asks him what he's currently researching. Jekyll answers, "Anti-virus. The universal panacea. One virus that can combat perhaps 20 diseases. I have produced a virus strain which will provide some immunity against diphtheria." Robertson then asks, "Just how long until you expect some results?" Jekyll responds with, "I hope to provide a more complete immunity against diphtheria within a year or two."

Robertson says, "A year or two? Then what, cholera? Another year or two, and then typhus, another year or two. Then Typhoid, influenza, yellow fever. My dear Jekyll, that race will be 40 or 50 years even before you've completed the experiment ... you'll be dead and buried long before it's finished." First off, Jekyll gets his virus and anti-virus mixed up. An "anti-virus" is an antibody (or antibodies) and certainly not a "universal panacea," a "cure-all." There are way too many viruses for one anti-virus to be effective. "One virus that can combat perhaps 20 diseases," though an interesting goal, is totally unrealistic. Viruses cause diseases, they do not combat them! Cholera, typhoid, and diphtheria are diseases that have just recently been eradicated and effectively controlled, so the "40 or 50 years" time line was too conservative.

Once Jekyll decides to "explore a new avenue" of research, "the secret of eternal youth," he goes to a morgue to obtain tissues (pituitaries? ovaries?) from female bodies. While doing so, he does not wear any gloves and gets his hands very bloody. So much for safety and caution around the infectious diseases he is initially trying to prevent.

After obtaining the necessary quantity of female tissues, Jekyll prepares a greenish liquid of about 50cc volume and drinks it. Within a few minutes he feels its effects and "changes" into a female, the "Mrs. Hyde," his "sister." His hair grows longer (about 10 to 12 inches—with curls!!), breasts develop (a nice, round "C" cup size), hips widen, and, as if all that isn't already hard to believe (here comes the topper), "she" suddenly has facial makeup—lipstick, rouge, eyeliner, etc.! An effective makeover, all from some drinkable hormones. Though hormones are powerful inducers of just about all biological responses, it is an inconceivable stretch to have a male change into a female and then back. Medically, this is called "feminization," which is the development of external female characteristics by a male.

The "Mrs. Hyde" character retains the surgical and medical skills of Dr. Jekyll, so the transformation is only a physical one and not a mental one. This implies that the hormones only affect skin, bone, and muscle tissues and not nerve tissues.

What Biological Science Is Necessary to Actually Achieve the Results in the Film: As Jekyll says, to make this all happen he needs "hormones ... female hormones"—and lots of them. The female hormones necessary are classed as estrogens. Then, to return back to Jekyll these hormones would have to be eliminated and their male counterparts available to reverse the changes. The male hormones necessary are classed as androgens (with the most potent being testosterone). Furthermore, genetically, males have an X and a Y chromosome and females have two X chromosomes. For Jekyll to undergo feminization, account would have to be taken for the change of the Y to an X chromosome. Perhaps Jekyll had an XXY genotype, which made him more readily susceptible to feminization.

What female hormones would be necessary to cause feminization? Estrogens stimulate secondary sexual characteristics and also control the course of the menstrual cycle. The most naturally potent estrogen available is called estradiol and is formed by the ovary and placenta. There is also progesterone (which is a pregnancy hormone), follicle-stimulating hormone, prolactin, and others. The ingestion of Jekyll's female hormone mix would stimulate the production of the others.

To revert back to a male, all Mrs. Hyde would have to do would be to simply wait. The ingested female hormones would eventually be degraded or eliminated, thereby diminishing their effects

and allowing the natural male androgens to take over. Therefore, the return to Jekyll would be a gradual one, at least in the world of reel science.

One aspect not shown nor discussed at all in this film is the status of the primary sex organs, the penis and testicles of Jekyll or the vagina, uterus, and ovaries of Mrs. Hyde. When feminization occurs and Jekyll becomes Mrs. Hyde, do his penis, testicles, and scrotum become absorbed like a tadpole's tail, or just go into the body like a turtle's head? Or are both a penis and vagina present, as in transsexual "she-males?"

Could It Actually Happen: The transfer of men into women and vice versa more or less does happen by the intervention of hormonal therapy and surgery, and they are collectively referred to as transsexuals. As discussed many times, the speed at which these changes occurs is what is doubtful. To surgically change is one thing. To biologically change is another matter completely. The mental state of being male or being female will not be addressed at all.

Project Vampire (1992)

Summary: Dr. Klaus, a vampire, heads Project Alpha, a program to develop a "superserum" that will give vampires a "key to longevity." This superserum gives vampires certain powers they normally do not have, such as the ability to exist in daylight. Project employees mutiny and eventually kill Klaus.

Screenplay: Peter Flynn.

Biological Sciences Principles Involved: Endocrinology. Biochemistry. Molecular Biology.

What Is Right with the Biological Science Presented: Since there is essentially nothing right about the presented biology in this film, this is as good a place as any to mention an interesting explanation behind the legends of vampires. A neurologist from Spain has speculated that the symptoms of rabies—the tendency to bite and an aversion to strong smells (garlic?) and mirrors—has an uncanny resemblance to the descriptions of vampires. Historically, there was a large rabies epidemic that spread throughout Eastern Europe, especially Hungary, during the early part of the 18th century. Shortly after this epidemic of "biting and various aversions," reports of vampires began to surface during the early 1730s. There are some amazing clinical correlations to be made here. Those afflicted with rabies suffer from insomnia and sometimes have increased sex drives. Vampires walk the night and their victims are usually women. Wolves and dogs, animals associated with vampires, are common carriers of rabies; so when Eastern European peasants observed the behaviors of rabid wolves and rabid humans, they came to the conclusion that vampires were present. Furthermore, rabies victims have trouble swallowing, and sometimes bloody saliva drips from their mouths! If you saw someone walking the night, stalking women, who was afraid of garlic and mirrors, and had bloody saliva dripping from their mouths what conclusion would you draw? This rabies explanation on the origins of vampires is certainly intriguing.

Perhaps Dr. Klaus is infecting his subjects with some form of altered rabies virus, and his "superserum" is able to counteract its effects. Interesting.

What Is Wrong with the Biological Science Presented: Way too many people think that scientists have all sorts of serums, "superserums," vaccines, and antidotes at their disposal. The truth of the matter is that these are few and far between. The major reason is not for lack of trying, but in unraveling the complexities of the human immune system by developing reagents that can optimally use and exploit what our bodies can handle.

Victor, one of the scientists at Project Alpha, escapes and is picked up by a nurse on her way to a hospital. She notes that Victor's pulse is a mere 58 and his body temperature is 10 degrees below normal. With a combination of those two values, Victor should have been dead. Normal pulse rates are usually, at resting, between 60 and 100, and over that with physical exertion. Well, Victor has been running, so his pulse should have been much higher. A 10 degree decrease in body temperature is considered a "moderate" condition of hypothermia, caused by excessive surface cooling; the patient would have severe chills but could survive.

Klaus has developed a "superserum" that extends a vampire's life. Victor explains how it "works" by saying, "…you're injected once, twice, maybe three times [by Klaus' superserum to become a vampire]. It takes a half day to a couple of days to take effect, depending upon your will power, your faith maybe[!]. All the patients [those who want to become Klaus' vampires] think it's a trendy way to extend your life maybe 50 years. But that's a crock. It alters your whole life. You become a vampire [there is a down side to everything!]. It's called a super tech way of creating vampires all over the world in rapid fashion. Their [Klaus and his wife] goal's everything, politics, business." Then, Victor says, "There's an antidote to the superserum. It lets the vampire withstand the ultraviolet light. Klaus calls it the daylight buffer. He has some kind of psychic power over the buffer and the superserum. It keeps the volatile molecular structure stable." An antidote could not keep any "volatile molecular structure stable." Antidotes (or antiserums) are used to remove toxic or problem molecules, not "stabilize" them.

The first time Dr. Lee Fong, the "genius chemist," is seen, he is typing on his home computer the following chemical reactions: H_2SO_4 (s) + HCl —> $4HSO_4$(s) followed by $3HCl$ (aq) + HNO_3 —> $3H_2$ + $2Cl^-$. First of all, these equations are not balanced (so much for the "genius chemist"). Then, why is he even doing these in the first place? They are high school simple and do not make sense in the context of the film.

Nurse Sandra believes Fong can concoct an antidote to the vampire serum and says, "He's done extensive work on DNA. Invented a virus he claims contracts on cancer cells and kills them dead." Anyone who has "done extensive work on DNA" must be a "genius chemist!" (The "brilliance" displayed by Dr. Lee "genius chemist" Fong reminds me of a quote from movie mogul Louis B. Mayer, who said, "Give me an intelligent idiot over a dumb genius." Fong is certainly a "dumb genius.")

Then Victor describes his predicament to Lee "genius chemist" Fong and says, "I need you to test my blood for the proper dosage [of antidote]. How long will it last? Will it kill me?" Fong then says, "Klaus, working with an unusual blood virus from Europe [what virus is that?]. Nobody believes his theory on eternal life ... unlimited power ... crackpot. Must go to university lab. Will have computer and test on blood and antidote."

Later, Victor is in Fong's apartment and types into his computer, "What is the correct dosage for prototype [i.e., superserum]?" The computer answers(!) with, "22ml for 2.13 hours duration." So Victor injects himself with the "correct" dosage. Unfortunately, he gives himself the 22ml volume using a 5ml syringe! While injecting this volume, Victor says, "22 milliliters for two point one three [2.13] hours"—again, from a 5ml syringe. Amazing.

What Biological Science Is Necessary to Actually Achieve the Results in the Film: Light, particularly ultraviolet light, can damage DNA and therefore our skin. An entire industry has developed in making a variety of suntanning solutions, blocking agents, etc., because they know that UV light is very damaging and too much exposure can potentially lead to skin cancer. In this industrial age, more and more of us are exposed to UV irradiation, and we must protect our delicate skin against these harmful rays. The notion that there exists some type of medication that can counteract the effects of the sun's more harmful rays is of interest. However, this medication should have been a topical cream or lotion that can be directly applied to the skin. Having to inject this protective substance into our bloodstream and have it go to the skin in sufficient amounts to actually do some good is ridiculous. Ultraviolet light penetrates the surface of our skin the distance of only a few cells, and an injected compound would have to travel through the blood system, unchanged, and find its way to skin cells in sufficient quantity to exert its protective effects. This would require very concentrated and very large doses. A few cc of volume simply is not enough.

Could It Actually Happen: European vampire legends have been with us ever since Vlad Dracul impaled his first victim in the Carpathian mountains. In modern times, vampire cults have sprung up thinking they need blood or blood products to survive. In fact, there are some now who are trying to find a bona fide medical explanation (see previous page) for vampirism, and attribute this to rabies, a neurological disorder. This is most fascinating, and it definitely puts a new spin on vampire legends.

5 SURGERY

Surgeons are a respected segment of society, and deservedly so. The sharpness of their knives and their delicate touch have relieved much suffering. Prior to the development of anesthesia, surgeons were little more that legitimate butchers. Twentieth century medicine and all the advancements described have made their profession the exalted one it is now.

In the realm of SF cinema the dominant use of surgery has been in limb and/or organ transplants. Arguably the best known example would be the Frankenstein Monster, a man of "many parts." Though organ transplantation has been attempted for centuries, it was not until the 1960s when a successful kidney transplant between identical twins was performed and the "modern era" began. So far, heart, liver, lung, kidney, pancreas, bone marrow, pancreatic islets, and skin have been successfully transplanted. Other organs will soon follow. In addition, "organ farms" will be established to provide the high demand for genetically matched transplants. The ability to design tissue, like organs or semi-organs from cloned and farmed cells, would give an enormous advantage. And behind all this is the surgeon doing his cutting and sewing.

Of all surgical procedures, those dealing with the head and neck are the most difficult. The main reason has to do with the numerous delicate muscles and connective tissues in this part of the anatomy. This, plus the fact that (Western) society uses the face as *the* major means (for better or worse) of assessing the personality and behavior of people. You mess with your face and your entire livelihood is at jeopardy, so surgeons have to be extra careful when operating here.

Another aspect of head and neck surgery has to do with the brain. Brain surgery has its own mystique, and requires a completely different set of procedures for success. The lessons of (Western) society tell us that you may have a beautiful face, but with no (functioning) brain you may as well be dead. So the combination of head and neck surgery, as well as brain surgery, makes everything very difficult. One of society's (mis)conceptions of a smart person is classifying them as a "brain surgeon." The truth of the matter is that there really isn't anything special about this area of surgery.

Which is why U.S. Patent number 4,666,425 is so interesting. Let me explain. I am listed as an inventor (so far) on five U.S. patents (plus one currently pending), and during the course of this procedure (dealing with patent attorneys, searching previous patents, etc.) I have glanced at a number of patents, most out of necessity (for background information, etc.) and some out of curiosity. While searching patent files, I came across number 4,666,425, and it is incredible in its implications. In reality, head (and brain) transplants are next to impossible, and I do not see any roads to success in the near or distant future. You can keep these cells and tissues alive, but a brain dead person does no one any good (not withstanding those who would like to keep bodies alive for organ "farming," as shown in the film *Coma*). In this case, proper brain and neurological function is far more important that simply keeping these cells alive. The title of patent 4,666,425 is simple: "Device for Perfusing an Animal Head." In other words, how to keep a human head alive. Perfusing is the scientific term for "feeding" the cells and tissues. Sufficient oxygen, nutrients, and blood flow to the brain will have to be maintained to keep a severed head "alive." (After all, even a severed head will need to eat!) I am flabbergasted that someone went to all the trouble and expense to actually patent such a procedure and concept. What is even more stunning is that the patent is good for only 27 years. After that, the technology falls into the public domain. It will be a lot more than 27 years before someone perfects the technique, not to mention why anyone would want to! It's utterly ridiculous, and such is the stuff of SF films—to do the utterly ridiculous. (I will leave it to someone else to place meaning on the "coincidence" of having the "666" number appear in this patent on head perfusion; 666 is the biblical sign of the beast or Antichrist.)

OH, I'D WHILE AWAY THE HOURS, CONFERRIN' WITH THE FLOWERS ... IF I ONLY HAD A BRAIN

The Scarecrow in the *Wizard of Oz* eventually gets his brain at the end of that wonderful movie, which was, for me, a highlight of that film. If it were only that easy. At least he had the sense to realize he needed a brain. Unfortunately, there are far too many humans who do not even know they need a brain. They just happily go through life without the foggiest idea of what is real and important.

Before we move on to the films in this section, let me spend a little time on the brain so you will get a better appreciation of what this is all about and perhaps why brain transplants are so difficult. The brain serves the body and the body serves the brain. If each is nice to each other then this is definitely a win-win situation. (I am reminded of a quip by inventor Thomas Edison, who disliked exercise. He said the body's chief job was to carry around the brain.)

The typical brain is about three pounds in weight and is encased in the skull. Upon examination it appears to be a convoluted mass of tissue. The bulk of the brain is called the neocortex and is proportionally larger in humans than most other animals. The brain is functionally divided into areas that control movement (the motor cortex), areas that respond to sensations felt on the surface of the skin (the somatic sensory cortex), visual images seen by the eye (visual cortex), and sounds detected by the ear (auditory cortex). Other areas are responsible for language and personality.

Just under the neocortex are the subcortical areas of the brain, which are involved in a variety of functions. One area, the thalamus, is responsible for relaying information from the sense organs to specific sensory cortical areas. The hypothalamus is responsible for the secretion of hormones for growth, reproduction, and metabolism. The striatum is responsible for the initiation and coordination of movement.

Underneath all this is the brain stem, an area that helps maintain motor systems, such as body posture and locomotor coordination. Areas within the brain stem also control breathing and heart rates. The brain stem is composed of the midbrain and the hindbrain. The hindbrain is further divided into the pons, the medulla oblongata, and the cerebellum.

The medulla oblongata controls autonomic and homeostatic functions of internal organs, including breathing, heart and blood vessel activity, swallowing, vomiting, and digestion. The pons also participates in the control of some of these activities. In essence, sensory data collection is the most important function of the medulla and pons. The primary function of the cerebellum is the coordination of movement. Information about the position of the joints, length of muscles, as well as sound and sight stimuli, are all processed by the cerebellum. If one part of the body is moved, the cerebellum will coordinate the other parts to ensure smooth action and balance.

Needless to say, damage, either slight or significant, will cause major alterations to these brain functions. Various physical and biological traumas to any of the anatomical regions of the brain or any of the peripheral nervous system can cause an imbalance in homeostatic functions. More to the point of the films discussed in this book, if all of the myriad of connecting nerve fibers are not aligned (or fail to function) properly, then the organism (read, creature) will have some serious biological problems.

Because the human brain is as complex as it is, the possibility of effective transplantations is problematical. Not only

are there the connections of the brain stem to the spinal cord to consider, there are also other nerve connections that control, among other things, sight, smell, heart, lung, and muscle movement. An absence of the sense of smell and facial expressions may explain the behaviors of some of SF cinema's creations. All it would take would be the improper connection or healing of certain nerves.

The Monster and the Girl (1940)

Synopsis: Good guy Scott Webster is framed by a gang of crooks and falsely convicted of a murder he did not commit. Webster is executed in prison. Dr. Parry obtains Webster's brain and transplants it into a gorilla. The Webster/gorilla then goes around and kills the crooks who framed him. After killing all these bad guys, Webster/gorilla is shot and dies.

Screenplay: Stuart Anthony.

Biological Science Principles Involved: Surgery. Neurobiology. Cell Biology. Immunology.

What Is Right with the Biological Science Presented: The brain transplant operating scenes are quite realistic for its time, 1940. The shots bouncing back and forth between the operation, the various pieces of apparatus, the heart and lung machines, and the clock showing the time going by are very gripping and add much excitement to the film. The audiences of 1940 would be quite taken by all this action. Authentic sterile procedures are seen, as well as the presence of an autoclave, the major piece of equipment used throughout the world to sterilize medical and scientific instruments and glassware.

The gorilla/man attacks a man and kills him. Shortly after that, the dead man is accidentally shot. The coroner examines the dead man and says, "There's no blood when the bullets entered the body. That means the heart had already stopped and circulation ceased." The coroner says this man was already dead when shot. Based upon this evidence, he is entirely correct; it's a good job by "Dr. Coroner."

What Is Wrong with the Biological Science Presented: Though significant strides have been made in the field of organ transplants (such as heart, lung, kidney, bone, and skin), the area of brain transplants is still unattainable at the beginning of the 21st century. More will be said about this when discussing the films *The Head* and *The Brain That Wouldn't Die*.

Transplantation of tissues or an organ (such as a brain) into a different species is called xenotransplantation. Of all the various transplantation procedures, cross species is the most difficult. The major problem has to do with tissue rejection by the host's immune response, and not with the actual surgical procedures. Of all the organs, skin is the most difficult to transplant, and the reason is immunological rejection. There must be accurate tissue matching of the histocompatibility complex (see below) for the transplanted tissues to be accepted. One way around this is to give the tissue recipient certain drugs that suppress the immune system.

During the brain transplant operation, only Parry and his assistant are present. This may be OK for simple surgical procedures, but for something as complicated and involved as brain surgery, there is no way only two people could successfully complete the task. A surgical nursing staff, anesthesiologist, and other assistants are always in attendance at these procedures.

Here is an interesting dialogue exchange between Parry and his assistant that deserves mention. After the operation, Parry says, "This night's [operation] will step him [the gorilla] up a million years in the pattern of evolution. The human brain, even more than the human heart, is God's greatest handiwork. [What about the human immune system?] Millions and millions of cells, each separate cell a treasure house which has guarded its own store of human passions, wit, wisdom, sin, repentance, envy, hatred, greed, and love." The assistant responds with, "Yes, but the ape. Will he know of this?" Parry says, "When he gives us the answer to that question we shall have a new chapter in scientific history." If the gorilla responds to *any* question, this would make "scientific history"!

What Biological Science Is Necessary to Actually Achieve the Results in the Film: No matter how you analyze the major plot point, a brain transplant, not to mention a xenotransplantation (see below), brings up two issues that need to be addressed. The first is the actual surgical procedures of a brain transplant. The second, and more risky (particularly for the long term survival of the patient), is overcoming the problem of tissue rejection by the host's immune system (and gorillas *do* have a valid and functioning immune system, very similar to that of humans).

The transplantation of a human brain (and therefore, human cellular antigens) into a gorilla would stimulate all the transplantation rejection mechanisms of the ape, thereby causing the gorilla to reject the transplanted brain. A xenograft is a tissue or organ from one species transplanted into another. Antibodies and cytotoxic T lymphocytes reject xenografts several days following transplants. Even with all the immune suppressive drugs available, the xenograft would still be rejected.

Could It Actually Happen: Even though newer and more complicated transplantation procedures seem to be reported on a daily basis, we have yet to solve the delicate problem of making nerve tissues "communicate" again after being "sewn together." Based upon what we know about the immune system, some foreign tissue rejection can be regulated and controlled to the point that they may become "routine." However, nerve grafting, especially involving something as complicated and fragile as the brain, is still a long way off. Not to mention the reason of why anyone would want to have their brain put into a gorilla in the first place. (Imagine a football team with the brains of humans and the bodies of gorillas playing a game. What a mess that would be! Or how about 500+ pound silverbacks as sumo wrestlers!)

In addition to this, there is the long standing biological "dogma" that you cannot grow new neurons in the brain once they have matured. For years it was thought that once all your brain cells, neurons, etc., have been produced, you will not get any more; and as you age, these brain cells die at an astonishing rate. Well, throw that dogma out the window. (I personally never did like "dogmas," because once you formulate one, exceptions and changes occur with advancing science and medicine, so that they become obsolete.) Scientists have now found ways to induce the creation of additional neurons in mature, even elderly, humans in at least one important part of the brain, a section of the hippocampus called the dentate gyrus. This offers great hope to those who are mentally challenged.

The Creature Walks Among Us (1956)

Synopsis: In this third film in the Universal Studios "Creature" series, a team of scientists go into the Florida Everglades in search of the Creature. After they capture him he is accidentally burned, and the scientists try to make him "human" through surgery. They want to convert a sea animal to a land animal. The gill-less creature escapes, wreaks some havoc, and returns to the ocean.

Screenplay and Story: Arthur Ross.

Biological Science Principles Involved: Surgery. Biochemistry. Hematology.

What Is Right with the Biological Science Presented: There is an interesting mix of scientists present: a geneticist, a "roentgenologist" (x-rays), a biochemist, and a physician. They interact well with each other and contribute meaningfully in dealing with the Creature.

While examining a blood sample of the Creature, the scientists note the red blood cells (RBCs) present. Dr. Johnson, the biochemist, says, "there's no nucleus to each corpuscle." This is correct. The only animal that has nucleated RBCs is the duck. To maximize the amount of hemoglobin in each RBC, the cells extrude their nucleus during development (which is why RBCs at blood banks have to be constantly replaced — short survival, only about 120 days long).

While trying to catch the Creature, the scientists douse the gillman with gasoline and set him on fire, causing third degree burns over his body. Back on the boat, the Creature is bandaged, and Barton says, "He isn't converting enough air into oxygen. His gills are too badly burned. He's dying of suffocation." (You do not "convert air into oxygen," but rather you remove oxygen from air for proper respiration. Gills are used for removing dissolved oxygen from water, not air. No wonder the creature had a hard time breathing.) Morgan responds, "But so slowly. He's getting a small air supply from some area." After this exchange Barton examines an x-ray of the Creature's chest and says, "We were right, there is a perfect lung formation. It shows much darker than average. They could be partially collapsed." The presence of both lungs and gills is seen in the

In **The Creature Walks Among Us** (1956) the Creature's gills have been surgically removed and his residual lungs allowed to develop. This scene of the Creature trying to "breathe" underwater without gills evokes great sympathy in the viewer.

African lung fish (which uses gills during the rainy season and lungs when the lakes dry up), so the presence of gills and lungs in the Creature is possible.

Further commenting on the chest x-ray of the Creature, Morgan says, "What's that black patch at the opening of the lung?" Barton says, "Not a typical human formation." This makes sense, and I am pleased this scene was included because, though a "throwaway line," it adds much authenticity to the Creature, in that of course he would have internal body structures that are "not a typical human formation."

Upon realizing the Creature has lungs, Johnson places a respirator over his mouth and says, "He is getting very little oxygen," indicating a problem. Barton quickly surmises the situation and says, "We'd better get those lungs inflated and working again. We'll do a tracheotomy immediately." They place a tracheotomy tube in the Creature's throat, and his chest immediately rises and falls in a breathing motion. When the throat is blocked (and the Creature may have had an anatomical structure that closed the throat during swimming) no air would get to the lungs, and a simple tube in the throat bypassed the blockage, allowing air direct access to the lungs. When the Creature actually starts to breathe, Barton says, "We are changing a sea creature into a land creature."

An EEG (electroencephalogram)—a technique used to measure and record the electric potentials of the brain—is obtained from the Creature. They note "gaps" in the recordings, and Barton comments, "He had a critically low supply of oxygen to the brain for more than an hour. It could have caused permanent injury." This is certainly true, though it would be anyone's guess how the Creature's brain would function and what areas, if any, would have been damaged.

While looking at another chart recording, Barton says, "The metabolism rate shows several sharp changes. It was the method of breathing…. We should have known. The step from fish to amphibian to mammal, it had to be the method of converting oxygen." Yes, an increase in breathing, meaning oxygen consumption, does increase the metabolism rate. Also, key to the evolution of fish to mammals was an efficient method of oxygen consumption.

What Is Wrong with the Biological Science Presented: To capture the Creature the scientists use liquid rotenone, which will "anesthetize him in a matter of seconds." Rotenone is an extremely toxic plant substance used by South American Indians as a fish poison, and is now primarily used as an insecticide. Rotenone is an inhibitor of what is called "Site I" in the mitochondria respiratory chain of oxygen breathing animals, which biochemically transfers electrons to molecular oxygen. Rotenone inhibits the ability to utilize oxygen, and in a large enough dose can cause death. Rotenone will not "anesthetize" but rather *kill* in a matter of seconds. When captured, the Creature is harpooned with rotenone spears, and more than likely this should have killed him.

The team of scientists locate a man in the Everglades who fought the Creature and cut him with a knife. Johnson looks at the knife and notices some blood still on the blade. A sample is examined under a microscope, and Dr. Barton, the physician, says, "The red corpuscle count checks with the Ocean Harbor figures, 35 percent. Halfway between the count in mammals and marine life vertebrates. Nature moving out of one phase into another." Though the RBC counts in mammals and marine life differ, there is no "halfway between" point. Also, if 35 percent were the halfway point, this means there would be the same amount above (70) and the same amount below (zero). The total absence of red blood cells (red because they contain iron atoms) in marine life vertebrates is wrong. Finally, the part of nature moving out of one phase into another is unsubstantiated.

Further discussion on the RBCs continues. Dr. Morgan, the geneticist, asks, "Are the corpuscles beveled?" Johnson responds, "No." Morgan then says, "Then the blood type is of a marine life animal." Whether RBCs are beveled or not has nothing to do with belonging to a marine animal.

Barton wants to surgically alter the Creature to learn how to adapt man to the conditions of outer space (a noble cause, but totally impractical). Barton says, "The Creature can be changed. We can make the giant step and bring a new species into existence.... We can create an entirely new form of life. We can change the blood texture, build up the red corpuscle count, then the gene structure has to be affected." Wrong on all accounts. First of all, the Creature essentially *is* a "new species," so why would they want to create another when they have one already? Changing the blood texture is an interesting concept. This could be interpreted many ways, including the texture of the proteins and other molecules coursing through the blood stream, the texture of cells (such as the white and red cells), and/or the texture of the serum and plasma. Either way it does not matter, since you cannot "change the blood texture," no matter how you define it, without a major change in the DNA of the cells and tissues that make up blood and its components.

Shortly after removing the bandages from the operated-on Creature, Barton says, "The fire burned away the outer scale. There's a structure of human skin underneath it. Two separate coverings. The way he had lungs and gills." To immediately say there is "human skin" present is absurd, and they push the Creature-as-man angle too much here.

During the boat journey back, Barton and Morgan have an interesting "scientist to scientist" conversation regarding their success with the Creature. Barton says, "We've found the secret. Change the metabolism and man will change." To this Morgan responds with, "As a geneticist, I know — the way any geneticist does — that nature hasn't created a new major type of animal on this earth for over 400 million years." Barton then says, "The creature's a new different major type." Morgan says,

"It's the interaction of heredity and environment for millions of years that makes a new species. We only changed the skin, not the animal." Well, changing metabolism will not fundamentally change man because, even though there is an enormous variation in life forms (from bacteria to plants to mammals), virtually all life on Earth is composed of essentially the same metabolism. Metabolically changing man will not physically change man (and vice versa). As a geneticist, Morgan doesn't know much. Nature has created countless new species within the past 400 million years, which is the mid–Paleozoic Era; since then we have had the Mesozoic Era (Triassic, Jurassic, Cretaceous) and the Cenozoic Era (the period of mammals), so plenty of new species have developed. However, the interaction of heredity and environment for "millions of years" does contribute to the creation of new species.

What Biological Science Is Necessary to Actually Achieve the Results in the Film: Surgery can only get you so far. The rest of the way would have to be modifications at the DNA level. Since neither extensive surgical procedures nor administration of gene therapy are seen, we can only guess at what was done to the Creature. Much of his skin is not badly burned, because shortly after he is set on fire he dives into the water, extinguishing the flames. The burnt portions of his outer body would have to heal, and assuming that both "human skin" and Creature "fish skin" are affected, then different procedures and materials would be needed for each skin type.

At one point Barton wants to "build up the corpuscle count" in the Creature; the most effective way to do this would be to use the hormone erythropoietin. This hormone is predominantly secreted by the kidneys, and it enhances the formation of red blood cells by stimulating precursor cells to grow and multiply. It is now made by recombinant DNA technology. By administering erythropoietin to the Creature, the red blood cell count would be increased.

X-ray results show the presence of lungs in the Creature. In previous films we saw the Creature on land, so having lung capabilities is not a surprise. The Creature spends most of his time underwater, but on occasions—when he has to be on land (why else would he have legs?)—his lungs serve him well.

The Creature would have to have a metabolism that is not overly susceptible to the poisonous effects of rotenone. An anesthetic works completely differently than a poison; an anesthetic is a drug that depresses nerve function, whereas a poison kills. The Creature would either have to have some respiratory enzyme that is rotenone insensitive, or have a completely different way of metabolizing oxygen that is unaffected by the poison. Since the Creature comes from the Amazon, and since rotenone is derived from a South American plant, perhaps the Creature has a natural defense against the poison.

Could It Actually Happen: Surgical alterations of existing species are technically possible. After all, cosmetic surgery is routinely performed on humans. Finding an organism like the Creature—with lungs, "human skin," and gills—is fantasy.

All in all, in reference to surgically changing the Creature from a sea dweller to a land dweller, Morgan said it best: "There is no short cut. You can't bypass nature."

Frankenstein's Daughter (1958)

(Note: Much has been written about Mary Shelley's *Frankenstein* and its impact on literature, society, and films. No matter where you look these days, there is some reference made to her creation. I would be remiss not to include at least some version of her inspiration in this book.)

Synopsis: Oliver Frank (aka Oliver Frankenstein, grandson of *the* Dr. Frankenstein) is working as a technician in the home lab of Dr. Carter Morton. On the side, Oliver has been doing experiments to revive the dead. Oliver kills Suzy, a family friend, with his car, grafts her head onto a (male) body he's pieced together, and brings "her" to life with electricity. The "she-male" monster escapes, wreaks some havoc, and is eventually killed (along with Oliver) in a lab fire.

Screenplay: H.E. Barrie, based (loosely) on Mary Shelley's *Frankenstein*.

Biological Science Principles Involved: Surgery. Neurology. Cell Biology. Dermatology. Transplantation.

What Is Right with the Biological Science Presented: There really is not much to talk about here, though the enthusiasm and zest for experimental work that Dr. Morton shows (even at his advanced age) is remarkable. His mannerisms are interesting, and he is frustrated when his experiments do not succeed as expected. All qualities of good (and real) scientists. The name of the compound Morton is using, "digenerol" (supposedly useful in preserving cells and tissues), is a wonderful name. It sounds real, like something you could pick up at the local pharmacy. "One bottle of digenerol, please."

What Is Wrong with the Biological Science Presented: All my comments on head transplants (see *The Head*), "grafting," and organ and limb transplants apply here. The overall lack of sterility of cells, tissues, syringes, and other equipment makes one wonder what kind of scientists Oliver and Morton are.

Morton explains to Oliver, "I'm on the threshold of developing this drug. Think

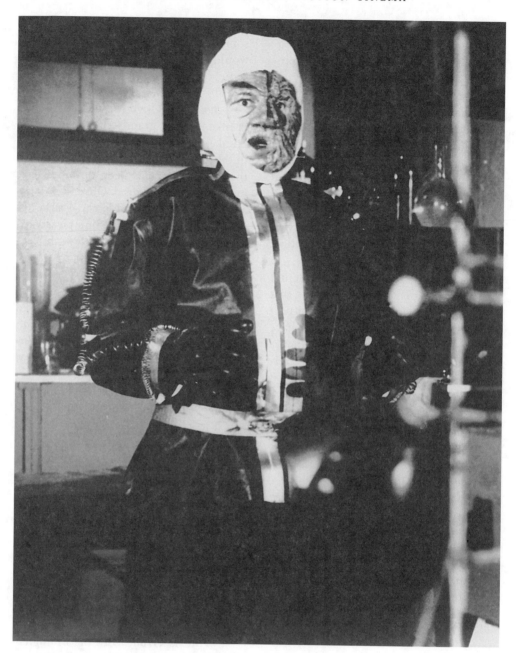

Frankenstein's Daughter (1958): he/she in all his/her glory. From the neck down it is male, but the head is female. Note the lipstick (which is supposed to signify female).

what it would be like. To be able to wipe out all[!] destructive cells and organisms that plague man. No disease. No destructive tissue or growth. Man would be ageless." Oliver responds with, "I'm afraid you're on the wrong track. Your formula may work on internal cells [called endothelial cells], but it causes violent disfigurement to sensitive exposed areas [composed of epithelial cells]." How did Oliver know this? Besides, no single formula would be able to "wipe out all destructive cells and organisms."

During his "spare" time, Oliver put together a body in a secret(!) room adjacent to Carter's home laboratory. All the body needs to function is a head/brain. How did Oliver prevent the cells and tissues of this body from decomposing? How did he prevent contaminations?

When Oliver attaches the head of Trudy, the girl he kills, to the body he put together, no sterile techniques are evident. Elsu, Oliver's assistant (and Morton's gardener!), says, "Your father and grandfather never used a female brain." Oliver responds with, "No, but now we're aware that the female brain is conditioned to a man's world. Therefore it takes orders where the other ones didn't.... We better hurry before the brain cells are damaged completely." Oliver zaps the completed she-male with electricity for several minutes and the body comes alive and walks around. Elsu notes, "She is nicer than the males your father and grandfather made. I really thinks she understands.... We've made a female being. She's more responsive to command." This brings up an interesting point. Though the creature's body is male, it is only the head/brain that is female. It is interesting that they use the pronoun of "she" when referring to the creature. What is "femaleness" and what is "maleness"? According to Oliver, it is not the body but rather the mind. We are who we think we are. Though the monster here has the body of a male, the mind is that of a female. It would be interesting to see which aspect would dominate should the creature have lived.

Speaking of being "conditioned to a man's world," one particularly humorous scene occurs when the she-male creature returns to Morton's house after escaping. To get back into the house the creature rings the front door bell! Courteous on her part.

Later a police detective catches Oliver and the she-male creature at the lab. After Oliver brags about his success in creating the monster, the detective says, "You have to use a human to make that." (Actually, several humans.) Oliver responds with, "The police have gotten scientific these days, haven't you?" It was a "sharp" detective to recognize that to create such a creature you need human parts!

What Biological Science Is Necessary to Actually Achieve the Results in the Film: My comments on *The Head*, *The Brain That Wouldn't Die*, and the *Bride* films equally apply here. Much biology is necessary to achieve these results. Cell preservation, electrical stimuli to restart cardiac cells and tissues, nerve regeneration and reattachment, plus organ transplantation are all necessary to explain the results here.

Compounds that can preserve cells and tissues are available. Keeping a body "alive" is no longer the problem it once was. However, this film was made in 1958, so many of the problems then have been solved in one way or another with today's technology.

To transplant a head onto the body of another would require innovative medical procedures, and key would be the maintenance of sufficient oxygen, nutrients, and blood circulation to the brain. First the patient is anesthetized (since Oliver uses the head of freshly killed Trudy, anesthesia is probably not used), and numerous machines monitor body and brain functions (ideally, throughout the procedure the brain would be cooled to 50–59°F to reduce oxygen demand). Then neck tissues, including all six major vascular structures (the jugular veins, the carotid arteries, and the vertebral arteries) are cut. The smaller vessels are tied off. Then the spinal vertebrae C-4 and C-5 are removed and metal plates/screws are put in place to provide support and connection to the body. The upper portions of the spine are connected first and held in place by the metal plates.

The major blood vessels are attached (sutured), followed by the vascular structures and remaining nerves, muscles, and skin. It is unknown what immunological tissue rejection will occur, since the brain is an immunologically privileged site, meaning it is somewhat protected from the immune response. The cells and tissues of the head and neck muscles could be a problem, however; and most likely it would require the use of drugs that suppress the immune system.

Could It Actually Happen: I have to admit I am intrigued about combining a female head (or brain) with a male body. Assuming the surgical and transplant problems are nonexistent, then what would occur should this happen? Cross-dressers and transsexuals would have a field day with this. After all, this is what many of them dream about. They feel they are either a female trapped in a male body or vice versa. Instead of going through all the pain and expense of having their bodies surgically and hormonally altered, they could just have one surgery to obtain what they wanted. (The problem here would be finding a suitable — and willing — body to go along with the procedure.)

The Head (1959)

Synopsis: Dr. Abel, a transplantation specialist, invents an operating table that does not need hands. Abel hires an assistant, Dr. Uud, to help him with his experiments. Abel has a heart attack and Uud, wanting to keep the genius of Abel's brain alive, removes his head (with the aid of the mechanical operating table). In the end, Uud goes insane and kills himself.

Screenplay: Victor Trivas.

Biological Science Principles Involved: Surgery. Cell Biology. Neurobiology.

What Is Right with the Biological

Science Presented: Abel says to Uud, "I'm particularly interested in the grafting of healthy organs to replace diseased ones." Organ transplantation is a very vibrant field, and much suffering has been relieved in those who have received transplants. Abel starts his work by experimenting on dog heads, so he has an effective animal model available. Working out some of the conditions and parameters on an appropriate animal model before proceeding with humans is typical of real science.

An important aspect of tissue culture work is the formulation of appropriate growth media and supporting serums, which contain all the necessary growth factors and essential nutrients to keep cells properly growing and alive. The "golden age" of this work took place during the 1960s through the early 1980s and culminated in the development of serum-free and protein-free media formulations. In anticipation of all this, Abel has formulated what he calls "serum Z" to "keep organs alive after separating them from their body." The concept of a "serum Z" is intriguing to me. A number of scientists have been actively working with various fluids and serums that could keep cells and tissues alive (especially intact organs) and viable for transplantation. Abel keeps his "serum Z" in large containers suspended from the ceiling in his operating room. Feeding nutrients to large masses of cells and organ tissues is called perfusion. You need some sort of precise pumping system to keep the fluids flowing smoothly and steadily into the cells.

(As an aside, while at UCSD I created a serum-free culture formula useful for growing human hybridoma cells. I call this formula "TABIE," which is an acronym for transferrin, albumin, beta-mercaptoethanol, insulin, and ethanolamine, which are the major components of the formula. For what it is designed for, it works very well.)

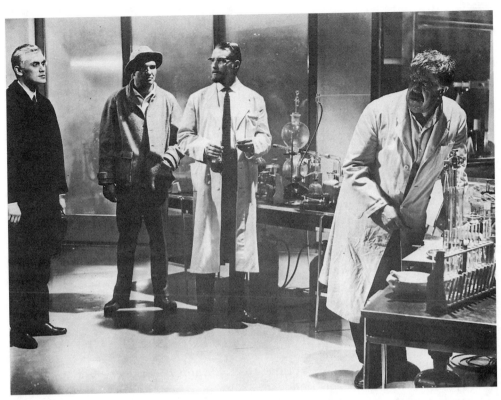

A scene from Dr. Abel's well-equipped home laboratory in *The Head* (1959). Abel, on the far right, dies from a heart attack, and Dr. Uud, on the far left, performs the necessary surgery to allow Abel's head to survive. As Uud says, "Your brain is important, the rest doesn't matter."

"You're a great man, a scientist; your brain may do great, the rest doesn't count"—as spoken by Dr. Uud to Dr. Abel's bodiless head. Having only the saved brains of famous scientists doing the thinking, and having nameless drones performing the work, is a well used idea in SF. (I always thought having the heads—and brains—of Albert Einstein, Groucho Marx, and Walt Disney still available for their comments and insight into life would be interesting fun!)

What Is Wrong with the Biological Science Presented: One of the biggest problems with severed heads is articulate speech. Proper speech needs air, expelled from the lungs, to pass through the larynx. Even if the neck is severed below the larynx, which does not appear to be the case here, there are no lungs present to provide sufficient air for speech.

The brain needs a significant source of nutrients to provide enough metabolic energy to function properly. Uud has "serum Z" hooked up to Abel's head for this purpose. Visible are several tubes coming out of the device holding the neck in place that "feed" nutrients to the head. EEG wires, to monitor brain function, are attached to the temple of Abel's severed head. Hanging bubbling fluids are present, which also go directly to the head. The head itself is set above a large fish tank–like container with more bubbling fluids. The bubbling is most likely to serve as a method of oxygenating the fluids (that, or just for looking cool!).

Uud performs another operation and places a nurse's head onto a dancer's body. The nurse has a pretty face and a curved, hunchbacked spine (she has scoliosis). In contrast, the dancer has a beautiful body. Uud performs the operation by himself and does his own anesthesia! Right after the operation, the nurse's head–dancer's body female immediately gets up and walks (without the scoliosis condition). This female has immediate head and neck movement (no visible scars and no post-surgical trauma!). The most amazing thing about this scene is that right after she gets up, Uud gives her a cigarette, which she smokes! It would be nice if all operations were that easy. (And whatever happened to the dancer's head/brain/mind?)

What Biological Science Is Necessary to Actually Achieve the Results in the Film: Enough nutrients would have to be constantly perfused to the delicate brain tissues to keep them alive and functioning. Judging by the large glass tank suspended above the head, there is a sizable source of fluids available. The composition of the fluid would have to contain a high amount of glucose (the primary energy nutrient for brain tissue), of at least two grams per cc. Also, high concentrations of vitamins, minerals, and other suitable nutrients would have to be present.

The question of articulate speech must be addressed. Abel spoke coherently, though a bit hoarsely, so a larynx must be present. The larynx is the anatomical organ of voice production, and is the part of the respiratory tract between the pharynx and the trachea. It consists of a framework of cartilages and elastic membranes, which are the vocal folds and the supporting muscles that control the position and tension of these parts. Since we see significant amounts of bubbling liquids under Abel's head, one could postulate that one of the tubes is connected just below the larynx (voice box) and forcing air into it, thereby providing enough air to pass to allow speech.

Could It Actually Happen: Organ transplants are becoming more and more

common. I do believe the day will come when brain transplants will also be successful. I do not know if head transplants will be done, since all you really need is the brain. Which would be easier, transplanting a brain (and having to attach all the cranial nerves) or re-attaching a head (with cranial nerves intact, but involving the spinal cord and all the veins and arteries)?

The day will come when actual speech will not be necessary. There will be an attachment of appropriate wires to brain tissues that will conduct electrical signals and be translated into speech. The brain will think and a computerized voice synthesizer will do all the rest.

Terror Is a Man (1959)

Synopsis: Dr. Gerard, a Manhattan surgeon, isolates himself on an island in the Philippines so he can conduct experiments on improving the evolution of man. Mr. Fitzgerald, the sole survivor of an exploded freighter, lands on the island. Gerard performs multiple surgeries on a panther in order to make it human. The panther-man is eventually shot and killed.

Screenplay: Harry Paul Harber. (Note: This plot is very similar to H.G. Wells' *The Island of Dr. Moreau.*)

Biological Science Principles Involved: Surgery. Neurology. Dermatology. Transplantation.

What Is Right with the Biological Science Presented: The extensive sterilization procedures shown are real and a pleasure to watch.

Philosophically, Gerard asks some interesting questions about the nature of man, such as, "What is a man?" and "Where does a species begin?"—questions humans have been asking for many centuries. Gerard says, "Man breeds animals for his own purpose, grooms them, modifies them; he speeds up the process of natural evolution. Why not use the same principle to improve the human race?" Why not indeed? To be sure, this has been going on for millennia. "You can't marry him (or her) because he's not good enough for you" is a statement said far too often, so subconsciously there is pressure to improve the genetics of our offspring. We want to marry the "right" person, with the (usually unspoken) notion that the resulting children will be genetically healthy and superior.

What Is Wrong with the Biological Science Presented: If you accept Gerard's premise of wanting to "create a higher, perfect man," then why start with a panther? What qualities of a panther would let him achieve his goals? Gerard surmises, "Man's mind is not his own. It is completely dominated by complexes, anxieties, fears, and prejudices on countless generations before him. That is why I have chosen the animal to be the father of a new race of man. He alone will have a new fresh mind capable of thinking his own thoughts with complete objectivity." If you could choose an animal to start a new race of man, which species would you choose? I would certainly not choose a panther.

Gerard says he has performed 53 major operations on his panther creature over the past two years, which amounts to an operation every 13 days! Unbelievable. That poor creature has gone through a lot of pain and stress, so its anger is understandable.

Near the end of the film the panther man attempts to say the word "man," and the implication here is the presence of vocal cords and the mental acuity to actually formulate the word. I wonder which one of the operations gave him this ability. That would have been a very interesting surgical procedure.

What Biological Science Is Necessary to Actually Achieve the Results in the

Film: The bulk of the surgical operations on the panther would have to involve bone and skin, not to mention brain surgery. Therefore, Gerard would have to solve the very serious problem of tissue rejections and neuromuscular interactions, and bone socket and joint replacements. Not to mention the pain involved from these extensive procedures.

Other aspects of surgical procedures, bone and muscle alterations, as well as tissue grafting and "morphing" have been discussed elsewhere.

Could It Actually Happen: Other films in this category attempt to change or alter man or other animals through the intervention of glands, serums, hormones, and/or DNA. Gerard attempts to achieve the same results solely through the use of various surgical procedures, which represents an interesting twist. Even Dr. Moreau uses both surgery and genetics. It would be far easier to achieve the desired results through manipulation of DNA than through the use of problematic surgical procedures.

The Brain That Wouldn't Die (1962)

Synopsis: Dr. Cortner and his fiancée take a drive up into the country. He crashes the car and she is accidentally decapitated. Cortner takes the severed head to his home lab and hooks it up to various tubes and fluids on a table, which keeps her alive. Cortner then looks for a suitable female body to which he can attach the head. In the end, Cortner's lab catches fire, killing him and the head.

Screenplay: Joseph Green, from an original story by Rex Carlton and Joseph Green.

Biological Science Principles Involved: Surgery. Neurobiology. Immunology.

What Is Right with the Biological Science Presented: The opening scenes, which take place in an operating room, are OK. There is one scene in which the father/son team massages a patient's open heart while they work on the brain to revive a particular patient. Open heart massages are somewhat common and, at times, quite effective in reviving certain patients. During this same surgery scene the young Dr. Cortner says, "Our bodies are capable of adjusting in ways we've hardly dreamt of." This is very true. The remarkable healing and restorative powers of our cells and tissues is truly amazing. There are natural biochemical functions that can readily repair most (moderate) wounds, regenerate some nerves, heal broken bones, repair muscle tears, and counter infections. There are limits, of course, but the body can often heal and restore itself.

The young Dr. (Bill) Cortner's assistant, Kurt, and the severed head (Bill's fiancée) have an interesting conversation. The head says, "Transplant my head onto another body ... but the tissues of my body [what body?] would reject the tissues of another [more like the other way around!], reject it as the foreign substance it is. The transplant would never take, it would never stay in place. My blood's antibodies would attack it as it would any invading matter." All of this, said in 1959 (though made in '59, the picture wasn't released until 1962), is as true then as it is now.

What Is Wrong with the Biological Science Presented: After the opening operating room scenes, the rest is all downhill. The errors are numerous. When Cortner picks up his fiancée's head and wraps it in his jacket, this would introduce an unacceptable amount of biological contaminations (such as bacteria, molds, fungus, and viruses). If there is just a small amount of bacteria present, the head would not survive; depending upon the strain, the contamination of a single bacterium could

expand and ultimately cause the death of the head. Furthermore, the blood loss and the amount of elapsed time without oxygen would result in a severe loss of brain function — and a very dead head.

In the lab the head is placed in a pan with liquid that is open to the air, demonstrating a complete lack of sterility. In spite of everything that happens, the head manages to retain all of her facial makeup, lipstick, eye shadow, rouge, etc.

The head talks, though with a raspy voice, and this problem has already been discussed above (see *The Head*). The problem is the necessity of pushing air over the vocal cords for speech. With no lungs there's no air, and with no air there's no speech. Furthermore, the head actually laughs! Wonderful stuff, though completely inaccurate. At least with the film *The Head* there is the semblance of air being pumped through tubes. In this film we do not even have that, so where the necessary air comes from for speech is anyone's guess. Furthermore, the head retains all of her cognitive abilities, including thought, reasoning, and psychic(!) powers.

Kurt, Cortner's assistant, says, "How long do you think we can keep her alive under these conditions?" Cortner says, "48 to 50 hours at the most. With her I'm using my new adreno-serum." Well, "adreno" means coming from the adrenal glands, which are flattened, roughly triangular glands situated on top of the kidneys. The primary function of the adrenal glands is the secretion of the hormones epinepherine and norepinephrine, along with some steroid hormones. Epinephrine (its scientific name is 4-[1-hydroxy-2-(methylamino)-ethyl]-1,2-benzenediol) increases the heart rate and force of cardiac contraction, brings about vasoconstriction (or vasodilation), relaxes bronchiolar (lung) and intestinal smooth muscles, affects the metabolism of glucose and lipids, and is used to treat asthma, glaucoma, and heart blockage. Norepinepherine is used in response to hypotension and physical stress. This is all fine and dandy, but what does it have to do with the physiology of a head that has no heart, minimal metabolism (compared to the body), and no lung activity?

In addition to this, Kurt tells the head that Cortner uses his "adreno-serum" on her, saying, "This serum injected into the blood stream affects the lymphoid tissues. Here, in the neck, the lymphoids that provide the antibodies for the blood that attack foreign transplanted matter." The head then says, "So that's the liquid in the blood that's being pumped into what's left of me ... this liquid that he's pumped into me, my brain burns with it [i.e., mental power] ... that same medicine that he's fed to me to activate my lymphoid tissues..." As far as is known, epinephrine does not activate lymphoid tissue and stimulate antibody formation. Compared to the rest of the body there are very few lymphatics in the head and neck. Furthermore, the relatively small amount of bone marrow present in the head is not enough to sustain a significant immune response. As such, this brings into doubt the problem of tissue rejection by whatever functional immune response is left in the head.

What Biological Science Is Necessary to Actually Achieve the Results in the Film: My above comments on the film *The Head* equally apply here.

The biggest obstacle to overcome would be the supply of enough nutrients to the brain to keep it functional. The other major problem is the time interval between the actual decapitation and the time Cortner is able to attach the life supporting apparatus to the head. This must be done within a very narrow eight minute window or the brain will cease to function normally. Perhaps the more imaginative of you could envision some sort of scenario

where the lack of appropriate oxygen to delicate brain tissues brought about some sort of hyper mental activity, which gave the brain some telepathic abilities so it could communicate with the creature locked behind the lab door.

Could It Actually Happen: Though I have learned to never say never, I have my doubts whether this could actually work. You may be able to keep the head's cells and tissues alive, but to have a functioning, thinking brain survive the trauma and be conscious is stretching reality, even for me, more than I am comfortable with. In the film *The Head*, its removal was done under controlled clinical conditions. In this film, the head was severed, probably not cleanly, by trauma (an automobile accident), so keeping it alive was most doubtful. However, if you believe patent number 4,666,425, then it could happen.

Astro-Zombies (1967)

Synopsis: (Note: No matter how you examine this film, it is downright weird. The plot synopsis simply does not do justice to the movie.) This mess of a movie has Dr. DeMarco (John Carradine) creating a series of "astro-zombies" he can control by thought wave transmissions, with the goal of having these astro-zombies work in the harsh environment of space so real humans would not be endangered. Astro-zombies escape and commit brutal murders in the neighborhood, which gets the attention of the CIA. Tura Satana leads a group of foreign agents who want the secret of the astro-zombies. In the end, mayhem breaks out and somehow everything is destroyed.

Screenplay: Ted V. Mikels and Wayne Rogers (who played "Trapper John" on TV's *M*A*S*H*).

Biological Science Principles Involved: Surgery. Photobiology. Cell Biology. Neurology.

What Is Right with the Biological Science Presented: Not much is right with the biology in this film. DeMarco says, "...this synthetic fluid [the red Kool-Aid–looking liquid] has the ability to feed body cells and keep them functioning as if in a living being." This is quite prescient for its time, anticipating all the work on serum-free and protein-free media formulations during the 1970s and 1980s. (I myself had a hand in some of this development work for the large scale production of human monoclonal antibodies. This work was in itself based upon the pioneering work of Dr. Gordon Sato, then at UCSD, who, as a molecular endocrinologist, developed all the formulations that are now routinely used in labs throughout the world in the growth and maintenance of cells and tissues in culture.)

What Is Wrong with the Biological Science Presented: The first time we see DeMarco he has his hand in what looks like a moderate sized fish tank filled with clear liquid and a heart. DeMarco is seen massaging the heart with his ungloved hand(!), and I can only imagine the level of contamination he introduces into the system. Also, DeMarco's assistant is seen extracting blood from a patient (victim?) with not a care about any semblance of sterile technique. I would guess their total lack of concern over sterile conditions has to do with a line of DeMarco's during the film. He says, "Not only have I found a way electronically to reactivate deceased body cells, I have also developed blood that is impervious to infection and disease and possesses the latent quality of instant coagulation." If DeMarco can keep away "infection and disease," then who cares about sterility? And as for "latent quality of instant coagulation"—that's anyone's guess.

DeMarco can do everything. In his spare time he develops a rudimentary mechanical heart (a very real and active element of cardiology) and is involved in developing thought wave transmissions by radio frequencies. Regarding this, one scientist comments, "Imagine feeding information from computers [via thought waves] into the brains of astronauts in orbital flight. In this way, knowledge from the minds of our top astrophysicists, aerospace medical scientists, and neurosurgeons could be combined and projected into the receiving device of a quasi-man [i.e., astro-zombie] in interplanetary space flight." I can see astrophysicists and aerospace medical scientists helping orbiting astronauts, but what does a neurosurgeon have to do with all this?

Also, the "quasi-man" in interplanetary space flight will have a stainless steel mesh stomach(!?), a synthetic electrogenic heart, a plastic pancreas(!), a cellulose liver(!), and silicon treatment of skin, making it impervious to micrometeorites!! A synthetic electrogenic heart, a plastic pancreas, and a cellulose liver are within the realm of possibility.

DeMarco's artificial heart is powered by solar power, meaning light (i.e., photons) is necessary to keep the heart pumping (pumping what?). The solar cells are on a device located on the foreheads of the astro-zombies. When one of the astro-zombies has his storage cell knocked off in a fight, he uses an ordinary flashlight and shines it onto the photocells on his forehead as a source of power to help his escape. In principle, this is possible; however, the amount of light energy coming from an ordinary flashlight (as measured in lumens), with two D sized batteries, would not give off enough energy to "power" a human body. Though an interesting idea, even with a 100 percent efficient conversion of flashlight energy, this is too much of a stretch to actually occur.

What Biological Science Is Necessary to Actually Achieve the Results in the Film: The implantation of electrodes and various wires into brain tissue is not that unusual, and could help many with brain dysfunctions. This was one of the ways neurosurgeons were able to map out regions of the brain and assign particular functions to them. My earlier comments on organ and brain transplants' nutrient media formulations all apply here too.

Photobiology is a rapidly growing discipline, with its "golden age" yet to come. The ability to harness light (either from the sun — as solar power — or by artificial means) and use it for work is intriguing. Several clinical procedures involve the use of light and are collectively referred to as photodynamic therapy. Certain drugs are activated when exposed to light and are used to control diseases as diverse as skin problems and cancer. The photocells of the astro-zombies would have photo sensors that could convert light energy into either physical energy and/or chemical energy.

Could It Actually Happen: The ability to transmit thought patterns into brains is in the realm of "impossible physics" and more the purview of *Star Trek* and "Jedi mind tricks" than any real biology. The unresolved question is one of distance. How far apart do the subjects need to be to receive the transmitted messages? And what is the rapidity of the sent messages? If you send the message in English, will it be understood in Japanese?

In the future we can imagine people with a variety of devices that harness light and convert it to do work. In this film, DeMarco developed a way to use light to keep a heart beating. This, of course, could be a real problem at night or in light starved areas (such as in caves or buildings). To accommodate this, there would have to be energy storage devices that could operate in the absence of light.

6 HEMATOLOGY

Blood, the "liquid organ," serves three primary purposes. The first is to transport oxygen, in the form of red blood cells, throughout the body's cells and tissues. The second is to transport white blood cells throughout the body to help defend against invading organisms and germs. The third is to transport molecules and nutrients throughout the body's cells and tissues to maintain proper health. All, of course, pumped by the heart.

Much of the fields of hematology and immunology overlap. The language and nomenclature of one is equally applied to the other. After all, the lineage of blood cells includes a myriad of cell types, the most dominant being the red cell (erythrocyte) and the white cell (lymphocyte). All of these diverse cell types originate from stem cells found primarily in the bone marrow. Stem cells are called pluripotent, meaning they can differentiate into different lineages, depending upon what molecular signal is used.

House of Dracula (1945)

Synopsis: An ensemble cast of Drac-ula, the Wolfman, and Frankenstein's Monster make an appearance in Dr. Edelman's laboratory. Edelman tries to develop a cure for Dracula's thirst for blood, a cure for Larry Talbot's lycanthropy, and the means to resurrect the monster.

Screenplay: Edward T. Lowe.

Biological Science Principles Involved: Hematology. Immunology. Infectious Disease. Parasitology.

What Is Right with the Biological Science Presented: The hematology and immunology concepts presented are satisfyingly accurate — and even more impressive knowing this film was made in 1945. The ability to use the human immune response to manage disease was very much a science fiction concept in the middle 1940s.

Baron Latos (aka Count Dracula) sought out Dr. Edelman to "effect a cure" and "to seek release from a curse of misery and horror." Recognizing a disease or affliction for what it is and seeking out a treatment are the first steps to obtaining a cure. Acknowledging that this "would be a challenge to medical science," Edelman further says, "cases have been recorded in which the victim, driven by some abnormal urge, actually believes that the blood of other people is necessary to keep them

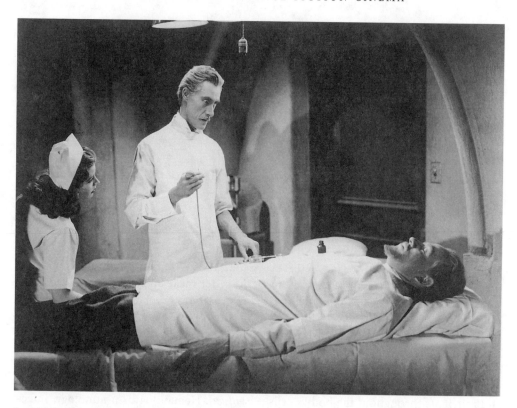

In *House of Dracula* (1945) Dr. Edelman (Onslow Stevens), on the examination table, is about to receive an injection/transfusion from Baron Latos (aka Count Dracula, played by John Carradine) himself. Human antibodies at work.

alive. Became psychological killers in order to obtain it. These beliefs probably upset their metabolisms, induced fixations, lustful appetites." Yes, certain diseases, whether biological or psychological, do bring about such behavior.

While examining a blood sample from Latos, Edelman recognizes that the observed parasite (see below) may be destroyed by using the power of the human immune response. After looking at the sample, Edelman tells his nurse/assistant to "make a culture of this and prepare an antiserum as soon as possible." This is certainly a reasonable approach, not only to control the production of the parasite but also to destroy it. While discussing these results with Latos, Edelman says, "The examination of your blood reveals the presence of a peculiar parasite, the form of

which I am completely unfamiliar. It's possible it may have something to do with your problem.... I am having an antitoxin prepared so that we may see." Edelman further explains that, "a pure culture of a parasite introduced into the parent bloodstream will destroy not only its own kind but themselves as well." In theory, this is correct (see below). This is, in essence, the basis behind vaccines. Vaccines exploit the power of the human immune response, so that when the "germ antigen" (in the case of Latos, the blood parasite) arrives, an immune response will be mounted against the invader and destroy it.

Reasoning that the human antibodies in Edelman's own blood may counteract the parasites in Latos' blood (a remarkably prescient observation), Edelman gives

Latos a transfusion of his own blood. Based on what is seen, it is difficult to estimate how much blood Edelman donates to Latos, though probably not much. Later, after a transfusion, Edelman examines another sample of Latos' blood and says, "This photomicrograph of your blood reveals an odd condition, one which I can't account for as yet. A different species of antibodies has appeared ... if a doctor effects a cure he wants to know how he did it." Latos replies with, "Which is of little concern to the patient so long as he is being cured." (Most real patients share this sentiment. They do not care how a certain medication works, just so long as it actually works!) Shortly after, during another visit, Edelman says to Latos, "You remember I was puzzled tonight by the new antibodies? I know now where they came from. They're from my blood. We may be on the verge of a major discovery. But to check my theory I am going to give you another transfusion." This time the amount is clearly seen, and about 10cc of blood is transfused. Again, Edelman theorized that his human antibodies would be effective against the parasite. Immunologically, this is all accurate.

After observing Larry Talbot turn into a werewolf, Edelman performs an examination on him the following day. Edelman says, "In your case, my boy, diagnosis is extremely difficult.... The examination discloses one condition — pressure on certain parts of the brain. This condition, coupled with your belief the moon can bring about a change, accomplishes exactly that. During the period in which your own reasoning process gives way to self-hypnosis, the glands which govern your metabolism get out of control. Like a steam engine without a balance wheel. When this happens, the glands generate an abnormal supply of certain hormones. In your case, those which bring about the physical transformation which you experienced."

Talbot responds with, "Explaining it doesn't help. [See above comments made by Latos, which echoes the same sentiment.] What can you do about it? Operate?" Edelman says, "A surgical operation to enlarge the cranial cavity is a long and dangerous one." Edelman then shows Talbot his laboratory warm room/incubator and says, "Under tropical conditions, what we've tried to duplicate here, this hybrid plant, *Cavaria formosa*, produces a mold in which we've been able to distill a substance which possesses the property of softening any hard structure composed of calcium salts—bone, for instance. With this substance it might be possible, without surgery, to reshape the cranial cavity and thus eliminate the pressure.... Unfortunately, it will take some time to produce the mold in sufficient quantity." Yes, certain molds do inhabit certain plants that may make a biological substance (most likely an enzyme) that does soften bone. This also represents one of the first cinema examples of biotherapy, using natural substances from our body to effect biological changes.

What Is Wrong with the Biological Science Presented: Edelman obtains a blood sample from Latos, and a "point of view" shot of this sample under a microscope is shown. The observed field seen has about 100 typical red blood cells present (RBCs), one polymorphonuclear leukocyte (or PMN in hematologist terms), and six bizarre-looking "parasite" structures, each wrapped around one RBC; about three fourths of the RBC circumference is covered with the parasite. The parasite appears as a long, thin arm that branches out to finger-like projections (either three or four "fingers" are present on each parasite arm). There is no such parasite, though there are plenty that do specifically attack RBCs (the best example is the malaria plasmodium sporozoite, which propagates inside RBCs).

After recognizing the existence of this parasite, Edelman tells his assistant to, "make a culture of this and prepare an antiserum as soon as possible." Culturing parasites is very tricky business, and the proper conditions must be met; trying to do this in culture dishes (scientifically called "in vitro") is very difficult, the biggest problem being which nutrients to use. Furthermore, to prepare an antiserum you must have enough sample to generate an effective immune response. If they have a difficult time growing the parasite in vitro, then they would not have enough sample with which to immunize and prepare the antiserum. In addition, the preparation of an effective antiserum would take months. The host animal (typically goats or rabbits) used to prepare the antiserum would need multiple immunizations with a parasite extract to obtain a good immune response. Therefore, it would take perhaps weeks to months to grow enough of the parasite to use for immunizations, and then months to actually prepare the antiserum. Meanwhile, Latos is still suffering and has the need to feed.

While examining another blood sample from Latos, Edelman says, "A different species of antibodies has appeared..." A different species would mean some other animal's antibody entered Latos' blood stream in sufficient quantity and stayed long enough that it could be detected. It is difficult to imagine how this could happen. What Edelman should have said is, "a different *form* of antibody has appeared," which, in this case, is Edelman's own antibody (resulting from a previous blood transfusion).

Edelman transfused some of his blood into Latos based on the theory that antibodies (i.e., antiserum) would destroy the parasite. In principle this is true. However, what is implied is that Edelman has antibodies to the parasite in his blood, which would mean he must have been infected with the parasites at some previous time! Antibodies are generated when prompted by an antigen. No antigen, no antibody. Since Edelman's blood contains antibodies to the parasite, he must have been exposed to it. If he was exposed, then why did he not present "Dracula-like" symptoms, as Latos clearly does? Since Edelman did have antibodies to the parasite, then one must conclude that the parasite is *not* involved in vampirism. However, at the end of the film Edelman becomes demented and vampire-like as a result of his transfusions with Latos. Edelman says, "My blood has been contaminated by the blood of Count Dracula" (presaging the now common knowledge of how infectious blood can be, HIV and AIDS being examples by which blood to blood contact is infectious). Perhaps there is some other component other than the parasite in Latos' blood that entered Edelman during a transfusion (Which was sabotaged by the devious Dracula; if done correctly, none of Latos' blood should have entered Edelman at all).

What Biological Science Is Necessary to Actually Achieve the Results in the Film: The immunological aspects of this film are intriguing, especially in light of the fact it was made in 1945. At that time immunology and hematology were not very well defined, and the film's speculations about the effectiveness of human antibodies is startling to see—clearly a case of yesterday's science fiction becoming today's science fact.

The parasite identified in Latos' blood deserves closer analysis. What would it take for this parasite to actually contribute to vampirism? Latos needs blood to survive, and the parasite appears to feed off RBCs, which does make sense. With enough parasites (the six seen on the microscope field early in the film would imply that Latos was literally filled with the creatures—throughout his entire blood supply and probably in a few organs, like the spleen and bone marrow), then Latos would suffer anemia-like conditions, and a "transfusion" of blood would certainly benefit him. Most likely the parasite population would increase and decrease, depending upon a variety of conditions. With the parasite population high, then Latos would be anemic and could have a severe need (masked as a craving?) for blood. If the parasite population was low, then he would not be anemic and his desire/need for blood would be reduced. Regarding the non-psychological traits of vampirism, perhaps the parasite secreted certain hormones that altered the metabolism of Latos, creating the creature that he is.

The development of an effective vaccine against a parasite is a long and tedious process, fraught with many unknowns, and only the most determined are involved in this work. Furthermore, when using the entire parasite to prepare the vaccine, there is no way to control for the most important antigen on which to focus the vaccine. Not all parasite antigens are the same, and the vaccine should be derived from the best antigen possible. The determination of this could take months, if not years (for example, after decades of work there still is not an effective vaccine against malaria), so for Edelman to "prepare an antiserum as soon as possible" could occupy the rest of his life — without any demonstrable progress. The key component here is time (or cinematime).

Edelman says, "...a pure culture of the parasite introduced into the parent bloodstream..." which is an accurate method for arming the immune response against the parasite's antigens. However, a necessary step is omitted. The scientific term is "attenuated parasite," meaning that, though intact, the parasite is not living and cannot reproduce within the body. (This same term also applies to other vaccines based on bacteria, viruses, molds,

etc.: "attenuated bacteria," "attenuated virus," etc.) You want the parasite's antigens to stimulate an immune response (and subsequent booster shots will provide long-term immune protection) without the biological threat of the parasite growing. There are many methods to do this, ranging from physically breaking up parasite bodies and fractionating the parts for immunization to using poisons or lethal doses of radiation to kill the organisms prior to their injection.

Regarding the ability to enlarge (slightly) the cranium of Larry Talbot with an extract from a particular mold, this extract would have to be either an enzyme or a special type of acid capable of dissolving bone. (An effective example is placing chicken or turkey bones in a container filled with vinegar for a few days. Later, the bones can literally be tied into a knot without breaking, demonstrating that some acids can weaken the strong bonds in bone and make them more pliable.) The enzyme would be more interesting, though the major problem would be getting the enzyme *inside* Talbot's head at the cranial areas that need enlarging. All of this is based, of course, on Edelman's diagnosis that pressure on the brain is causing a hormonal imbalance, which results in lycanthropy. Pressure on the pituitary gland and the hypothalamus can cause metabolic and psychological alterations, some of which can be severe.

For Edelman to identify his own antibodies in Latos' blood would require some very sophisticated experimentation. At the time, Edelman would have used techniques called gel electrophoresis and gel immunoprecipitation. These techniques separate proteins (antibodies are proteins) based on their size, their electrical charge, and ability to precipitate an antigen in a gel.

Edelman would set up "Ouchterlony plates" to analyze the antibodies within

Latos' blood. Edelman would centrifuge the blood sample, obtain the clear serum, and place a drop into a hole in a gel substance, the Ouchterlony plate. Adjacent to this hole is another antiserum that may recognize the blood sample. If it does, then precipitin lines form, which look like a crescent moon between the two holes and are easily visible. Based on these results, Edelman concludes that his own antibodies (precipitin lines would have formed between his blood and Latos') are present in Latos' blood. This is reasonable, since human antibodies can be detected for weeks after a transfusion.

Could It Actually Happen: Antitoxins, or, more specifically, human antibodies, are currently being prepared and are being used. This film was made in 1945, and about 45 to 50 years later human antibodies are being used in the clinic, and much worldwide research is being done in this area. This represents one of the more remarkably accurate insights into human biology by screenwriters.

Unfortunately, infectious agents are in the blood supply, and only constant vigilance and endless testing of samples will help ensure a clean and uncontaminated supply. To be sure, contaminations from blood do happen.

NOT OF THIS EARTH

(Background information): Like the *Island of Dr. Moreau* and *Fly* series, we are fortunate in having two versions of Roger Corman's *Not of This Earth*; the first was made in 1957 and the (good) remake came in 1995. (Actually, there is a third version, made in 1988, starring former porn actress Traci Lords, which adds nothing new and is definitely the weakest of the three.)

These two versions, separated by nearly 40 years, provide an interesting opportunity to compare and contrast the biological science in each. Were any of the advances during this 40 year time interval presented in the 1995 version?

Not of This Earth (1957)

Synopsis: An alien, calling himself Mr. Johnson, comes to earth to acquire human blood for his home planet. He needs human blood to survive, so he hires a nurse to give him transfusions. Johnson obtains blood from several human victims and disposes of their bodies in a basement furnace. Johnson's hearing is sensitive to loud noises, and after being chased by a policeman on a motorcycle his car crashes, which kills him.

Screenplay: Charles B. Griffith and Mark Hanna.

Biological Science Principles Involved: Hematology. Cell Biology.

What Is Right with the Biological Science Presented: After Johnson attacks his victims he inserts a tube into their necks and removes their blood. The best choices here are either the external jugular vein or the common carotid artery, so either way, Johnson got it right. Since this is best done with someone with a pumping heart, Johnson leaves his victims alive long enough to allow the natural physiology of the heart to pump out the blood. If he killed them right away, then their heart would no longer be pumping, making it very difficult to extract blood in the quantities he needs.

When he first feels "weak" Johnson goes to a hospital and asks for a transfusion. Imagine yourself walking into a hospital emergency room and asking for a transfusion! Well, Johnson gets the same response, and he puts a mental "whammy" on Dr. Rochelle, who subsequently becomes his "slave." Johnson tells Rochelle he is "type O" blood and then gets his transfusion.

Mr. Johnson (Paul Birch, right) and the mysterious vitamin fluid that he regurgitates in *Not of This Earth* (1957).

After running some tests, Rochelle visits Johnson's home and tells him, "Your blood is different than any I have studied in my entire career." Johnson asks, "In what way?" Rochelle says, "First place, no man on earth should be able to live with such a low count of red corpuscles as you have. Second place, your blood's behaving in an impossible manner. The agglutinin's breaking down, destroying the basic structure of the blood itself. The result is ... evaporating blood."

A "low count of red corpuscles" is called anemia. Anemia is any condition in which the number of red blood cells (or hemoglobin) falls below certain standards, which vary, depending upon the size and condition of the person. Anemia is frequently manifested by a pallor of the skin, a shortness of breath, palpitations of the heart, lethargy, and fatigability. There are several types of anemias, due variously to blood loss, problems of cell and pigment production, lysis of certain cell types, failure to produce or renew red blood cells, and failure to generate new hemoglobin, the oxygen-carrying protein. Johnson could have had any one or any combination of these maladies. Since he appears to be very mobile and active (not lethargic or easily fatigued), he must have one of the other conditions.

"Evaporating blood" is a very interesting concept and is a good term describing what could be going on. The modern term for "evaporating cells" is called apoptosis. Apoptosis, pronounced as either ap-o-to'sis or ap'op-to'sis, is called programmed cell death, or cell suicide. When a certain antigen on the surface of cells, called the "FAS antigen," is activated, a signal is sent into the cell that starts a complex cascade of events which culminates in its fragmentation into small particles for reabsorption and reutilization; in essence, the cell kills itself. Apoptosis was not recognized as such until the early 1980s, so congratulations to the writers of this film (in 1957!) for accurately describing, decades ahead of its time, a bona fide mechanism of how cells naturally die. (There are those in the cancer world who think that tumor cells do not undergo natural apoptosis and therefore do not naturally die, giving rise to cell populations that continually grow and become cancers. I too am a believer in this concept.)

During a conversation with his nurse, Johnson says, "...since cancer tracks radioactivity, then the cancerous tissue itself may be charged with a negative energy. Possibly that might lead to a cure." Well, cancer does not "track radioactivity," but the idea of cancer cells being "charged with a negative energy" is interesting. It so happens that cancer cells are indeed negatively charged! All cells have on their surface a class of proteins called glycoproteins, meaning they are proteins with carbohydrate ("glyco") molecules attached to them. One carbohydrate molecule in particular, called sialic acid, is negatively charged, and cancer cells have an overabundance of this sialic acid on their glycoproteins, which gives them a net negative charge. This concept has been exploited by some cancer researchers in designing certain therapies. Again the writers say something correct!

To explain all the blood problems, Rochelle offers the following explanation: "The [patient] has lived in an area that's been constantly charged with radioactive material. It was this atmosphere that affected the blood ... in a place where continuous nuclear detonations have taken place over a period of years. An area of all-

out nuclear warfare." Rochelle's mental light bulb then goes on, and he calls him "an alien." Yes, excessive radioactive contamination does affect the blood in many ways, chief of which is the inhibition of what we call hematopoiesis, the formation and development of new blood cells. There are, unfortunately, far too many documented, real examples of problems in blood formation and development in those exposed to excessive radioactivity. Even those patients undergoing bone marrow transplantation have total body radiation to destroy all their own blood cells before they receive the transplant.

What Is Wrong with the Biological Science Presented: After Rochelle takes the first blood sample from Johnson for analysis, the physician puts a sample under a microscope and, unfortunately, a point of view shot of the field is seen. Present are crystals(!) and a unicellular organism known as a paramecium! A paramecium is an abundant freshwater holotrichous ciliate (i.e., possessing hair over its entire body) that is slipper shaped in appearance and often big enough to be seen by the naked eye. This creature inhabiting a blood sample is ludicrous! While looking at this "blood" sample, Rochelle says, "Fantastic. Agglutinin disintegrating at an uninterrupted rate, resulting in the cellular destruction of the cellular structure of blood. It's impossible." An agglutinin is an antibody that causes clumping of particles and/or cells that stimulated the formation of the agglutinin in the first place. An agglutinin causes aggregations not disintegrations. Disintegrating agglutinins would mean that there would be no clotting, so wounds would not heal and all cellular matter would be dismantled into soluble components—all at a fantastic rate.

For Johnson's blood transfusions, Rochelle tells the hired nurse to "administer 500cc of type O every night until further orders from me." Without missing a beat, the nurse calmly asks, "What's wrong with him?" Rochelle responds with, "There are indications of internal hemorrhage." Five hundred cc of blood a night is incredible! (This is a little more than a unit of blood.) The old adage of what goes in must come out applies to liquids. If 500cc go in, then somewhere 500cc must come out, so Johnson would be urinating all day! And hemorrhage is the release of blood, either natural or forced (as in a rupture), from blood vessels. Johnson's blood vessels must leak like a sieve for him to need 500cc a day. Furthermore, if he does need that much a day, the transfusions should be done in a hospital so the physicians can keep a closer eye on him should complications occur. Finally, transfusions are typically done with a 12 gauge needle, which is relatively large. Most injections in humans are done with 21 to 24 gauge needles, and diabetics give themselves insulin injections with 30 gauge needles (so small that they hardly feel it). A 12 gauge will leave significant scar marks at the insertion point in the skin, and to have this done once a day would not allow enough time for the injection wound to heal properly. (When I donate units of blood [this should not be done more frequently than once a month, and it's best to wait six weeks or more], 12 gauge needles are used, and believe you me, those do hurt, so getting one a day would be very uncomfortable.)

Johnson's job on Earth is to study "six phases of Earth's sub-humans." The leader of Johnson's home planet explains, "Your [Johnson's] mission on this globe is to be accomplished in five out of six phases. In the first, you will study all characteristics of the Earth's subhumans. In the second phase, you shall increase the quantity of Earth's blood, which you are transmitting to Devana [the alien home planet]. For phase three, we must have a live specimen, a subhuman to be used in vivisectory research. You are phase four, in which Earth

blood value will be determined by your survival or your death. If Earth blood preserves your life, phase five will be the conquest, subjugation, and pasturing of the earth subhumans. Phase six will be the utter obliteration of this planet if you die." The easiest way to "increase the quantity of Earth's blood" would be to have more "sub-humans," so have all women become pregnant.

As a source of nutrition, before Johnson drinks a glass of water he first places a tablet into the glass, which darkens the water. The nurse is curious about this and takes a sample of what she calls "black water" to Rochelle for analysis. Later, Rochelle says to her, "Well, the compound's fantastic. Not only does it contain every vitamin known to man but a few I've never even seen before. And it has the basic food structures concentrated with bulk, roughage, energy, and diet control. All in the same molecular structure." A vitamin is an organic substance essential for normal metabolism, and in insufficient quantities a person could suffer deficiency diseases. There was no way Rochelle could have identified vitamins he had "never even seen before." If he had not seen them, then how could he have known they were vitamins in the first place? The concept that everything in the "black water" had "the same molecular structure" is ludicrous. Vitamin structure alone is highly varied, since we have the water soluble ones (the B and C vitamins), fat soluble (A, E, and K), and those resembling steroids (vitamin D), not to mention whatever molecules are involved in "bulk, roughage, energy and diet control." Some vitamins are small and simple, like vitamin C (ascorbic acid), and some are amazingly complex, like vitamin B12 (cyanocobalamin).

What Biological Science Is Necessary to Actually Achieve the Results in the Film: Just about all of the biology presented in this film involves various aspects of blood and its components. Since Johnson's home planet is saturated with radioactivity, they would need blood to survive. (This is, of course, assuming their biochemical makeup is nearly identical to that of humans, so much so that our blood would be compatible with their own physiology.) There are three major components in whole blood: red blood cells, white blood cells, and molecules. Most likely Johnson needs the red blood cells, or erythrocytes, the most. Therefore, he needs cells for hemoglobin to carry oxygen. To manufacture erythrocytes our body uses a protein hormone called erythropoietin. This hormone is secreted by the kidneys and stimulates the release of stem cells, the precursors to erythrocytes, from bone marrow and causes them to mature into functional red blood cells. What Johnson really needs is not the actual red blood cells themselves but enough of a supply of erythropoietin, so the "sub-humans" could have their bodies manufacture their own erythrocytes.

If Johnson needs white blood cells, also called lymphocytes, then his immune system is malfunctioning. In a sterile environment you can live without lymphocytes (like children who live in "plastic bubbles"). Perhaps Johnson needs the lymphocytes to boost his immune response. Another major type of white blood cell is the megakaryocyte, which gives rise to platelets, those irregular shaped cell fragments necessary for blood clotting. Since the comment is made that Johnson has "internal hemorrhage," then his clotting mechanisms have gone haywire and he may need platelets for natural blood clotting mechanisms to properly function.

Could It Actually Happen: The problem of aliens visiting us and taking our blood is unrealistic. Excessive radiation exposure does alter blood and can cause anemia, cancer, or both. The incidence of blood problems from those affected by the atomic bombs dropped during World War II, the nuclear testing practices of the USA and other countries, and nuclear accidents (such as that of Chernobyl), are sufficient proof that radiation poisoning is nasty. Most of these high dose exposures are fatal, and low dose exposures do cause all sorts of chronic and long-term problems.

Not of This Earth (1995)

Synopsis: The overall plot, including the main characters' names, Mr. Johnson and Dr. Rochelle, is identical to that of the 1957 version (see above).

Screenplay: Charles Phillip Moore, based on the 1957 screenplay by Charles B. Griffith and Mark Hanna.

Biological Science Principles Involved: Hematology. Biochemistry. Physiology. Virology.

What Is Right with the Biological Science Presented: After examining Johnson, Rochelle tells the nurse, "He has a rare form of hemophilia and needs frequent transfusions." Hemophilia is an inherited disorder of blood coagulation, primarily in males, manifested in a permanent inability to form hemorrhages due to a defect in the clotting mechanisms. They are unable to heal blood vessel wounds, either internal or external, so they are at a serious risk of literally bleeding to death, even from the smallest of cuts or wounds. Hemophiliacs do indeed need frequent blood transfusions.

During a conversation between Johnson and his home planet, the alien official says, "The plague goes stronger with each moon. Have you found a cure?" Johnson answers with, "Their [humans'] blood and life essences have renewed my capabilities, if only for short durations. I will be sending more units for study. As for a cure, I remain hopeful. Their blood and life force are a temporary reprieve. Our survival lies in a cure." Interesting stuff here. First of all, based on what the alien official (Johnson's boss?) says, they too have a moon, which probably influences them like ours does us. Human blood apparently has everything these aliens are looking for. However, since our blood only provides a "temporary reprieve" and is good "only for short durations," they have to analyze our blood's components to discover which element or elements they need to survive their plague. This suggests that there are a combination of cells and/or molecules they need and not just blood for blood's sake.

After some experimentation Rochelle tells Johnson his blood is different. Johnson says, "Different in what way?" Rochelle says, "In the first place, HIV is transmitted by body fluids. The virus in your blood is airborne." Johnson replies, "Is it contagious?" Rochelle says, "I wish I knew. What I do know, this virus requires that an extremely rare element be present in the blood if it's to survive. I also know that the only blood I have ever tested that contains this element is your blood. So, Mr. Johnson, either your case is one in a trillion or you are not of this planet." Johnson replies with, "Yes ... this virus, you can stop it?" Rochelle says, "Possible, but I'll need help ... specialists, computer time, research facilities." Later, after some more tests and experimentation, Rochelle says, "I think I've found a way to knock out this new virus. The protein that carries it is very basic. If we eliminate the protein, the virus can't survive. Not only that, it can be knocked out by exposure to radiation." Well, all of this tells us a lot about Johnson's predicament. During the last 20 years or so, very rarely has HIV or AIDS been mentioned in science fiction films, so this one is definitely different. Since there are only about six billion people on earth, "one in a trillion" is an exaggeration, though

many, myself included, overemphasize facts to make a stronger point; this is called hyperbole. Rochelle, like any real scientist, knows his limitations, and when necessary he seeks out the help of colleagues ("I'll need help ... specialists ... research facilities"). Finally, many viruses bind to receptors (a special class of proteins) on the surfaces of cells, which is how they get inside to integrate with the host DNA. For example, HIV binds to what we call the CD4 receptor on T lymphocytes, which is how that virus enters those cells and eventually causes their destruction. If you eliminate the protein to which the virus binds itself, then the virus will be knocked out. This is the basis for some forms of therapy for AIDS.

During a conversation between Johnson and his nurse he asks, "Will you answer for me a medical question ... autoimmune diseases. They are new to this world and they come at a time when billions of breeding humans are despoiling this world of all other forms of life. So, is it possible this world sees humans as a virus destroying its body, so then it fights back with these new fatal diseases? It's vaccine against the human virus." Interesting stuff. Imagine, good ol' planet earth ("Mother Earth") as a living organism unleashing new forms of "vaccine" (such as plague, AIDS, and other diseases) to get rid of us humans, the troublesome "virus." Most interesting. This is a concept that many people do agree with, though not many of them are scientists. An autoimmune disease is any disorder in which the loss of function or destruction of normal tissue occurs from the person's own immune response. Common examples are systemic lupus, thyroiditis, and rheumatoid arthritis. Essentially, you recognize your own cells and tissues as foreign and destroy them, very much like the rejection of an organ in an organ transplant that did not "take." It is important to note that many autoimmune diseases are not fatal. The implication by Johnson is that they are.

What Is Wrong with the Biological Science Presented: After removing about 500cc of blood from his first victim, her body, in a matter of moments, becomes all shriveled, like a mummy's—emaciated, thin, and with dry skin. The removal of such a relatively small amount of fluid from a body should not have caused that effect, though it does look cool.

When Johnson first visits the hospital for a transfusion he says, "I need an input of blood." If I heard someone phrase it that way, I would certainly question the sanity of the patient. Rochelle rightly asks Johnson for a blood sample for analysis for typing (which blood group does Johnson have, etc.), and at first Johnson refuses. Then, to accommodate Rochelle, Johnson takes a scalpel and makes a deep cut in his forearm to supply a blood sample. When doing this, Johnson says, "My blood is bad," which is better than saying "my blood is ill," as said in the 1957 version of this film. Right after making the deep cut, the wound on his forearm quickly heals. Johnson's wound-healing mechanisms must be extremely rapid for this to occur.

After the first transfusion, the nurse says, using her best bedside manner, "you were down nearly a quart," which is an interesting, though outmoded, way to put it. Johnson replies with, "The deficiency was one and a half liters." She, a nurse, is on the arvoirdupois (or American) system and he is on the metric system. Well, one quart is about 0.95 liters so the nurse is way off. One and a half liters is about 1.6 quarts, not "nearly a quart."

After eating, Johnson regurgitates some black viscous liquid ("smells bitter, like chemicals"), and the nurse takes a sample to Rochelle for analysis. This is interesting, and body fluids do tell a lot about our health (or lack of it). Just a few drops of blood or bodily fluids are all that is necessary to make an analysis. As determined by Rochelle, the black liquid from Johnson has the following values:

compound	Johnson	normal human
glucose	1000	100
urea nitrogen	100	7–18
creatinine	0.0	0.7–1.3
lactate	15,000	4.5–19.8

Other values, such as total protein (6.7), albumin (4.7), and globulin (2.0), are within normal human range. To have a fluid glucose level of 1000 is ridiculous, and is about the consistency of pure maple syrup! Lactate is a breakdown product of glucose; and at least that makes some sense, with his impossibly high glucose levels. Even so, that much lactate is definitely life threatening. Also, with his urea nitrogen level as high as shown, he probably did not urinate for weeks! If a physician obtained those levels from a real patient, the doctor would declare a medical emergency because these values are life threatening.

After obtaining these values, Rochelle reports them to the nurse, saying the black fluid is composed of, "amino acid, protein based. Hemoglobin plus bile, digestive enzymes. There's some choice components that I can't even identify. It's like some crazy gastric bouillabaisse." The phrase "gastric bouillabaisse" is disgustingly descriptive and apt.

What Biological Science Is Necessary to Actually Achieve the Results in the Film: The comments made for the 1957 version of this film also apply to this version. For human blood to provide the "temporary reprieve" Johnson claims it does, then their alien metabolism must be very similar to ours. As such, they should also be susceptible to many of the diseases and infections that plague mankind. Most likely Johnson is immune to some and highly susceptible to others. This probably represents the biggest single threat to the invading aliens.

Could It Actually Happen: The comments above for the 1957 version also apply here.

Blade (1998)

Synopsis: While pregnant, a woman is bitten by a vampire, and her baby grows up to become Blade, a vampire hunter with special powers. Blade uses a variety of devices to kill vampires. Blade's friend, Whistler, develops a serum that protects Blade from blood cravings. Blade confronts a group of vampires and kills them all.

Screenplay: David S. Goyer, based on a character created by Marv Wolfman and Gene Colon for Marvel Comics.

Biological Science Principles Involved: Hematology. Molecular Biology.

What Is Right with the Biological Science Presented: A vampire is brought to a morgue, apparently killed by being burnt to death. Blood and fluid samples are taken by a pathologist and hematologist for analysis. The pathologist says to the hematologist, "Did you check the chem panel? Blood sugar is three times normal, phosphorous and uric acid are off the charts." One of the major functions of pathologists is to analyze the body's fluids for specific contents. Deviations from normal values typically indicate or support certain diagnoses. Blood sugar (I digress, but this is probably a mistake; a pathologist talking to another colleague would most likely have said "blood glucose" instead, since this is the more accurate term and certainly one used in scientist-to-scientist interactions) is typically around six to ten grams per liter of blood, and three times this is not unreasonable; most likely this vampire has low levels of insulin and is di-

abetic. Phosphorous is a metabolite found primarily in the urine. Normal values are in the range of 0.4 to 1.3 grams produced per day. The normal values of uric acid are between four and eight grams per liter of urine. These two metabolites could very well be "off the charts." In addition to being a diabetic, this vampire, with his excessive uric acid levels, probably also has a severe case of gout.

The pathologist carefully examines the mouth region of the burnt vampire corpse and says, "Maxilla looks a little deformed. There's some odd muscle structure around the canines." The maxilla is the bone around the upper teeth area, extending into the eye and nose regions. The vampires have retractable canine teeth, so a "deformed" maxilla would be necessary to house these, and an "odd muscle structure" would be needed to extend and retract the teeth.

When beginning the autopsy on the burnt vampire corpse, the pathologist performs the perfunctory Y-shaped cut on the chest cavity, which is accurate.

While looking at a blood sample from a vampire, Curtis, a pathologist, says, "Look at the polys, they're binucleated." The humor of this was lost on over 99 percent of the people who saw this film. "Polys" is a medical slang term for polymorphonuclear leukocyte, which is a white blood cell (leukocyte) with various forms of nuclei. Many of these nuclei are indeed "binucleated," so the pathologist was, in essence, stating the obvious. "Look at the polys, they're binucleated" is like saying "See the ocean, it's wet."

An interesting concept in this film is treating vampirism as an immunological disorder. Blade keeps getting immunizing injections of "alium sediment, garlic" to help ward off his blood cravings. Like with many injections, Blade develops an increased resistance to the injected garlic, requiring larger doses for effect. Also, it is explained that the vampires go into anaphylactic shock, another immunological disorder, when exposed to silver.

Anaphylaxis is an allergy based immunological reaction that, in severe cases, can cause death. The term anaphylaxis is commonly used to describe the immediate allergic reaction to an antigen, characterized by contraction of smooth muscle and dilation of capillaries due to the release of highly active biomolecules (such as histamine, bradykinin, and serotonin) upon the binding of the antigen (in this case, silver) to a class of antibodies called IgE. The release of these highly reactive biomolecules can cause shock, due to the immediate fluid imbalance. Anaphylaxis can be local and confined to a certain area of the skin of the sensitized person or more general and affect the entire body.

Since it is shown that these vampires are sensitive to silver, an effective "vampire mace" is used, composed of silver nitrate ($AgNO_3$) and essence of garlic. Silver nitrate is a common chemical with many uses (grains of silver are the primary light-grabbing emulsion on black and white film). Silver nitrate also heavily stains skin a dark brown, which lasts until the stained skin cells are sloughed off.

The explanation given about Blade's history is intriguing. His need for blood had "taken hold at puberty," which is interesting. Puberty is the stage when a child becomes a young adult, characterized by the change in hormonal levels. The changes in hormones could have brought about the secondary changes for becoming a vampire. Because of these and certain other genetic changes, Blade could withstand garlic, silver, even sunlight. Furthermore, his wounds would completely heal within 24 hours.

The pathologist refers to a chemical, called EDTA, as an "anti-coagulant, used to treat blood clots," which is correct. EDTA is a chelating agent primarily used to remove multivalent cations (like magnesium, calcium, and iron) from solution. EDTA is used throughout the world in biomedical labs as a water softener, to help stabilize some drugs, to remove certain metals from bone, and as an anti-coagulant. Calcium ions are necessary to help catalyze blood clotting, and removing calcium with EDTA will inhibit clot formation. EDTA stands for ethylenediamine tetraacetic acid.

A favorite exercise of the natural scientist is to give newly discovered species a Latin name — one word for the genus and another for the species. For example, the scientific name for man is *Homo sapiens*. The vampires in this film are also given a genus/species name, which is "*Hominus nocturna*," which translates as "night man."

What Is Wrong with the Biological Science Presented: At a club for vampires, blood is seen coming out of ceiling sprinklers, coating all those dancing. The blood is obviously fake. It is not viscous enough and appears to be colored water. Fake blood concoctions have been around a long time (one of the best is red food dye mixed with diluted, clear Karo Syrup), and some better formulation should have been used. Also, the color of the blood is off and far too red in tone.

When the hematologist looks at a dead (burnt) vampire blood sample under a microscope, she says, "The red blood cells are biconvex, which is impossible." Though red blood cells do indeed come in a variety of shapes, all due to certain diseases (such as sickle cell anemia), "biconvex" is not one of them.

It is shown that the vampires are very sensitive to sunlight and ultraviolet rays. U.V. ray exposure causes immediate blistering of vampire skin. Yes, some humans do experience skin blistering when exposed to sunlight for extended periods of time, and that is the problem here ... time.

U.V. light would not have this severe blistering effect in mere seconds.

A vampire cop keeps blood frozen in liquid nitrogen in the trunk of his squad car. Liquid nitrogen has a temperature of about −180°C, so this is very cold and requires effective insulation; even the most efficient containers lose a few liters of liquid nitrogen a day as evaporation. As seen, the cop keeps whole blood in plastic "unit" bags in his trunk. This is the wrong way to store whole blood, not to mention the impracticality of dealing with liquid nitrogen.

The hematologist asks, "Why do vampires need to drink blood?" Whistler, a friend of Blade's, responds, "Because their own blood can't sustain hemoglobin." The hematologist then says, "Right, so it's a genetic defect, just like hemolytic anemia. That means that we have to treat it with gene therapy. We infect the victim's DNA with a retrovirus. They've been using it on sickle cell anemia." Earlier it was stated that vampire red blood cells are "impossibly biconvex." No matter what their size and shape, RBCs do contain hemoglobin. Whether that hemoglobin is completely functional, 75 percent functional, 50 percent functional, etc., is unknown and depends upon the disease. Hemolytic anemia is any anemia resulting from an increased rate of red blood cell (erythrocyte) destruction, which would subsequently mean the presence of free hemoglobin. RBC destruction could be a result of iron deficiencies, endocrine problems, malnutrition, lack of cell proliferation, and/or increased cell death. It is not just "a genetic defect." Gene therapy will be common in the not too distant future, especially for sickle cell anemia.

What Biological Science Is Necessary to Actually Achieve the Results in the Film: During pregnancy, Blade's mother is bitten by a vampire. For Blade to be affected by this would require some biological material, most likely DNA (as a virus?), to transfer through the placenta and directly into the developing fetus, which becomes Blade. Many proteins and viruses do not cross the placenta barrier (an example of real DNA that does pass from mother to child is, unfortunately, HIV and AIDS). Whatever vampire DNA was passed on to Blade was not expressed until the onset of puberty ("taken hold at puberty"), linking his "pseudo-vampirism" to hormonal changes.

During his battles with vampires, Blade sustains a variety of wounds that heal themselves within a day, exhibiting fantastically rapid wound-healing mechanisms. The clotting of blood, the recruitment of fibrin and fibrinogen, the cross linking of proteins, and the growth and doubling of new cells to seal up the wound would all have to work within a few hours. Normally, these processes take days. Most human cells double within 24 hours, which is certainly not enough time for millions of cells to form and seal.

Structurally, red blood cells have a biconcave appearance, where the center of the cell is not as thick as the outer periphery of the cell. This is due to a complex network of proteins connected underneath the surface membrane. For vampire RBCs to be just the opposite—"biconvex" (as stated by the pathologist)—it would require the center of the cell to be significantly thicker than the outer edges. For this to happen the cell would have to swell considerably in volume—the equivalent of going from a round flat pillow to a beach ball. There are a number of biochemical transport proteins on the surface of each RBC that keeps the volume of each cell a constant value. These systems could have failed in vampires, with large volumes of water entering each cell and causing the swelling. RBCs of this size would have a difficult time moving through tight capillary vessels, causing clogging and localized pain. Also, a vampire's oxygen exchange for CO_2 may not be as efficient, which could be why they crave blood (to get "healthier" RBCs as a source of hemoglobin or as a source of whole, oxygenated blood).

During the autopsy the pathologist notes a deformed maxilla and "odd muscle structure around the canines." For this to occur in vampires would require new bone synthesis to reshape the maxilla to accommodate the lengthened canine teeth, and the presence of whatever musculature was necessary to allow the lengthening and retraction of these teeth.

Building up resistance to any antigen (in Blade's case, garlic) takes a series of injections, with increasing doses to "tolerize" (i.e., to literally make tolerant) the individual to the particular antigen. Unfortunately, this is also a two-way street, in that you could likewise build up a tolerance to a medication, so that over time you would require a larger dose to get a response. In Blade's case, this affects his resistance to a serum that eliminates his craving for blood; he needs larger and larger doses to stave off his craving.

How could a vampire explode when injected with about 10cc of EDTA? An interesting question. As discussed above, EDTA binds (chelates) various positively charged metal ions, effectively removing them from use. This could be good or bad, depending upon what metal ions were being removed. RBCs have surface proteins that keep an equilibrium between the water inside the cell and outside. When these surface proteins are altered and this equilibrium is significantly changed, dramatic changes can occur with the RBC. When all ions are removed from the outside of RBCs by EDTA, the surface proteins no longer function properly, which allows water to enter cells until they literally burst. This is called cell lysis and is an easy way to eliminate RBCs. When the

vampires are injected with a 10cc volume of EDTA, they explode moments later. For this to happen, the EDTA would have to immediately bind up all the divalent metal cations in the vampire's body, causing the mass destruction of their red blood cells. This mass destruction, or lysis, of trillions of RBCs could have caused their bodies to explode.

In the end, Blade asks the hematologist to help him "make a better serum" that would counteract, suppress, or alter his cravings for blood. First of all, what does he crave? Is it just RBCs, or hemoglobin, or white cells, or the clotting factors and other proteins, or cytokines, or nutrients in serum, or all the above? Each of these would involve different aspects to a developed serum and would be critical for a successful formulation. If Blade simply craves hemoglobin, then this would be the easiest to overcome. He probably needs something as complex as an actual cell, like a red blood cell, so he needs this cell to perform certain biological functions to sustain (vampire) life. Perhaps his RBCs are "biconvex," too big to fit in tight capillaries, and he needs normal RBCs to perform this function (at capillary junctions arteries become veins, oxygen is exchanged for CO_2, and respiration continues). A "better serum" could be composed of the hormone erythropoietin, a hormone that generates new red blood cell production, and used on Blade to enhance his own RBC levels, thereby alleviating the need or "craving" for someone else's blood.

Could It Actually Happen: Vampires, as presented in this film, do not exist, nor would they explode. Allergies to silver and garlic, as well as sensitivity to ultraviolet rays, are somewhat common. Also, EDTA is a commonly used reagent, and I offer my congratulations to the creators of this film for their novel use of it.

7 MICROBIOLOGY

IMMUNOLOGY

The greatest battles of all time were — and are — waged within our bodies. Our cells, tissues, antibodies, cytokines, and other molecules have fought the never ending battle with the antigens of the "evil empire." The "Force" is definitely with our immune system! Cancer, autoimmunity, infectious diseases, and allergies are the major battle fronts that bring into play an impressive number of biochemical ordinance and tactical cellular maneuvers.

Animals have either a natural or acquired resistance to a disease, germ, or antigen. Either a subclinical infection with a stimulating agent, or deliberate immunization (such as with a vaccine) with antigenic substances prepared from it may render a host immune. Because of immunologic memory, the immune state is heightened upon second exposure of individuals to the immunogen. The individual may become immune as a consequence of having experienced and recovered from an infectious disease. An extreme case of subsequent exposure could result in anaphylaxis, a condition of immediate, and potentially life threatening, immune response. (Common examples are those sensitive to bee stings or penicillin.)

Reactions of the animal body to challenge by an immunogen constitute an immune response. This response is expressed as antibody production and/or cell-mediated immunity, or what is collectively called immune tolerance (which is a carefully regulated response of lymphocytes to self antigens). Immune response may follow stimulation by a wide variety of agents, such as pathogenic microorganisms, tissue transplants, or other antigenic substances deliberately introduced for one purpose or another. Infectious agents may also induce inflammatory reactions characterized by the production of chemical mediators, such as cytokines and/or growth factors, at the site of injury.

All in all, the immune response is quite a power unto itself, capable of incredible preciseness and amazing broadness in its various activities.

Man Made Monster (1941)

Synopsis: "Dynamo Dan" McCormick has developed a carnival act that involves giving himself high doses of electricity. Because of his "immunity" to electricity he is

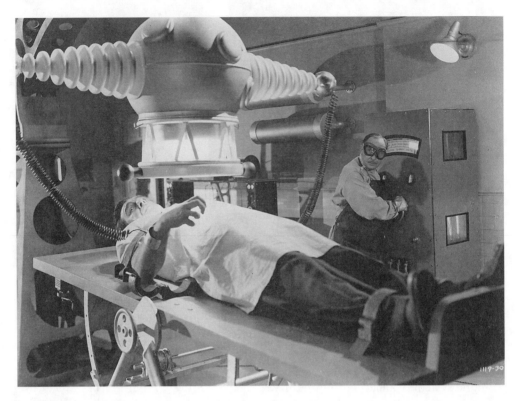

Dynamo Dan (Lon Chaney, Jr.) on the "electrothermostatic table" being given another electrical immunization booster in *Man Made Monster* (1941).

the only survivor on a bus that crashes into a high tension power line. Anyone who super-charged McCormick touches dies. McCormick eventually dies when his insulated suit catches on barbed wire, which drains away his electrical power — and his life.

Screenplay: Joseph West, based on the story "The Electric Man" by H.J. Essex, Sid Schwartz, and Len Golos.

Biological Science Principles Involved: Immunology. Cell Biology. Electrobiology.

What Is Right with the Biological Science Presented: McCormick is known as "Dynamo Dan, the Electrical Man." He developed a carnival act and says, "I fool around with storage batteries and stick my fingers in light sockets, make sparks jump between my hands." This is certainly plausible, though I personally could not do it.

There is no question that some people can handle more electricity than others. (I am reminded of an incident while I was in college. I had a deck of cards "box" that, when opened in a certain way, delivered a good shock from two 1.5 volt AA batteries inside, attached to about 100 yards of wound copper wire. It was quite effective, and I personally could not handle the shock. Well, one of my friends, who went on to become a successful physician, opened the box and just kept on holding it without letting go! I was incredulous. I thought that perhaps the batteries were dead, but I tried it myself afterwards and received the usual uncomfortable shock. This effectively demonstrated to me that some can handle more electricity than others. But I digress...) Like with many things in life (such as our immune systems), some can handle larger doses of antigens than others.

In this respect, all humans have biochemical individuality.

The concept of building up an "immunity" to electrical current is of interest. Over time, with careful control you could handle more electricity. The parallels in immunology are remarkable, and (just like an exposure to an antigen develops a tolerance) more exposure to electricity could result in a build-up of tolerance. During one intelligent exchange between Lawrence (a doctor investigating Dan's electrical "immunity") and McCormick, Lawrence says, "Maybe you've built up an immunity to electricity." McCormick says, "What's that?" Lawrence says, "Immunity? Ordinary fatal doses of electricity can't hurt you." McCormick responds with, "Oh, you mean kinda like I was vaccinated against it." Lawrence says, "Some cellular or glandular changes have taken place which renders you immune. I would like to find out what that is. Just take your blood count, examine your muscular co-ordination, and study your reflexes. If we can find out what it is that produces this immunity against electricity, we might have the means of saving the hundreds of lives lost every year through accidental electrocution." In this context, immunity is meant as "resistance" and not an active process of our body's immune system. In simple terms, it is a useful metaphor or analogy to describe what is observed with McCormick and electricity.

Electrobiology is a real and fascinating aspect of biological science. There is no doubt that electricity influences us all. You need look no further than our own heart, which steadily beats from electrical impulses. Electricity influences us in more ways than suspected, and more and more is being learned about how it affects our lives. During one scene, Lawrence's niece picks up a textbook with the title *Electro Biology* (a nice touch) and says, "When a scientific discovery is announced to the world it must be proved beyond chance." Though that does overstate it a bit, at its core it is true.

While examining a blood sample of McCormick's under a microscope, Rigas (Lawrence's assistant) says to Lawrence, "Seems way below normal in corpuscle count." With all the electrical zapping McCormick gets, this is not surprising at all, and he could have been slightly anemic.

Here is another exchange between the two electrobiologists over Rigas' theories. Lawrence says, "I think you're mad." Rigas responds with, "I am. So was Archimedes, Galileo, Newton, Pasteur, Lister, and all the others who dared to dream. Fifty years ago a man was mad to think of anesthesia. Forty years ago the idea of operating on the brain was madness. Today we hold a human heart in our hands and watch it beat. Who can tell what tomorrow's madness may be." Unfortunately, this is all too true.

What Is Wrong with the Biological Science Presented: The basic premise of this film is McCormick surviving a 100,000-plus volt jolt of electricity from a high tension power line. The five others in the same bus all die from the electricity, and he alone survives. This is not plausible. No matter how immune one is to electricity, a jolt of that magnitude would be fatal.

Rigas, the "mad scientist" in this film, proves it by saying, "I believe that electricity is life. That men can be motivated and controlled by electrical impulse supplied by the radioactivities of the electron. That eventually, races of pure men could be developed, men whose only wants are electricity. By successive treatments their bodies will be so electrolyzed that they are no longer subject to the pains and frailties of ordinary mankind." Well, electrons do not have radioactivities. Radioactivity comes about through the decay of an atom's nucleus, not its electrons. Electricity can be used as a powerful motivator, via cattle prods or tazers, but having electricity as a man's "only wants" is ludicrous. This provides an interesting image of men snacking on a bag of AAA batteries with battery acid dip!

To administer electricity to McCormick, Rigas straps him to a table and attaches electrical leads. At first Rigas gives McCormick 25,000 volts, enough of a jolt to knock anyone on their keester! Dynamo Dan just briefly passes out(!) but quickly recovers and is okay. Rigas gives him enough of a dose to help "build up his immunity." Whenever McCormick tries to touch objects, sparks of electricity come off his fingertips. No way. (Trivia buffs may find it interesting to note that the gauge used here to monitor the voltage is the exact same one later seen in other Universal films, such as *Frankenstein Meets the Wolf Man*.)

Later we see Rigas write in his notebook: "Dan McCormick is a perfect subject for proving my theory. His immunity is growing greater. Today I gave him five times the usual amount of electricity before he fainted." Giving someone enough of anything until they fainted would be a malpractice attorney's dream! Even later Rigas writes: "The subject is slowly but surely coming to depend on the doses of electricity. They are his motivating force. Fainting spells have entirely disappeared. The change is becoming apparent. Without electricity he is a walking shell, waiting for the life-giving current." In effect, Rigas makes McCormick an electricity junkie, existing only for his next fix.

After receiving the maximal electrical dose (at least maximal according to the gauge, since the needle is in the "maximum" red zone), McCormick breaks free of the straps holding him on the table and literally glows. Plain and simple, this glowing is reel biology. (Both phospholuminescense and chemiluminescense, the nat-

ural glowing seen in such organisms as the firefly and deep sea fish, work on entirely different principles.)

Realizing that a man with that much energy has to be somehow contained, Rigas has McCormick put on a rubber suit, which covers him from foot to neck, the rubber acting as an effective insulator. While looking at a glowing McCormick in the rubber suit, Rigas says, "Look at him, the worker of the future, controlled by a superior intelligence." So much for an egomaniac.

Later, when the authorities come to investigate Rigas' lab, they see the elaborate examination table Rigas uses to zap McCormick and ask what it is. Rigas says, "That's an electrothermostatic table. We've succeeded in curing many malignant diseases with electrical heat." Light and some of the heat given off by certain forms of light, such as infrared or ultraviolet, are used in some medical procedures. However, I am not aware of any malignant diseases (i.e., cancer) being "cured" by electrical heat.

About Rigas' notion that men can be controlled by electricity, Lawrence says, "This theory of yours isn't science, it's black magic." Theories are theories and black magic is black magic. A theory is a reasoned explanation of known facts or phenomena that serves as a basis for investigation. There is nothing in that definition that impacts on black magic. Conversely, there is nothing in black magic that has to do with theories; either it works or it doesn't.

What Biological Science Is Necessary to Actually Achieve the Results in the Film: Both the heart and nervous system of humans depend upon the conductance of electrical impulses for proper function. To be able to withstand the amounts of electricity given to Dynamo Dan McCormick would require some extraordinary physiology. Of all the potential problems (other than cardiac and nerve pulses) associated with chronic high dose electricity — like the destruction of hair follicles (electrolysis) — the most life threatening would be electrodesiccation, which is the destruction of blood vessels (usually in the skin but also in the surfaces of mucous membranes). Monopolar high frequency electrical currents will damage blood vessels, resulting in severe debilitation that could threaten the life of the subject. Perhaps Dynamo Dan had extra fat pads or thicker sheaths surrounding his nerve fibers to withstand the excessive electricity he received.

Lawrence comments to McCormick that "some cellular or glandular changes have taken place which renders you immune." The cellular changes would have to involve some ability to channel the electricity to other sources. Perhaps McCormick has the ability to effectively ground himself, thereby allowing the electricity to harmlessly dissipate to other structures. In the body are electrolytes, which are compounds that conduct electricity in solution. Perhaps McCormick had an excessive amount of electrolytes in his blood, tissues, and cells that acted as a buffer of sorts, enabling him to withstand higher voltages. Since proteins themselves can be considered electrolytes (they are electrically charged in the body's fluids), then McCormick may have had mutated proteins that could also absorb excessive electricity and, in essence, "render him immune."

Could It Actually Happen: As stated, there are some individuals who can handle more electricity than others. Though you may be able to handle more, you will not glow as a result. However, like anything, given a significant enough dose, even those with a high immunity will suffer the consequences. It is unknown, however, if someone can actually build up an extensive immunity to electricity.

The Brain Eaters (1958)

Synopsis: A cone-shaped object from the Carboniferous Period (about 300 million years ago!) appears out of the earth. Inside the object are hairy parasites whose mission is to take over the world. To control humans, the parasites attach themselves to the back of people's necks. The cone is eventually electrified, thereby killing all the parasites inside.

Screenplay: Gordon Urquhart (it is suspiciously similar to Robert Heinlein's famous book *The Puppet Masters*).

Biological Science Principles Involved: Parasitology. Biochemistry.

What Is Right with the Biological Science Presented: One of the first humans attacked by a parasite is the town's mayor, which makes sense; if you control those who control the town, then you control the town. After the mayor dies, Dr. Kettering performs an autopsy on him and discovers the parasite attached to the back of his neck. In describing the parasite, Kettering says, "That thing on the back of the mayor's neck had two piercing instruments. They attached themselves to the central nervous system at the base of the neck. We don't know how it worked, but when the thing was crushed and the instruments withdrawn, they secreted something in the form of an acid, and this acid destroyed the mayor's nervous system. So … death would have ensued in about 24 to 48 hours — just enough time for the acid to do its work. Once this thing attaches itself to the victim's back, well, the victim isn't human anymore." All of this is interesting and very descriptive. The parasites attaching themselves directly to the victim's nervous system would allow precise control over the body's thoughts and movements. The use of acid to kill the victim is an interesting survival mechanism. The acid could work like a venom by destroying the myelin sheaths surrounding nerve fibers, thereby effectively killing the human victim. Some venoms and acids are slow acting on tissues, so the 24 to 48 hour time frame seems reasonable.

After cutting off a piece of a parasite, Kettering observes that it is still moving. His assistant asks, "How long can it do that?" Kettering responds, "Until the cellular structure begins to break down I suppose." Though true, this would also apply to just about all biological specimens. When the cellular structure breaks down, all you are left with is a pulpy mess that will eventually dehydrate.

Kettering adds, "In feeding, the mouth parts rupture the cells, convey the food to the stomach by a pumping action." There are many species on earth that use this process for feeding, so this is accurate. Insects, arthropods, and others (like starfish) all feed in this way. While saying this, a piece of a parasite gloms onto Kettering's forearm and (painfully) begins to rupture his skin. Kettering, ever the quick thinker, takes a nearby lit Bunsen burner and burns off the creature. Those lit Bunsen burners do come in handy at times!

Later in the film, Kettering explains to an investigating team, "They're parasites. That means they need something or someone to live on. On their own, most parasites would die." All true. The Mayor's son then says, "They [the parasites] tried animals. Why didn't they settle on animals?" Kettering responds with, "That's the rub, they wanted more than just life. They tried animals through ignorance. They didn't understand earthly form, didn't know which animal, including man, was best suited for this environment, so they experimented. Trial and error." Kettering's assistant says, "You mean they can think? They chose the mayor; that shows they can think." This is an interesting exchange, and it demonstrates that these parasites are intelligent enough to manipulate their environment.

Physically, the parasites appear to be about 8 inches long, about 2 inches wide, and are covered with fur/hair. On the front they have two long white "antennae," which they use to puncture the backs of their victims' necks. These puncture holes are about one inch apart and about one third the distance below the hair line, near the C2 to C4 cervical vertebrae. It sounds ridiculous, but these parasites make a hissing sound. The parasites are carried around in glass jars filled with milky white liquid. This fluid is probably a food source and contains appropriate nutrients for them to feed on.

Later in the film, a man, Professor Helsingborg (a "professor of biochemistry"; cinema biochemists are a special breed!), comes out of the cone after being in there for five years. He has a parasite attached to him. Shortly after surfacing, the parasite leaves him. When asked why the parasite left the professor's body, Kettering says, "A car with a bad engine, would you buy it? He's got a bad heart. It's the same thing." This also demonstrates the intelligence of the parasites. When a body no longer serves them or does not function properly, they abandoned it, as in the case of the professor. This is also true with real parasites. If their host is dying they will seek out a new host.

What Is Wrong with the Biological Science Presented: While dissecting a parasite, Kettering wears no gloves to protect his hands from its acids. He should have been completely covered. While doing the dissecting, Kettering says to his assistant, "This is a piece we got off the Mayor. Reflex action like a snake. Cut a snake in half and the two pieces go off in different directions." No, cut a snake in half and it dies. However, a worm called a planaria will go off in two different directions when cut in half.

After the parasite leaves Professor Helsingborg, and just before he dies, he talks about the parasites. Kettering asks him, "Are the parasites from the cone?" Helsingborg confirms this and says, "200 million years ago the coal and oil forming period began. Geologists refer to it as the Carboniferous Age. It was the age of insects, giant dragonflies, two feet in wingspread. All kinds of insects, mammoth in size." The quick-witted mayor's son then asks, "You mean the parasites are from the earth? They survived in the earth all this time?" The good professor must have realized how utterly ludicrous this is, because he dies right after this, failing to answer any more questions. First of all, let's get our geology right. The Carboniferous Period is in the latter part of the Paleozoic Era, between 285 and 360 million years ago; 200 million years ago was the Jurassic Period in the Mesozoic Era. The Professor should stick to his biochemistry. The Carboniferous Period, so named because of the extensive coal deposits in rocks of that age, was indeed the time when the first amphibians and reptiles appeared. (Coal is the carbonaceous residue of plant matter that has been preserved and altered by heat and pressure.) Since all organic matter of that period is now coal (or oil), there is no way biological life could have survived that long!

What Biological Science Is Necessary to Actually Achieve the Results in the Film: It is unsure what it would take to have a functioning biological life form exist under the earth for 300 million years. Not only is this a life form, but it is a parasite at that, meaning that for it to survive it must have a host. What kind of host could survive along with this 300-million-year-old parasite? Perhaps the parasites were in some sort of suspended animation in a pocket of protective rock that, as a result of geologic activity, comes to the surface in 1958. OK, then how to explain the metal, cone-shaped "home" for the parasites? From time to time the parasites could

have come to the surface to search for new hosts, but not for 300 million years!

Could It Actually Happen: Parasites are indeed everywhere, and we do not want to get rid of those that are actually beneficial to various species. In this respect, some parasites are necessary.

You need not worry about 300-million-year-old Carboniferous parasites coming up from the ground and attaching themselves to the backs of our necks. (This reminds me of an incident involving my daughter. She had a case of ringworm, a fungal parasite called tinea that infects the keratin component of hair, skin, or nails. Tinea is easy to treat. She had a quarter-sized lesion on the back of her neck, just below the hair line, near the C3 cervical neck vertebrae — and I wondered if it was the mark of a "Brain Eater!")

INFECTIOUS DISEASES

An infection is a multiplication of some sort of parasitic organism (a virus or a bacterium can also be considered a parasite) within a body. This organism typically enters, invades, or inhabits another body, causing infection and/or contamination. Some infections take over the entire body, and others affect a specific organ, like the brain, lungs, or liver. The world's most deadliest infectious disease is tuberculosis. Approximately one third of all people on Earth are infected with tuberculosis, and about three million die every year from this disease!

The Angry Red Planet (1959)

Synopsis: A rocket expedition goes to Mars, and her crew of four encounter carnivorous plants, a giant creature called a bat-rat-spider-crab, and a huge amoeba/jellyfish–like organism. Of the crew, two die, one is "infected" with Martian life,

The bat-rat-spider-crab creatures found on Mars (aka *The Angry Red Planet*, 1959). The interaction of a variety of DNA elements (genes) from a variety of species could give rise to such creatures.

and the fourth is in shock. The woman in shock recovers and tells of their expedition in flashback.

Screenplay: Sid Pink and Ib Melchior.

(Note: Man has had a love affair with the planet Mars for centuries. Earth's interest peaked when Percival Lowell described "canals" on its surface and thought of sophisticated cultures and bizarre life forms. Ray Bradbury's *Martian Chronicles* ushered in another burst of interest, and during the summer of 1998, when the Mars Rover kissed the rock "Yogi," earthmen once again dreamed of what secrets that planet has yet in store for us. I envy those lucky ones who will some day place footprints on its soil.)

Biological Science Principles Involved: Microbiology. Infectious Disease. Biochemistry.

What Is Right with the Biological Science Presented: After landing, Professor Gitelle, the "designer of the Mars rocket and world's foremost authority on space and rocketry" (and who smokes a pipe on board the flight!), says to Dr. Ryan, the "brilliant young authority on the sciences of biology and zoology": "You take a microbe count." That is exactly what should be done. Assess what type of life forms are present before walking on the surface.

While Ryan is doing the microbe count, Gitelle says to O'Banyon, "The atmosphere is pretty much like we thought — thin, extremely thin. Not enough oxygen to sustain us, but undoubtedly enough for some kind of native animal life." (Right after this O'Banyon says to Jacobs, when looking out a window at the Martian surface shortly after they land, "With all that vegetation out there, there's bound to be something alive." On

Mars, apparently, plant vegetation is not considered "alive!")

One of my all-time favorite SF creatures is the "bat-rat-spider-crab" seen in this film. The only reason I mention this creature in this section is not because it could literally exist, but to demonstrate the point that life on other planets will indeed be combinations of what we are familiar with. Legs, body armor, appendages, eyes, hair/fur coverings, etc., are essential parts of biology, and, to be sure, the combinations of these will be unique to each planet's life forms.

Regarding the giant amoeba that attacks the crew and the rocket ship, Ryan says, "I'm sure its a unicellular animal. The two areas inside it must be the nucleus and the contractile vacuoles. Like an amoeba, a giant amoeba. One single cell without intelligence, without a nervous system at all. Reacts completely on instinct to external stimuli. The amoeba engulfs its prey and digests it with extremely strong acids." This is all true of amoebas. However, this one is larger than the rocket ship! They eventually escape by sending a large electric current to the hull of the ship, which repels the amoeba, suggesting that it is sensitive to electricity (like much of life on Earth).

Back on Earth the doctors examine O'Banyon's infected arm. Dr. Gordon says, "An enzymatic reaction. A minute particle of the amoeba creature must have reached Tom's skin, and it's growing, literally eating his tissues." The use of electricity to repel the amoeba on Mars gives the doctors a clue about how to fight the infected arm. Gordon says, "Any kind of electric shock strong enough to kill the amoeba will also kill Tom." Ryan then says, "We've been attacking the alien amoeba as if it were a disease. But it isn't. It's an animal, an animal with instincts. And the most important of all, a will to act." Gordon replies, "It only makes it harder to destroy." Ryan then

says, "And gives it a vulnerability we also have, that of making the wrong choice. Look, we have two identical tissue cultures there, both infested with our own microscopic amoeba and placed very close to each other. One we left alone. The other we subjected to light, periodic electric shocks. Before long, all the amoeba on the irritated culture had made their choice. They moved to the nearby undisturbed culture." Gordon answers, "Then that is what we have to do. We will prepare a large tissue culture and place it next to the infected arm, then subject Tom to electric shocks, just short of being harmful to him." In doing this, the infecting amoeba leaves O'Banyon's arm and he is "saved." (Please note that the use of the phrase "tissue culture" is a misnomer here. It would have been more appropriate if they had said "agar plates" or "cell culture media," since amoeba are not thought of as tissues.)

During the film's final fade-out, we see O'Banyon awake and lying on a hospital bed. At the foot of his bed is a chart that reads "Temperature Chart" and shows a gradual decline in his temperature, suggesting that he spiked a temperature during his "infection," and when "saved" his temperature slowly returned to normal.

What Is Wrong with the Biological Science Presented: The first view of the rocket and her crew is on their return journey to Earth. After landing, the recovery team grabs Ryan as she exits the ship. These recovery personnel have no gloves, helmets, suits, or masks on. So much for sterility and caution for the recovery crew. O'Banyon has some sort of green, jelly-like substance on his arm — obviously some sort of infection/contamination — and the surrounding people take no special precautions. While looking at O'Banyon's arm, the recovery manager says, "Anything that can be done for him will be done." Ryan responds with, "How can anyone cope with that?" So much for confidence.

While doctors are examining O'Banyon's infected arm, they have the following interesting dialogue exchange. Doc Number One says, "Dr. Gordon, that growth. What are we up against?" Gordon replies, "I don't know." Doc Number Two then says, "It's spreading rapidly." Doc Number One says, "Do you have any idea what it might be?" Gordon replies, "No, I haven't ... yet. If we only knew how or by what he was infected with we might know how to combat the disease, but we are working in the dark." While this dialogue is going on, Gordon takes off his examination gloves and drops them into a bag a nurse (ungloved and unmasked) is holding. All in all, very poor containment conditions for a potentially serious infectious disease. While the doctors are busily contaminating everything with O'Banyon's infection, the General, in an amazing fit of sobriety, says, "Suppose this alien infection spreads to all of us. Every moment counts." That is why he is the General.

Storage space and cargo capacity is severely limited inside space capsules. Astronaut Alan Shepard went to great lengths just to bring a golf ball and club on board his flight to the moon. Weight is that precious. Well, the Mars flight "electronics and radar expert," Sam Jacobs, is seen reading the pulp digest magazine *Super Fantastic Science Fiction Stories* on board! On the cover of this issue is a large creature chasing a girl and the following captions "The Monster and the Martian Maid," "Loathsome Beasts," and "Weird Monster." Perfect reading material for a lengthy journey to Mars.

As ridiculous as this sounds, the Mars crew are all wearing street shoes on the flight, and they continue to wear them when they walk on the surface of Mars! It is unknown what microorganisms were brought along with them and left in their shoe prints on Mars.

On the surface of Mars we see an extensive and diverse plant life. Shrubs, palm fronds, trees, ground cover, moss, ferns, leaves, vines, etc., are everywhere. Ryan examines a plant leaf and says, "All the characteristics of plant life but hardly any chlorophyll. And there seems to be an indication of a nervous system." Yes, plants are green because of chlorophyll, and chlorophyll is green because of the magnesium ion held in the heme groups (similar to [red] iron held in blood heme). However, these heme groups more than likely have a different metal ion, because they are a different color, so Ryan's comment that Mars' plants have "hardly any chlorophyll" is incorrect. Also, just by looking, there is no way she could have concluded that Mars' plants have a "nervous system."

Later, Ryan spots a large Venus fly trap-like plant and approaches for a close look. The plant moves a foot-like tentacle, which wraps around Ryan and pulls her into its leaves. Then the plant makes growling noises! After being rescued, Ryan says, "A giant carnivorous plant that feeds by trapping animals and digesting them live." (They also find bones [!] at the base of the plant. This should have been a remarkable discovery. If there are bones, then there was a body that covered the bones. And if there is a body, then this is a bona fide Martian "animal!") After examining the plant, Gitelle says, "This is more than just a plant. It's a low form of neuromuscular vegetable creature." Gitelle should stick to his rocketry work and not deal with biology.

Back on the spaceship O'Banyon asks, "What could control all life here?" Ryan replies, "It could be some super intelligent community mind, I suppose." (?!?!) Gitelle adds, "Like the inexplicable mysterious control which keeps a colony of ants functioning in perfect unity back on Earth." (As stated, the professor should stick to rocketry!)

While exploring again, the crew comes upon an enormous lake, which has "no abnormal radiation." They all get in an inflatable rubber boat and row out on the surface. Large buildings, about "...a half mile tall," are seen at the opposite shore. Ryan puts her gloved hand in the water and says, "feels kind of oily. Heavier than ordinary water." Gitelle says, "It probably has an entirely different mineral content." (Way to go, professor!) Ryan adds, "I am sure it couldn't sustain life. At least life as we know it." Well, a large amoeboid creature comes out of the lake and attacks the crew. The amoeba chases them and they rush back to the rocket ship. As they are entering the ship the amoeba surrounds it and while closing the door, Jacobs is caught by the creature and ingested, clothes and all. Part of the creature touches O'Banyon's arm and eats right through the clothes and skin. This is the infection O'Banyon brings back to Earth with him.

What Biological Science Is Necessary to Actually Achieve the Results in the Film: For bona fide life as we know it to exist on Mars, it would require the ability to exist at extremes of temperature, with a minimal availability of water, and in a drastically reduced oxygen atmosphere. Of the three, the extreme of temperature is the easiest, closely followed by scarcity of water. Here on earth, biological life, both plant and animal, does exist within the North and South poles and in the driest of deserts. Adaptive mechanisms and behaviors have evolved over the millennia to permit life to exist at these extremes. Oxygen "shortage" on Mars is a problem and would take some very special and unusual biochemistry to permit complex life forms to exist. However, here on Earth we have anaerobic bacteria that exist without oxygen and in an oxygen-free environment. There are even life forms on Earth that exist by consuming sulfur instead of oxygen. If complex life forms evolved on Mars based on the biochemical principles of anaerobic bacteria, then perhaps something interesting could live there.

Giant unicellular amoebas existing on Mars are an interesting concept. The diminished gravity on Mars, combined with the lessened partial pressure of the atmosphere, could allow larger unicellular organisms to exist. What primarily limits their size is the fragility of their plasma membrane, that part of the cell that holds everything together (much like a sack holds all of its contents inside). Should the sack tear, then its contents would come out. Even considering all this, an amoeba about the size of a five story building is just too much to justify.

Assuming this amoeba does exist, there is no problem with it ingesting and digesting unfortunate Sam Jacobs, clothes and all. Something that size would have developed biochemical mechanisms to allow it to digest all sorts of things, since when it slithers around on land it would pick up a variety of debris, which it would need to handle.

The use of electricity in dealing with this amoeba is interesting. All biological organisms do respond to electricity in one way or another. If the charge is significant enough, then cells and organisms will move away (assuming they can). This could have been a very neat way of getting the infecting amoeba part off of O'Banyon's arm. However, the concern is if some of the amoeba DNA is able to successfully integrate into his cells and tissues, then what, if any, would be the consequences? He should have been kept in quarantine isolation for some time to see what would happen. Who knows what alien DNA would do when combined with human DNA.

Could It Actually Happen: Man will some day leave footprints on the surface of Mars. Unfortunately, a biologist need not come along, since no life will be found there. In theory, much of what is talked about could happen, but in reality it won't. Alack and alas. No "five armed ongollas" will appear, as suggested by Sam Jacobs, the pulp sci-fi reader of the Mars rocket ship crew.

"Space Brain" Episode of *Space: 1999* (January 1976)

Though the films discussed in this book were first shown on the big screen at your local movie theater, the following is an exception, it is an episode of *Space: 1999*, and first shown on the small screen in January, 1976. This is the only TV episode discussed in this book and the reason is quite simple. My scientific field of expertise is with antibodies, and this particular episode discusses that specific topic in an interesting way. To be sure, there are quite a number of other television series and episodes that deal with interesting aspects of biology, but this episode in particular deals with antibodies, so it is included.

For those of you not familiar with the program, the premise of the TV series *Space: 1999* is a simple one. The Earth's moon is used as a nuclear waste storage dump. After about a 20-year buildup of accumulated atomic waste, all the radioactive material explodes on September 13, 1999, sending the moon and its inhabitants out of Earth's orbit to wander in space, experiencing one adventure after another. Those who live on the moon are inhabitants of a colony called Moonbase Alpha.

Space: 1999—"Space Brain" episode (first aired in USA during January, 1976)

Synopsis: A gossamer-like space organism called a "space anemone" threatens to destroy Moonbase Alpha. It has already destroyed a space ship and possessed the mind of one of the crewmen. As a defense mechanism, the organism sends out foamy material called antibodies to those on Moonbase Alpha. The moon and the colony are covered with this antibody foam. Eventually, the moon steers clear of the space organism, avoiding a collision.

Teleplay: Christopher Penfold.

Biological Science Principles Involved: Immunology. Biochemistry.

What Is Right with the Biological Science Presented: After the inhabitants realize that the Moonbase is being contacted by some sort of organism, a scout space ship is sent to investigate. The pilot reports, "It's like a giant space anemone. It's pulsating. Strange shapes falling around us." In an immune response, when the host organism perceives some sort of threat it mounts an appropriate response, typically in the form of antibodies to attack the "threat." This organism behaves in this fundamental way. It thinks the scout ship is a threat and sends the equivalent of "space antibodies" to neutralize it. The "strange shapes" are wispy tendrils, like cobwebs, that attach to the ship and completely coat it, thereby rendering it "harmless." Basically, this is an immune-like response on a planetary scale! It was pretty neat by TV standards.

What Is Wrong with the Biological Science Presented: The space anemone sends a meteorite to the moon. It is retrieved and brought inside the Moonbase for analysis. The meteorite looks like a four-to-five foot in diameter rock with some yellow spaghetti-like noodle strings wrapped around it. The base physician/scientist reports, "I've got some early findings on this stuff [the noodle strings]. It's a piece of the coating that I took from the surface of this meteorite. It's organic." The commander says, "Alive?" After an affirmative, Victor the physicist says, "Weight, 328 tons[!]; essential elements—

titanium, stainless steel, aluminum, glass, carbon filters, plastics, nuclear fuel cells, and a small amount of human tissue." That meteorite is certainly well traveled!

A Moonbase pilot, Kelly, goes on a space walk to investigate the space anemone. Some of the wispy antibody material gets onto him and takes over his mind. A doctor says, "Those brain patterns [of Kelly's] are fantastic for a man who's totally anesthetized. His brain activity is phenomenal, but his breathing is back to normal." Another doctor says, "His heart and lungs have adjusted to what is going on inside his brain. He's suffering these non-stop flow of impulses and ideas because that part of his cerebellum which controls his will is failing its function. My hope is to stimulate the cerebellum and restore balance. Now, if we don't achieve that very soon he will simply burn himself up." Though it sounds interesting, it is completely wrong. Later, Kelly is awakened and says, "What's happening? You must not touch my brain." Too bad TV is so formulaic.

The antibody material itself looks like foam. Victor the physicist says, "It's the same material we found that crushed [the space ship]. It's reverted back to its original form ... but it's highly unstable. We don't know why, but its chemical structure changes. It gains incredible weight and density. In sufficient quantity, this foam as you call it could crush anything." Imagine, an antibody, a protein, that has those properties! Antibodies are not unstable, but remarkably stable (even under very harsh conditions). Though their chemical structure does indeed change, primarily because of genetic variability (there can be up to 10^{15} different forms!), they do not physically change as implied in this episode. Antibodies certainly do not "gain incredible weight and density"; for that matter, nothing does! To do so is beyond biology and physics as we know it. There

is a concession though, that if a "sufficient quantity" of antibody fell on a human, say 10,000 kilograms, it would crush you!

The base commander eventually figures out that the space anemone is trying to make the moon avoid a collision with a force field, and the antibody foam is a signal. The commander says, "It's a living organism. Like a brain. Pulsating with life and light. It's the center of a whole galaxy. Maybe even hundreds of galaxies, planets, stars, strange life forms. And in the middle of it all is this brain." An interesting way to describe a galaxy!

The commander further says, "...hurtling towards that brain is our moon. Now, the [destroyed space ship] was just a fragment, so the brain surrounded it with antibodies and rejected it. But our moon is a million times bigger than that." The space brain then sends wispy antibodies and a huge amount of foam coats the moon and the base. Some of the wispy antibody foam completely bypasses the moon, does not touch it, and continues out into empty space (where does it go?). The moon eventually goes through the space brain, and the antibody bombardment stops. The Moonbase Alpha crew has an incredible amount of antibody foam to clean up, and where do they put all that, since there is literally tons of it everywhere?

What Biological Science Is Necessary to Actually Achieve the Results in the Film: To stimulate an immune response, an antigen must be present and recognized as such. In this episode, the scout space ship is recognized by the space anemone as the "antigen," and the foam antibodies attack it. Later, this same space anemone recognizes the moon as the "antigen" and sends antibodies after it too. This is all reasonable. Antigens do come in many sizes and shapes. They can be as small as a few molecules to something as large and complex as an intact cell. Using this analogy, the scout ship was a small "molecule" and the moon was an "intact cell." There is some internal logic to this, and it makes sense.

What is unknown here is the behavior of antibodies in the vacuum of space. When water molecules and air are removed from proteins (an antibody is a protein), they form different crystal structures (and revert to their natural shape when remixed with water). Also, when proteins are rapidly mixed with air (or oxygen), they form bubbles. What happens here is that oxygen causes the protein molecules to lose their natural shape or conformation, sort of like foaming action, though not as extreme. When the wispy antibody molecules from the space anemone/brain enter the Moonbase, the oxygen in the air causes it to foam. Since this foam is also seen on the surface of the moon, then when the wispy material comes in contact with anything it immediately foams. This bit of biology would require the waving of a magic wand, since there are no known examples of this occurring.

Could It Actually Happen: The premise of *Space: 1999*, that our moon could leave earth's orbit and aimlessly wander the cosmos, is absurd. Though the idea of storing nuclear waste on the moon is an interesting one, the expense of doing so would be prohibitive. Furthermore, the atomic explosion massive enough to rip the moon away from Earth's gravity would have to be so enormous that it would also rip apart the moon.

Coming in contact with alien life forms that perceive humans as "antigens" and mount some sort of anti-antigen defense (aka antibodies) is plausible. In this case, antibodies are used figuratively and not literally, though the principle is the same.

PARASITOLOGY

Parasitic diseases constitute one of the most serious health problems of today. It has been estimated that over one billion humans have been infected by some sort of parasite. That is an incredible statistic. In almost all cases, parasites come from contaminated water and foods.

A parasite is an organism that lives on or in another and draws its nourishment from its host. There are quite a number of different parasites; some are beneficial and some are harmful. The beneficial ones are referred to as having a commensal relationship with the host. In commensalism, a symbiotic relationship is established in which one species derives benefit and the other is unharmed. For example, the bacteria that inhabit the intestines of humans help in food digestion and some vitamin production. Another beneficial relationship is called mutualism, which is a symbiotic relationship in which both species derive benefit. Metabiosis is a form of parasitism in which one species is dependent on another for existence and survival. Symbiosis is the association of two or more species for their mutual benefit. In reality, most parasitism is multiple, in that parasites from many species parasitize a single host. It's sort of like my three children (all different species!) constantly parasitizing me, the host.

As you can imagine, the host-parasite relationship is amazingly complex. The mechanisms by which parasites evade a host's immune system, their complicated life cycles, and other survival traits are testaments to the strong hold these organisms have.

Major groups of human parasites consist of protozoa, nematodes, trematodes, cestodes, and arthropods. Protozoa are single-celled organisms that have a complex functional system capable of reproduction, digestion, respiration, and excretion. Examples are malaria, toxoplasmosis, and pneumocystis.

Nematodes are worms, such as flatworms and roundworms. These organisms are multicellular. Examples of diseases are hookworm, trichinosis, and ascariasis.

Trematodes are flukes, so named because of their prominent suckers. The only ones that are a problem for humans are the digenetic trematodes, which reproduce sexually in adults and asexually in larvae stages. All of these digenetic forms are leaf-shaped and are hermaphrodites (both male and female reproductive organs are present in each worm). The best known example causes schistosomiasis.

Cestodes are commonly called tapeworms because of their ribbon-like appearance. Their length varies greatly and can be from microscopic to 15 meters long!

Parasitic arthropods are ticks, mites, bedbugs, fleas, and some flies and mosquitoes.

Dark Breed (1996)

Synopsis: A space shuttle with six astronauts on board crashes into the water near a Long Beach wharf. The astronauts are infected with a space parasite that gives the humans incredible strength and the ability to shape change. The infected astronauts are eventually located and destroyed, with the help of another alien.

Screenplay: Richard Preston, Jr.

Biological Science Principles Involved: Parasitology. Physiology. Molecular Biology.

What Is Right with the Biological Science Presented: The comments above on parasites and parasitism apply here. As astronaut Cutter says, "The whole [shuttle] crew is infected. I don't know how." Though a cop-out for an explanation, it is effective in dismissing a lot of (expensive) action that would have been nice to see. (How did they get infected?)

While holed up in a warehouse, the infected astronauts talk amongst themselves. At this time the parasites have not yet taken full possession of their biological functions, so the astronauts know what is happening to them. They talk about being "possessed," and one of them says, "They can control us at will. They are parasites, we're the hosts." At least they are cognizant enough to know the score.

During a realistic autopsy on a burned infected astronaut, Dr. Kline performs the typical y-shaped surgical procedure to open the chest cavity to begin her examination. After she opens the chest cavity area, the internal organs are actually seen to move! Some creature with a prehensile tail jumps out, à la *Alien*, and attacks the doctor, though she remains unharmed. The creature then immediately decomposes. After the doctor calms herself, she says, "I know why Omega [a government organization trying to capture the creatures] wants one of these organisms. My God, full grown, they'd be incredible killing machines." Though I personally do not like the philosophy of this, it is an accurate statement, and I wonder what programs and/or agencies the government actually has to look into these things.

A "good alien parasite," called "a Watcher," whose job is "to destroy the dark breed," explains to Dr. Kline where they came from. The "Watcher" says, "My race were once parasites, with conscience, infesting the galaxy, moving from host world to host world. We were a cruel and murderous race in the old days. We changed, became a society of peace." Kline asks, "How long to they [the parasites] require the host body?" Watcher replies, "It takes 84 hours for their bodies to reach maturity and for them to adjust to the new environment." Kline then asks, "Can I assume that the dark breed require the body for the entire incubation period?" The Watcher says, "Yes. If they leave the body prematurely it means near instant death." (What is "near instant death?" Is it the opposite of "far away from a lingering death?") This does make internal sense within the confines of the film's premise.

What Is Wrong with the Biological Science Presented: The infected astronauts have super-strength, while not appearing overly muscular; it must be quality, not quantity. When the astronauts try to escape in a stolen van, a military man shoots a bazooka at it, blowing it up. The astronauts are not harmed in the action.

The infected astronauts have reptile-like eyes, in that the opening of the iris is vertical and not round, as in a human eye. This would imply that the parasite does more than simply live within the natural biology of the host; they also take over and radically alter physiology.

One of the astronauts is in another car crash and ends up in a hospital emergency room in a coma-like state. Something crawls down *inside* of his right arm. He partially awakens, then something (which looks like a spine with bones, tendons, etc.) crawls up inside his neck to his head. He convulses, then fully awakes. He demonstrates incredible strength and is shot several times while escaping, indicating that whatever possesses him is capable of handling severe trauma without suffering any biological consequences.

In previous chapters I discussed the biological problems and limitations of shape-changing, sometimes called allometric growth. The infected astronauts show remarkable abilities to rapidly metamorphose into *Predator*-like creatures. During one scene one of the creatures "hatches" out of an infected astronaut. The alien's prehensile tail comes out of the coccyx area of the astronaut first, followed by the rest of its body. The creature's head is large, with a ribbed exoskull. It also has small arms and hands with talon-like claws and sharp nails. The jaws open and a whip like tongue comes out. The creature's face looks very similar to the alien in the film *Predator*. The most incredulous part of all this is that the alien's body is larger than the astronaut's body from which it just hatched, representing remarkable accelerated growth!

What Biological Science Is Necessary to Actually Achieve the Results in the Film: Parasites being parasites, they would have a difficult time altering human biology in the way shown. To justify much of what is seen with the infected astronauts, the parasites themselves could have some type of virus infection that they transmit to the humans. Alien viral DNA could do all sorts of things. It could have been this virus(es) that alters human physiology, and not the parasite itself. Or, more probable, the parasite itself acts in unison with the virus (or viruses) in some sort of symbiotic relationship to bring about the observed changes.

It is interesting that the infected astronauts have reptile-like eyes. The iris is vertical and oval in shape. This type of eye structure would be useful to "see" different aspects of the electromagnetic spectrum above and beyond the frequency of visible light. Perhaps they are heat sensors or can detect infrared light, thereby giving them an interesting survival characteristic.

Could It Actually Happen: Sadly, a space shuttle has already crashed, though none of the astronauts survived. Whenever man does encounter other life forms, parasites, and "unfriendly DNA" will be a serious problem, one which we will have to deal with in some sort of real way.

Shape-shifting and hyper allometric growth will not happen. Human physiological limitations are too inhibitory.

VIROLOGY

A virus is a term used to describe a group of infectious agents that are unable to grow or reproduce separately from living cells. Virology is a very broad based discipline, which includes the domains of molecular biologists, geneticists, pharmacologists, microbiologists, immunologists, and epidemiologists.

The field of virology is quite complex and has a large nomenclature, or classification, associated with it. Viruses are classified by host (e.g., plant, insect, rodent, bird), by disease, or by vector (e.g., arboviruses).

There are also viruses that are primarily animal viruses that accidentally infect humans. Examples are some forms of herpesviruses and rabies virus.

To further classify viruses, they can be described as being DNA viruses (e.g., poxviruses, herpes viruses, and parvoviruses), RNA viruses (e.g., rotavirus, reovirus), DNA and RNA viruses (e.g., hepatitis B virus and lentivirus, more commonly known as HIV), and subviral agents, such as viroids, satellites (hepatitis D), and prions (Creutzfeldt-Jakob disease).

To be sure, as time goes on, new viruses will be created and/or developed that will cause global catastrophic and epidemic problems. Most of these viruses will be contained and controlled.

Last Man on Earth (1964)

Synopsis: A plague ravages mankind, and the sole survivor is Robert Morgan. The plague turns those infected into vampire-like zombies. The zombie vampires only come out at night, which leaves the daytime available for Morgan to explore and defend himself. In the end, the zombies kill Morgan.

Screenplay: Logan Swanson and William F. Leicester, from the novel *I Am Legend* by Richard Matheson. (Note: The name Logan Swanson is a nom de plume for Matheson. He was unhappy with the film, so he used a fictitious name in the credits.)

Biological Science Principles Involved: Virology. Immunology. Microbiology. Biochemistry.

What Is Right with the Biological Science Presented: Mankind has been affected by various plagues since recorded history, and the Old Testament of the Bible describes several of these. Moses inflicted

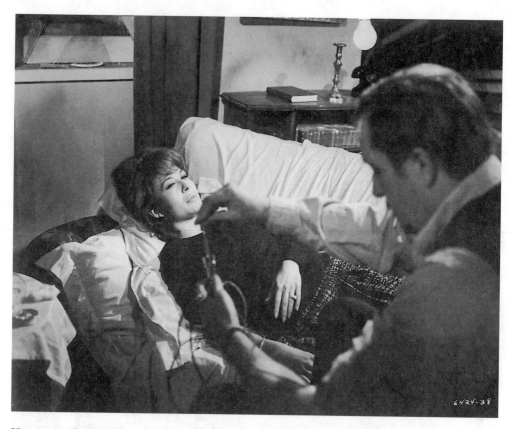

Human antibodies at work. As the *Last Man on Earth* (1964), Morgan (Vincent Price, right) transfuses his blood and serum, which contain antibodies (in essense, he is transferring his "immune system"). Currently, therapeutic protocols are being implemented that use human antibodies and other aspects of the human immune system and the results are very promising. Morgan was ahead of his time.

plague on Pharaoh Ramses II before the Exodus. In modern times some would call AIDS and HIV a plague. Let us examine what a plague is.

A plague is any disease of wide prevalence that results in excessive mortality or death. The best examples are the plagues of the Middle Ages that decimated Europe, in which the bacterium *Yersinia pestis* was transmitted to man by the fleas of rodents, primarily rats (rats have yet to live down that reputation). Clinically, plague sufferers show signs of high fever, toxemia, prostration, minute hemorrhagic spots that erupt, lymph node enlargement, pneumonia, and hemorrhage from mucous membranes. All in all, it is an ugly

way to go. In man, plague comes in four different forms: bubonic (the most common, marked by extensive inflammation of internal tissues and glands), septicemic (a generally fatal form with high levels of bacteria growth and excessive toxemia; the toxemia comes from breakdown products of bacteria, commonly called endotoxins), pneumonic (a progressive and generally fatal form marked by excessive buildup of fluids in the lungs, which makes it hard to breathe, chills, high fever, and bloody fluids coming from the mouth), and ambulant (a mild form of bubonic plague marked by mild fever and tissue swelling).

The plague of this film appears to be bacterial. Once infected, humans behave like vampires in that they only come out at night, are repelled by garlic, and cannot look in mirrors. If you accept the premise of vampires, then the plot of this film makes sense. Furthermore, the infected vampire humans are physically and mentally weak, like an animal after a long famine, since they walk slowly and are lethargic. Most likely they ran out of fellow humans to feed on, so they do not have the energy to do anything strenuous.

During an early phase of the plague, Morgan discusses with his wife and Ben, a colleague, the nature of the disease. They first speculate that the disease is "carried on the wind," which, for airborne diseases, is certainly a real threat. Morgan says, "I just can't accept the idea of universal disease. The germ is visible under a microscope, but it's not like any bacilli ever known. It can't be destroyed by any process we've been able to uncover." This conversation would also apply to AIDS. It too is a universal disease and difficult to destroy.

In a conversation between Morgan and Ben, Morgan is skeptical that infected humans are coming back as vampires. Ben says, "Why are the infected people always so tired in the daytime? Why can't they stand the sunlight? Why are they only seen at night?" Morgan, convinced an infectious agent is the cause of the plague, points to a specimen on the microscope and says, "Is this bacilli or isn't it? And this bacilli is found in the blood of every infected person." Morgan, ever the skeptical experimentalist, needs more facts before he can accept Ben's conclusions. The best scientists in the world are healthy skeptics, so Morgan's attitude is real.

During a conversation with a colleague, Morgan says, "...theory is the beginning of solution." Theory is a reasoned explanation of known facts, which serve as a basis for discovery. Thinking of a theory as the "beginning of solution" is an interesting way of putting it.

The plague appears to be human specific, since during the film dogs are seen who seem perfectly fine, and therefore immune to the plague. If dogs are immune, then are there other animals unaffected? Most diseases are species specific, otherwise everything on earth would be infected with what everything has. Unfortunately, neither apes nor monkeys are seen, because it would have been interesting to discover if they were immune or infected. Imagine vampire gorillas!

For most diseases there is a subgroup of individuals who appear immune to its affects. This is true, and this concept is presented in this film. While on one of his daily sojourns, Morgan comes across a female who appears unaffected, since she is seen during daylight. During a conversation she asks Morgan why he is immune to the plague. He says, "A long time ago, when I worked in Panama, I was bitten in my sleep by a bat. My theory is that the bat had previously acquired the vampire germ. By the time it had entered my blood it had been strained and weakened by the bat's system. As a result, I have immunity." A lot of interesting, and correct, biology is implied here. It is true that some "germs" are weakened when they pass from body to body, since each host's immune system does alter it somewhat, making it less infectious. The major implication here is that Morgan's immune system, both his human antibodies and cellular interactions, acted in such a way that they were able to recognize and effectively destroy the plague germ(s).

In an attempt to cure this woman, Morgan gives her a transfusion of his own blood. Apparently it works, because after the transfusion the woman is no longer repulsed by garlic and she can look at herself in a mirror. Morgan says, "It worked. The antibodies in my blood worked. My blood has saved you." (Note that the transfusion worked immediately!) In effect, Morgan's human antibodies, the ones his (white cell) lymphocytes generated in response to the bite of the vampire, germ carrying, Panamanian bat, are able to inactivate and destroy the plague. That is how antibodies do work, and it's satisfying that a 1964 movie got this right.

What Is Wrong with the Biological Science Presented: At his lab, Morgan says to his boss, Dr. Mercer, "The bacilli are multiplying." Mercer answers, "That kicks the bone marrow theory in the head." (It is unclear what he means by this, since infections do not originate from the bone marrow.) Morgan responds with, "This specimen shows a higher white count than when I put it on the slide. Those cells are still living off one another." Mercer replies, "You stay on this virus theory until I decide it's exhausted." White cells, also called lymphocytes, do not multiply when prepared for analysis on a microscope slide. Typically, the cells are "fixed" and stained with various dyes to distinguish them from each other, so they can't possibly grow. If cells were still "living off one another," then they would be "eating each other" to grow, and if they were eating each other then their numbers would diminish, not increase. Finally, if the problem is a bacillus, then what does a "virus theory" have to do with it?

The woman Morgan meets at the end of the film explains that though she is infected she is able to withstand its effects by giving herself injections to suppress the plague in her body. She tells Morgan, "I take defibrinated blood, plus vaccine. The blood feeds the germ, the vaccine keeps it isolated and prevents it from multiplying." Fibrin is an elastic protein derived from fibrinogen by the action of thrombin, all of which are involved in blood clotting. Defibrinated blood has lost its ability to coagulate. A vaccine is any preparation intended to activate the immune system to provide prophylactic protection against its

original host form. Why she needs defibrinated blood is unknown, since heparin was (and is) available, which is an excellent anti-coagulant. There is no need to remove fibrin from blood. The type and nature of the vaccine is not specified, but this really does not matter, since vaccines do not keep germs "isolated." Rather, vaccines allow the immune system to destroy germs when they appear in the blood system.

What Biological Science Is Necessary to Actually Achieve the Results in the Film: Infected humans are afraid of sunlight, so they have what is called photophobia, which is a fear of light, or heliophobia, which is a fear of the sun. These infected vampires also have an aversion to mirrors, which is called spectrophobia. These are real phobias and could be either mental conditions, physical conditions, or a combination of both.

One thing not discussed in this film is how the plague is transmitted from human to human. Since it is alluded to early in the film that in Europe the disease is "carried on the wind," then the germ must be either airborne itself or carried (vectored) by something that can easily travel through the air, such as a mosquito, fly, tick, mite, or even a flea. Any one of these vectors can effectively carry the pathogen. Furthermore, the germ could have been carried by mechanical means, such as on the clothes, skin, or other objects that are readily carried or transported.

Blood transfusions are given routinely, primarily to deliver hemoglobin carrying blood, not as a source of human antibody as in this movie. Morgan claims that he has immunity to the plague pathogen because of the bat bite he received in Panama. Let us examine this more carefully. In blood, humans have about 10 grams per liter of gamma globulin, the component that contains human antibody. Assume that about one percent of Morgan's circulating antibody is to the plague pathogen (a little high, but this will serve our purposes; after all, he is actively immunized and the pathogen is still around, constantly challenging his immune system), then he would have 0.1 grams of antibody per liter of blood. 0.1 gram is the same as 100 milligrams or the equivalent of about 0.003 ounces! Morgan is seen transfusing about 300 milliliters of his blood into the woman, so this would mean he gives her about 0.033 grams (or the equivalent of about 0.001 ounces)—that's one thousandth of an ounce! That 0.033 grams is then diluted into the woman's six liters of blood in her body, giving her a final concentration of about 0.0055 grams per liter, or 0.0000055 grams (5.5 micrograms) per milliliter of blood. Patients who routinely receive gamma globulin injections typically receive anywhere from 100 milligrams to one gram per injection, and this woman receives less than one-thousandth of that. For that single transfusion to work, Morgan's human antibodies must have been incredibly powerful! (I wish my human antibodies were of that caliber!)

Could It Actually Happen: Depending upon your point of view, some would say that a plague (AIDS) is currently among us, so yes, it could happen. However, though AIDS (or HIV) does make you physically and, eventually, mentally weak, those infected are not allergic to garlic, afraid of sunlight, or unable to look at mirrors.

Horror of the Blood Monsters (1972)

Synopsis: Dr. Rynning leads an expedition to an alien planet in the "Spectrum" solar system to investigate the source of a vampire plague infecting mankind. Rynning discovers the problem to be a virus that is unable to survive in Earth's atmosphere.

Screenplay: Sue McNair.

(Note: Critics call this film one of the "all-time worst" ever made. It was released under several titles: aka *Vampire Men of the Lost Planet*; *Horror Creatures of the Lost Planet*; *Creatures of the Prehistoric Planet*; *Creatures of the Red Planet*; *Flesh Creatures of the Red Planet*; *The Flesh Creatures*; *Space Mission of the Lost Planet*. Such is the life of an Al Adamson film. He almost makes Ed Wood look competent.)

Biological Science Principles Involved: Virology. Immunology. Physiology.

What Is Right with the Biological Science Presented: Rynning takes blood samples from each of his crew for analysis to determine the cause of the infectious vampire plague, and this would have been a natural thing to do. To one of the crew members Rynning says, "Look at the microscope." After doing so, she says, "I don't understand. There's no microorganism." Rynning replies, "Check the leukocyte count." (Leukocytes are a type of white blood cell commonly called lymphocytes.) The woman says, "Oh no. There are hardly any red corpuscles left in this blood. Whose is it?" Rynning answers, "Yours. All your blood samples show identical characteristics. The white corpuscles are devouring the red ones." If true, then the woman has a case of hemolytic anemia, which is an increased rate of destruction of erythrocytes, or "red corpuscles." This would cause all sorts of problems, such as shortness of breath, palpitations of the heart, lethargy, and fatigueability. One of the major jobs of "white corpuscles" or leukocytes is to destroy cells in the body. This is a natural occurrence and part of the normal physiology of all animals, including man. In severe cases anemia does result. This woman does show some signs of having an anemic condition, and her "white corpuscles," as a result of the Spectrum planet's virus, could have caused this.

What Is Wrong with the Biological Science Presented: Where to start? First off, one of the astronauts actually smokes cigarettes while in space flight!

At the beginning of the film we hear a voice-over that sets the stage for the action to come. The voice apparently comes from a distant planet and says, "Scientists of this planet [Earth] cannot destroy me. The infected blood of the vampire [from his planet in the "Spectrum" galaxy] was carried to Earth millions of years ago by the Tubitahn vampire men of a distant galaxy far beyond this solar system." If the infected blood was brought to Earth millions of years ago, then some sort of manifestation of it would have been seen. Why did this infected blood take so long to "appear?" To do so would mean it was hidden somewhere, which does not make sense.

The "Spectrum" planet the astronauts land on is constantly being bombarded by cosmic radiation. This radiation mutates some of the Tubitahn "cavemen" who inhabit the planet, causing them to develop into vampire-like people. They have incisor fangs/teeth that are about two inches long, and a 10-inch-long snake-like appendage coming out of the top of their left shoulder. The purpose of this "shoulder snake" is not explained.

Later in the film, after Rynning figures out that something in the Spectrum planet's atmosphere is causing the vampire-like symptoms, he explains to his crew, "Deadly virus entered the system through the respiratory tract with the air they breathe. Not only it destroyed the blood balance, it also destroyed the chromosome balance. Those poor devils living there won't last much longer." One of the crew members then asks, "But what about us? We have it [the virus] in us now too."

Rynning replies, "We'll be all right. The virus can't live in the earth's atmosphere. It hasn't done us enough damage." It would have to be a very serious virus to cause anemia *and* a chromosome imbalance, meaning it alters the DNA content of cells. If it did alter the DNA content of cells then they would not be "all right!" If the virus cannot live in the earth's atmosphere, as stated by Rynning, then why do they come to the planet to look for the virus in the first place? If the crew is suffering from anemia, then the virus *has* done them "enough damage!" Also, according to the voice-over during the beginning of the film, "the infected blood of the vampire was carried to Earth millions of years ago." Well, Rynning says, "the virus can't live in the earth's atmosphere." It should be one way or the other, not both.

What Biological Science Is Necessary to Actually Achieve the Results in the Film: The premise of this film is that a space virus comes to Earth (even though it was "millions of years ago") and causes the appearance of vampires. Having a virus be the cause of vampirism is an interesting idea. A virus could cause an anemic condition, which is why vampires need blood to sustain themselves. The virus could alter the DNA of leukocytes, thereby causing them to destroy or lyse red blood cells; some manifestations of this would be diagnosed as autoimmune disease. This destruction of erythrocytes would be caused by an immune mechanism in which antibodies are generated to antigens on the surface of red cells, which then activates a cascade of proteins and enzymes that ultimately destroys the erythrocyte. This does occur within our bodies, but the process is highly regulated, and usually no problems occur. The space virus could alter this natural process and speed it up, causing an imbalance of destruction and replenishing, so the destruction mechanisms far outpace the replenishing. Or the virus could interfere with the replenishing mechanisms, so those naturally destroyed red blood cells are not replaced. Either way, the end result is anemia.

Could It Actually Happen: Though remote, there is the possibility of alien DNA coming to Earth. What is unknown is whether that DNA will be intact, not to mention functional. If you believe the well publicized 1997 story about fossilized microorganisms embedded inside a Martian meteorite that came to Earth, then there could be other instances in the past — or yet to come — in which infectious alien DNA could be a problem for humans. However, there is no need to go into a panic over this. Some even think that alien DNA — in the form of HIV — has already landed on Earth. As far as is known, none of those with AIDS experience vampire-like symptoms.

Outbreak (1995)

Synopsis: An African monkey carrying a deadly virus is smuggled into the U.S. and ends up in a small California town. Those infected with this rapidly spreading, mutating virus develop a severe form of hemorrhagic fever. Many of those infected die painfully from the disease. The military is called in to handle the difficult situation. An antidote to the disease is eventually found and used to save mankind.

Screenplay: Laurence Dworet and Robert Ray Pool.

Biological Science Principles Involved: Virology. Immunology.

What Is Right with the Biological Science Presented: The film opens with the following quote by Joshua Lederberg, Ph.D., Nobel Laureate: "The single biggest threat to man's continued dominance on the planet is the virus." His accurate quote is both sobering and chilling. One need

look no further than the current AIDS problems throughout the world. The HIV virus is decimating much of sub-Sahara Africa, in spite of the worldwide effort to combat it. Many worry about what will come after HIV?

The procedures, steps, protocols, and mannerisms of all the scientific personnel in this film are authentic looking and impressive. At first blush I would be happy to have any of these people working for me in my lab.

Ebola, Lassa, and Hanta viruses are very real and very deadly! They all cause hemorrhagic symptoms, which is simply a loss of blood through either ruptured or unruptured blood vessels. With the loss of enough blood, you will die. Viral hemorrhagic fever is caused by a number of different viruses in the families Arenoviridae, Bunyviridae, Flaviviridae, and Filoviridae. (Virologists spend a lot of time naming and classifying viruses. The strange names they give viruses are no different than the names particle physicists use to describe their "toys": charm, gluons, hadrons, etc.)

Majors Casey and Salt explain hemorrhagic fever as follows: "When the patient first gets the virus he has flu-like symptoms, and in two or three days pink lesions begin to appear all over his body, along with small pustules that soon erupt with blood and pus. A kind of milky substance begins to form. These particular lesions, when they become full blown, feel like mush to the touch. There's vomiting, diarrhea, bleeding in the nose, ears, gums, the eyes hemorrhage, the internal organs shut down, they liquefy." All in all a pretty nasty way to go.

The film's first viral outbreak of Ebola, which was shown not to be airborne but rather requiring direct human to human contact to spread. This is very similar to HIV, which also needs direct human to human contact to spread.

This Old World monkey is the host/carrier of the Motaba virus in *Outbreak* (1995). From this little monkey comes about 200 liters (53 gallons) of high-titer antisera!

All viruses (and other infectious diseases, for that matter) need a host as a carrier. For some viruses, monkeys, particularly the African green monkey, are very suitable carriers. (One real outbreak at Marburg University in Germany resulted in a case of highly fatal hemorrhagic fever among handlers and laboratory workers of green monkeys. It is mistakes like this that demonstrate the seriousness of these viruses.) A carrier is any person or animal that literally carries a specific infectious agent in the absence of any visible clinical disease, and serves as a potential source of infection to others. One example of a famous carrier many may be familiar with is Mary Mallon, aka "Typhoid Mary," an immigrant Irish woman who spread typhoid fever through her cooking of various puddings and cakes during the years of about 1900 to 1938, when she finally died. She definitely had typhoid but did not present any symptoms of the fever and was isolated for years on North Brother Island on the East River in New York. Wherever she traveled she infected those around her with typhoid fever, and several died as a result of exposure to the typhoid bacillus.

During the film it is suggested that the "Motaba" virus has mutated. Originally it is not airborne and only transmitted by direct human to human contact. Then we "see" the virus contaminate a group of people in a room (a movie theater) by dissemination via a sneeze. Little vapor particles are strewn about from the sneeze and carried by air currents to others. Therefore, the virus does mutate and spreads through the air. This is, of course, the most deadly means of spreading germs, since there is no practical way to stop this. Major Salt isolates the new strain of virus and compares it to the old strain. There is a distinct difference in what is called the "viral coat," since "spikes" are now visible on the new strain. Major Casey says, "The protein coat has changed, which allows it to survive longer in the air." Sam then says, "So it spreads like flu." Yes indeed, viruses do mutate and new strains occur all the time. For example, the HIV virus has mutated and different strains have been discovered, which makes a single effective treatment difficult.

Since there is a new mutated strain of the virus, Sam and his staff speculate that the host animal, the monkey, is carrying both strains— the regular and the airborne version. This could be true. Since the Motaba virus starts out in a monkey and is transmitted to man, it is referred to as being zoonotic. Zoonotic viruses cross species barriers. Typically, most viruses are confined to one genus; those that cross species barriers cause the most problems, and therefore the most morbidity and mortality. You should avoid these viruses at all costs.

When the end credits roll, it is a pleasure to note the creators of the film acknowledging those companies who supplied the lab equipment. These companies are Forma Scientific, Inc., Savant Instruments, Beckman Instruments, Inc. (Arnold O. Beckman is an incredible philanthropist in the world of biomedicine; I wish there were more like him), Nuaire, Inc., Carl Zeiss Equipment, and International Equipment Co. All of these companies are real, and I have personally used equipment from each one of them in my research. If you can, support them all.

What Is Wrong with the Biological Science Presented: While looking at a virus particle under a high powered electron microscope, Major Salt says, "In the space of an hour a single virus(!) has invaded, multiplied, and killed the cell [a normal, healthy kidney cell]. In just over two hours its offspring have invaded nearby cells, continually multiplying." First of all, an electron microscope is a microscope that uses electron beams with wavelengths thousands of times shorter than visible light, thereby allowing much greater resolution and magnification. With this instrument, individual virus particles can readily be seen. In the preparation of samples to be analyzed for electron microscopy, a process is used that prevents any metabolism or life to continue. The sample is not only embedded in resin but also sliced to around five microns (one micron is 10^{-6} meters) in thickness, guaranteeing nothing will survive. And if that was not enough, the sample is then ultra cooled and placed in a vacuum for analysis. Nothing will survive this procedure, so having Major Salt comment on seeing the virus "invade, multiply, and kill" a cell under the electron microscope is ridiculous!

During a conversation with General Billy, Sam says, "We've got baseline information on it [the virus]; we've got the bug growing. We've got most of the protein isolated; we'll have an antibody test within a week. Casey has put the bug in rodents and rhesus, and if everything goes well, we'll map this guy to its last gene." Though you can isolate viral protein, get virus growing in small animals, develop antibody tests, and genetically map it "to its last gene," this work takes months and months, not the hours and days shown in the film. Growing the virus in rodents is a complete waste of everyone's time. Hemorrhagic fever viruses do not "grow" in rodents.

Right after the above exchange, Sam tells Robby, a co-worker, that after testing the virus he has a lab full of dead animals that "failed to respond to endoDNAse, acyclovir, and ribovarin." Though these compounds are used to interfere with the replication of viruses, they work on humans and not rodents. No wonder he has a lab full of dead animals.

When speculating that the host monkey is carrying both strains of the virus, Sam says, "The host is carrying antibodies to both strains." The reason for saying this is that since the monkey survives, then its immune system must be keeping the virus in check, and the most convenient way to do this is by antibodies (and another class of lymphocytes called "T–cells"). Well, not necessarily so. There are two major aspects to our immune system: the antibody response and the cellular response. The cellular response (i.e., certain T–cells) could easily be destroying newly made viruses, thereby allowing the monkey to survive with the virus in its system. It is somewhat surprising this aspect was not discussed in the film.

During one of the testing scenes, one of the government workers, wearing his isolation suit, accidentally rips a valve open on his suit and exposes himself to contaminated air. He later dies of the virus. This most likely would not have happened in real life because these isolation suits are pressurized, meaning that with any tear air would exit, not enter. Air exiting at a fast rate would not let a virus particle enter against that force. The worker gets out of the room fast enough that there should not have been a problem.

General Billy tells Sam that the army has developed an antiserum to the Motaba virus, and this serum is called "E–1101." The army develops Motaba for use as "the perfect biological weapon" (but the virus mutates—so much for army planning!), and E–1101 is the antidote. After learning of the existence of E–1101, Sam tells Major Salt to "use E–1101 as a road map to synthesize an antiserum. We've got an awful lot of people here [in Cedar Creek, California]." Ever the good soldier, Salt says, "I'll copy it big time." Sam then says, "I mean, I want liters of it." You just do not go out and make "liters" of an antiserum with the snap of a finger nor the bark of a commanding officer. It takes several months to make an effective antiserum, so in the meantime all the people of Cedar

Creek would have died, not to mention the rest of mankind exposed to airborne virus!

Obeying orders, Major Salt hooks up a peristaltic pump to the host monkey to extract its blood (serum). Now, this is *one* small old world monkey that has no more than a total of one liter of blood in its entire body, and Salt has to make "liters!" Good grief! To make this even more foolish, Salt obtains about 100cc of pure serum(!) from the monkey and uses this on one of the Motaba victims. Sam hooks up a plasma bag containing the 100cc of serum and is seen squeezing the bag to make the fluid enter the patient faster! Squeezing the plasma bag is downright absurd, especially by Sam, a physician who should have known better. Right after this, Sam tells Salt, "You have the lab geared up [to make more antisera]. Make more, we've got a town waiting." Now, all of these liters from *one* single old world monkey! As an immunologist, I am still laughing at the thought of that.

Major Salt, a major in the army, is seen doing all the lab "grunt" work, work that technicians should have done. There is no way a major in the army would have done all this work by himself. Personally, I would love to have a technician who worked as fast and was as capable and competent as Salt was.

To cap this all off, after the townspeople are recovering from the antiserum Salt made from the little monkey, Sam comments that the antiserum is being "cranked out by the liter" and that *each* patient is being given a dose of "200 cc." Here is some simple math. Cedar Creek has a population of 2,400 people, and let us assume that half of them are contaminated (probably all of them are, but I will be generous here) with the virus. If each receives 200cc, then for 1,200 people Sam would need 240 liters of antiserum! All of this coming from one little monkey. I really feel sorry for him.

What Biological Science Is Necessary to Actually Achieve the Results in the Film: There are a variety of useful treatments available to combat viruses, and in some (severe) cases an antiserum would be called for. However, the generation and stockpiling of antiserum is not a trivial matter. The two major factors here would be time and, of course, money. It takes months and months to generate a workable antiserum. Most antiserums are made in goats, though there are some human antiserums available — and these are commonly referred to as "gamma globulins." To prepare gamma globulin, human blood is removed, and the serum component, the fraction containing the antibodies, is collected. From a human you should get no more than about 500cc (which contains about 5–10 grams of antibody) once every two months or so. Then the serum is usually pooled to make a larger batch. Needless to say, all this material is endlessly tested for safety reasons, and that costs money. After all, would you want HIV-contaminated serum? I think not.

Because of the laborious, time consuming, and costly way to produce effective human gamma globulin, there is work currently going on all over the world to bypass this process. This research involves the generation and production of human monoclonal antibodies, my particular field of specialty. I anticipate that human monoclonal antibodies will eventually eliminate the need for gamma globulin preparations. Much needless suffering will be eliminated when these human antibodies are readily available.

In addition to antiserums, there are other methods and treatments available which have been effective against certain viruses. Some pharmaceutical drugs, such as acyclovir, ribovarin, and protease inhibitors, have been effective in stopping viruses from replicating. A combination of drugs and human antibodies may make for a relatively virus free future.

Could It Actually Happen: Yes. Viral epidemics are real, and AIDS is an example most are familiar with. Viruses are transmitted by human contact and in the air we breathe. Medicines have been, are being, and will be developed to combat these threats to mankind. Hemorrhagic fever is a serious problem if not sufficiently contained. It is unfortunate, but infectious diseases will pose serious consequences to the ultimate survival of humans, and Dr. Lederberg's words may be prophetic. The best defense to infectious diseases is the human immune system.

BIOCHEMISTRY

Humans have five major senses: sight (ocular), sound (acoustic), smell (olfactory), taste (gustation), and touch (tactile). Of these five, most SF films have to do with sight and sound (for obvious reasons). We get to see the titular creature of these movies and we hear the dialogue and music presented. Also, for obvious reasons, our other senses, those of smell and taste, are just about impossible to adequately convey on the movie screen. Often times you see actors wrinkle their noses over some foul smelling substance, and we certainly see them eating. What one enjoys another may find unpleasant, since both smell and taste are highly subjective. The senses of taste and smell are biochemically and mentally intertwined. We smell what we taste and taste what we smell.

SMELL / OLFACTION

One advantage of animation is that from time to time we *see* odors, such as the off-white misty trails seen in the "Pepe Le Pew" cartoons when they want to show skunk odor wafting hither and yon. Mists and clouds are occasionally shown in SF movies, but we can only judge them by the responses of the actors.

We can identify (olfactorily speaking) with films that have hospital settings, because most of us are familiar with the distinctive "clean" odor of hospitals. The same can be said for outdoor scenes in forests or at beaches. The scent of pine trees and misty salt air is quite distinctive. However, the smell of a mad scientist's lab is simply lost to most people, since they have never been in labs. Believe me, there is a significant difference between an organic chemist's lab and one of a molecular biologist! Organic chemistry labs are usually filled with the noxious odor of pyridine, while the molecular biologist often times has the odor of mercaptans (sulfur smelling beta-mercaptoethanol used in the analysis of DNA and proteins) permeating his or her lab. After a while you get used to these odors (sort of like garbage collectors becoming accustomed to the various odors of their profession).

There may be a few other films that involve odors, but one of the most memorable was the interactive John Waters movie *Polyester*. I attended this movie during 1982 in San Diego. Though *Polyester* is not SF, it is about fantastic elements. (For those of you familiar with John Waters movies, I need not explain). As I entered the theater showing *Polyester* I was given a card about 10 centimeters by 20 centimeters in size. On this card were 10 circles, and at various times during the movie you were given a signal to scratch one of the circles and smell the released odor — sort of like a "scratch and sniff" concept. The odors ranged from mild (food) to pleasant (perfumes) to disgusting (fart and rotten eggs; after all, this is a John Waters movie!). This movie engaged sight, sound, and smell. It was a first for me, and I am somewhat surprised no one else has taken the idea any further.

The study of the sense of smell, olfactology, though somewhat straightforward, has a huge economic impact worldwide. The perfume industry alone is a multi-billion-dollar-a-year enterprise. All of this attention for such an anatomically small area!

The olfactory region of our bodies is located near the superior nasal concha in the nasal cavity. Incoming air is circulated around the olfactory region by the natural vortices created within the upper nasal cavity. The olfactory apparatus itself is composed of a series of cells situated in the mucous membranes of the nose, and are directly attached by nerves to the hypothalamus and thalamus regions of the brain. Biochemically, an odor molecule stimulates an olfactory cell receptor, which in turn stimulates olfactory glomeruli, tufted cells, mitral cells, and granular cells. These diverse cell types help to translate a particular odor signal to the brain for interpretation: was it a good odor or was it a bad odor.

The smallest measurable unit of smell is called the olfactie, and keenness of the sense of smell is measured by an olfactometer. Needless to say, the levels of sensitivity are quite varied from person to person. Some people can pick out very dilute odors, say, one part in a billion, while others can only detect, say, one part in 10,000. Still others can distinguish between

odors with only one atom's difference, while others cannot do that at all. Biochemically, the olfactie binds to a receptor, which initiates a rapid cascade of events. It is these receptors and associated nerve interpretations that are highly varied. In simple terms, odors are highly subjective. On planet Earth the animal with the keenest sense of smell is the moth. Some species of moth can detect a single molecule to distinguish between odors!

Odors have received very little attention in SF films (or any films for that matter) for all of the reasons discussed above. Which is why the film *The Devil Bat* is of interest and represents some intriguing reel and real biological science. The main scientist uses the powers of odors for nefarious means. The biochemistry of odors, which receptors are involved, and how these signals are translated in the brain is a very active field of study and research.

The Devil Bat (1940)

Synopsis: Dr. Carruthers (Bela Lugosi), a research scientist, develops formulas for exotic perfumes, creams, and shaving lotions. His partners are getting rich from his formulas and not sharing the wealth with him. Carruthers creates giant bats who attack and kill persons wearing a certain type of shaving lotion. In the end, one of these giant bats kills Carruthers.

Screenplay: John Thomas Neville, based on an original story by George Bricker.

Biological Science Principles Involved: Biochemistry. Olfaction. Physiology.

What Is Right with the Biological Science Presented: Carruthers' main job is to make exotic formulations for his cosmetics company, Heath Cosmetics. Throughout the film he goes about a variety of ways to generate, study, and analyze his new formulas, and all of this looks authentic. He correctly appears as a scientist who thoroughly enjoys what he is doing. To support this, one of Carruthers' partners says, "He [Carruthers] doesn't like visitors when he is experimenting." Most scientists, including me, do not like to be interrupted when busy in the lab "experimenting." We like to continue uninterrupted in what we are focused on, and distractions are exactly that — distractions.

The main theme in this film is the sense of smell, and it is unfortunate that we the audience cannot participate in this interesting aspect of the film. I have often wondered what the formulas developed by Carruthers actually smell like.

Carruthers must have studied the biochemistry of olfaction with his bats for some time to be able to understand how to create a special formula that stimulates the bat to recognize — and hate — the particular odors he develops. Carruthers dips a cotton ball in some particular shaving lotion and lets the bats smell it. This irritates the bats, and Carruthers says to them, "Good. You have not forgotten. You hate this strange oriental fragrance even while you sleep. Now, if you detect the fragrance in the night when you are fully awake, you will strike!" It is a brilliant idea to put the particular odor so irritating to the bats into shaving lotion — which the future victims so willingly splash on the tender, freshly shaven parts of their necks. The bats, using their sense of smell, hone in on the odor and slash the neck area (i.e., the jugular area) of their victims, killing them. This is a most interesting way to exploit the biochemistry of olfaction.

The police eventually figure out that the shaving lotion must have something to do with all the killings and have it analyzed. A cop says to Layton, a reporter, "Here's the chemist report on that shaving lotion." After examining it, Layton says, "I see he couldn't break down one of the ingredients." The cop replies, "Yes, he said it must be some element with which he's not familiar." This "element" is the secret ingredient Carruthers uses to antagonize his bats. Whatever olfactory receptor the bats have to this "element" affects them enough so that they risk their lives to attack those who have it on their necks. It must be powerful stuff, because the victims only put a little of it on their throats. This demonstrates that the bats have sensitive olfactory receptors to this particular odor and are able to track it down from miles away.

To explain Carruthers' motivation in killing his partners, there is the following conversation. Morton, Carruthers' partner (and the head of "Heath Cosmetics") says to Carruthers, "You've had a lot of fun in your laboratory [you bet!] doing experiments, dreaming up something new. You're a dreamer, doc. Too much money is bad for dreamers." Carruthers replies, "So, you try to pay me in flattery, telling me that I'm a dreamer. Well, I do dream. Dreams that you could never guess." Morton then says, "Your nerves are frayed, doc. Now calm down. You've been working too hard on your formula." Carruthers says, "Formula. That's but child's play for a great scientist. Your brain is too feeble to conceive what I have accomplished in the realm of science." Carruthers is referring to his studies on the biochemistry of bat olfaction. Quite frankly, though interesting, it is certainly *not* something great. Then again, no matter how trivial, all scientists, real and reel, think that what they are doing is always "great."

Eventually, Carruthers is hoisted on his own petard when the reporter, Layton, who figures it all out, splashes some of the shaving lotion onto the scientist's face. Soon after, a giant bat swoops down on Carruthers and kills him.

What Is Wrong with the Biological Science Presented: As Dr. Carruthers,

Lugosi plays a deliciously demented scientist. For example, when he is zapping one of his bats to get it to grow to gigantic size, he says, "Ah, my friend, our[!] theory of glandular stimulation through electrical impulses was correct. A few days ago, you were as small as your companions [other small bats]." A bat and a human who develop a theory together ("our theory") is quite touching to see. (From time to time I have been seen talking to my experiments and various pieces of equipment. However, I never referred to them as "our!")

Carruthers takes his bats to his electrical lab and attaches electrodes to each of its legs. After injecting them with his glandular extracts he then turns a few dials, flips a few switches, and zaps the bat with electricity, thereby causing the bat to significantly grow in size. The bats end up being about two feet long from head to tail. Their wingspan is even more impressive. No gland extract in combination with electricity can bring about such dramatic physiologic changes.

What Biological Science Is Necessary to Actually Achieve the Results in the Film: To create giant bats would require the use of bat growth hormones. Carruthers does not detail the source nor composition of the glandular extracts he uses on his bats, but it would make sense if he uses glands from bats. Most likely this growth hormone comes from bat pituitary glands. It appears the bats increase their size about four fold, so it would take a lot of bat pituitary glands to do the job.

The use of electricity probably serves no useful biochemical purpose on the bats. However, as a method to reinforce the behavior of the bat to recognize a particular odor as "bad," the electrical stimulation probably works. Whenever Carruthers presents the target odor to the bats he zaps them with electricity to help them "remember" the unpleasantness of the odor, thereby making them angry enough to seek out whomever has that odor on them. Since the odor is on the victims' necks, the bats go there and bite hard enough to sever the jugular vein. Those would have to be pretty angry bats. As a result, the victims bleed to death.

Biochemically, the nature of the odors is important. Since animal species react favorably to pleasant odors and unfavorably to unpleasant odors, most likely Carruthers used some particular odor molecule (the chemist's "element with which he's not familiar") that is neutral to humans and unpleasant to bats. To work this all out would require some reasonably sophisticated biochemical analyses.

Could It Actually Happen: Creating giant bats from gland extracts and electricity will not happen, so you need not worry about this.

Animals, and certainly humans, can be behaviorally trained to respond to different odors. After all, there are all those drug sniffing dogs that go through airports, and humans in the perfume industry who can readily detect one-carbon-atom differences in fragrances. However, it would take extraordinary training and discipline to train an animal to kill over a particular odor, not to mention determining the biochemical mechanisms of which odors to use.

TASTE / GUSTATION

Many films have scenes with actors going through all sorts of eating rituals, from very formal affairs to eating on the run, from dining alone to feasting in the presence of thousands. For the most part we give very little thought to these, since eating is essentially no big thing. After all, stating the obvious, we have to eat to survive.

The act of eating is called gustation. Taste is the sensation provided by the stimulation of the gustatory nerve endings in the tongue. The tastes of bitter, sour, salt, and sweet can be readily distinguished by the taste buds in our tongue. The receptors for sweet and salt tastes are near the tips of our tongues, and the receptors for bitter and sour tastes are near the backs of our tongues. The three main nerves that are stimulated by tastes are the chorda tympani, the glossopharyngeus, and the vagus. (Ironically, all these names are not particularly "tasty.")

Tastes, like smells, are also highly subjective. Furthermore, the differences in tastes vary between species. This should be relatively obvious. Which brings us to species not of this Earth. It should also be obvious that extraterrestrial species would have different eating and taste habits than us Earthlings. I certainly would not expect a Venusian to enjoy chocolates as much as I do. In fact, chocolates may even be poisonous to them (as they are to Earth's dogs).

Implied in the eating process is the obtaining of certain nutrients, such as minerals and vitamins. Vitamins are discussed in some detail in the entry for the film *Not of This Earth* (1957 version). Suffice it to say here that we cannot live without vitamins. And neither can aliens!

Vitamin manufacturers have gone to great lengths to package and market their products. They want us to take them "one-a-day," as chewable, as health supplements, in the shape of amusing characters (the Flintstones, dinosaurs, etc.), multi-colored, specialized tablets, fortified, etc., etc., etc. Basically, all vitamins are the same, though the manufacturers will debate this till the end of time. The structure of vitamin C (ascorbate) is the same, the structure of vitamin E (tocopherol) is the same, as are all the rest of the vitamins. The differences are in how they are packaged and formulated.

In the realm of SF cinema, the nature of aliens and the nutrients they require are as varied as those here on planet Earth. Most likely, because of their different metabolic makeup and requirements, these aliens would have radically different metabolic needs than humans. A vitamin for them could be something poisonous to us. The film chosen to describe such interesting and diverse metabolic alien needs is an all-time favorite, and I vividly remember seeing it for the first time in a theater as a five-year-old child (it still seems like only yesterday!). This film is one of the best by Ray Harryhausen.

20 Million Miles to Earth (1957)

Synopsis: A spaceship returns from Venus carrying a capsule containing a gelatinous egg. The spaceship crashes in the Mediterranean off the coast of Sicily. The egg hatches, releasing a creature (the Ymir) that doubles in size every day. The Ymir is captured and then escapes, killing people and destroying parts of the countryside. The Ymir is eventually cornered in Rome and shot to death.

Screenplay: Bob Williams and Christopher Knopf, based on a story by Charlotte Knight.

Biological Science Principles Involved: Biochemistry. Nutrition. Physiology.

What Is Right with the Biological Science Presented: During the beginning of the film a narrator says, "Great scientific advances are often times sudden accomplished facts before most of us are even dimly aware of them." This also applies to small and moderate "scientific advances."

The canister carrying the Venusian egg is interesting. The canister, marked with "USAF Project 5," clearly indicating who it belongs to, is a glass tube with a radius of about 10 inches and a length of

The newly hatched Ymir creature, who came *20 Million Miles to Earth* (1957), gets his first taste of Earth's growth-promoting atmosphere.

about 18 inches. There are metal closures at each end of the tube, and inside is an opaque substance. A boy finds the canister washed ashore and is easily able to open it. Out comes a large jelly-like mass with some sort of animal species encased inside. The boy wraps it up in his jacket and takes it to Dr. Leonardo, a professor of zoology who is (conveniently) visiting nearby. All of this action is quite reasonable, and the canister looks "real" for what it is.

In the hands of Leonardo, the creature (Ymir) "hatches" out of the egg. At first the Ymir is about 12 inches tall. The creature reacts to the overhead room lights and covers its eyes. Leonardo then puts the Ymir in a cage and covers it with a cloth. The idea of the creature reacting negatively to the strong light suggests it must have sensitive photoreceptors in its eyes. This

light is "alien" to the Ymir, and its negative reaction to this makes sense.

Once the authorities know this creature is on the loose, they come onto the scene. Dr. Youle, a scientist from the military, says, "Our task is to discover in what physiological way life is able to survive and to flourish there [on Venus]." Though life as we know it here on Earth would not survive on Venus, there could be other forms of life there, and Youle would be correct in wanting to understand how life is "able to survive and to flourish there."

While roaming the countryside the Ymir goes to a farm to apparently look for food. (After all, if the creature grows as fast as seen it must have incredible hunger pains!) What is interesting and very telling here is that the creature passes up horses, sheep, and chickens. The Ymir is truly alien, because these animals are not tempting food sources. Rather, the Ymir is seen eating a bag of flour and some corn. Perhaps the creature is a vegetarian.

A group of humans attack the Ymir in a barn, and both bullets and a pitchfork have no detrimental affect on it. However, the Ymir does scream in apparent pain when the prongs of the pitchfork enter its back, suggesting that the creature does have a nerve system.

Youle finds a notebook kept by the chief scientist of the rocket ship expedition that went to Venus. While on Venus, this scientist must have studied the Ymir creatures because he made notes of the diet of these creatures. The chief scientist notes that, "The basic diet of these creatures is sulfur, raw sulfur." This is interesting and clearly demonstrates that an alien form of life would also have alien metabolism. (Actually, a diet of sulfur is not all that alien on Earth! Read below, gentle reader, to learn why. Just so you all know, sulfur is the eighth most abundant element in our bodies.)

Another passage from the notebook is, "On Venus we discovered, quite by accident, that these creatures are extremely susceptible to electric shock, and that controlled voltage can paralyze them." This is an interesting insight into what makes the Ymir's nerve system function. The creature is also afraid of fire.

After another day, the Ymir is seen near the boiling sulfur pits of Mt. Vesuvius. At this time the creature is about 10 feet tall and maybe 20 feet long. The Ymir needs his sulfur fix. A helicopter drops some bags of pure sulfur on the ground to lure the creature out into the open. While it eats some of this (high grade?) sulfur, the helicopter drops a wire mesh over the creature and zaps it unconscious with electricity. This method of capturing the Ymir is quite effective.

The captured Ymir is brought to a large warehouse and studied by a team of scientists. After a few days there is a press conference, and a reporter asks a colonel in charge of the creature, "How do you account for its astonishing rate of growth? Is that normal on Venus?" The colonel responds, "No it isn't. The scientists here believe that the Earth's atmosphere has upset its metabolic rate. The more air it breathes, the more tissues it builds, the bigger it gets." This explanation shows intelligence and insight. Later, during the same press conference, the colonel, when asked how the creature was kept subdued, says, "1800 volts of electricity keeps it knocked out." Electrical leads are attached to the creature, and a constant current is being sent to the Ymir, thereby keeping it unconscious. This effectively gives the scientists an opportunity to study it carefully.

When asked about details of the creature, a scientist says, "The creature's olfactory system is more highly developed than any known on this planet." Youle then says, "We've discovered that the creature's respiratory system includes a sort of a fibrous filtering element which blocks out all of the poisonous vapors on Venus." A reporter then asks, "Gunfire has no effect on the beast. Why?" Youle says, "This beast has no heart and it has no lungs. It has instead a network of small tubes throughout its entire body. Hence, firearms effect no great damage." This is an interesting lesson in Ymir biology, and it all sounds very plausible. Venus does indeed have, by Earth's standards, a poisonous atmosphere, so the Ymir would naturally have developed a mechanism to filter out the "poisonous vapors on Venus." Our kidneys, lungs, and livers are essentially filtering organs that remove or alter many potential poisons from the environment, so I would imagine that the Ymir would have a filtering system too. Since there is no heart, then there is no "blood" to pump through the Ymir. In animals, blood is primarily an oxygen carrier, and since the

Ymir does not have pumped blood, then gunshot wounds would indeed have no effect.

And speaking of Ymir biology, the colonel says, "They're [the scientists] feeding the creature a compound of sulfur [with a huge syringe that holds about 200cc of fluid]. Sulfur serves it as our vitamins do us." This is a fascinating bit of biological science.

What Is Wrong with the Biological Science Presented: The growth rate of the Ymir is astonishing. It literally doubles in size every day! On Earth, the fastest growing life form is the blue whale, and no way does that animal double in size every day. So, the next morning, after Leonardo puts the Ymir into its cage, the creature has significantly increased in size and is almost three feet tall! Later that same day, the creature is about four feet tall and strong enough to break out of its metal cage. (While escaping, the Ymir's claw grabs Leonardo's daughter's arm, and she says, "its claw was so strangely hot.") To increase in body mass you need, of course, to ingest a food source to provide the bulk necessary. We do not see Leonardo feed the creature.

While roaming the countryside the creature is seen stopping at a river bed and apparently drinking some of the water. The temperature on Venus is so hot that no water would exist in liquid form, so water should have been alien to the creature. Perhaps the nature of water piqued its curiosity and it stopped to see what this strange liquid was. Anyway, this scene does not fit with the nature of the creature.

Youle explains that the creature does not have any lungs, so its breathing mechanisms are different than Earth animals. Well, during one particular closeup, the Ymir's chest is clearly seen to expand and contract several times, as if it were "breathing." So much for that. (Technically, it was a "tour-de-force" of stop motion animation by master artist Ray Harryhausen to show the Ymir "breathing.")

The electricity to the Ymir is accidentally cut off and the creature immediately regains its faculties. (If I were knocked out by a steady dose of electricity I would be a little sluggish. Then again, I do not have Venusian metabolism.) After escaping, the Ymir is strong enough to break through a cement wall of the building where it was kept. Venusians have remarkable recuperative powers, though they are not perfect, since the creature is ultimately destroyed by a bazooka blast to the chest.

What Biological Science Is Necessary to Actually Achieve the Results in the Film: The Venus we knew in 1957 is not the Venus we know today. (And the Venus we will know in, say, 50 years from now will also be different from what we know today.) The surface of Venus is most inhospitable to life as we know it on Earth. The surface temperature is so hot that carbon based life would not survive, nor would water exist in liquid form. The atmosphere is composed of acid vapors highly caustic to terrestrial life.

On Earth there are life forms, called extremophiles, which do exist in very harsh conditions—consisting of absence of all light, temperatures in excess of 750 degrees Fahrenheit (about 400°C; water boils at 212°F, or 100°C), and corrosive acidic conditions—and can live off of metals and sulfides. However, these organisms are predominantly bacteria and not multi-celled animals, though some bizarre invertebrates, such as certain tube worms and some clams, do exist in these environments. These worms have intestinal bacteria that live off of hydrogen sulfide, a compound poisonous to just about all of earth's surface species. These primitive bacteria are classified as belonging to the archaebacteria group. So, right here on Earth we have examples of life forms that do feed on sulfur for energy and metabolism.

Sulfur is found in abundance on Venus, so whatever creatures do exist there could have evolved in a way that they use it for their metabolism in a manner similar to those sulfophiles here on Earth. The Ymir is seen consuming large quantities of sulfur near the sulfur pits of Mt. Vesuvius, and it is lured into a trap by feeding it bags of the chemical. Sulfur is most likely its main food chemical, like carbon is the main food chemical for the majority of earth's animals.

Pain is an unpleasant sensation mediated by nerve fibers to the brain. The Ymir does experience pain, as clearly seen when it is struck by a pitchfork, so it must have some sort of nervous system. Also, the creature is paralyzed from being zapped by electricity, so Ymir physiology is clearly influenced by electrical current. Therefore, the Ymir has nerves and a brain capable of assimilating those sensations, since the creature produces appropriate reaction responses.

It is stated that the Ymir has "strangely hot" claws, so its internal metabolism must generate a lot of heat. This is reasonable because of the tremendous growth of the creature. To double in size every day would require an enormous amount of metabolic processes, and these do create heat, so the Ymir's basal metabolic rate must be very high indeed. In addition to this, the Ymir may also have a slight fever. In animals, including humans, a fever is a complex physiologic response characterized by a rise in body temperature. The elevation of body temperature is a mechanism to recruit other physiological aspects of the body to help counteract whatever is causing the fever. The Ymir could have developed a fever from being exposed to Earth's environment. An increased metabolism from both a fever and rapid growth could be the cause of the Ymir's "strangely hot" condition.

Regarding Ymir metabolism, it is stated that "the more air it breathes, the more tissue it builds." On earth we understand how oxygen is utilized and metabolized. On Venus there is very little free oxygen in the atmosphere, so its use would be radically different than on Earth. Perhaps oxygen serves as a growth factor to the Ymir, and with the abundant amounts on Earth the creature's metabolism reacts in a positive, accelerated manner. Oxygen readily combines with sulfur to make sulfur dioxide and sulfur trioxide. These sulfur-oxygen molecules, when in the presence of water, make strong acids. It is these acids which may have created the increased Ymir metabolism. Very interesting and very alien!

The description of the Ymir's respiratory system is interesting. A "network of small tubes throughout its entire body" could be similar to the tracheoles of Earth's insects. Perhaps the Ymir developed a mechanism to efficiently utilize some gaseous molecule, an oxygen equivalent (hydrogen sulfide gas?), and the network of tubes is the best means to distribute this gas throughout its body.

Could It Actually Happen: We have sent spaceships to Venus and, so far, no life forms of any recognizable kind have been found. To be sure, if life on that planet were found, then it would be very alien indeed!

ENTOMOLOGY

Of all the science fiction films I have seen since I first started watching them in the 1950s, I have a special place in my heart for giant bug movies. This is where the acronym of "B.E.M," which stands for bug-eyed monsters, comes from. To me, the bigger the bug the more fun the film! Bugs or, more accurately, insects, are the dominant animals on planet Earth. About 90 percent of the phylum Animalia are invertebrates, and of these, about 80 percent are insects. There are about six billion humans on Earth, and there are one million insects for each one of us. This makes a whopping total of 6×10^{15} insects!! Of these, most are ants.

As a child I intuitively knew that big bugs just could not happen; after all, if they were "real" then where were they? I had no problem believing in aliens and spaceships, but big bugs just did not seem possible nor reasonable. However, this did not prevent my thorough enjoyment of this subgenre of SF films. It wasn't until much later in life, when I began to seriously learn some of the simple laws of biology, that I realized that insects bigger than say, half a meter, just could not and will not happen.

One of the limitations on insect size is their respiration capability. Like all ani-mals on Earth, they too need oxygen to survive. Oxygen for respiration in insects (including ants, ticks, mosquitoes, etc.) is physically transported by tracheae, an internal system of air-filled tubes, to within a couple of cell diameters to each individual cell in their bodies. These tracheae are exquisitely interconnecting tubules that arise from paired, lateral openings called spiracles and terminate in fluid filled tubules called tracheoles. The passage of air into the tracheal system is regulated by the spiracles. Overall, the tracheal system creates a large surface area of permeable tissues to allow the efficient exchange and diffusion of oxygen. The tracheoles start out at 350 micrometers in length and about one micrometer in diameter and eventually taper to 0.2 to 0.1 micrometers in diameter. Through repeated branching the tracheae become smaller in diameter and terminate in tiny subdivisions.

Respiration by diffusion is the key here. Insects have no active system, like the lungs and oxygen-carrying hemoglobin of vertebrates, so they must rely on the laws of diffusion to transport oxygen to their cells and tissues. If you calculated oxygen consumption, diffusion rates, and measurements of tracheae size you would realize that diffusion alone could supply insects of no longer that 3 millimeters. Ventilation (i.e., movement of air through the tubules) can make this somewhat more efficient. Motions of the body or churning of internal organs of active insects incidentally moves air through their interconnected anatomy. Air flow through the system is greatly accelerated by pumping movements of the abdominal segments, creating inhaling and exhaling-like effects. Even so, the tracheal system imposes maximum limits to the size insects can attain. Diffusion aided by ventilation is adequate over distances measured in millimeters, but not more than a few centimeters. Alas, unless some additional system for cellular respiration is available, insects shall forever remain small.

It may interest you to know that the deadliest organism on planet Earth is the mosquito. These creatures can kill something up to 5000 times their size! So get your mosquito repellent out and be ready to zap those critters. They are pests in every sense of the word, and personally it would be a much better world if *all* "skeeters" were wiped off the face of (or under) the Earth! Mosquitoes, like vampires, live only to suck blood. In addition, you should also know that only female mosquitoes suck blood. Males don't and instead feed on plant nectar and other liquids. If a mosquito lands on your body looking for a meal, you know it is a female. Phylogenetically, mosquitoes belong to the order Diptera (same as flies) and to the family Culicidae.

In this section of the book five bug films are discussed: *Them!*, *Ticks*, *Skeeter*, *Mosquito*, and *Mimic*. Yes, there are many others, but it is these five I feel are descriptive of this subgenre. This "gang of five" covers it all, from the first, *Them!* (and one of the best), to one of the most contemporary, *Mimic*.

Them! (1954)

Synopsis: A series of deaths occur in the New Mexico desert, and the local authorities call in some experts from Washington, D.C. The deaths are determined to be caused by giant, mutated ants (call them gi-ants!), a result of atomic bomb testing at Alamogordo. Entomologists, working with the army and FBI, track down the gi-ants and destroy their colony.

Screenplay: Ted Sherdeman, adaptation by Russell Hughes, from a story by George Worthing Yates.

Biological Science Principles Involved: Entomology. Genetics. Mutagenesis.

What Is Right with the Biological Science Presented: All organisms, ants included, need to eat, and our first exposure to the gi-ants is the destruction they cause by looking for food — in particular, sugar.

The local coroner performs an autopsy on the body of a man killed in one of the gi-ant attacks and says, "Old man Johnson could have died any way of five ways. Neck and back broken, chest was crushed, skull fractured, and here's one for Sherlock Holmes. There was enough formic acid in him to kill 20 men." Quite a descriptive way to detail someone's death. The primary poison of bees, ants, and wasps is indeed formic acid. Formic acid is a one-carbon acid (with the formula CH_4O_2) and has a very distinctive odor. Mammals have a difficult time metabolizing one-carbon compounds, which is why they are poisonous, and their injection into our bodies can cause a lot of pain and even, in sufficient quantities, death. The key scene in which the entomologist has the little Ellison girl smell some formic acid — which dramatically revives her from her shock, resulting in her screaming the famous quote, "Them ... them!" — is a very interesting (and practical) way to test the hypothesis that ants are involved.

The gi-ant of *Them!* (1954), *Camponotus ficitus,* forages for food. To maintain the size shown they must consume a large quantity of food every day.

The main entomologist called in to investigate the scene in the New Mexico desert is given his correct title when he's introduced as "one of the world's greatest myrmecologists." Myrmecology is the study of ants of the phylogenetic family Formicidae. Those are words most people do not hear in their everyday lives. In real life, the scientist Edward O. Wilson of Harvard University, a Pulitzer Prize winner, is certainly the "world's greatest myrmecologist." (Perhaps Professor Wilson was influenced by this film in his youth?)

The reel entomologist of the film, Dr. Medford, locates a gi-ant "footprint" and says, "It's gigantic ... over 12 centimeters! That would make it about two and one half meters in length. Over eight feet!" Yes, a 12 centimeter "footprint" would make the ant about eight feet long. After killing one of the ants, Medford says, "Ants use their mandibles to rend, tear, and jolt their victims. But they kill with that [pointing to huge stinger], by injecting formic acid. We must find the colony."

While out in the desert searching for ants, Medford asks, "Has there been any report of a strange mound? A cone-shaped structure?" He is looking for the gi-ant's nest, which indeed is a large, cone-shaped mound. While searching for the colony, the helicopter pilot says, "How many giant ants do you think will be in it?" Medford says, "If they follow the usual pattern of their species, the nest, depending upon its age, may contain from several hundreds to several thousands.... Ants don't like the heat of the desert. They forage only between sunset and dawn, when it's cool. So half the colony wouldn't even be inside the nest tonight. Our best chance would be during the hottest time tomorrow. They haven't changed in form or habits in more than 50 million years. Ants don't see well at all. They hear, smell, and locate objects entirely with their radar-like antennae. Queens live quite a long time. They continue to lay eggs from the one mating for from 15 to 17 years. Ants are savage, courageous, and ruthless fighters." Quite a bit of interesting — and correct — ant lore.

What Is Wrong with the Biological Science Presented: In the earlier introduction to the insect films I mentioned the problems and limitations in their size. It all has to do with respiration. Because of the biological limits of oxygen diffusion through cells and tissues, insects have remained small. Their exoskeletons can handle more weight and size, but since they

have no lungs they do not have the ability to "breathe." Ants of the size shown are fantasy.

The main action of this film takes place near the White Sands, Alamogordo, area of New Mexico, the same area of the first atomic bomb tests. It is the radiation that has given rise to the mutated gi-ants. During one conversation, Medford asks, "In what area was the atomic bomb exploded?" Graham, the FBI agent responds, "Right here, in the same general area, White Sands [which was located about six miles from the gi-ant location]." Medford then replies, "1945, that's nine years ago. Yes, genetically it is certainly possible." If it took nine years for the mutations to manifest themselves, then why haven't any problems been reported prior to that?

Medford's daughter comments on the sparse amount of food in the desert and says, "Rather slim pickings for food, Dad. They [the ants] turn carnivorous, what for lack of habitual diet." The daughter also hears weird noises that are attributed to the mutated ants and consist of shrieks, vibrations, intonation, and sinusoidal tones.

The biggest biology blunder of all in this film (other than the impossible size of the ants) is the taxonomic identification of the gi-ants themselves. After killing one, Medford looks at it and immediately says, "*Camponotus ficitus.* One of the family Formicidae ... an ant! A fantastic mutation. Probably caused by lingering mutations from the first atomic bomb." Ants of the genus *Camponotus* are called carpenter ants, primarily because they are found around sources of wood. Well, in the New Mexico desert there is very little wood, and Medford could not have found a *Camponotus* in this hot and arid climate. (Most ants cannot survive in temperatures over 40 to 45 degrees Celsius, and it certainly gets that hot in the New Mexico desert! Furthermore, ants from the genus *Camponotus* would certainly not be able to survive at all in that heat. Their habitat is moist and relatively cool wood.) If you include all the described and non-described species of ants, you have over 10,000 varieties! Even the venerable Professor Wilson of Harvard would have had a difficult time instantly naming a giant desert ant as *Camponotus*! This is one case where the creators of a film tried to sound more authentic than necessary. However, about 99.99999 percent of all the people who have seen this film over the years probably could not care less about this mistake.

In talking of how to destroy the ants, Medford says, "Some species of desert ants dig down as deep as 30 feet and more. Flood the nest. Ants won't come through deep water. They breathe through their sides. We then drop cyanide gas to kill them." Yes, desert ants (not *Camponotus*!) do dig deep, and if they were 8 feet long then, to be sure, they would dig much deeper than that. After gassing the ants, the protagonists notice that there are "no winged ants in the nest anywhere ... only worker ants," meaning the queen ant has escaped. A single queen is capable of laying "thousands of eggs." After much searching, they locate the queen and her new colony in the sewers of Los Angeles, representing quite a distance to travel.

What Biological Science Is Necessary to Achieve the Results in the Film: The increased ant size is attributed to atomic bomb radiation. This premise can be accepted, and there have been many documented cases of radiation damage to DNA resulting in all sorts of biological problems. It is implied in this film that the size of the ants is a gradual increase, and this too is acceptable biology.

For the ants to exist at the size seen, we would have to account for their metabolism — respiration in particular. The "out" here is radiation. The genes of an ant are quite diverse, and since radiation-in-

duced mutations do occur, then not only are the genes that determine size altered, but those that involve oxygen consumption have also been altered. I do not mean to imply that these ants developed lungs (see the entry on *Mimic* for that problem). As mentioned above, insect (and ant) respiration occurs by transporting oxygen through an internal system of air-filled tubes called the tracheae to within a few cell diameters of each cell. (This is efficiently done in mammals through the use of oxygen-carrying hemoglobin.) Either one of two things (or perhaps a combination of both) would have to occur for the gi-ants to "breathe": The mutated ants must have somehow significantly increased the number of trachea within their bodies, thereby making more tubes available for oxygen transport; or they have developed a completely different means of getting oxygen to all their cells and tissues. If more trachea are present, then the ant's body cavities would be more hollow and they would weigh less (since there would be less tissue mass). That would be a good thing.

Could It Actually Happen: Mutations in animals and insects are a real phenomena. However, the vast majority of these mutations are lethal, and the organism does not survive. Mutations occurring on the single gene level are more problematical and do indeed happen. However, an entire species being affected as the ants just could not happen. Furthermore, why were only ants affected by atomic blast radiation? There are perhaps thousands of different life forms, from other insects to animals to plants, in the White Sands area, so why weren't they affected too?

Ticks (1993)

Synopsis: Backwoods marijuana farmers spill some toxic chemicals into the ground, resulting in arachnid ticks mutating into softball-sized creatures. The mutated ticks attack and kill several people at a nearby camp. The ticks are eventually killed by fire.

Screenplay: Brent V. Friedman.

Biological Science Principles Involved: Entomology. Molecular Biology. Pharmacology.

What Is Right with the Biological Science Presented: The most satisfying aspect about this bug film is the relatively small size of the mutated ticks. Instead of showing some enormous tick (though they, unfortunately, do so at the climax), the creators of this film kept it pseudo-realistic by making the insects about six to eight inches long, which is much more believable than an eight-foot-long ant!

Toxic chemicals, some of which are later identified as being herbal steroids, leak from a vat onto a small tick larva. If extensive DNA mutations are going to occur, then having them happen at the larva stage does make some sense. As the larva grows, more toxic liquid spills on it. In due course, more larvae are exposed to the toxic liquids, and they also mutate. It is later shown that these larvae hold several eggs and are found in all sorts of places (inside closets, hanging from tree branches, on fallen tree trunks).

Ticks are arachnids because they have eight legs and therefore phylogenetically belong to the class Arachnida (spiders, mites, scorpions, phalangids, etc.) and order Acarina, which is specifically ticks. What is interesting about ticks is that some species populations are actually stimulated by pesticides, resulting in an increased rate of reproduction! In light of the toxic exposure seen in this film, that certainly makes sense.

What Is Wrong with the Biological Science Presented: The tick larvae are shown to be about the size of a football and full of a large amount of slimy mucus, which most likely serves as a source of nutrients. Where does all this liquid come from? Rain? (We do not see it rain.) Tree sap? (What about the larvae inside a closet? Where did it get its liquid?) Furthermore, what is the carbon source that provides the body mass of not only the ticks but also the larvae?

One of the ticks attacks a dog and kills it by getting completely under its skin. The dog is taken to a local veterinarian. After a cursory examination the vet says, "There's some sort of mass under the sternum." The vet tries to use a syringe to obtain a blood sample for analysis and says, "Can't seen to find any plasma … something drained your dog of all its blood." After some effort the vet eventually fills the syringe, but "something" in the dog's belly keeps sucking the syringe blood back into the body. The vet subsequently pulls out a large tick, about 6 to 8 inches long. The humorous part here comes when the tick escapes with the 30cc size(!)syringe stuck in its back. This tick is seen crawling up the smooth walls of the vet's office. The vet steps on the tick, squashing it, and being the curious sort, begins to dissect it. The abdomen of this tick is filled with a red mucoid liquid, which I took to be semi-processed dog blood. After the examination, the vet says, "*Xyities tamini.* Judging from the mandibles and pseudo hair, a wood tick … severely altered, but a tick all the same. This specimen has been covered with something [the vet got some on her gloved fingers, then brought it up to her nose to sniff], possibly an herbal steroid. It's illegal, but some of the farmers use it on their marijuana fields to accelerate growth. From your description of the dog's behavior [excessive twitching during its death throes] this [steroid] may have even strengthened the tick's neurotoxin.… When a tick bites it numbs you so you don't feel it. In some cases it can produce an hallucinatory state." If tick juice were hallucinogenic, then you can bet someone, somewhere, is using it as a recreational drug.

A tick bites one of the campers, and he is able to remove its body. In doing so, a large amount of thick red goo (blood?) comes out of the tick body. That much blood cannot be removed so quickly. Unfortunately, the tick head lodges in the camper's thigh, eventually killing him. Later, the tick "molts" away the camper's skin, and a gigantic tick, about three feet long, splits open the body from the inside and emerges. This giant tick is eventually killed by fire.

What Biological Science Is Necessary to Achieve the Results in the Film: During insect larvae development a large number of genes are being turned on and off to help regulate the growth of the larva into an adult insect. During this phase a mutagen could significantly alter the growth hormonal levels, resulting in a larger insect. In the fruit fly, for instance, such viable mutations as an extra eye on the end of antennae, or an extra set of wings, have been created. Even a modest increase in size has been observed. But a ten-fold increase in size would require similar internal organ, neuromuscular development, and other physiology coordination to occur.

Could It Actually Happen: This film seems to be somewhat plausible. Under the right growth conditions an insect larvae (tick, whatever), when exposed to some mutagenic toxin and hormone, could potentially transform into something larger and meaner. Of course, all sorts of genetic conditions would have to be satisfied, but it may be possible. Finally, all ticks are parasitic during some part of their lives.

Skeeter (1993)

Synopsis: A company, in cahoots with the government, hides some nasty toxic waste drums in a mine shaft located some-where in the Southwest desert. Mosquitoes find the leaky drums, ingest some of the toxic liquid, mutate into foot long skeeters, and attack the residents of a local small town. The skeeters, their nest, and eggs are eventually found and burnt.

Screenplay: Lanny Horn and Clark Brandon, based on a story idea by Joe Rubin.

Biological Science Principles Involved: Entomology. Genetics. Mutagenesis.

What Is Right with the Biological Science Presented: The skeeter eggs and subsequently hatching larvae are shown to be on the surface of stagnant water pooled in the mine shaft. (Mosquito larvae will only hatch on the surface of stagnant water.) The toxic drums are leaking directly into this water, easily contributing to the mutagenic effects. Since the toxic leaks are isolated and only seen in this water, then other species were perhaps not affected by the mutagens. At least this is internally consistent.

The local coroner, Wyle, examines some of the skeeter victims and notes, "There's something consistent with the two bodies. Welts. Like you get from an insect bite. These [welts] are too large to explain." At least the coroner knows something is up and is able to identify the welts, though she does not (then) believe they come from insects.

What Is Wrong with the Biological Science Presented: The size of the skeeters is almost too big (though they are smaller than those in the following film *Mosquito*), but perhaps they could have survived. They appear to be about six to eight inches long. As discussed above, insects this size would have problems with their respiration. The skeeters are seen to fly about as normal mosquitoes, though perhaps a bit too fast. In one scene a boy on a motorcycle barely outruns the attacking (and hungry!) critters.

During one particular attack, a man and his daughter are inside a car and the skeeters bombard the windows, splattering themselves all over, trying to get inside to feed. This behavior does not make sense. These skeeters are like kamikaze pilots seeing how much of themselves they can spread on the car windows.

Some of the animal carcasses are so drained of fluids from a mosquito attack that they look almost mummy-like in their emaciation. It would take quite a number of mosquitoes to drain animals of that much fluid. A horse or cow contains as much as 15 to 20 liters of blood, and that would require a lot of mosquito bites.

What Biological Science Is Necessary to Achieve the Results in the Film: Normal-sized mosquitoes growing into the reel skeeters of this film would require the same changes in DNA I have often stressed. Everything would have to function normally.

The proboscis, the piercing aspect of the (female) mosquito mouth, would have to be sturdy enough to deeply pierce the skin of their intended victims. The apex of the piercing organ would have to retain adequate tensile strength to be able to penetrate enough of the skin to not only obtain the necessary blood volume to survive, but to also survive the physical aspects of the skin penetration itself. Needles, after a while, do become blunt, and the skeeter would need some method of renewing the cells and tissues of this organ for survival.

Could It Actually Happen: Based on the fairly reasonable size of these skeeters, and the fact that the toxic drums only leak into one confined area, the mutagenic results are biologically tolerable. However, mosquitoes of this size would have some trouble flying, particularly after gorging themselves on blood and taking on the added weight. As repeatedly stated, DNA mutagenesis of this extent is highly doubtful.

Mosquito (1994)

Synopsis: A spaceship crash-lands on Earth in a small pond on a farm. A mosquito lands on the arm of a dead alien and sucks its "blood," becoming infected and mutating into a larger version of itself. As a result, a large colony of mosquitoes hatches and attacks several humans. Finally, the mosquito nest is blown up.

Screenplay: Steve Hodge, Tom Chaney, and Gary Jones, from a story by Gary Jones.

The opening of this film is, without a doubt, inspired by the George Pal film *The War of the Worlds*, itself based on the H.G. Wells story of the same name. In the famous Wells story the invading Martians are defeated not by any weapons of destruction, but rather by "God's tiniest creatures," bacteria. At the end of the Pal film a hatch from a crashed Martian flying saucer opens to reveal a thin, slimy, alien hand and arm; it reaches out, briefly moves, then stops, indicating the creature has died. The opening of *Mosquito* also features a crashed flying saucer, a hatch that opens up, and an alien hand and arm (very similar in appearance to the one shown in Pal's movie) reach out, briefly move, then stop. Then a mosquito lands on the arm and sucks the alien's blood, thereby causing the mutations that follow.

Biological Science Principles Involved: Entomology. CULFology. Genetics.

What Is Right with the Biological Science Presented: A young couple are driving on a country road when a huge mosquito flies into their car window, splattering itself. The insect's proboscis impales itself in the radiator, causing a significant leak. The woman immediately knows what it is, saying, "...this looks like a proboscis—the mouth part of an insect used for feeding." So she knows some insect anatomy.

Later in the film, this same female sees one of the mosquitoes and says, "*Aedes aegypti* ... only females suck blood ... I don't know why it's so big. Could be some sort of genetic defect or toxic pollutant." To be able to give the genus and species name of the mosquito is remarkable, so this woman had to have known more than her share of entomology. Also, her speculation about "some sort of genetic defect or toxic pollutant" is exactly what I would have said.

In addition to the above, this intelligent female entomologist also says, "The thing I find so strange is that mosquitoes, real ones, I mean the little ones, suck blood from a human just once and they take the blood and they nourish their eggs with it." Yes indeed. These reel mosquitoes would need quite a lot of blood to nourish themselves and their huge nest.

What Is Wrong with the Biological Science Presented: The mosquito proboscis that impales itself in the car radiator early on in the film would have to be very strong to do that. The car is going no more than 45 mph and the mosquito much slower, so the combined relative speeds of the two would not have been enough to justify the penetration of the proboscis completely through a metal radiator. Later in the film, a pack(!) of mosquitoes attack a camper vehicle and push their probosci through the walls of the camper, through its windows, etc., indicating that not only are the probosci very sharp, but the insects are strong enough to apply the necessary force to actually penetrate some very hard and durable materials! Furthermore, during the attack on the camper the mosquitoes show intelligence by going for and puncturing the (spinning) tires, thereby causing the camper to crash.

The mosquitoes are up to about three feet in length, and their sword-like probosci appear to be about 18 inches long and about two inches in diameter. All in all,

these are rather serious weapons! When these reel mosquitoes attack humans they appear to remove about two to three liters of blood from each victim. Humans have about six to eight liters of blood, so taking 25 to 50 percent of this volume is silly.

The reel mosquitoes of this film are identified as being "*Aedes aegypti*," which is the yellow fever mosquito. What the yellow fever mosquito is doing on Midwest farmland is not explained. If this were true, then someone would notice local residents coming down with yellow fever!

Dr. Parks, an air force scientist specializing in meteors, investigates the crash site. His primary investigational tool is, believe it or not, a Geiger counter! Parks explains that his counter, "monitors different levels of alpha and gamma rays. Basically, stray radiation." Well, basically, Parks is completely wrong. Whenever Parks finds a dead body (from a mosquito attack) he tests the victims with his Geiger counter and notes that the bodies are "covered with radiation." For one particular victim, Parks says, "Just as I thought. Those mosquitoes are making these [victims] radioactive." The bodies seen are mummy-like, emaciated and sucked dry of most of their bodily fluids. In doing so, the reel mosquitoes would have injected very little radioactive matter into the victims, certainly not enough to register on something as crude as a Geiger counter. Mosquitoes remove fluids, they don't add them, so they could not have placed much radioactivity into their victims.

The female amateur entomologist notes that the mosquitoes exhibit intelligence in their attack methods. She says, "These things don't seem to stop after just one take. Their motive seems to be to kill." If true, this would indeed make these reel mosquitoes a major threat to mankind.

What Biological Science Is Necessary to Achieve the Results in the Film: What is implied in this film (though not implicitly stated) is the compatibility of the alien DNA with mosquito DNA. The alien DNA has to successfully integrate into the mosquito DNA in a functional manner for the results to have any meaning. Furthermore, the alien must have either some blood-like components and/or cells that the mosquito ingests during the bite, thereby obtaining the DNA. (Is there an attractant [pheromone?] on the alien skin that causes the mosquito to land in the first place?) The implications of this are profound. Exobiologists have speculated on the nature of life in the universe, and if some of that life is based on carbon (why not?), then there must be some sort of DNA equivalent whereby a series of molecules are capable of self-replication and coding for life forms. The surprise is not that alien life forms have DNA, but rather that this alien DNA is readily compatible with DNA from Earth! This would mean that life forms from Earth are capable of translating and transcribing alien DNA, have all the necessary enzymes and growth factors to do this with high fidelity, and create proteins that can function in meaningful ways. All in all, a tall order.

If a mosquito from Earth is so affected by the alien DNA that a larger mutated form results, then how about other species who obtain this DNA. For example, how would other insects, pond algae, bacteria, or nearby plants that have the alien DNA incorporated into their systems respond? Not to mention, say, humans who survive a mosquito attack and have some of the alien DNA injected into their bodies from the bite. Would these humans and other species so affected grow to fantastic size?

For the large size of the mosquitoes to occur, then the alien DNA must have altered the normal growth processes of this Earth species. Either excess growth hormones would be made in larger supply, or the genes that make them are never turned off, so the organism never stops growing.

For the alien DNA-infected mosquitoes to have such strong probosci would also imply other interesting biology. Perhaps there are other forms of strong collagen fibers incorporated into that piercing organ to allow it to withstand metal and glass and still retain its sharpness and tensile strength. There is also the possibility that the probosci have some type of enamel outer layer, similar to a tooth, composed of hydroxyapatite, calcium, and magnesium carbonate, mixed in with collagen to give it its tensile strength. When you mix in some alien DNA then just about anything can happen. And speaking of proboscis, the original Earth mosquito's proboscis must have either been strong enough to penetrate the crashed alien's skin, or the alien's skin must have been soft enough to allow easy penetration for the successful removal of its DNA.

It is noted by Parks that the victims of the reel mosquitoes are radioactive. For this to occur the mosquitoes would have to be carrying a very high level of radiation within their bodies; and each time they suck blood from a human, enough of this radioactivity would have to be left behind for a Geiger counter to detect it. With that much radioactivity it is amazing that these mosquitoes do not crash and burn! It is anyone's guess where this radioactivity comes from. Most likely from the surrounding environment (if this is true, then the entire place should have been shut down and decontaminated!). No way could it have come from the alien DNA. At best, the alien DNA codes for the means to acquire and live with that much radiation, not to manufacture it in the quantities suggested.

Could It Actually Happen: For the very interesting premise of this film to come true, Earth would have to be visited by DNA-compatible aliens. Some fervently believe that we already have.

My previous comments on the film *Skeeter* equally apply here.

Mimic (1997)

Synopsis: In attempting to cure a cockroach-derived children's plague, entomologist Dr. Susan Tyler inadvertently creates giant killer cockroaches, which infest New York City, particularly the subway system. The giant cockroaches are hybrids between mantids, termites, and humans. Some of the giant insects mimic a human form. Eventually, the hybrid insects are destroyed by fire.

Screenplay: Matthew Robbins and Guillermo del Toro, based on the short story "Mimic" by Donald A. Wollheim.

Biological Science Principles Involved: Entomology. Molecular Biology. Biochemistry.

What Is Right with the Biological Science Presented: Regarding the insects, everyone hates cockroaches, including me, so they get that right! And the genus name for the common cockroach is *Blattodea*, so they get that right too.

The plot of this film presents a scientifically complex story line and the verisimilitude of the science is gratifying to see. First of all, Tyler herself plays a credible entomologist, and her words and actions are of someone who cares about her profession and is clearly passionate about insects. It is refreshing to see a female in a role such as this.

During a discussion with two young boys about a termite nest, Tyler says, "If anything happens to insect nests, the entire colony would die out." This is true. She also explains that it would be best to kill only fertile males, so the entire colony would die for failure to reproduce. Also true.

At her home Tyler talks to her physician husband, Dr. Mann. Mann says, "You said the ones released only had a lifespan of six months." Tyler responds with, "We engineered them to be sterile adults. The Judas' were not supposed to last past one generation. The one I examined today was

a baby. They were designed to die. They are breeding." Engineering sterile insects is a common practice, and in San Diego where I live there is a program to introduce sterile "medflies" into the environment in the hope that this fruit-destroying species will breed itself onto the endangered species list. And yes, mutations do occur, and those sterile can somehow mutate into a breeding species.

While cleaning a subway sewer a blue collar worker comes across an (adolescent?) insect body about three feet long, and this is brought to the attention of Tyler. The sewer worker comments, "If it's got more than four legs it's not a mammal. It's a lobster, right?" Though humorous, it is this kind of thinking that is disturbing. More people, including your "average Joe," whom this sewer worker represents, need to be aware of more general science. His comment, "It's a lobster, right?" just shows what respect writers of SF films have for the common man.

While examining this same "lobster," Ostes comments, "Look, the [internal] organs are perfectly formed. They were functional. I'm guessing here ... but this thing is not just some random mutation, it's a highly evolved soldier cast. Formidable killer. It couldn't have developed in a vacuum. It's part of a colony." How correct he is. No way could such an organism have developed all by itself. A vibrant colony with others of similar ilk must also be present for such a creature to exist.

What Is Wrong with the Biological Science Presented: A cockroach infestation has hit Manhattan, and a disease (called "Strickler's Disease") only affects children, resulting in thousands of deaths. Since neither a cure nor a vaccine is available, the Center for Disease Control (CDC) decides to go after the disease carrier, the common cockroach (genus *Blattodea*). There is no such disease as Strickler's Disease (at least not yet, anyway).

During an opening speech by Tyler, she explains, "Since [cockroaches] have been proven to be virtually immune to chemical control, we had to find a new avenue of attack. With the aid of genetics labs across the country we recombined termite and mantid DNA to create a biological counter agent. A new species to be our six legged ally in wiping out the roach population. We call it the Judas breed. Once in contact with the Judas' secretions, the common roaches were infected with an enzyme which caused their metabolism to go into overdrive. No matter how much the common roaches ate, every last member of their nest starved to death in a matter of hours." The combination of termite and mantid DNA will not provide any selective advantage and certainly no "biological counter agent." The big assumption here is that cockroaches, to be affected, will have to come in physical contact with the Judas species. Furthermore, one just does not go out and "create a new species." Existing species can be modified, even mutated to something very different, but we cannot create new ones! In addition, it is implied that the enzyme secretions will enter the roaches and be functional. Enzymes are proteins, and all organisms have mechanisms that degrade ingested proteins, the cockroach is no exception. Ingested enzymes will be immediately digested, degraded, and broken down into harmless amino acids for reutilization. Therefore, coming "in contact" and "infected with an enzyme" just will not happen.

Tyler goes on to add, "The transfer of recombinant genetic material from termites and mantids into Judas breed will allow rapid enzymatic change ... showing 100 percent sterility in all Judas females. Utilization of suicide gene ... leading to a life expectancy of 120 to 180 days." While saying this, Tyler takes some Judas insect secretions and places a sample on some pH litmus paper. The resulting pH test sample matches the Judas species released in Manhattan three years previously, indicating the species has indeed survived. Litmus paper is a fairly crude test and is used to measure the relative acidity or alkalinity of solutions. It is certainly not indicative of any species of insect, nor is it an indication of the survivability of an organism.

One of the major cinema taboos has to do with the endangerment of children. It is very rare to see a child hurt or threatened in any way. Not only is this taboo broken in this film, it is shattered! Two boys, while searching the subways of New York for insect eggs, come across an adult Judas bug, human looking in size and appearance, which is holding a dead dog and feeding on it. The adult bug attacks and actually kills the boys!

Late in the film, when we finally see an adult Judas insect, it is about six feet tall and looks like it is wearing an overcoat. I have already commented why insects cannot be that size, primarily due to respiration problems; however, the adult Judas has something which may have allowed it to get that big: lungs! Tyler, her husband, a policeman, and a civilian are trapped in an abandoned subway car and are attacked by the mimic insects. The policeman empties two clips of ammo into one of the bugs before killing it (30 rounds of ammo will stop anything!). While looking at the bullet-opened bug carcass, Tyler says, "These are lungs." Her husband, a physician, says, "Biology 101. Insects don't have lungs. It's what limits their size." The amount of DNA necessary for cockroaches to develop lungs is incredible, and no way could termite, mantid, and roach DNA evolve into something with lungs! In addition to this, Tyler says, "Secretions are the same. When I increased the Judas' metabolism, I must have sped up its breeding cycle. We're talking tens, hundreds of thousands of generations. Who knows how many mutations." Mann says, "How could the Judas evolve into this?" Tyler responds with, "Think generations, not years. It took only 40,000 generations for apes to turn into humans. We changed its DNA ... I mean we don't know what we did." Other than the "40,000 generations for apes to turn into humans" comment, which is probably correct, everything else is wrong. A generation is about 25 years so 40,000 generations is about a million years, and some anthropologists think that was enough for *Homo sapiens* to evolve from ape-like ancestors.

To justify the title of the film, near the end Tyler says, "Sometimes an insect will evolve to mimic its predator. A fly can look like a spider, a caterpillar can look like a snake. The Judas evolved to mimic its predator ... us." Though it is stretching the point a bit, with enough alcohol (or drugs) in your system you could probably look at some species of fly and perhaps see a spider, or believe a caterpillar to be a *very* small snake, but for an insect to mimic a human is beyond ludicrous!

What Biological Science Is Necessary to Achieve the Results in the Film: The actual insertion of functional DNA genes into other species, such as a termite's and/or a mantid's into a cockroach, is no longer a problem because the biological science necessary to achieve this is currently available.

The engineered(!) Judas species secretes some enzymes that are able to infect roaches and cause their metabolism to "go into overdrive," resulting in "every last member of their nest starv[ing] to death in a matter of hours," no matter how much the roaches eat. For this to occur, the ingested enzymes would have to be resistant to the natural degradative actions of roach digestion, meaning other degradative enzymes, acidic pH in the roach gut, and other biochemical reactions. Biochemically, to ingest protein and still starve to death involves what we call "futile cycles." In simple terms, this is the equivalent of spinning one's wheels. While doing so you spend a lot of energy and go nowhere. Biochemically, energy is expended in these futile cycles, usually involving glucose metabolism and the "Krebs cycle," and metabolism is in "overdrive"—yet no net energy is obtained. Normally, ingested protein is broken down into its individual amino acids, and these amino acids are either reutilized or enter the metabolic Krebs cycle and are metabolized for energy. In futile cycles the same events occur, but no net energy is obtained and the necessary enzymes are out of whack and literally spin around. A metabolite is broken down and rebuilt again, burning up energy in the process. It's similar to digging a hole then filling it, digging it again and filling it again, etc.; you get nothing done but you do burn a lot of energy in the process. In one respect, this is a dream of many individuals looking for weight loss programs; eat all you want and literally starve. That is not a healthy way to go.

Could It Actually Happen: The day will come when certain genes will be introduced into other species, especially insects, for control and regulation aspects. If necessary, perhaps termite and mantid DNA could actually be inserted into roach genomes. Even so, there would have to be a very compelling reason for scientists to do this, which would most likely be population control.

Regarding the development of large insects that mimic man—and those who develop lungs—you need not fear, since this will not happen.

11 SHRINKOLOGY

The next three films have to do with "Shrinkology," the science of being and becoming small. How small is small? The old adage that size is relative equally applies here. One man's David is another man's Goliath. The best example is Jonathan Swift's *Gulliver's Travels*, where a man of the same size appeared completely different to the Lilliputs (as large) and the Brobdingnagians (as small). The smallest animal in the kingdom Animalia is the tiny spider mite, which is a small white fleck to the unaided human eye and is Godzilla-size compared to a single bacterium; so yes indeed, size is relative.

The question "how small is small?" is like the sands of time, ever shifting and ever changing. The field of nanotechnology is completely changing our perspective of small. Levers, gears, and latches are constantly getting smaller and smaller. Even "molecular machines" are now down to the size of a single protein that can act as a motor. But what about actual biological life? How small can this be? Viruses have been classified as "on the verge of life," primarily because they cannot self-replicate —*the* key distinction that separates non-living things from living things. The smallest bacteria is about one micron long,

but my interests are in the kingdom of animals and not prokaryotes nor protozoa (both single-celled organisms). Therefore, how small can you make multicellular organisms so that they still function? There must be a head, a body of some type, and appendages. These next three films touch on this concept, and I find that intriguing.

When referring to Shrinkology there are two ways to go. If the number of atoms (or individual cells) of an organism are the same when it shrinks, then the weight will remain unchanged. What this means is the density of the organism will increase. For example, one of my favorite comic book superheros, "The Atom," works in this manner. His mass of about 180 pounds is a constant, and when he becomes smaller his weight stays the same. This has provided some very entertaining and interesting plot lines over the years.

However, when an organism shrinks and its number of atoms also decreases, then there will be fewer cells and it will weigh proportionately less. Of the two scenarios, I prefer the latter because it does not invoke some weird physics and biology as we know it here on Earth. The atoms remain atoms and not some super dense atom with diminished electron orbitals such as you would find within a cosmic black hole.

Regarding the film *Fantastic Voyage*, there are two things that stand out in my mind and deserve special comment. One is the "author" of the work. After the movie came out, Dr. Isaac Asimov was asked to write a novelization of it. In my opinion, no one but the "good doctor" could have done the job that he did. I was 15 years old when I read that book and I found it utterly fascinating. Because Asimov did such a good job, people often think that he himself conceived of the plot, and that the movie was based on his work. In reality, he was just a "hired gun" to write a credible book based on the film.

The second thing that stands out in my mind regarding *Fantastic Voyage* was the impression it made on my father, a pathologist. It was very easy to talk him into taking me to that film, and I have very clear and vivid memories of the drive back home after seeing it. My dad was very animated and excited about what was shown within the human body by that film. He was telling us which parts were good, which were okay, and which were not. In hindsight, that critical analysis of his more or less set the gears in motion in my mind that have culminated in this book. Once again, Dad, thanks for being there!

The Devil-Doll (1936)

Synopsis: Lavond, an escaped convict who was unjustly accused, seeks revenge on the three partners who swindled him and set him up. Lavond happens upon a scientist at his home who has developed a method for making miniature animals and people. Lavond and the scientist's wife, Malita, enact a revenge plot involving miniature humans and end up poisoning two of the partners. The third partner, fearing for his life, confesses, thereby clearing Lavond's name.

Screenplay: Garrett Fort, Guy Endore, and Eric Von Stroheim, from a story by Tod Browning.

Biological Science Principles Involved: Shrinkology. Physiology. Endocrinology.

What Is Right with the Biological Science Presented: The motivation of Marcel (the scientist) is honorable, but (like with all cinemascientists) out of high aspirations and lofty goals are sown the seeds of trouble. As Marcel explains to Lavond, "Millions of years ago the creatures that roamed this world were gigantic. As they multiplied, the earth could no longer produce enough food [not true!]. Think of it, Lavond, every living creature reduced to one-sixth its size, one-sixth its physical need. Food for six times all of us. Lavond, you know that all matter is composed of atoms and all atoms are made of electrons. Well, I've found a way to reduce all atoms in a body simultaneously to any desired degree and still maintain life.... Only, in reducing the brain all records are wiped off, no memory left, no will of its own. A creature capable of responding only to the force of another will." That is a remarkable explanation.

To activate the lab apparatus, Marcel goes through quite an elaborate system of body movements—turning handles, connecting tubes, adjusting valves, etc.—that give the impression he certainly knows what he is doing. Marcel simply tinkers with his lab "toys" until he gets them to work, a process more common in the real scientific world than you perhaps imagine.

What Is Wrong with the Biological Science Presented: Marcel wants to shrink everything to one-sixth its natural size, making a six-foot-tall man only one foot high. Why only one-sixth? Why not one-twelfth or one-twenty-fourth, thereby making even *more* food available for the masses? Marcel did not think this all through very carefully because the machines

The Devil-Doll (1936): In his home lab, Marcel (Henry Walthall, right) is about to give life to one of his miniature creations. Visible in the background are well stocked reagent shelves.

of man are designed for our current size. How would a foot-tall man operate a car or fire a weapon? Steering and touching the gas pedal of a car would be challenging (to say the least), not to mention handling the recoil from a rifle. A foot-tall man firing a full sized high powered rifle would completely destroy his shoulder! Not to mention using the (gigantic) farm machinery necessary to till the soil, harvest full sized corn, or can fruit. The list goes on and on.

The actual shrinking process itself is a combination of physical and chemical processes. No comments on the physical aspect will be made, since they are outside the limits of this book. Suffice it to say that the people are placed under some sort of light source, which affects their shrinking. The chemical aspects, however, are inter-

esting. Marcel develops some liquid solution that he both sprays over and injects into the people (or animals) he wants to shrink.

A 22 gauge needle is used to inject the solutions into the miniature people. Now this is a one-sixth body, so a 22 gauge needle would leave a tremendous hole in their arms! How is the bleeding stopped? What kind of scar tissue forms over the injection site? A body that small receiving even a 100 microliter volume injection would have too much liquid to handle. To make this work Marcel would have to develop instruments that are of the same scale as the people he shrinks.

What Biological Science Is Necessary to Actually Achieve the Results in the Film: To reduce body size has been, in principle, the Holy Grail of the weight loss industry. That billion-dollar-plus industry is constantly looking for easy, safe, user friendly ways to reduce body size. (I am not distinguishing between total body mass, size, or fat; whatever your shape or size, just imagine it to be five-sixth smaller.) Bone, muscle, skin, organs, etc., would have to be done "simultaneously," as Marcel explains. If not done simultaneously, then the person would not survive. To reduce that much mass (five-sixths of your body) so quickly would give off a tremendous amount of heat, and that alone would probably kill the person, so a system would have to be put in place that could siphon off the produced heat. Marcel could have used the mist spraying technique to allow the released heat to be absorbed by the moisture.

Given a six-foot man with a weight of 200 pounds, approximately 166 pounds would have to be removed if he is to be reduced to one-sixth his size. That is a lot to just "remove" without surgery! To reduce that much body mass, hormones would have to be used. This is where the injection would come in. The injected fluid would have to contain some sort of hormonal mixture that activates a number of enzymes, which in turn would diminish body mass and metabolism. After all, if a tadpole can "shrink" its tail (actually, absorb), then an animal (with appropriate hormones and enzymes) could also do the same (at least in principle).

Could It Actually Happen: Instead of decreasing the size of animals so there would be plenty of food, Marcel should have thought about leaving the size of animals the same and increasing the size of food. Then there would be plenty for all. In reality, this is what much of the agricultural industry is aiming at. More productive use of farming land, better yields, and bigger foodstuffs will benefit all.

The use of hormones to reduce body size is fraught with physiological problems, and I just do not see it happening. Furthermore, the FDA would have a very difficult time approving such a system. To reduce your body size you essentially have two choices. Do not eat as much or exercise more. Of the two, I would highly recommend you exercise more. The third option, of course, would be to eat less *and* exercise more. Your body will thank you.

The Incredible Shrinking Man (1957)

Synopsis: While out on a boat on the ocean, Robert Carey is exposed to a radioactive cloud. As a result, Carey begins to grow smaller. At first he notices his clothes no longer fit and that he has lost some weight. Over time he becomes smaller and smaller, and eventually he is small enough that first a house cat and then a spider become a serious threat to him. The film ends with Carey disappearing from view and, in a voice-over, espousing on philosophical matters of what it means to be infinitely small.

Screenplay: Richard Matheson, based on his novel *The Shrinking Man.*

Biological Science Principles Involved: Shrinkology. Cell Biology. Physiology. Biochemistry.

What Is Right with the Biological Science Presented: Unlike the film *The Devil-Doll,* in which the shrinking procedures are very rapid and occur in a matter of moments, the shrinking in this film occurs over months. At first the shrinking is slow, but it eventually picks up speed, which is exactly what would be expected (if real). This is one of the more pleasant aspects of the film.

Early on, Carey says he has "...been six feet, one inch since 17." At the doctor's office he measures out at five feet, eleven

Robert Carey (Grant Williams), about three inches tall, is about to do battle with a tarantula in *The Incredible Shrinking Man* (1957).

inches. To explain this "modest" height problem the doctor says, "There are a number of things which could cause such errors [in measuring height]. For example, if you stood erect you'd measure out as taller ... because people actually decrease in height during the day. You see, the body weight actually compresses the spinal discs, the bones, joints, and so on." All of this is certainly correct.

Later, Carey's clothes are very loose and "too big." A week after the doctor's visit, Carey has lost another four pounds. His wife kisses him without stretching, and Carey says, "You used to stand on your toes to do that [and he had his shoes on!]. I'm getting smaller every day."

During the second visit to the doctor's office, the physician compares two chest x-rays, measures bones, and says, "I needed two full sets of pictures, taken sev-

eral days apart. I had to compare them before I could be sure. You are getting smaller. I don't profess to understand it. There's no medical precedent for what's happening to you. I simply know you're getting smaller. The x-rays prove it beyond any doubt." Two important things are presented here. First, the doctor uses a very simple and effective means of establishing whether Carey is indeed shrinking, namely, the use of x-rays. Second, the doctor is honest in saying he does not know why Carey is getting smaller. Most doctors claim to know everything and pontificate on all sorts of reasons so that they will sound authoritative. This doctor readily admits his lack of understanding, and that is refreshing to hear.

During a voice-over, while Carey is seen undergoing multiple physical examinations, he says, "Then began an extensive series of tests. I drank a barium solution and stood behind a fluoroscope screen. They gave me radioactive iodine and an examination with a Geiger counter. I had electrodes fastened to my head. Water restriction tests, protein bond tests (?!), eye tests, blood cultures, x-rays and more x-rays. Tests. Endless tests." All of this looks very convincing and quite real. As a result of this a doctor comes to him and says, "Now don't be despondent Mr. Carey. At least we found out what is happening to you. Gradual loss of nitrogen, calcium, phosphorous." To shrink in size you would have to lose significant bone mass, and calcium and phosphorous would be key to that happening. At least the doctors recognize this phenomena for what it is, a degenerative disease, the correct diagnosis. To be able to effectively treat a disease, the physician must first know what the malady is so he can prescribe the correct therapy. (For what it is worth, I have never heard of "protein bond tests" — that is a new one for me.)

Later, in the doctor's office we have the following interesting exchange. The doctor asks Carey, "Have you ever been accidentally exposed to any kind of a germ spray? In particular, an insecticide, a great deal of insecticide." Carey then relates an incident that happened about two months previously in which he was accidentally sprayed by a truck spraying trees. The doctor then says, "Something happened to that insecticide after it was in your system. Something fantastic and unprecedented. Something which in layman's terms so affected the insecticide that from a mildly virulent germ spray it created deadly chemical reversal of the growth process. Have you been exposed to any type of radioactivity in the past six months?" After thinking about this Carey responds with, "The mist [on the boat]." In "layman's terms" this is called mutagenesis, which is the production of genetic alterations

through chemicals and/or radiation. The mist radiation could have set the stage, and the insect spray could have been the catalyst that caused the genetic alterations to occur. In theory this scenario is plausible.

Carey's final soliloquy is worth noting and attests to the interesting psychological state of his mind. Though he is becoming too small to be visible to the naked human eye, his mental acuity is apparently still functioning. At film's end, Carey narrates an extensive voice-over, saying, "I continued to shrink. What was I, still a human being or was I the man of the future? If there were other bursts of radiation, other clouds drifting across seas and continents, would other beings follow me into this vast new world? So close, the infinitesimal and the infinite. But suddenly, I knew they were really the two ends of the same concept. The unbelievably small and the unbelievably vast eventually meet. Like the closing of a gigantic circle. I looked up as if somehow I would grasp the heavens, the universe, worlds beyond number. God's silver tapestry spread across the night. And in that moment, I knew the answer to the infinite. I had thought in terms of man's own limited dimension. I had presumed upon nature that existence begins and ends in man's conception, not nature's. And I felt my body dwindling, melting, becoming nothing. My fears melted away and in their place came acceptance. All this vast majesty of creation, it had to mean something. And then I meant something too. Yes, smaller than the smallest, I meant something too. To God, there is no zero. I still exist." That is quite a mouthful. Some beautiful imagery is seen while Carey intones what I feel to be one of the most powerful statements man can make. When faced with the most difficult of choices, and the immovable force of fate and time, man always philosophizes about his place in the cosmos. This has been going on ever since primitive man looked up to the heavens and began to question and dream. (All of this from writer Richard Matheson.)

What Is Wrong with the Biological Science Presented: One of the multiple tests performed on Carey is a "paper chromatography test." This procedure involves the separation of chemical substances and particles by differential movement through a liquid two-phase system. The moving phase is a liquid and the stationary phase is the paper. The sample to be separated is added to a sheet of specially absorbent paper, and the sample elements least soluble migrate the least, while those elements most soluble migrate the most, resulting in a separation of the individual components of the test sample. In Carey's case, the sample is probably his serum. At the time this film was made, paper chromatography was a popular method of analysis, though it is quite outmoded today and used only in special circumstances.

The doctor uses the paper chromatography test to "tell us why" Carey has a "gradual loss of nitrogen, calcium, and phosphorous." When analyzing the results, the doctor says, "I think the strips should be dry by now. We should find phospholipid, amino acids, cholesterol, creatinine, and protein. These are the elements most commonly found on the strip." Yes, those elements can be found on paper chromatography strips; however, not at the same time and certainly not on the same strip! Phospholipids and cholesterol are fats, and a completely different liquid phase is needed to separate them; the liquid is typically a chloroform/methanol solution. The other elements, amino acids, creatinine, and protein, though similar, also require a different liquid phase separation system. Proteins are done separately and are in a class by themselves. Creatinine can be classified as an amino acid, so this can probably be done on the same strip. Please note that there are 20 common amino acids found in proteins. To have all of these procedures done on a single paper chromatography strip is ridiculous. Furthermore, paper chromatography is mostly a qualitative test and not a quantitative test. Though it is interesting to see paper chromatography, this is just far too much to ask from such a simple test.

This paper chromatography bit is not yet done. After carefully examining the paper strip the doctor says, "Wait a minute, this one doesn't belong. It certainly doesn't belong." The doctor then looks at the strip under a microscope! Is the doctor blind? The resolution of paper chromatography is so crude that you can observe the results clear across the room; using a microscope is laughable.

To make this even more unbelievable, the doctor then tells Carey, "Our analysis [the paper chromatography test] shows it's [i.e., shrinking] a rearrangement of the molecular structure of the cells in your body." Carey's wife, who is also in the doctor's office listening to this entertaining explanation, responds with, "You mean like a cancer?" The doctor says, "No. More like an anti-cancer(!) causing a diminution of all the organs proportionally." Though the concept of "anti-cancer" is interesting to me, that is really the wrong way to think about shrinkology. (The word tumor, which means a "swelling," is synonymous with cancer, so anti-cancer could mean an anti-swelling. In this case, perhaps the doctor has it right, since an anti-swelling could mean a shrinking. However, cancer typically means uncontrolled growth, so anti-cancer would then mean anti-uncontrolled growth, which in turn would mean controlled growth. In Carey's case, this has little meaning. It would have been better if the doctor had used the term "anti-tumor.")

In an effort to combat the shrinking, the doctor develops an anti-toxin, which in itself is interesting. A toxin is a substance that is poisonous or noxious and has specific biochemical effects on individual cells. The result(s) of a toxin exposure is essentially a one-time effect, whereas the radioactive mist and insecticide spray combination results in genetic mutations that are long term, if not permanent; so, strictly speaking, an "anti-toxin" is not what Carey needs. Even the word "vaccine" is inappropriate, since his problems are genetic and not the result of some substance (i.e., toxin) coursing through his blood. Most likely, Carey would have needed some sort of gene therapy to permanently overcome the genetic problems of physiological imbalance.

One aspect not discussed in this film, and one which is important, is that of his mental state. As a healthy adult he appears to be reasonably intelligent. As he becomes smaller the number of his brain cells would also decrease — that is decrease, not diminish. If they decreased, then he would perhaps lose some of his memory or other body functions that his autonomic and sympathetic nervous system would involuntarily regulate. As he becomes significantly smaller, it is shown that he still uses his mind for not only problem solving but also to maintain a normally functioning body. With such a smaller body something would have to give in his mental capacity. His cerebral cortex, cerebellum, et al., would have to proportionately diminish, and for him to maintain all of his normal functions with this going on is too difficult to accept. With a decreasing mental capacity occurring over several months, it is an interesting exercise to analyze which parts of the mind would go and in what order. There would have to be both qualitative and quantitative differences.

What Biological Science Is Necessary to Actually Achieve the Results in the Film: The question is a simple one. What physiological and biochemical processes are necessary to lose body mass and actu-

ally shrink? The answer is also simple. The processes would have to be hormonal. The biggest problem in shrinkology is that of bone resorption. To understand that, it would help to know something about the structure and makeup of bone.

In man there are over 200 separate bone structures. Bone is a hard connective tissue consisting of cells embedded in a matrix of mineralized ground substance and collagen fibers. These fibers are composed of a form of calcium phosphate, similar to hydroxyapatite, as well as a substantial amount of carbonate, citrate, sodium, and magnesium. Bone is composed of about 75 percent inorganic matter and about 25 percent organic material. Also, bone consists of a dense outer layer of compact inorganic material (referred to as the cortical substance) covered by the periosteum, while the inner area is a loose, spongy organic material; the central area of long bones (such as the femur) is called the marrow. The toughest job would be to get rid of a lot of inorganic matter, in the form of calcium. There are biochemical ways of doing this, and there are degenerative diseases in which bone resorption does occur. The term for this is called osteophagia, which means the eating of bones. A bone cell called an osteoclast (which is a large multinucleated cell, possibly of monocyte origin) functions in the absorption and removal of bone tissue. There would be a vitamin D deficiency, the mobilization of the hormonal effects to remove calcium from bone, and then a shrinking of their size. The months this would take are completely in line with the time frame depicted in the film.

While all this bone resorption (osteophagia) is going on in Mr. Carey's body, his other cells and tissues would also have to concomitantly diminish in size. These effects are much easier to rationalize than the bone resorptions and also require hormonal intervention. There is a general process called apoptosis, which is essentially a form of cell suicide. In apoptosis, a cell literally falls apart and its individual components are absorbed by other cells. In Carey's case there would be no absorption, and the cell matter would have been eliminated by normal bodily functions. All this non-reused body tissue would have to go somewhere, so Carey must have had some very large bowel movements for a few months. An interesting image is him looking into the toilet bowl after he had done his business and wondering where it had all come from.

In addition to all this, his basal metabolic rate would also have to increase. His body's physiology would have been "hyper" to burn off the excess fat, protein, and carbohydrates generated from the cellular apoptosis mechanisms. As a result, he would have periodic "hot flashes" as his body's temperature increases from time to time to accommodate the heat generated from all the enzymatic reactions (which do generate heat), due to all that cellular metabolic activity.

Could It Actually Happen: In some respects, this does happen, primarily in older people in which bone resorption does occur. However, this bone resorption does not occur in a uniform manner. As such, some sections of bone become more brittle than other sections, often resulting in fractures, breaks, and a lot of pain. In Carey's case, his entire body shrank at a completely uniform rate, which is the most unusual aspect of his predicament. In that respect it could actually happen. However, neither general organ resorption nor shrinking occurs.

Fantastic Voyage (1966)

Synopsis: A Soviet agent defecting to the U.S. is wounded by Russians, and an inoperable, life threatening blood clot forms in his brain. The only way to save him is to miniaturize a team of scientists to enter the agent's blood stream and destroy the clot. Once inside the agent's body the team is threatened by his natural biological defenses. The clot is eventually destroyed, and the team makes it out of the agent's body in the nick of time.

Screenplay: Harry Kleiner, adapted by David Duncan, based on a story by Otto Klement and Jay Lewis Bixby.

Biological Science Principles Involved: Shrinkology. Physiology. Immunology.

What Is Right with the Biological Science Presented: General O'Brien, the military man in charge of the project, says, "The only way we can reach that clot is from inside the brain." Since the agent's clot is located deep inside the cerebrum, it is inoperable (at least by 1966 standards). Using stereotaxic mapping of the agent's brain, they determine the clot is on the left side. "The only way to reach it [the clot] is by the arteriole system," so the miniaturized Proteus submarine is injected into the carotid artery, the best route to get into the cerebrum, where the clot is.

To make the job easier the agent is made hypothermic to slow down his heartbeat, circulation, and other general physiological processes, which is a good idea. Just before the operation we hear the vital statistics of the agent. "Blood pressure holding steady at 32 per minute ... respiration is down to six a minute ... the hypothermia is holding him at 28 degrees centigrade." All reasonable.

The navigator of the sub's crew says, "[the] lymphatic system drains off excess fluid ... without it we'd all blow up like balloons." That is correct.

What Is Wrong with the Biological Science Presented: There is some confusion regarding the agent's diagnosis. At first it is called a brain tumor, then it is called a blood clot. The difference is not

Fantastic Voyage (1966): the Proteus Submarine, with various clotted fibers and human antibody complexes strewn about. These clumps will be an irritant, and an inflammatory-like response could occur.

trivial, and the physicians should have been able to distinguish this. Though both are life threatening, the brain tumor is definitely the biggest problem, since the tumor cells could spread (metastasize) to other parts of the body, whereas the clot would be confined to the area of origin and treated with anti-coagulants. A blood clot is coagulated blood and consists of a soft, jelly-like mass of converted fibrinogen to fibrin that has entrapped red blood cells in its matrix. The problem with a blood clot in the brain is that it could interfere with critical blood flow and result in a debilitating stroke or even death.

The Proteus sub is nuclear powered and is tracked like any radioactive tracer. There are all sorts of problems with this. Since the sub is "miniaturized," its nuclear power source would also have been miniaturized. The physics of this is, of course, impossible; but assuming it could happen, then I doubt if the radioactive decay detectors would be sensitive enough to pick up the miniaturized decay particles, making the precise anatomical location of the Proteus sub impossible.

The major drawback to being miniaturized is the 60-minute time limit. Apparently, after 60 minutes everything that is miniaturized returns to its normal size, including the sub and its crew. The General says, "You must be out within 60 minutes. After that you are in danger of attack. Banisch's [the agent] natural defenses … white corpuscles, antibodies. Once you begin to grow you become a menace to the body and you trigger them off." The biggest problem would not have been the agent's "natural defenses" but the size problem of the sub and crew enlarging and blowing a large hole in the agent's body!

The enlargement happens in a matter of seconds, much too fast for any sort of immune response to occur.

One of the major concerns with the biomedicine in this film is the apparent lack of sterile technique. Prior to entering the sub, the crew of five enters a "sterilization chamber." Such chambers are not 100 percent efficient, and all it takes is *one* contaminating bacteria to cause problems. And what about all the myriad components of the Proteus sub? The outer hull could have been scrubbed clean, but would it have been 100 percent effective? For the actual miniaturization, the sub is shrunk and placed into a syringe and shrunk again. The assistant who puts the syringe plunger and the needle onto the miniaturized syringe uses ungloved hands. Furthermore, the syringe needle is uncapped! No way is this 100 percent sterile. As if that isn't enough, later in the film some of the crew exit the sub and swim in the agent's blood fluids. The crew members are covered with standard scuba gear on their bodies, with the exception of their hair and hands, the two parts of the body that would cause the most problems! Blood fluids come in direct contact with their hair, and during some of this action some of the hair follicles (or eczema scalp cells) slough off. (What happens to this sloughed hair when the 60-minute time limit expires? Those follicles should have increased to their natural size and would have caused all sorts of clogging problems. Also, what about any bacteria, viruses, etc., which are also attached to the hair and scalp? Those left behind would have increased to their natural size and could eventually have been life threatening. Finally, what about the crud located under the fingernails of their ungloved hands? What would happen to that stuff after 60 minutes?)

When the miniature Proteus and crew are injected into the agent's carotid artery, very few red blood cells (RBCs) are seen in the fluid. Typically, there are at least 10 million RBCs per milliliter of blood, and nowhere near that amount is seen. Perhaps the agent had severe anemia. When the Proteus enters a vein, the RBCs actually look blue! In addition to this, the RBCs seen are too amorphous and jelly-like; in real life, RBCs are fairly rigid in form, though quite flexible.

The size of the miniaturized sub appears to be about five times larger than the RBCs. When entering a capillary blood vessel, a normal RBC has to squeeze through. Well, the sub has no problem navigating the capillary bed. While in the capillaries, RBCs are actually seen to change from blue to red as they are reoxygenated, which is silly. Upon seeing this, a physician comments, "The engineering of the cycle of a breath."

At one point the sub is sidetracked into the lymphatics, which are a series of vessels that carries the lymph. In turn, the lymph is a clear, transparent, and faintly yellow fluid collected from the body's tissues and is eventually added to the venous blood circulation. Also in the lymph are lymphocytes, the cells of the immune system, and a few red blood cells. While the ship is in the lymphatics, seaweed-like reticular fibers clog the sub's intake valves and vents. The crew has to make an unscheduled excursion outside the sub to clear the debris. While they are in the fluids, antibodies are seen attacking a bacteria cell. The antibodies are seen as complexes. Normally they exist as individual molecules. The antibodies are also seen moving through the body's fluids very rapidly, like a guided missile. In reality, they move as fast as the general flow of fluids.

Regarding the Raquel Welch antibody scene, in which she causes an irritation and triggers an antibody response, the on board physician says, "If the antibodies reach her they will attack her as if she were bacteria." Antibodies also attack body-sized cells, viruses, and other cellular components, in addition to small bacteria. Finally, after the antibodies do reach her and cover her body, she says, "They're tightening. I … can't … breathe." Just like a boa constrictor. (On a personal note, I was 15 years old, with raging hormones, when I saw this film, and the scenes of the crew pulling off the "antibodies" attached to Welch, especially those on her breasts, sure got my blood boiling! In my professional career, in dealing with human antibodies I think of this scene often, but I digress…) The antibodies that attack Welch are seen as relatively large, compared to her body, and are strung or hooked together like a string of pearls. This just does not happen.

The crew eventually makes it to the clot and destroys it with a laser. The laser is used in the fluids of the body, and the liquid may have had negative effects on the power of the emitted light.

The biggest problem I have with the biological science in this film occurs after the crew zaps the clot and a large white corpuscle (a lymphocyte) "attacks" the sub, dissolving it! I never heard of a lymphocyte dissolving metal. Not only that, what would happen to the miniaturized

metal atoms after the expiration of the 60 minute time limit? These atoms should return to normal size, thereby causing an interesting death scene for the agent.

What Biological Science Is Necessary to Actually Achieve the Results in the Film: The best way to dissolve a blood clot would be to use enzymes, especially those that work on fibrin. There are a few good ones available, such as "TPA" and a form of collagenase, which are routinely used on heart attack patients to prevent the clotting of blood. These could be introduced into the body, using the natural blood flow to let the enzymes go to the lesion and dissolve the clot. The best way to use a laser would be to employ fiber optics, small light-carrying fibers that bend and angle light to the place you want it to go, in this case the brain blood clot. Only a small amount of the clot is dissolved, enough so the rest can be absorbed by the body.

Could It Actually Happen: Miniaturization is impossible and would require a completely new set of physics for this to happen. The use of nanomachines to do the work of the sub and its crew is not that far off in the future. Using miniaturized machines combined with single molecule "clot busters" is certainly possible.

12 CULFOLOGY

Biological life comes in many shapes, sizes, and forms. The rich diversity of life that has evolved on this planet is truly awe inspiring. For every adversity over the eons Mother Nature has found a way to overcome it. The true power of DNA to adapt and modify itself is, unfortunately, appreciated by far too few people.

CULFology, the study and analysis of Creating Unusual Life Forms, is one of the cinemascientists' favorite pastimes. The creation of life forms in general has been going on for some time in many laboratories throughout the world. The major difference is in creating intelligent life forms that are capable of sustaining life all their own. Real scientists are a long way from achieving that goal. And it *will* be reached, to be sure. The applications are endless, so once all the appropriate genetic elements are understood, then CULFology will stop being a reel science and become a real science.

In some respects it already is real, though under a different name. Cryptozoology is the science of "hidden animals," such as the Yeti and the Coelacanth. The word "cryptozoology" first appeared in print in 1959, so it is a relatively new discipline. What makes an animal of interest to cryptozoologists is that it is unexpected. Quite frankly, there are some legitimate scientists who view cryptozoology with skepticism and treat it as a sort of "pseudoscience."

What is created and how it was created are of interest to the CULFologist. The life form started with just serves as a basis to build on. The changes made can be either surgical or genetic, or perhaps both. To confront these issues in real life would be interesting, especially with respect to which would be easier, surgery or genetic alterations. Surgical changes would be immediate, whereas some genetic alterations could take months or perhaps even years to occur.

The Killer Shrews (1959)

Synopsis: Dr. Craigis, on an isolated island, develops a serum that transforms normal sized shrews into killer shrews (which look suspiciously like dogs). Craigis wants to control animal size, and therefore metabolism, diet, and overpopulation. The shrews kill some people, and a few of the humans are able to escape the island in a boat.

Screenplay and Story: Jay Simms.

Biological Science Principles Involved: CULFology. Genetics. Physiology.

What Is Right with the Biological Science Presented: Selective breeding programs to enhance species have been ongoing for centuries, so, in principle, there is really nothing new here.

It is stated that shrews (genus *Sorex*; species *soricidie*) must eat their own body weight every few hours. This is true because of the shrew's small size. With mammals, especially small ones, their body size is a problem. This mostly has to do with maintaining homeostatic body temperatures. Since mammals are warm blooded, they generate a lot of body heat, and this usually dissipates out of the body through natural openings and pores in the skin. The bigger the mammal the more "insulation" there is from the body's mass; this insulation helps to maintain the body's internal heat. Small mammals, like the shrew, have to consume a lot of food to maintain their body heat because they have very little insulation to keep the heat in. This is why the shrew and others, like the kangaroo rat, have to constantly eat. As Craigis correctly says, "Among mammals, the smaller the size the higher the metabolism and the shorter the life span." Later, Dr. Blaine, Craigis' assistant, says, "In controlling the size factor we seemed to have crossed some of the other characteristics." This is the equivalent of a scientist saying, "oops."

The scientific progress of Craigis comes about in spurts and not all at once, as seen in other films discussed in this book. While discussing a long lived (normal sized) shrew, Craigis says, "Not the breakthrough, but it certainly sets our course. They have a birth cycle of 10 to 14 days, and using them we can establish traits. We can trace their progressions through a number of generations over a short period of time." This is one of the main reasons many biomedical scientists use small rodents—because of their short breeding times and the ability to analyze traits over relatively short genetic distances. All of this is a reflection of real science and well done.

As mentioned, shrews are voracious eaters. In addition to the above, Craigis also has this to say about shrews, "They are not climbers, they are diggers. They are like cannibals, will eat each other if hungry enough. To survive, they must eat three times their own weight in food every 24 hours or starve. Some call them bone eaters."

Blaine is ever the consummate scientist. He is bitten on the leg by one of the giant, poison-laden shrews, and while he is dying he types out on a typewriter what his clinical symptoms are and how he feels. What a dedicated scientist!

What Is Wrong with the Biological Science Presented: In explaining his work, Craigis says, "I am attempting to decrease the size by maintaining a low metabolism and result in a longer life span." The reason Craigis is doing this is, "Overpopulation. Not a problem now, but it will be in time. If we are half the size we are now, we could live twice as long on our natural resources." Interesting logic, being able to live twice as long if we were half the size we are now. If true, then dwarfs and midgets should be able to live twice as long as fully grown adults!

One common problem in reel science is called linear extrapolation. Attributes are expected to remain the same when organisms increase or decrease in size. This is simply not true. As an organism significantly increases its body mass it does not have the same movements nor appetite. Conversely, as an organism significantly decreases its body mass it has more mobility and must feed more frequently.

Craigis says, "Six months ago we managed to isolate the path to control their size. Two litters were born. Six individuals kept for study. They were the size of buckshot at birth. Their rate of growth was abnormal. They continued to grow, grow. They were mutants, but they inherited all the negative characteristics of their breed. Somehow they managed to escape, they dug through the dirt floor." Ann, the daughter of Craigis, says, "There are 200 to 300 giant shrews out there [beyond the fence], monsters weighing between 50 to 100 pounds. They are beginning to starve." The implication behind this dialogue is that the giant shrews have maintained their same feeding habits. Therefore, if each weighs between 50 to 100 pounds then they need to consume between 150 to 300 pounds of food a day! No wonder they are starving. That is a diet for a whale, not a dog-sized shrew.

Blaine comments, "Think what would happen if we could isolate and identify the inheritant factor in each gene." Well, each gene *is* an "inheritant factor," so there is no way to separate one from the other.

One of the residents of the island, Mario, is bitten by a giant shrew and dies. During an autopsy on him Blaine says, "Extremely high poison content in the shrews' saliva." Craigis responds, "Several weeks ago I concocted the most virulent poison I could with the materials I had at hand [which wasn't much, judging by what he has in his "lab"!]. We put it about as bait. Mario was killed with that poison." Blaine then says, "Doctor, I wonder if you thought the system of the sorex enabled them to assimilate the poison. It remained in the salivary glands of their jaws. Isn't that wonderful?" Hmmm. Craigis then says, "This indicates that we can't afford to get even so much as a scratch from these animals. They are more poisonous than snakes." Swallowed food does not remain in the salivary glands of the jaws but goes through the body's digestive system and then perhaps is excreted in the glands. Also, the relatively small amount of the ingested poison would be diluted by the shrew's body, so a vanishingly small amount would have ended up in the salivary glands. It is doubtful if this would have been enough to kill a man.

At the end of the film, once Craigis and a couple others are safely off the island, he says, "In 24 hours there will be one shrew left on the island, and he'll be dead from starvation. An excellent example of overpopulation." Cannibalism is not a very good model of overpopulation.

What Biological Science Is Necessary to Actually Achieve the Results in the Film: The major premise of this film is increasing the size of shrews to serve as a model of overpopulation. Though this is an interesting idea, there are better ways of going about obtaining data on overpopulation than making dog-sized killer shrews!

Growth hormone (called somatotropin in humans), and its various species specific versions, is the major hormone responsible for the size and shapes of animal bodies. After a certain age, the production of growth hormone ceases and the resulting body remains essentially the same throughout the remainder of its life. In rare instances growth hormone production does not stop but continues in some fashion, or has stopped but somehow becomes reactivated. In humans, cases of this are called acromegaly, where peripheral body parts, such as the head, face, hands, and feet, undergo progressive enlargement. To develop dog-sized shrews, Craigis would have to make sure shrew growth hormone is constantly available. The problem here is that growth hormone primarily works on bone and not on organs. Though the shrew body may have increased in size, many of the internal organs would have remained relatively small. In the long run, the shrew would not have been able to survive this problem.

Could It Actually Happen: Shrews are just a few inches long, and to genetically breed one to be the size of an average dog is asking way too much of good ol' Mr. DNA. Doubling its size is a bit of a stretch, but more than a ten fold increase is out of the question. This will not happen. Having a mammal unaffected by a poison that affects other mammals also will not happen. CULFology in the shrew world is currently beyond the limits of biology as we know it.

The Crawling Hand (1963)

Synopsis: An astronaut returns from space and crashes on Earth, severing his arm. The arm goes on a rampage, killing and infecting others with some sort of weird type of cosmic radiation. The arm is eventually found and destroyed.

Screenplay: William Idelson and Herbert L. Strock, from an original story by Joseph Cranston, Malcolm Young, and William Idelson.

Biological Science Principles Involved: CULFology. Physiology.

What Is Right with the Biological Science Presented: The arm seen is essentially severed at the elbow. A severed arm and hand moving about is not as difficult as perceived, and the physiology of this happening is not that much of a stretch (see below). However, crawling all over town is another matter entirely.

Paul, a teenager, is nearly choked to death by the arm. As a result of being touched by the arm, some of its "cosmic radiation" transforms Paul into an aggressive youth. Later, Paul, as a result of the arm's cosmic ray effects, has developed a

fever of "104." Consequently, this high body temperature "burns out" these cosmic ray effects, turning him back to normal. There are a number of instances where fever does bring infections to a rapid end, so this could be correct, and a temperature of 104 would certainly burn out whatever was there.

What Is Wrong with the Biological Science Presented: Here is a somewhat lengthy discussion between Astronaut Lockhart, out in space, and Dr. Weisberg and Steve on Earth that is full of all sorts of faulty biology. Lockhart is having problems, and his oxygen supply has run out. On Earth, Weisberg asks Lockhart, "How long have you been without oxygen?" Lockhart responds, "20 minutes[!]". Instead of talking back to Lockhart, Weisberg asks Steve, "How can a man continue to function without oxygen for 20 minutes? Something kept him functioning." Steve says, "An oxygen substitute?" Weisberg then says, "I think what kept Lockhart going was life, an independent vital force, something kinetic. Living covers a lot of territory. What makes life? A certain particular combination of molecules or carbons or silicons or nitrogen or any number of these things. And certain temperature. Mixed well, but this mass, swirling together in tiny orbits fuses these things into a precise energy relationship which we call life. What happens when we send a man up there. See, we just don't send a man in a rocket. We send up living cells, molecules, bacteria, germs, we throw in radioactivity. We introduce all these to cosmic rays. Do we upset this balance? Do we start a cycle? Does a living cell from Earth romance a cosmic ray and give birth to an illegitimate monster who makes his nest in Lockhart? Anything evolving so rapidly couldn't live very long." It is amazing that Steve stayed awake while listening to all this, not to mention the poor astronaut running out of oxygen!

First of all, the maximum amount of time the human brain can retain its functions without oxygen is about 8 minutes. Any longer than that and the brain will begin to lose vital functions, and approaching 20 minutes will certainly result in brain death. There is no way Lockhart would be coherent enough to answer "20 minutes." Yes, there are oxygen substitutes, such as chlorofluorocarbons, but those are not available to Lockhart. About the only thing right in the above monologue by Weisberg is the statement that more than just a man is sent into space. Other organisms, both inside and on Lockhart's body, also go up with him. However, none of these will sustain his life without oxygen.

Regarding the actual arm itself, it is seen moving all over the place, through the concerted efforts of its hand and fingers. The fingers grab the ground or other objects and slowly inch its way forward. The arm crawls onto a woman's bed while she is sleeping and chokes her to death. The arm also attacks others by grabbing their necks. All of this directed movement implies some sort of intelligence. Where is the "brain" located in this severed arm? Is there a rudimentary bundle of nerve fibers giving instructions?

This arm also emanates some sort of strange cosmic radiation, because those who come in direct contact with it immediately begin to act weird. One teenager, Paul, who is touched by the arm, begins to choke a man but does not kill him. Also, near the end of the film, two cats find the arm and lick off some of the blood on it and eat some of the tissue. The cats immediately become very aggressive and begin to fight each other.

Astronaut Lockhart crash lands, and the resulting accident severs his arm. No mention is made of his other body parts. Since his arm has a life of its own, inference can also be made that other body parts should behave exactly like the arm. Did a leg move about — or his other arm? What about a foot? And finally, did he have a "crawling penis?"

What Biological Science Is Necessary to Actually Achieve the Results in the Film: There are two points of concern here. One is the intelligence shown by the arm in its directed movements, and the second is the source of energy the arm uses to move.

The arm would not need a lot of "brain power" to do its thing. A small bundle of nerves is all it would take, and this could be some sort of nerve rewiring as a result of some cosmic ray exposure Astronaut Lockhart experiences in space. The directed movement of the arm implies some sort of sensory input because the arm "knows" how to find its victim's necks and choke them. The nerve fibers located on the fingers could have "searched" the victim's body until it located the neck region. (If I felt an arm groping along my body, I would not have idly watched it make its way to my neck. You can bet I would have yanked the arm off and flung it as far away from me as I could!)

For the arm to actually move would require muscular contractions along the forearm, tendons, and all the muscles in the hand. All muscle and tendon movements require energy, and since there is no obvious food source for the arm it must obtain its metabolic energy from the breakdown of carbohydrates, lipids (fats), and proteins already stored in the arm tissue. This would be OK for a while, until all of the tissues are "used up" as an energy source. Then the arm's movements would considerably slow down. The arm's exposure to cosmic radiation would make a negligible contribution as an energy source for muscle movement.

Could It Actually Happen: Cosmic radiation exposure to space travelers is a potentially serious problem and one that

NASA is keenly aware of. However, its effects on biological processes is poorly understood. Even so, I seriously doubt that this form of radiation will affect a severed arm in the manner shown in this movie. (Without meaning to be disrespectful, in keeping with the theme of this film, maybe there are parts of the astronauts from the exploded "Challenger" space shuttle that are crawling on the floor of the Atlantic Ocean off of Cape Canaveral.)

Island of Terror (1966)

Synopsis: In an attempt to develop a cure for cancer, research scientist Dr. Phillips accidentally creates silicate creatures on a remote British island. These silicate creatures have tentacles and a protective turtle-like carapace shell. They attack and suck out all bone matter from their victims. In the end, the creatures are destroyed by radioactive strontium–90.

Screenplay: Alan Ramsen and Edward Andrew Mann.

Biological Science Principles Involved: CULFology. Oncology. Biochemistry.

What Is Right with the Biological Science Presented: The main diet of the silicate creatures of this film is bone. Stanley (a doctor called to the island to investigate) is asked the question, "Do you know of any disease that can completely dissolve human bone?" and he responds, "No," which is true (the key word is "completely"). However, there is the disease, osteophagia, which is an eating of bone, usually brought about by mineral deficiency. However, this is a degenerative disease that occurs over a long period of time and not the cause of an organism, especially a silicate. (For a more detailed discussion on bone, please see the entry for *The Incredible Shrinking Man.*)

While examining one of the deboned victims of the silicates, Stanley says, "Here's something interesting. There are a series of tiny punctures in this dermal segment [a section of skin]. Punches are all over the body. It's possible some kind of enzyme was introduced in the body through these punctures. Some organism producing an enzyme went in. Not a trace of calcium phosphate in his body." Dr. West, a colleague, replies with, "Then this enzyme, or whatever it is, seems to attack and break down the calcium phosphate, a major component of human bone." This is all certainly plausible. Enzymatic action could have resulted in the "attack and breakdown" of bone, and this is an intelligent bit of dialogue.

The idea of Phillips "creating living cells ... [to] attack cancer" is interesting. During the 1980s investigators developed a procedure called "LAK cell therapy," which is an abbreviation for Lymphokine Activated Killer cells. LAK cell therapy involves the use of a patient's own lymphocytes ("living cells") to attack and kill their own cancer cells ("attack cancer"). The LAK cells are removed from a patient, trained to "recognize" and "kill" the cancer cells, then grown in large quantities to be given back to the same patient as a therapy. The LAK cells are cytotoxic or destructive to the cancer cells. Though currently labor intensive and laborious, LAK cell therapy is a very promising procedure. As has been said before, you wait long enough and science fiction will become science fact.

The radioactive atom strontium–90 is known to cause some bone damage when in high enough of a dose. A dog eats a batch of strontium–90(!) and is subsequently attacked and killed by a silicate. Since the silicate consumes the radioactive strontium–90 in the dog's bones, the creature dies. This is plausible. Well, the quick-witted scientists on this island then obtain some more strontium–90 from Phillips' lab and injects it into a herd of

A tentacle of a silicate creature is about to enzymatically digest another victim on the *Island of Terror* (1966). The bones of victims are completely absorbed through the octopus-like suction cups. How these hard, tortoise shell-like creatures manage to climb walls (or trees) is not explained.

cows. When the silicates attack the cows they consume the contaminated cow bones. As a result, the silicate creatures die. The idea of using an organism (cow) as a vehicle to dupe the silicates into ingesting the radioactive bone matter is intelligent.

Finally, in so many SF films the main "creature" only "feeds" on humans and ignores other potential food sources, in particular other animals. In this film the silicate creatures attack anything that contains bones in a nondiscriminatory way. Whoever and whatever is in their path will be attacked and consumed, which is what would happen.

What Is Wrong with the Biological

Science Presented: The dialogue between the scientists in this film is amusing. During one series of experiments Phillips says to his colleagues, "Potential across the cell membrane must be maintained during irradiation of the nucleus. Is the tri-template [?] complete?" Another scientist says, "The paper applicator has been corrected." A third scientist says, "The histoconnect [?] problem has been solved." Responding to all this meaningless jargon, Phillips says, "If we are successful today, it may well be we have the cure for cancer." It is virtually impossible to irradiate a cell nucleus without irradiating the rest of the cell. I have no idea what a "tri-template," nor what a "histoconnect problem" is.

As a result of the above described experiment, in which Phillips and his colleagues are searching for "the cure for cancer," they accidentally create the silicate creatures! This is one of the most outlandish leaps in all the films described in this book. From a cure for cancer to living forms based on the silicon atom! Unbelievable!

Throw all logic, chemistry, biochemistry, and biology out the window for the moment and just accept the concept that these silicates have indeed been created. These creatures attack all animals, such as humans, horses, cattle, etc., and dissolve and consume their bones. Therefore, these silicates are unable to distinguish bone from different species. The first human victim found has all his bones missing, and a constable describes the results by saying "the body is all like jelly. No face, just horrible jelly, eyes like mush." Certainly an uncomfortable way to go. Without knowing it is the silicate creatures who kill this man, a doctor, when he sees this body, says, "This 'disease' may be virulent and contagious," which is an interesting thing to say when confronted with a corpse in this condition.

While examining Phillips' lab, a radiation storage room is seen with a very impressive steel door, thick enough to stop most radiation. However, this storage room is made out of not-very-thick stone walls, so the advantage of having a radiation leak–proof steel door is defeated with the stone walls. Some forms of radiation will leak through stone, and strontium–90 is one of those.

After finding these silicate creatures, the residents of the island know they are in trouble. Drs. Stanley and West go to Phillips' lab and begin to go through his notebooks to learn more about these creatures in the hopes of finding some way to destroy them. After inspecting the notes, West says, "Phillips was certainly working on cancer research. He was trying to create some form of living matter to counteract the cancer cells." Stanley says, "He may have succeeded in creating some form of life there in his lab." After more notebook reading, Stanley then says, "...an overdose of radiation. Attempting to get the nuclei to fuse. Look at this protein structure, it isn't adenosine triphosphate!!!" And this comes from "England's most eminent pathologist!" Adenosine triphosphate or ATP is the primary energy source of all cells and is the nucleic acid adenosine with a triphosphate acid esterified at the 5' (five prime) position. There is no excuse for looking at a complicated protein structure and confusing it with ATP. This is like looking at a car and saying, "it isn't gasoline!" (Gas runs a car and ATP "runs" proteins.)

As if the above gaff on ATP isn't enough, Stanley, the "eminent pathologist," says, "In order to understand the nature of cancer, Dr. Phillips was trying to create living cells. Cells that he hoped would attack the cancer. He based his creation on the carbon atom, which is the basis of all life on this planet. He did not succeed. But what he probably succeeded in creating was some form of life based on the silicon atom. These silicates, as we call them, eat animal bone, human bone. They have an external skeletal structure and divide every six hours. There are 64 silicates now [at noon] and 128 by 6 pm this evening ... 256 by midnight. And if the multiplication continues, by end of the week there will be about a million of them." If this linear growth is true, then this tells us the first silicate was created Sunday night, and if they did double every six hours then there would be 1,048,576 silicates by midnight the next Saturday. The flaw in all this is assuming the silicates have a steady diet of bone with which to nourish themselves. The island where all this takes place is tiny and does not have a sizable enough population (including all humans, livestock, and small bone-containing animals) to achieve such progressive growth. Since Stanley is the "eminent pathologist" in England it makes one wonder how really competent all the other pathologists are.

There are not enough words to describe the idiocy of creating an anti-cancer life form out of carbon and ending up creating a life form out of silicon. The silicates are physically interesting creatures. They have a hard carapace shell, similar in style and shape to a turtle shell, which is able to withstand an axe blow, shotgun blasts, and a Molotov cocktail bomb. All in all, this silicon stuff is impressive. They also have a single tentacle-like appendage which they use to suck out bone matter from their victims. In addition to all this, they make weird noises of tonal intonations and echoes with vibration sounds. When the creatures divide they literally split in two and out comes a secretion similar to an opaque yellowish noodle soup ooze. Quite disgusting looking. And if all that isn't enough, they do not move very fast (anyone could easily outrun them) and are able to climb trees!

What Biological Science Is Necessary to Actually Achieve the Results in the Film: To go from carbon to silicon is beyond the realm of biological science and is in the world of fantasy and atom-smashing physics. The improbability of that is beyond anything sensible and completely outside the bounds of this book.

Since the silicates have an exclusive diet of bone, this indicates that something in the biochemical composition of bone is necessary for the survival of these creatures. Since these creatures are made of silicon, then calcium and/or phosphate (the major chemicals in bone) are required to help in the biochemical design of silicon life forms. Bone is also composed of other atoms and molecules, like carbon, nitrogen, oxygen, minerals, and metals. Some

of these can serve the function of vitamins or growth factors for the silicates.

It is stated that the silicates use "some kind of enzyme" to dissolve animal bone. The enzyme(s) could have been made out of carbon, which functions as is and has the capacity to catalyze reactions using silicon atoms. There is some precedence for this because there are some polysaccharide structures found in mammary (breast) tissues that do contain silicon, so it is a metabolically active atom in mammals. The enzymes could catalyze silicon atoms to serve as cell and tissue "scaffolding" to support the silicates' bodies and their heavy outer shells. The presence of both silicon and carbon molecules is not incompatible, and a combination of them is most likely what these creatures would be made of.

Could It Actually Happen: Creating anti-cancer treatments out of living cells is an active program going on in many oncology labs throughout the world. The real science behind this work makes sense to me, and many future cancer patients will benefit from this type of therapy.

Creating life forms out of silicon will not happen on Earth, so no need to worry about a silicate creature eating all your bones.

Sssssss (1973)

Synopsis: Dr. Stoner, a herpetologist, develops a procedure that can change a human into a snake. The reason being to create a new species capable of surviving catastrophes of the future. Eventually, Stoner is bitten by a snake and dies.

Screenplay: Hal Dresser, story by Dan Striepeke.

Biological Science Principles Involved: CULFology. Herpetology. Endocrinology. Physiology.

What Is Right with the Biological Science Presented: Ever since the Garden of Eden snakes have gotten a bad rap, and they have yet to live this down. Many people are genuinely afraid of snakes and have no idea which ones are harmless and which are poisonous. During a university lecture, Dr. Daniels says, "Here we have two of the most commonly confused snakes ... in the case of the poisonous coral, the red and yellow bands touch. Whereas, in the case of the non-poisonous king, the red and yellow bands are separated by black stripes. A good way to remember that is the old folk saying, 'red touch yellow, kill a fellow.'" This is all true. When I was a child I learned a different folk-saying, "yellow next to red, you're dead; yellow next to black, you're okay, Jack." Either way, good words to live by.

On the chalkboard in Daniels' classroom are various renderings of snake anatomy, such as a head and a description of vertical scales, all of which are accurate. Though completely irrelevant to the plot and action, these chalk renderings do add a certain amount of unspoken verisimilitude.

During a conversation between Stoner and Daniels, Stoner describes himself by saying, "The theories I have originated are now being considered by world medical opinion ... I've got 30 years in the field of venom research. I've got seven books, 63 articles and monographs." All in all, impressive credentials for a herpetologist, making Stoner someone who would be well known in his field of specialty.

Stoner says to Blake, a new lab assistant from the college, "The fear that most people have of snakes is based on the same misunderstanding they have about any other minority group. If they're told that one member is harmful, they generalize and believe they're all dangerous." Unfortunately, this is true and a fact of life.

We see Stoner (Strother Martin) actually handle a Mamba snake and extract its venom. All the procedures and techniques are real and effective. Stoner "catches" the snake directly behind its jaws and has the snake bite into a rubber septum–covered glass vessel, thereby effectively extracting its venom. After this Stoner has the snake force fed with a syringe-like device, with a tube inserted into the mouth instead of a needle. Stoner says the meal "contains a pre-measured diet of milk, eggs, vitamin concentrates, liver, gelatin, bone meal, and chicken blood." A good, sensible diet for the snake.

Stoner gives Blake multiple injections, and the technique used is excellent. After an injection Stoner uses a sterile cotton ball swabbed in alcohol (from a typical brown plastic dispenser) and efficiently wipes off the needle stick area.

In general, immunizations are an excellent method to stave off certain diseases. In Western culture, most infants are immunized against tetanus, polio, diphtheria, etc. Usually, a single injection is all that is necessary, and occasionally, years later, a booster is given. Stoner has the right idea in saying he is giving Blake immunizations against venom, and in some cases it would work.

A snake, being a reptile, is cold blooded, meaning their body temperature is dictated by their environment; the warmer it is the more active the snake. As Blake is slowly transforming, he develops chills and complains that the room temperature is too cold, signs that he is losing control of body temperature physiology. Accepting the premise of the film, Blake's internal temperature going haywire would be expected. Reptiles are cold blooded.

The transition of Blake to a snake is gradual, and that makes sense. The first changes are some moderate skin shedding, then, as Stoner says, "slight flattening of the nostrils, eyelids beginning to recede..." Then, as I would expect if real, there would be an acceleration of the changes as Blake becomes more and more snakelike. As Stoner says, "[after several days] the evolutionary process should accelerate greatly. Cataclysmic changes should occur." Accepting the premise, this seems reasonable.

What Is Wrong with the Biological Science Presented: Stoner explains to Blake that the "black mamba secretes enough venom in a single bite to kill 10 men. His venom is neurotoxic, inhibiting the breathing and affecting the vagus nerve that controls the heartbeat. The victim's heart beats wildly and he usually succumbs within an hour to symptoms that appear very much like a heart attack." The vagus also controls the pharynx, larynx, trachea, lungs, and the gastrointestinal tract, so more than just the heart would be affected.

In the venom storage room Stoner says to Blake, after obtaining a venom sample, "dry freeze it [venom] into crystals, just like coffee, then it's blended and ground, shipped to pharmaceutical firms and research laboratories, where it is used as coagulants and pain relievers and in the treatment of certain blood diseases." Most venoms are not dry frozen but rather stored in a refrigerator or in an ultra-cold freezer (around −80°C). "Blended and ground" is Stoner's way of saying that the different batches of venom (surely from the same snake, taken over time) are mixed together for uniformity. Neither pharmaceutical firms nor research laboratories would use snake venom as a coagulant or pain reliever. Snake venom does not work that way. However, if leukemias and lymphomas can be considered "blood diseases," then venoms have been used for treatment. The best example is cobra venom toxin (see the entry for *The Undying Monster*), a compound I have personally used in my own research.

Under the guise of "immunization is an occupational necessity," Stoner administers a series of injections to Blake. Stoner uses a small needle (about 30 gauge) and about 3cc volume for each injection. Subsequent injections are called "booster shots." These injections are clearly fake because the skin surface is pushed in as the needle touches it; ordinarily, the needle would easily enter the skin, with no "pushed in" effect. Also, Stoner says, "...booster shots. Every few days for the next month or so..." Booster shots are generally given only once, and months (sometimes years) after the initial injection. A booster "every few days" would have been a wasted effort and could have potentially put Blake's immune system at risk.

Blake's slow metamorphosis into a snake is interesting, though the rapidity of the final changes is nonsense. After some injections, Blake's facial skin, the upper epidermal layer, starts to peel off, as well as skin on his back, some of which comes off in large sheets. Stoner comments, "It's a perfectly natural reaction to cobra inoculation. The venom burns off the superficial layers of skin, much like a sunburn, only from the inside. It's the same principle that allows a cobra to shed its skin." Though the explanation sounds perfectly sensible, especially the sunburn part, it is incorrect. Immunization mechanisms occur within the body (especially with immune response related cells and tissues) and not in the skin. Cobras, or any snake for that matter, shed their skin because they outgrow the old one. Regarding the principle of skin shedding, if applicable in this case, then Stoner's implication is that Blake is "growing" out of his current skin and needs it replaced. Not true.

Regarding Blake's drop in body temperature, Stoner notes on a tape recorder, "David [Blake]'s body temperature is dropping at the rate of three degrees a day. It should stabilize at 80 degrees [Fahrenheit] by the end of the week." Starting at 98.6 degrees and dropping to 80, at three degrees a day, would take six days. Earlier it was stated that Stoner would give booster shots "for the next month or so," so the time frame does not match.

One of Stoner's former lab assistants "disappeared" and ends up as a side show attraction at a local carnival as the "snake man." Blake has "failed" at trying to turn him into a snake. Physically, this snake man has a pasty, light green skin, large scales over his nose, upper lip, and on upper shoulders. He has no eyebrows, some minimal "Friar Tuck" hair on his head, one arm that tapers to the elbow, and a torso that goes to his butt with no legs. Finally, he has blue eyes.

During the finale, as Blake is turning into the snake, Stoner says, "You are the first creature of the next evolution, who will survive pollution, the holocaust, the famines, the plagues that will make man extinct. You will survive and multiply." No, that will probably be the cockroach. Blake's body mass dramatically and rapidly decreases during his concluding transformation into a snake. What happens to those pounds of body mass that disappear in seconds?

And, finally, what would happen to Blake's consciousness? As his brain diminishes in size, would he lose all his memory; would he have any dim recollections of being human; what instincts would surface?

What Biological Science Is Necessary to Actually Achieve the Results in the Film: To convert a human into a snake would take a lot of hormones and fundamental changes in anatomy and physiology. Gone would be the arms and legs; the rib cage would have to extend all the length of the body; the skull, maxilla, and jaw bones would dramatically change; muscle structure would be significantly altered, and many of the internal organs would also have to change. In principle, this is possible, simply because such transformations already occur in nature, such as the change of a caterpillar into a butterfly. During that metamorphosis the dramatic changes of the caterpillar have been studied and the bio-

chemistry of the transformation somewhat understood. Hormones are at the core of these changes. And so it would be with Blake. Stoner has to inject some form of snake DNA, which integrates into Blake's DNA, thereby producing certain hormones that cause the physical changes seen in Blake. These snake hormones would have to completely reshape bone and transform skin. Given enough time, perhaps some changes could be engineered, but certainly not as rapidly as seen in the film.

Blake's transformation initially starts with subtle changes in his skin, and then, as time goes on, more dramatic changes occur. Blake's jaw is seen to widen, his snout elongates, his legs fuse together(!), his collar bones taper, but his eyes remain circular and blue. The outermost layers of skin would have to harden more and possibly thicken into scale-like structures. At first, this process would be slow, as more and more of the surface skin changes are initiated; in essence the changes would occur in a sort of geometric progression, a little at first and then a lot at the end.

Resorption of tissues is seen in nature with the developing frog, since tadpoles absorb their tail as they grow. Not only are cells and tissues absorbed, but tail bone as well, so, in principle, Blake's cells, tissues, and bone could have been absorbed (though not as rapidly as shown). As the absorption processes are taking place, new (snake) tissue and bone would take its place. It would have to be a well coordinated biological effort; the enzymes that absorb bone would have to be gone by the time new snake bone is being generated, so the new bone would not also be absorbed.

Could It Actually Happen: Converting a human into a snake will not happen. No hormones are currently available that could accomplish this. Also, no one would go to all the trouble, primarily because there is no money to be gained from the effort.

13 LIFE CYCLES

Alien (1979)
Aliens (1986)

Life's most distinctive component is its ability to reproduce itself ... exactly. Man begets man and dog begets dog. In even simpler terms, like begets like. This is referred to as heredity. Though offspring show individuality and variations, they do resemble their parents. And parents pass on coded information to their offspring in the form of genes, and genes are nothing more than segments of DNA, so DNA begets DNA. Each gene's sequence codes for different pieces of information, which is not only expressed in each organism or life form but is also passed on to subsequent generations. This passing on of our genes to offspring is called inheritance, and inheritance is the *precise* replication of any given species' DNA. One set of DNA gives rise to another set of DNA, et cetera, et cetera. This passing on of DNA, genes, or inheritance from parent to offspring, one generation to another, is called a life cycle. Life cycles are generation-to-generation stages of the reproductive history of any given species.

In asexual reproduction, such as in single-celled organisms like bacteria or yeast, a single organism is the only parent and passes all copies of its genes (or DNA) on to its offspring. The offspring are *exact* copies of the parent, much like a cloned species is an exact copy of the original.

In contrast, sexual reproduction usually results in greater variability because the resulting offspring is a combination of two parents, or two sets of genes (or DNA). The genes or DNA of each parent co-mingle to establish unique patterns that, though distinguishable from the parents, nevertheless contain elements of each. For example, some siblings do indeed resemble each other, and in certain ways resemble their parents; blue eyed parents tend to have blue eyed offspring, and tall parents tend to have tall offspring.

In humans, cells other than sperm and eggs have a total of 46 chromosomes (each sperm and egg has 22 chromosomes, plus either a Y or an X chromosome — the ones that determine maleness or femaleness; XY is male and XX is female), which are actually two sets of 23 chromosomes, one set from a father and the other from a mother. So, in humans, the 46 chromosomes are from two sets, one set of 23 (22 plus either an X or a Y) from one parent and the other set of 23 (22 plus an X or a

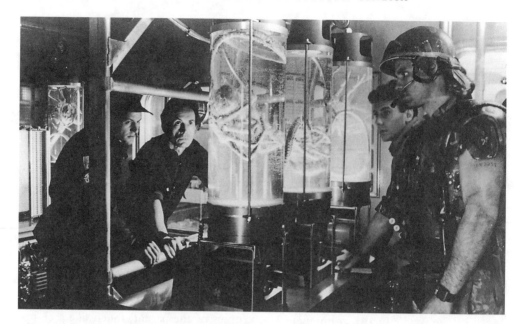

Aliens (1986): Stasis tubes containing the "face hugger" phase of the Alien life cycle. This phase of the Alien requires a host to implant its DNA.

Y) from the other parent. As a human (or any organism for that matter) develops, the chromosomes are passed on with amazing precision to all cells of the body. Even though a muscle cell is different from a liver cell, which is different from a brain cell, they are all composed of the *same* DNA. What makes them different is that different genes are expressed in each cell, so only muscle DNA is expressed in muscle cells, liver DNA expressed in liver cells, and so on. How these traits are passed on from one generation to the next, which are dominant and which are recessive, which are characteristics and which are traits, which determine pedigrees, and which are genotypes and phenotypes, though important to the geneticist, is beyond the scope of this book. Suffice it to say that DNA is DNA, and the odds of predicting which genes will be expressed are currently at the cutting edge of genetic science. As we more clearly understand how genes function and are regulated, much of the SF described in the films detailed in this book will become tomorrow's science. Another

biological revolution will come to pass during the next few centuries as genes can and will be controlled. To be sure, there will be those who violently oppose such meddling ("man was not meant to mess with either Mother Nature or God"). However, our health will be dramatically improved by gene manipulation.

So, as humans we obtained our DNA from our parents (both good and bad), and we will pass this DNA on to our offspring. And so goes the cycle of life. Sperm cells donate one set of chromosomes and egg cells donate the other set of chromosomes. The two sets of chromosomes combine (a fairly sterile and unromantic way of referring to sexual intercourse) and are sorted by a combination of three separate mechanisms: independent assortment of chromosomes, crossing over, and random fertilization. The manner in which these three mechanisms interact is what makes each of us unique individuals. As a result of these mechanisms there are literally trillions and trillions of combinations, so it's no wonder siblings are different from each other!

Which brings us up to one of the more interesting life cycles in SF cinema, namely, the *Alien* films. With the same concepts of life cycles discussed above, how does this relate to the main antagonists of this film series? Conceptually, the life cycle of an Alien is composed of both a sexual phase and an asexual phase. The sexual phase starts with an adult male who mates with a queen. The queen lays her eggs, which hatch "face huggers." The face hugger alien begins the asexual phase. The face hugger latches onto another species and assimilates its DNA with the host. As a result of this DNA mixing, a "chest burster" alien emerges from the host and grows into an adult, completing the cycle.

We can learn some interesting biological science by examining this life cycle more closely. Though not readily obvious, the most dramatic element of an Alien life cycle is the absence of sexual intercourse during one key phase of its life cycle; this would be the asexual phase. Animals on planet Earth combine sperm and egg, which grow into adults of the respective species. In the *Alien* films there is an additional step that does not involve sexual intercourse. And therein lies an interesting example of a complex life cycle that does not involve sex, as is traditional for Earth animals. Because there are two separate phases, one sexual and one asexual, we refer to this as digenetic.

In the *Alien* films, the creature form known as a "face hugger" latches onto the face of the target species and inserts part of itself into the victim's mouth (maybe that is sex from the Alien's point of view). As a result, the Alien either takes DNA from the host or adds its own DNA to the host, resulting in the growth of what is called a "chest burster." Like a uterus or womb, the host's body serves as a source of nutrients and protection from the environment. After a somewhat short incubation time, the chest burster is "born" by literally bursting out of the host's chest area. This chest burster then grows to an adult. As an adult Alien, this creature then (probably) mates with the queen Alien (there could be any number of ways this could happen), who then lays eggs. It is from these eggs the face hugger emerges when a new host is within range, thereby completing a most interesting life cycle.

To discuss this further, we will make some reasonable assumptions. First of all, the Alien must have DNA, since it effectively combines with and assimilates humans (and their DNA). However, it should be noted that Alien DNA has the ability to effectively combine with virtually any species. (This is referred to as a xeno-species, meaning the combining of two radically different species into a viable mixture capable of reproduction; unlike the sterile mule, which is a cross between a horse and a donkey and is incapable of reproduction). In the *Alien 3* film, Alien DNA is seen to not only combine with human DNA but to also combine with dog DNA. The key to the survival of the Alien species is that its DNA can adapt to *any* species, which is a stunningly powerful survival characteristic. Also, since the adult form, whether derived from a human or a dog, is similar in overall shape (as exemplified by the domed head and retractable teeth), then there must be some strongly dominant genes being expressed. Furthermore, since DNA is passed on from generation to generation (for example, we all have some of our grandparents' characteristics), then the Alien must have DNA from assimilating previous species, whether from planet Earth or elsewhere. The DNA from many species was combined to make the Alien the force that it has become. In one respect, the Alien was able to take the strongest — that is, the most viable — genes, which ensures survival no matter how hostile the environment. As a molecular biologist, the implications of this are most interesting. What are the genetic controlling elements that allow the co-regulation of xenospecies of DNA? Are they, in principle, similar to humans, or do they have a radically different mechanism of function? How do the cells and tissues of the two species interact as a cohesive, viable unit? Does the Alien have something like a liver or kidney, which can compliment human livers and kidneys?

Another interesting assumption about this life cycle has to do with Alien sex. As presented, there is both a sexual and asexual component to their life cycle. The adult "male" Alien must mate with an Alien queen to propagate the species. Whether this is by actual sexual intercourse as we understand it or by some other means, such as how Earth's fish or amphibians simply co-mix sperm and extruded eggs, is a moot point. Alien male DNA must combine with Alien queen DNA in whatever way they choose, so that two gamete cells combine and form an embryo/egg. Since the Alien species has, more than likely, assimilated DNA from a variety of species, then its somatic cells probably have an enormous number of chromosomes, many more than the 46 humans have.

Somehow, the Alien has the ability to find the best genes it can in the "species du jour" and incorporate these genes into its own genome and life cycle, making it one of the most powerful and dominant species seen in SF cinema! No matter what the environment or situation, the Alien has the genetic capacity to survive.

What is interesting in all this is that the Alien life cycle is not really unique, since there are examples and parallels here on good old planet Earth. For example, the life cycles of blood flukes, the slime mold, and that of the malaria mosquito are surprisingly quite similar. These organisms have both a sexual and non-sexual component to their life cycle, are digenetic, and

need another species to complete their own cycle. Both blood flukes and malaria mosquitoes need humans to propagate their species. The malaria mosquitoes inject their eggs or sporozoites into the blood stream of humans, and blood flukes also inhabit humans, releasing their fertilized eggs into the environment through human fecal waste.

Flukes (the common name for members of the class Trematoda and phylum Platyhelminthes, which are flatworms) are soft-bodied worm parasites that live in and on other animals. In the adult stage they are internal parasites involving humans and, moving on to their final host, snails. Many have suckers for attaching themselves to hosts (like the Alien face hugger, which also attaches itself to its host), and a tough outer covering to shield them from sometimes harsh environments inside the bodies of their host animals (Aliens also have a tough outer exoskeleton that essentially serves the same purpose). Flukes have a complex digenetic life cycle whereby their life cycle alternates between sexual and asexual stages. Many species of flukes require an intermediate host animal, such as a snail, in which larvae develop before infecting another host (man) to complete its life cycle. In the sexual stage the fertilized eggs of females exit man in their fecal body wastes and develop in water into ciliated larvae. These larvae then enter snails, where asexual reproduction produces swimming larvae (called cercariae) that in turn infect humans. Usually, people working in irrigated fields contaminated with feces are exposed to the fluke larvae, which penetrate human skin and blood vessels. (An estimated 200 million people worldwide are infected with flukes, resulting in body pains, anemia, and dysentery.)

The malaria life cycle is quite complex and composed of an exogenous phase (sexual cycle in the mosquito, called sporogony) and an endogenous phase (asexual cycle in humans, called schizogony). Malaria has a cyclopropagative transmission process, meaning that the plasmodium parasites change in form and function as they invade and multiply within various organs of hosts. Malaria is a disease caused by the presence of these plasmodium sporozoites in human red blood cells, usually transmitted to humans by the bite of an infected *Anopheles* mosquito (all biting mosquitoes are females) that previously sucked the blood from an infected human. The plasmodium is an extremely invasive parasite (like the Alien) and spends most of its time inside human liver and red blood cells. The malaria life cycle begins when a plasmodium parasite enters a mosquito body by biting an infected human. Once the plasmodium parasite is inside the mosquito, gametes form and fertilization occurs within the mosquito's digestive tract, resulting in a zygote. The zygote grows, releasing thousands of sporozoites that migrate to the mosquito salivary gland. The mosquito then bites another human, thereby infecting him. These sporozoites then enter human liver cells via the blood system, develop into merozoites, and are released, which in turn infect red blood cells. Inside red blood cells, these merozoites then divide asexually into great numbers and break out of the blood cells, causing various fevers and chills. Some of the merozoites develop into gametocytes, which complete their life cycle in a new female mosquito. All in all, malaria is caused by a red blood cell cycle, a liver cell cycle, and a mosquito gut cycle. Complex indeed.

And this all brings us back to the Alien. The Alien is also cyclopropagative in that it changes in form and function as it invades and multiplies within its hosts. Once the face hugger attaches itself to its host, cells from the Alien (i.e., Alien DNA) enter the host and develop into the so-called chest burster. In this respect, humans (or another species, terrestrial or otherwise) serve as a vector to transmit their species for the propagation of its own kind. To grow, the developing chest burster must utilize terrestrial atoms and molecules, such as carbon, hydrogen, oxygen, nitrogen, etc., and minerals as a source of nutrients. The development of whatever the face hugger deposits into its host would have as complex a life cycle (cyclopropagative) as the fluke and malaria processes discussed above. The face hugger–chest burster phase would be the asexual phase of its life cycle. At the right moment of growth, the chest burster exits its host to grow into an adult to eventually mate with a queen (sexual phase).

Taking a somewhat speculative leap in logic here, it is reasonable to assume that if a sexual/asexual life cycle involving at least two different species is common on Earth, then species not of this Earth, based on DNA, may also have evolved such life cycles as powerful survival traits. And the Alien life cycle is one of the most powerful in all of SF cinema.

14 REANIMATED BRIDES

Many critics believe, myself included, that the film *The Bride of Frankenstein* is one of the best examples of horror cinema. Much has been written explaining this, and I need not waste space to further delve into what has gone before. However, in keeping with the theme of this book, there is some interesting biological science discussed (or implied) in this film that does deserve analysis. Furthermore, with poetic license in mind, there is an interesting "remake" of sorts in Brian Yuzna's *Bride of the Re-Animator*. The 54 year time difference in the two films is telling, and like the *Island[s] of Dr. Moreau*, *The Blob*, and *The Fly* films, there are significant gaps between the original and the remakes, in that much biology has been added to the more modern versions, making them somewhat interesting in the level and degree of the science presented. Let's take a closer look at our beautiful Brides. The biological science parallels between those two wonderful films are most intriguing.

Setting aside the obvious differences in graphic surgical scenes between these two films, there are some interesting ob-servations to make. The '35 *Bride* was born of electricity, whereas the '89 *Bride* was born of biochemistry, a neurotransmitter muscle stimulant. The '35 *Bride* had an intact and functional brain for coordination, whereas the '89 *Bride* had body parts that were independent of a controlling brain.

For the times they were made, the respective laboratory *Bride* sets are some of the most impressive in all of SF cinema. For a 1935 electricity motif, that set is unsurpassed (with the possible exception of the derivative *The Bride*, in 1985), and for a 1989 biochemical analysis and synthesis motif, that lab is excellent for scientist Herbert West's goals.

The 54 year difference between the two films is most dramatically shown during the surgical scenes. Blood, tissues, body parts, and organs are strewn about in West's lab and are virtually absent from Frankenstein's lab. Even the fundamental science has dramatically changed. Electricity held more of a fascination for 1930s audiences, primarily due to the booming radio markets; 54 years later, audiences were more sophisticated in their science, so something more challenging than an electrical storm was needed — and a neurotransmitter was a reasonable choice.

The Brides are assembled with a combination of limb and organ transplants and plastic surgery. The history of each of these goes back to ancient times. There is evidence, primarily from the Edwin Smith Papyrus, that plastic surgery was practiced by the ancient Egyptians as early as 2400 B.C. Physicians have known from ancient times that limb transplants would not work. Religious texts offer evidence of limb transplants that did not succeed. Starting in the 15th century, medical texts began to explicitly state that limb transplants were "impossible." It wasn't until the 20th century that even the reattachment of a detached limb from the same animal has been possible, and not always with complete recovery. Even with the elimination of immunological problems, the ability to successfully attach all vessels, nerves, sinews, tendons, and muscle in complete working order is a laborious task with no guarantees. Modern medicine has now made it possible to perform many of the surgeries implied in these films.

Bride of Frankenstein (1935)

Synopsis: Frankenstein's monster survives the devastating fire of the original film. Dr. Pretorious, a colleague of Dr. Henry Frankenstein, is independently conducting experiments on the construction of artificial life. Pretorious uses extortion, by kidnapping Frankenstein's wife, to induce him to help in the construction of a mate for the monster.

Screenplay: William Hurlbut, suggested by the original story written in 1816 by Mary Wollstonecraft Shelley, and adapted by William Hurlbut and John Balderston.

Biological Science Principles Involved: Surgery. Physiology. Cell Biology. Transplantation.

What Is Right with the Biological Science Presented: In terms of actual science there is very little presented. Only two main sequences have any real substance, one less than the other. The most realistic is the scene involving the beating human heart encased in a large glass vessel. This vessel is initially sealed, at least demonstrating some semblance of sterility, and the heart (freshly obtained from an unwilling victim) is immersed in an opaque liquid. Inserted in the liquid are electrodes that monitor the beat and rhythms of the heart — in essence, an early version of an EKG machine. While looking at the heart, Frankenstein says to Pretorious, "It's beating, but the rhythm of the beat is uneven." In response, Pretorious says, "Increase the saline solution." From this Frankenstein adds about 50cc of "saline solution" through a funnel directly into the heart vessel (at this point, sterility issues are over). Pretorious then says, "Is there any life yet?" Frankenstein replies with, "No. Not life itself yet. This is only the simulacrum of life. This action only responds when the current is applied." At this, Pretorious responds with, "You must be patient. The human heart is more complex than any other part of the body." Of special note here is that during this film sequence Frankenstein wears rubber surgical gloves, demonstrating some semblance of sterile procedures usually lacking in most SF films.

Heart rhythm is determined by electrical conductivity and the electrolyte fluids in the body; sodium (i.e., "saline solution"), being a key component, keeps the beating steady for the life of the person. Heart physiology, as studied by cardiologists, is an exciting discipline. The heart itself is a muscle and a highly regulated organ. Heart transplants involve a complicated

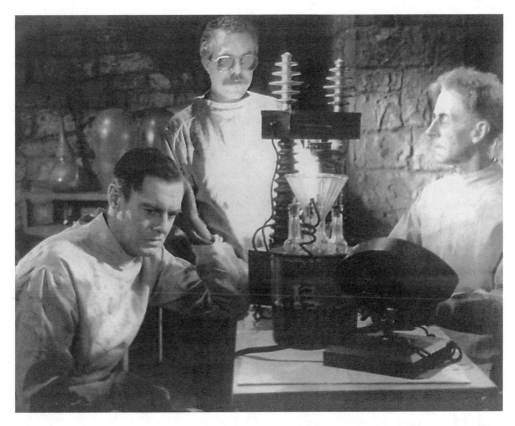

Bride of Frankenstein (1935): The three scientists in discussion over the apparatus containing a beating heart — "Not life itself ... only the simulacrum of life," says Dr. Frankenstein (Colin Clive, left). An early cinema example acknowledging the importance of proper conduction of physiological electrical impulses in the rhythm of heart beats.

array of equipment and procedures to keep it viable and beating.

The second sequence of interest takes place in the laboratory of Pretorious. Here, while talking about his experiments on creating a form of life, he hints at cell culture techniques. Pretorious says to Frankenstein, "While you were digging in your graves, piecing together dead tissues, I, my dear pupil, went for my material to the source of life. I grew my creatures. Like cultures. Grew them as nature does, from seeds." He is, of course, referring to the homunculi he creates, and as the philosophy of the time implied, life is indeed spawned from "seed." Cell culture techniques during the 1930s were primitive at best, not to mention at the time the film is

set. The majority of what is now known as tissue culture techniques was not worked out until the 1950s. During the movie's time period, vitamins, nutrients, culture medium, and growth factors were unknown, and concepts like "vital fluids," life "ethers," and "glandular effects" were the norm. The concept of "grew them ... from seeds" is a wonderful expression of what, in principle, does indeed happen. The seeds Pretorious is referring to are undoubtedly sperm and egg.

Though subtle, an interesting aspect is the scene of the Monster finding the blind hermit in the woods. Fresh from being newly created, the Monster has yet to eat, and when he comes upon the hermit the Monster is ravenous with hunger.

When the hermit offers bread, broth, and drink, the Monster hungrily consumes it all, indicating that the Monster needs sustenance, which is something we rarely see in SF films. Life, no matter how created, needs energy to survive. Hunger certainly does modify animal behavior, and the Monster's hunger brought him to the hermit's food.

Finally, after the Bride is brought to life, several closeups of her face are shown, and her head is seen to jerk rapidly from side to side (this head jerking is also seen in *Bride of the Re-Animator*; see below). In medical parlance, this jerking is referred to as titubation, which is a tremor or a shaking of the head, and is of cerebellar origin. Perhaps not all of the Bride's brain is completely formed, and a problem with her cerebellar region is such that titubation-like head jerking results.

What Is Wrong with the Biological Science Presented: Most of what is wrong with the biology in this film is what is implied: transplantations, heart growth and maintenance, cultures from "seeds" to grow a brain, sterility, and homunculi as miniature humans. Of these, transplantation science has come the farthest and quite possibly could happen as implied.

During one conversation with Frankenstein, Pretorious says, "The heart is more complex than any other part of the body"; in actuality, the brain is (the heart is the second most complex part of the body; the most complex cell is the sperm cell). The reason Pretorious says this line is because, at the time, much belief was put in the heart as the "seat of life." Furthermore, when Frankenstein moves the heart jar from its table to the Bride's body, the glass container is open to the air, which could have resulted in serious risk of contamination. A contaminated heart in the Bride's body would not have lasted very long.

Shortly before the climax of bringing the Bride to animated life, when her body is just about all sewn together, Pretorious says to Frankenstein, "All the necessary preparations are made ... I have created by my method a perfect human brain. Already living but dormant." Later, Pretorious says, "Isn't it amazing, Henry, that lying here within this skull is an artificially developed human brain. Each cell, each convolution ready, waiting for life to come." Maybe someday scientists will figure out a way to actually grow a brain, but that really is not the point. What is missing and absolutely critical is memory, both learned and instinctual. Without any stimulus or learned responses, how does a newly minted brain know anything — from simply what visual input is (or means), to how to respond to others and the environment, to how to do something as simple as walk? With no memory, one is at a loss to explain the Bride's behavior when she first sees the Monster. Why did she scream when she has no reference about looks, males, or what simple touching is?

The homunculi created by Pretorious could have been done in two ways, both of them unrealistic. The choices are either reduced cell size or reduced cell number. For example, the adult human liver is composed of about 10^{11} cells. Do the miniature homunculi have livers composed of 10^{11} miniature liver cells, or of, say, about 10^9 cells? Because of the given size of tissue cells, shrinking them is beyond any sort of current science and a highly improbable scenario. More likely, the liver is reduced in cell number (like the size of a mouse liver, smaller but capable of everything a human liver does) and not in cell size. This discussion is important because of how Pretorious says he "grew my creatures." To start from "seed" to grow his miniatures, the cells themselves would not shrink per se but just be reduced in number. Another way of saying this is that the size difference is quantitative and not qualitative.

What Biological Science Is Necessary to Actually Achieve the Results in the Film: Transplantations require a variety of immunosuppressive drugs. The growth of a human brain to full size would require a knowledge of neurobiology currently beyond what is now known. Cell culture techniques are currently available to maintain the viability of certain organs, but to grow a brain from "seed" would require the ability to activate, regulate, and control certain genes of nerve tissue. Precursor cells, such as multi-potential stem cells, could be stimulated with the right combinations of gene regulatory elements to ensure the development and growth of brain tissue. Whether this tissue would be a fully developed and anatomically correct brain, with "each convolution ready, waiting for life to come," though possible, is improbable with current technology.

The growth of miniature homunculi people (forget about the miniature mermaid!) is an interesting possibility. This begs the question of why would anyone *want* to (for another analysis of this concept see the entry on *The Devil Doll*).

Could It Actually Happen: Organ, bone, and tissue transplants are very common, and most of a human's body can be transplanted from matched donors. Currently, transplants from unmatched donors are not possible, but there may come a time when this could be possible, most likely from a combination of better immunosuppressive drugs and effective gene therapy (whereby tissue rejection mechanisms are severely reduced or eliminated altogether). As already mentioned, the area yet to be successful is that of brain transplants. It would be easier to transplant organs, tissues, and bones to a particular body than add a new brain to a different body. Homunculi, as the term is defined, cannot happen.

The Bride of the Re-Animator (1989)

Synopsis: Doctors West and Cain are once again teamed together, this time to create the titular creature of the film. The procedures are graphic, with several "attempts" at creating artificial life, most of which go awry. West uses his "re-animation reagent" to bring the Bride to life.

Screenplay: Woody Keith and Rick Fry, story adapted from H.P. Lovecraft's "Herbert West — Re-Animator" by Woody Keith, Rick Fry and Brian Yuzna.

Biological Science Principles Involved: Surgery. Transplantation. Cell Biology. Physiology. Neurobiology.

What Is Right with the Biological Science Presented: The various surgical scenes of assembling the Bride are the most interesting. Even though many of the scenes are quite graphic, they are realistic. Hip replacements are common, and the replaced bone socket (the femur head with the pelvic girdle) is typically made of metal, and the arm and leg joints (where the humerus contacts the radius and the ulna) of the Bride are also metal. The metal clamps used to hold skin flaps and muscle together are visibly present. The Bride here is assembled in stages, which was not actually seen in *The Bride of Frankenstein*. The assembled nature of the Re-animator Bride is what it would actually look like if this was done for real.

One interesting problem discussed by West and Cain has to do with the sequence of re-animating the Bride's extremities. As Cain says, "She's going to be uncontrollably spastic. Unless we re-animate all the limbs at the same time they'll separate." To this West responds with, "That's why we inject directly into the heart. The circulatory system should distribute the reagent to all the various limbs and affect re-animation concurrently." Assuming the heart would work(!), and assuming all the major blood vessels (the circulatory system) were connected (highly improbable), this would be an effective way to achieve what he wants, since the pumping action of the heart would effectively and quickly distribute the reagent to the limbs for coordinated movement.

One of the ancillary benefits of the reagent is its preservative properties. This is interesting because there are such preservatives in nature, though none as strong nor as effective as West's reagent. Many of the organs and tissues of the assembled Bride, especially her heart, which came from Meg Halsey (a character from the prior film, *Re-Animator*, 1984), are well preserved due to their contact with the reagent. Preservatives are compounds that chemically interact with biological cells and tissues, thereby keeping them in as natural a state as possible. Because the organs and limbs are preserved in a freezer, the liquid contents of the cells and tissues would be intact and ready for thawing. The preservative could have acted like an "antifreeze" protein, which are somewhat prevalent in nature.

In the nicely designed basement laboratory of West and Cain they are seen creating some of their "reagent." One interesting aspect of this reagent is that it works in a dose-dependent manner, indicative of a wide variety of medications and indications. The larger the tissue mass or body part, the more reagent is necessary to induce animation. To prepare some fresh reagent, West opens up the chest cavity of a freshly killed lizard and, after removing some tissue, says, "The amniotic fluid of the Cuzeco iguana ... with that we add the muscle proteins of myosin, actin, and tropomyosin ... and then our 'reagent.'" Amniotic fluid is the innermost liquid within the embryo/fetus sac. This fluid is protein and nutrient rich, and includes a variety of hormones. Muscle proteins

myosin and actin are the two protein molecules that make up the thin and thick filaments of muscle. Thin filament of muscle fibers is composed of two strands of actin and one strand of tropomyosin, regulatory proteins coiled around one another. The thick filaments are staggered arrays of myosin molecules. The cyclic interaction of the shortening and lengthening of these coils gives muscle movement. Skeletal muscle only contracts when stimulated by a nerve cell called a motor neuron.

Gloria, a terminal patient at the hospital, dies, though Cain and West try to revive her. They first open her chest in order to massage her heart. This procedure is graphically accurate — from the realistic scalpel chest cut, to using a bone saw on the ribs, to the final rib separating vice. After she dies, West removes her head and brings it to his lab as the final piece for his Bride.

While the Bride is in the later stages of assembly, there is an IV fluid bag attached to her arm. She did need fluids to replace those being rapidly lost from other leaking areas. The body is kept on a bed of liquid nitrogen or dry ice as a preservative. Ultra cold therapy does have advantages in cases where blood flow needs are a concern.

What Is Wrong with the Biological Science Presented: First up, there is the re-animating "reagent." One of the tenets of biology is that "the sum of the parts do not make the whole." Separate components do not work by themselves, and the separate components in the reagent could not animate muscle movement.

One of the biggest problems confronting West and Cain would be the state of preservation of the tissues they use to assemble the Bride. The fresher the tissue, the less likely it would malfunction. Some of the Bride's parts are much older than others, so this would have an effect on movement.

The first demonstration of the effectiveness of the re-animation reagent is the scene in which West combines five separate fingers, along with an eye and optic nerve, into one unit. After West adds the reagent, this finger creature comes "alive" and crawls around on the fingertips, with the eye providing direction. There is not enough nerve tissue for the eye's input to be translated as a neuromuscular impulse and sent to the muscles in the fingers for any meaningful (and directed) movement to occur.

Graves, the pathologist, injects some of the reagent into the base of a head belonging to Dr. Carl Hill, a character from the original *Re-Animator* film. Graves and Hill are colleagues. After a second injection of reagent, the head of Hill recognizes Graves and says, "That seminar in Zurich. Your theory of reconciling creationism with the origin of disease, totally idiotic." Absolutely idiotic! Speech occurs when air is forced out of the lungs and over the vocal cords. Since Hill is all head and no lungs, then no speech would have been possible. Given that, the perceptive cognitive ability and insightful thinking capacity of Hill's brain, several months after being beheaded, is, unfortunately, reel biology.

The muscle proteins West adds into the "reagent cocktail"—actin, myosin, and tropomyosin—are indeed the proteins that make up muscle, but when mixed together they do not make muscle tissue. Perhaps they may be of some benefit in helping certain muscle repair mechanisms, but essentially the inclusion of these proteins would really serve no advantageous purpose.

In describing the Bride's body parts, West says to Cain, "Feet of a young ballet dancer who ended her life when she lost her ambition. These legs walked the streets. You remember the hooker who was killed in E.R. by her pimp last week? Think of all the bodies these legs were wrapped around. And here, the womb of a virgin, struck down before tasting the pleasures of life. The arms of a waitress. The lawyer's hand." In total, the Bride is composed of at least seven different people. Since the circulation system is shown to work, then the tissue rejection component of the immune response would cause a massive cellular response that could destroy critical cells and tissues. If the circulation works, then the immune response would also work. And therefore these problems would be insurmountable without the aid of massive doses of immunosuppressive drugs.

After re-animation the Bride sits up, jerks her head from side to side in a titubation-like tremor (similar to the Lanchester Bride in *Bride of Frankenstein*), and then stiffly walks. Moreover, she also speaks. Her torso is composed of multiple exposed tendons and muscles, fluids are draining from everywhere, and the look on her face is like one who's in shock. If she has any sort of nerve function she must be in terrific pain, with all the exposed cells and tissues, nerve fibers, muscle, tendons, and bone.

What Biological Science Is Necessary to Actually Achieve the Results in the Film: The biggest hurdle to overcome is the nature and composition of the re-animation "reagent." What would this material have to be to work in the way implied in the film? First, let us examine what the intended goal is. Interpreting "re-animation" literally, then it would be giving life back to living flesh. Life has many meanings, so in a way, reanimating a body part is giving some form of life, which, in this case, would have to be defined as movement. If it moves, it has life. Directed or intelligent movement are not as important. Movement requires muscles, and muscles work by being activated by nerve connections. The firing of these nerve connections will make muscles move, a finger bend, an elbow or knee bend, arms lift, head move, etc. In this sense, the reagent would have some sort of neuromuscular impulse stimulating property. What mediates these impulses are what are collectively called "neurotransmitters," which are chemical messengers released from one cell (usually a nerve) to stimulate an adjacent cell (usually a muscle cell). These chemical messengers range from small molecules, like amino acids, to more complex organic structures, such as peptides. It is these neurotransmitters that nerves use to stimulate muscle to move. The reagent could have some sort of novel neurotransmitter that is independent of nerve function and "fires" off the muscle by itself. If the muscle cells are stimulated to move by chemical means, instead of by coordinated electrical impulses from nerve cells, then the herky-jerky, semi-spasmodic limb movement seen would make sense. As a chemical, the reagent would eventually deplete itself, so it would have to be used again and again for continued effectiveness.

Another aspect about this is the level of pain experienced by the Bride. Is she in a lot of pain, minimal pain, or no pain at all? It is hard to say. She is probably at the no pain at all level, because who knows how the Bride will respond once fully animated. With pain eliminated, then her natural movements and instincts would take over. The level of pain can be controlled (by endorphins), and the nerve cells that convey pain can be selectively killed, so that no sense of pain is transmitted. West could have easily done this.

In addition to the neurotransmitter effects of the reagent, West also adds amniotic fluid. In this fluid are a variety of nutrients, vitamins, proteins, cells, and other organic matter which could provide all sorts of benefits to the effectiveness of the reagent. The addition of the muscle proteins, myosin, actin, and tropomyosin, could be used to replenish whatever dam-age the constant chemical firing of muscle contractions by the reagent's neurotransmitter had caused.

Another significant problem to overcome would be the ability to coordinate the gross motor body movements in such a way that walking, standing, sitting, etc., would all be possible. After being re-animated, the Bride makes numerous jerky movements, as though in spasmosis. Taking the success of the reagent at face value, then all the limbs would have been re-animated at their extremities. The wrists, elbows, shoulders, hips, knees, ankles would all want to go their separate ways; there would be no coordinated movement. For coordinated body movement there would have to be some sort of controlling center, the brain, which would have to function well enough to do this. The head of the recently deceased Gloria was quickly rushed to West's lab for the connection surgery. In all of this surgery with re-animated tissue, sterility would not be a concern, so the connecting work could proceed unimpeded.

By eliminating the tissue rejection capacity of the immune system, the reagent, if it exists, could re-animate any body part irrespective of what other body part it is attached to. This does give rise to interesting, Hieronymous Bosch–like imagery. West, ever the experimentalist, has made a variety of "experiments" to test his various reagent batches. Seen are a head/foot combination, an upper male and upper female torso attached together (with their four arms serving for crawling), an upper male torso with feet instead of arms, a cat with a human head, etc. Without a central controlling brain, these "experiments" have no sense of direction or purpose, but simply flail about.

Could It Actually Happen: In principle, enough surgical and biological science is currently available that the assembly of (living) body parts is a possibility.

The advances being made in the use of electrical impulses to coordinate muscle movement in paraplegics and quadriplegics are examples of what will ultimately come, a blurring of the fields of robotics and surgery to create artificial and enhanced bodies. With current understanding, the function of the brain is key to the success of this goal. After all, brain dead bodies have been kept alive for years, so that is no longer a problem. A functioning brain must be available to properly coordinate the body parts.

SYNTHETIC SKIN

Synthetic skin is an interesting concept. And why not?; it would be useful technology. It doesn't take much imagination to see all sorts of uses. The concept of artificial skin dates back to at least the late 17th century, when water lizard skin was applied in the care of certain wounds. Wound healing, burn victims, repairing aged skin, and even cosmetic improvements would be routinely performed should some sort of synthetic skin be readily available. What was pure fancy in 1932 is essentially in practice in the 1990s. This century will see dramatic improvements in the use of skin, and we may even see the re-defining of what skin actually is. The field of dermatology is entering an interesting golden age of sorts and is now divided into medical and surgical specialties. Dermatologists are the ones who have recently developed cutaneous laser surgery, micrographic surgery, and a whole assortment of cosmetic surgical developments to keep many fit and trim.

Some examples of what has been used as artificial skin are virtually any animal skin (a xenograft), plastic sprays, sponges, and fresh skin from cadavers (called an allograft). (Cadaveric skin is an interesting possibility, especially in the temporary coverage of large wound areas. However, problems of availability, disease transmission, immunological rejection, not to mention limited shelf life, forced the development of alternatives.)

Back to our anatomy. By definition, skin is the tissue layers above the superficial fascia, where the muscles and nerves lie. Tissues below the fascia would not be considered skin. Another consideration is the placement of skin over the fascia or the placement of skin over an already existing skin layer. In other words, is there skin or tissue over the muscle layer, or is the muscle layer exposed? This involves the thickness of skin needed. Since skin is composed of layers, then which layers are needed to satisfy the requirements for "synthetic skin?" The upper layer is the epidermal and the next is the dermal, which functions as the site of vascularization. In the absence of the dermal layer the epidermal layer eventually sloughs off. Synthetic skin in the truest sense should be as close to real skin as possible.

Techniques are being developed that provide a three dimensional stroma scaffold (a user friendly polymer), thereby allowing the growth of thicker sections of cells. Depending upon which layer or layers of skin

265

are damaged or need replacing, there will be some form of "synthetic" skin available at the thickness required.

During the 1970s methods were discovered which allowed the culturing of sheets of epidermal cells, thereby allowing the ability to grow several layers in different sizes in clean, sterile, and reproducible environments. Technically, these epidermal cells are keratinocytes. The key in this case is that the particular patient donate a small skin biopsy, so that about two to three weeks later there will be available an entire body's worth of epithelium. In some burn cases this is of major benefit. In cases of elective cosmetic surgery, some skin can be prepared in advance to ensure the "taking" of the tissue, since it would be the patient's own cells. The field is rapidly advancing, as new culture techniques, especially in the area of organ culture, become available

Many good things have, so far, come out of the field of artificial skin, with more on the way. A bovine (cow) collagen-based dermal analog that quite cleverly biodegrades over time while encouraging organized dermal tissue regrowth (this stuff could be placed over wounds as a temporary measure) is one such example. This analog is also extensively used in soft tissue augmentation. Another example of the benefits of artificial skin is all the work done with silicone as an alternative epidermal substitute. Silicone behaves very much like skin, in both mechanical strength and protection from fluid loss. Unfortunately, it is only temporary. However, the use of silicone in certain cases could be the difference in the protection of the wound and underlying tissues and their loss or substantially reduced function.

Though skin does indeed play a major role in SF cinema, the use of synthetic skin has played a surprisingly small role in these films. Which is unfortunate,

since the cinematic possibilities are extensive. Like in the 54 year gap in the *Bride* films, the two films dealing with synthetic skin have a significant 58 year gap in their production. And it shows. The '32 skin looks like putty, whereas the '90 skin looks like skin.

Doctor X (1932)

Synopsis: Dr. Xavier is the head of the "Academy of Surgical Research." Bodies have been showing up, and the killer is one of the Academy members. Xavier sets up an elaborate device to discover the real killer. The killer develops synthetic flesh as a method of disguise.

Screenplay: Robert Tasker and Earl Baldwin, based on a play by Howard W. Comstock and Allen C. Miller.

Biological Science Principles Involved: Autopsy. Physiology. Cell Biology. Dermatology.

What Is Right with the Biological Science Presented: The morgue scenes for the early 1930s are realistic and impressive. The life of a pathologist is fraught with unpleasant vapors, messy cutting, and body after body. What is present in this morgue fits very well with a real life morgue of the time.

The biomedical library looks impressive, with high walls jammed with assorted books, notebooks, journals, and records. Also present are a massive globe and a skeleton (naturally). In another area an anatomical model of an eye is seen, with the orbit muscles displayed.

In reference to the caged animals kept in his lab, Dr. Haines calls them, "Mankind's benefactors." On a personal note, I thought this is a wonderful tribute to the countless small animals who have helped advance biomedicine. In my own research I have used a number of rabbits, rats, and mice to help answer some critical

Doctor X (1932): The impressive, large, and well equipped home lab of Doctor Xavier. Most of the interesting pieces are in the chamber in the left background.

questions. These animals certainly are my "benefactors."

In Wells' lab is seen a sealed container, demonstrating some interesting sterile technique, that contains a pinkish liquid. In the world of tissue culture this probably is some phenol red dye, which is a very good indicator of the pH value of the media. The pinker the color of the media the higher the pH value, and the more orange/yellow the color the more acidic the pH; when too yellow, the media should be replaced with fresh.

During the time period in which the film is set, discovery of new cellular anatomy was a vibrant and exciting reality. (Ultimately, in real science, the work done in cellular anatomy around this time netted Palade, Christensen, and Claude the 1974 Nobel Prize.) During one scene Professor Haines excitedly shows Xavier, "a new type of brain cell" under the micro-

scope. This would be something of significant interest at the time, and the two scientists' child-like behavior is justified (though the real reason is a ruse to get them away from the police).

While explaining synthetic flesh, Wells says, "For years I've been searching to find the secret of living, manufactured flesh. I went to Africa to get samples of the human flesh that the natives eat ... living flesh from humans for my experiments." There is an interesting concept here, which needs to be amplified, based on the fact that not all skin is the same. Skin from the leg would be different from skin from the upper back, etc. (The only real difference is in the thickness of certain layers.) Wells reasoned that African cannibals must "naturally" have selected for the best flesh, and he thought that if he used this same flesh area then his own research would benefit. It's interesting deductive reasoning to rationalize a certain goal. (This falls under the category of "the end justifies the means.")

What Is Wrong with the Biological Science Presented: When scientists blurt out long and complicated names, the audience automatically believes the words because of who it comes from. Some of these words are real and some are reel. As long as these words sound good and flow off the tongue, then they are used. Lionel Atwill has a way of pronouncing multisyllabic words with interesting emphases. As Xavier, he points to an area around the neck and says, "stratocleavomastoid." Only Atwill can make that made-up word sound wonderful. It took a cop to point out the obvious, apparently missed by the pathologist (highly unlikely), when he says, "And what do you think of this incision at the base of the brain?" Xavier responds, "Obviously made by some type of scal-pel [deliciously pronounced as two distinct words by Atwill, the master] used for brain dissecting." As further understatement in a case he just acknowledged now belongs to a coroner, Xavier then says, "But it is peculiar that this left deltoid muscle [around the collar bone] should be missing ... this is cannibalism." These two facts are critical to this case and should have been stated first. Sloppy pathology. To further add to this, when Xavier does his autopsy he does not wear any gloves, which all pathologists since the 19th century have worn.

Shown is a tour of the labs of the research institute. In Professor Wells' lab is seen a large glass cylinder containing a beating heart in a liquid. Wells says, "I've kept it alive for three years by electrolysis." This is ludicrous. The heart may have beaten for some time (minutes, hours, or even days), but the constant threat of contamination of tissue over a three year period is unacceptable.

Dr. Rowitz' specialty is light, and he explains, "I have an interest in the light qualities of the moon. If you might suffer sun stroke, might you not suffer some similar evil from the rays of the moon?" To which a cop says, "Moon stroke, you mean?" Rowitz responds with, "Exactly. What we call lunacy." The concept of lunacy in relation to the full moon (so many people "swear" certain behaviors are influenced) has been debated since the dawn of mankind, and all the studies have shown that the full moon does not bring about mental illness. Lunacy due to the rays of the moon is itself lunacy.

Wells, who has an artificial left hand, is seen removing it and attaching another, which is composed of "synthetic flesh." He then places the synthetic hand in an electrical device, and the current makes the hand come alive. For electricity to affect the "hand" this way, it would require the presence of nerves; otherwise, moderate exposures to electricity would have virtually no effect. Based on the use of electricity, then there must have been neuromuscular interactions within the hand. Wells then takes some clay/paste-like material and rubs it over his face and head. He does this while peering over a steaming vat. Synthetic skin grows in layers, not gobs, and it is certainly not applied like makeup. Other than for obvious horrific effect (which is quite effective), Wells' application of the synthetic flesh to his own face during the climax makes no sense. More importantly, how would Wells have his synthetic tissue production system setup at Xavier's home without Xavier knowing about it?

The actual application of the synthetic flesh material to Wells' face and head is done in a very non-sterile manner. Not only does synthetic skin neither behave nor look like putty, it cannot be rolled on in clumps and then smoothed out. Also, why did Wells need to cover his hair with the synthetic flesh? This is pointless.

What Biological Science Is Necessary

to Actually Achieve the Results in the Film: There are two main areas of interest in this film. The first is the astonishing ability of Wells to keep a beating heart "alive for three years by electrolysis." Though the cylinder contains what appears to be culture media and electrodes attached to the heart, it is sealed, which demonstrates an acknowledgment of sterile needs and conditions. A heart is primarily muscle tissue that needs to be well fed to keep it healthy. The beating action is brought about by a coordinated electrical stimulus. To actually keep a heart beating for a three year period would require absolute sterile conditions. The culture media would have to be changed at least once a week to maintain optimal nutrient consumption. The cardiology of the heart is far beyond the scope of this book. Suffice it to say, artificial hearts and heart transplants are becoming more and more routine, so keeping a beating heart alive for extended periods of time is not unreasonable.

The second main area of interest is the synthetic skin itself. What would it have to be composed of to work as seen in the film? For Wells, the synthetic skin serves more as a makeup disguise (cosmetics) than as any particular help to wounds and burn victims. As seen, the synthetic skin has the composition of a squishy putty. It is placed on the intended area to be covered and spread around for the desired consistency and smoothness. Because it is so pliable, neither facial movement nor details are lost. However, putty is not skin. To function as seen in the film, perhaps the skin could be prepared as individual cells, much like bricks for a wall (or amino acids for a protein), and kept this way in humidified containers. After exposure to air, the cells congeal and form up, elbow to elbow, into stratified sheets, much like bricks cemented to form a wall. After a period of time the new skin cells could become vascularized and permanently attached.

Could It Actually Happen: The future will only see an increased use of "synthetic flesh," only it will not be scooped out of containers and rubbed over the area of coverage.

Darkman (1990)

Synopsis: Dr. Westlake is attempting to develop a form of liquid skin. While he works in his lab, some crooks break in, kill his assistant, set the place on fire, and blow it up. Westlake survives the explosion but has burns over about 40 percent of his body. After being treated in a burn unit, he escapes, sets up a new lab, gives himself a new face with his liquid skin, and goes after the crooks.

Screenplay: Chuck Pfarrer, Sam Raimi and Ivan Raimi, Daniel Goldin and Joshua Goldin, story by Sam Raimi.

Biological Science Principles Involved: Molecular Biology. Dermatology. Cell Biology. Endocrinology.

What Is Right with the Biological Science Presented: The "Hayflick limit" is known in biology as the number of doublings a normal cell, such as a fibroblast or an epithelial cell, can achieve within its lifetime. Without some sort of genetic intervention, as in the case of genetically transformed cancer cells, normal cells are unable to double beyond that finite limit. This has profound implications in the field of aging research. Our normal cells cannot live forever. For Dr. Westlake to say that his "liquid skin" destabilizes after 99 minutes is sort of correct. However, the 99 minute limit is bogus and far too restrictive.

As discussed above, synthetic skin development is a very active and exciting area of research, not only at the academic university level but also at the corporate level. There are biotechnology companies that

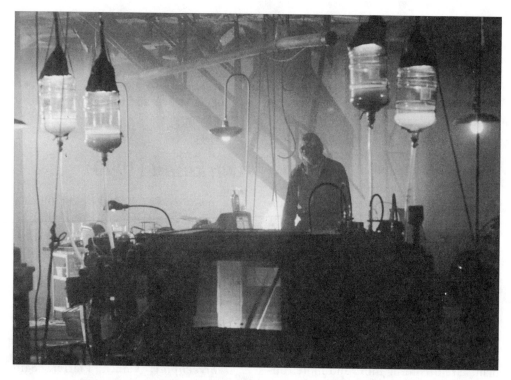

The second laboratory established by Dr. Westlake (Liam Neeson) in *Darkman* (1990). This one was "low budget," as exemplified by the creative use of watercooler jugs to help feed his tissue regeneration research.

specialize solely in the area of providing artificial skin, and significant progress has been achieved in this area — so much so that many burn victims and others, such as those with congenital defects and certain skin disorders, can be readily patched together again. Their future will be much brighter with the advances made here.

The manner in which Westlake is treated as a burn patient is accurate (with one significant exception performed by the attending physician, which is described below).

What Is Wrong with the Biological Science Presented: Though there are computer programs that can easily scan a photo of a face and create it in three dimensions, they are not (yet) able to create this image out of real, viable skin. The mold machine shown in this film is fascinating to watch, and there will come a day

when this will certainly be possible. However, it is doubtful if it will ever be as fast as seen, simply because it does take a finite amount of time for skin cells to duplicate themselves. It could take a few days, but not the few minutes as shown in the film — unless there is some mechanism by which individual cells are stored in containers with nozzles that release just the right amount of cells. Upon exposure to air these cells could attach and congeal.

Early on in the film, Westlake looks into a microscope, and a point of view shot of this is seen. The artificial skin cells appear to look like unciliated paramecia, which are oblong, rounded, single-celled protozoans. Skin cells are attached to each other and are typically seen in sheets (sort of like a cobblestone street), not as individual cells. Even forgiving the "single cell status," the paramecium-like cells seen have some ill-defined internal structures and no visible nucleus, which makes me wonder what exotic biological entity they really were. Also, they appear to have significant Brownian motion, which is random movement, and rotate a lot. At the 99th minute these cells are seen to burst; this is a common thing to do with cells, and is accomplished by significantly changing the osmolarity of the liquid around them. The easiest way to do this is by adding more salt (sodium ions) to the solution.

We get a little bit of insight as to why the cells destabilize at the 99th minute when, during one such experiment, the lights in Westlake's lab go out and the cells appear to survive beyond this time limit. Westlake says, "The dark, of course, the dark. I think the synthetic cells are photo-sensitive. What is it about the dark? Why are they still stable? At least we know it's all about light." It would have made better sense if Westlake had said, "what is it about the light" instead of his comment about the dark. Photosensitivity of skin is a well documented phenomenon and has to do with the amount of ultraviolet radiation absorbed by the skin cell's DNA. With too much UV radiation, the DNA is broken up and the cells eventually die. Furthermore, a skin pigment called melanin, a metabolite of amino acid synthesis, is also formed by the actions of UV radiation. The amount of melanin pigmentation generated is a direct relation to the amount of UV radiation the skin receives; in simple terms, this is called a tan and a "sunburn" when you get too much.

Just before the bad guys blow up Westlake's lab, they beat him up and throw him into a large vat filled with some type of culture fluid (his "secret sauce" for feeding his liquid skin?). While in this vat of liquid, Westlake grabs two large electrodes with his hands, which "fries" his skin and tissues, exposing tendons, muscle and bone. After the lab explosion, Westlake is treated at a hospital burn center. When next seen, he looks like Kharis the mummy, all wrapped up in white gauze bandages. A doctor comes by with a group of interns and explains his case to them. After explaining how to minimize the pain of burn victims, the doctor says, "…we sever the nerve at the spinefalanic tract, which as you know transmits neural impulses of pain and vibratory senses to the brain. No longer receiving impulses of pain, you stick him with a pin and he can't even feel it." As the doctor says this, she sticks a huge needle, about a 12 gauge size and two inches long, directly into his upper thigh! Needless to say, Westlake does not flinch. After that demonstration of excellent bedside manner, she continues with, "As in any radical procedures, there are serious side effects to this operation. When the body ceases to feel, when so much sensory input is lost, the mind grows hungry. Starved of its regular diet of input, it takes the only remaining stimulation it has—the emotions—and amplifies them, giving rise to alienation, loneliness. Uncontrolled rage is not uncommon. Now surges of adrenaline flow unchecked through the body and brain, giving him augmented strength. Hence, the restraints." Unbelievable!

In the second lab Westlake sets up, he programs his computer to make a duplicate of his face. The computer responds by informing him the process will take "571 hours and 57 minutes." Some simple math reveals this to be about 23.8 days of continuous computer time!

What Biological Science Is Necessary to Actually Achieve the Results in the Film: As stated earlier, the biggest problem with the "liquid skin" concept is the time element. Skin is a very complex organ (see the section on dermatology) composed of several different types of cells, not a single type as implied in this film. Once the skin is in place on his face, the cells would have to be sufficiently vascularized to receive nutrients via blood vessels for proper function. (But for only a 99 minute survival time, blood vessels are not necessary.) Furthermore, the numerous facial muscles would have to be adequately connected to the skin in order to display proper expression, like smiling, frowning, eye movements, etc.; this aspect is never addressed in the film.

Could It Actually Happen: As stated, artificial skin is a reality and is being applied to patients all over the world. As more and more sophisticated methods are utilized, these procedures will become more routine. In the long run, perhaps you will be able to significantly alter your features to make them more "easy on the eyes."

Appendix: Accuracy of Laboratory Sets

The laboratories presented in the films discussed in this book have been arranged in chronological order, which provides some interesting insights. The level of sophistication and detail in the lab sets is very indicative of the times in which the films were made, and not necessarily an indicator of when the film's cinema time takes place. Futuristic plots to advance the action are unrelated to the lab details. Irrespective of when the cinema time occurs, there is usually a variety of glassware, flasks, beakers, solutions, reagent bottles, chemicals, microscopes (which varied wildly in size and sophistication; see below), and the proverbial lit Bunsen burner strewn about on various lab benches. Some of these items are arranged in meaningful and scientifically accurate ways, and some make no sense at all and are just placed where the filmmakers thought they would look the most interesting.

An interesting observation when viewing all the labs in sequence is the separation of those sets before the so-called "DNAge," when molecular biology and the manipulation of genes have become dominant, from those after DNA manipulation and gene splicing have become commonplace. The SF cinema demarcation of "B.D." (before DNA) to "A.D." (after DNA) seems to be around 1985; lab sets before this date were primarily composed of elaborate and exotic glassware scattered about on lab benches, and SF lab sets after this date tended to have more machinery and testing apparatus, which are present in real labs. In reality, depending on how you look at it, the DNAge either started in 1953 (my preference), when Watson and Crick correctly described the structure of DNA, or in 1972, when the first genes were cloned by Paul Berg. SF films made before, say, 1985 had typical lab sets that showed all sorts of glassware, usually with multicolored liquids ("eye candy" that served no practical purpose), and some instruments. After that, when at least the term DNA is known by just about everyone, the lab sets took on an entirely different look. To be sure, even SF films made during the 1990s still had the proverbial lit Bunsen burner and Rube Goldberg–like glassware setups, usually only found in the most sophisticated organic labs, so for the most part the set directors decorated

273

lab sets with visually appealing items that have little or no bearing on the level of science (or cinemascience, for that matter) presented.

In general, cinema lab sets in SF films made after 1985 have sophisticated instruments on lab benches, the presence of *plastic* containers and disposable supplies, and a higher sense of verisimilitude. It is the presence of plastic containers (many of which are disposable) around the middle 1980s that provides another demarcation point, separating "old" labs from "modern" ones.

Films made in the 1940s have lab sets that feature equipment and setups that are "state-of-the-art" for the 1940s, and films in the 1950s have lab setups that are typical for that decade, and so on until present times. Even those films that are period pieces, such as *Dr. Jekyll and Sister Hyde* (a 1971 film set in the late 19th Century), have a lab setting that sport some modern conveniences instead of sticking to those things in use during its cinema time. During the 1990s SF films show a dramatic shift in the use and understanding of DNA and what it can do. Even still, most of the sets are just assembled with little real sense. Exceptions are *Deep Red*, *Proteus*, *Outbreak*, *The Island of Dr. Moreau* (1996 version), and *The Relic*; these films have outstanding lab sets that are not only visually stunning but amazingly accurate. In other words, the scientific items presented in these films — glassware, equipment, instruments, etc. — are justified in what science is being presented and/or discussed on the screen. As a professional scientist, I would be quite happy to work in any one of them.

One of the most dramatic set pieces in SF films involves the microscope. When the audience sees a cinemascientist gaze into the optics of a microscope, they have the sense that something interesting was observed, which justifies his actions. In the films discussed in this book the sophistication of the microscope varies dramatically — from an embarrassingly cheap dime store kiddie 'scope (e.g., *The Wasp Woman* and *Astro-Zombies*) to astonishingly expensive versions only seen in the most sophisticated research labs (e.g., *Frozen Alive*, which features a fluorescent microscope, and *Jurassic Park*, which displays an imaging microscope). The latter could be worth by itself more than the budgets of many of the films discussed! Also, the microscopes are either of monocular style, meaning one eyepiece, or binocular, having two eyepieces. It should be obvious that the binocular microscopes are the preferred variety because of ease of observation; there is no squinting nor blocking of an eye for viewing. The microscope to a biologist is like a gun to a cop or a horse to a cowboy. You never see one without the other.

Another aspect worth commenting on is the use or, more often than not, lack of use of sterile procedures. Most SF cinema that deals with biology has two major flaws when it comes to sterile procedures. The first has to do with the use of syringes. Invariably, the cinemascientist has a syringe in hand with no covering on the needle, nor do they accurately insert or remove the needle from the (usually) human arm. It is the "open" needle that is the most problematical. In the atmosphere are any number of causative agents, such as bacteria, viruses, fungi, yeast, particulate, etc., which can easily glom onto a needle; when entered into flesh and tissue these can introduce the unwanted invader. The wrong agent can cause a variety of symptoms, even death, so those needles must be covered until immediate use, and only after the stick area has been adequately swabbed with alcohol for proper sterile procedure. Also, the needle point can be radically different, depending on the intended purpose. For most needle sticks the standard 12°–14° bevel penetration point is used. For intravenous use a short bevel point of 15°–19° is used, and an intradermal or intramuscular injection has a bevel of about a 30° angle. Other points are a closed pencil point and a deflected septum point, so not all needles are alike! Finally, prior to about 1980, most syringes used were made of glass, and after this date most syringes were made of disposable plastic. The glass syringes needed to be sterilized before each use, while the disposable plastic syringes are designed for one time use, then to be thrown away.

The second lab procedure that represents a total lack of sterility is the use of open topped containers. Cultures, jars, flasks, beakers, plates, and other instruments are seen being carried around without a thought about what can grow in these things. An open container with any sort of liquid will eventually grow something! For a demonstration as to what can readily grow on anything open, all most people need to do is look no farther than their own refrigerators. Food items left alone for as few as a couple of days demonstrate some sort of biological growth, so these microorganisms are everywhere. Cinemascientists have the worst sterile technique, and most people viewing these procedures mistakenly think that there is no problem.

COMMON PIECES OF EQUIPMENT

Spread throughout the various labs in SF cinema are some common bench decorations. Items in these labs include various pieces of glassware, such as beakers, flasks, retorts, Dewars, volumetric containers, titration columns, and condensers, many interconnected with tubing. Some common equipment found on bench tops are water baths, pan balances, microscopes, ring stands, mixers, hot plates, monkey bar setups and the occasional centrifuge and spectrophotometer. Items to be found on the floor are gas cylinders, incubators, autoclaves, and various electrical apparatus.

Flasks come in all sorts of shapes and sizes. A flask is a small container, usually of glass, used to hold liquids, powders, or gases. Some common varieties are a Dewar (a two walled container used for keeping liquids at a constant temperature, usually low — as in liquid nitrogen), an Erlenmeyer (a broad based flask with a conical body and a narrow neck; it is so designed so its contents can be shaken or stirred without spilling), Fernbach (used in culture fermentations where a large bottom surface area is needed for optimal gas exchange), Florence (a globular, long-necked flask), and volumetric (a calibrated flask to measure or deliver a specific volume of liquid). A beaker is a glass vessel with a lip or beak for ease in pouring various liquids; since the 1970s many beakers are made of plastic. A retort is a glass vessel, used for distillation, with a round bottom and a long side-armed neck coming outward. A condensor is used for cooling a gas into a liquid or a liquid into a solid; it's made of glass and usually has two walls, one for actual condensation, while the other, separate, portion has water running through it to enhance the cooling process. A titration column is a volumetric column used to analyze or assay a known strength of a solution by finding its end point or the concentration by which a measurable reaction is reached.

Water baths are vessels containing water at a certain temperature to either warm up or cool down another immersed container. Pan balances, or electronic balances, are very sensitive measuring instruments for weighing out amounts of solids or liquids. Most common balances can easily weigh out micrograms to nanograms. The high end sensitive balances can even weigh out vanishingly small picogram amounts.

Other common pieces of lab equipment peppering cinema benches are ring stands, which are used to support glassware over some sort of heating device, usually a Bunsen burner, but it can also be a hot plate.

Gas cylinders are thick walled metal containers that keep a particular gas in high pressure for whatever use it is intended. On top of these cylinders are regulators that release small, controlled amounts of the gas. Common contents of these cylinders are oxygen, air, carbon dioxide, nitrogen, oxyacetylene, hydrogen, and inert gases, such as argon and helium.

I would be remiss if I did not say a few words about Robert W. Bunsen, the German chemist (1811–1899) who invented the burner named after him. The Bunsen burner, present in just about every SF film with a lab bench (and *always* lit!), is a gas lamp supplied with lateral openings to admit sufficient air so that the gas is burned more efficiently, thereby providing a very hot flame with very little luminosity. Bunsen burners are indeed used all over the world but are not used as often as shown in SF cinema — and are *never* left unattended.

THE LABORATORY SETS

Island of Lost Souls (1933)

For the 1930s, Moreau's laboratory setting looks okay. There are surgery tables, large operating lamps, various bottled chemicals and reagents, assorted apparatus, a microscope, and glassware spread about in meaningful ways. Not much screen time is spent in his lab, but what is seen is convincing.

The Devil-Doll (1936)

The lab is located in the house of scientist Marcel. This is quite a sophisticated setup for the mid–1930s, and even more impressive when you consider that it is all held within a relatively small house out in the middle of nowhere. Present are multiple huge glass jugs of colored liquid, extensive glass apparatus hooked up the jugs, shelves full of glassware (beakers, flasks, test tubes), the ever present (lit) Bunsen burner, various pumps, reagent bottles, chemicals, scattered notebooks, an anatomy poster, etc. To add a nice homey touch to the whole thing, the lab is adjacent to the kitchen in the house. You could do an experiment and get a snack, all within about 15 feet of space!

The Man Who Lived Again (1936)

There are two labs shown in this film. The first is in the home of Dr. Laurience and primarily consists of wood tables that serve as benches, shelves with books, chemicals, assorted glassware, beakers, flasks, etc. Also present are various electrical gadgets and apparatus. One of the more outlandish items present is a fish tank–like apparatus containing a human brain. Not seen, though certainly implied, is a vivarium that houses at least two chimpanzees. All in all, quite an impressive home lab.

Laurience is offered a position at the famed "Haslewood Research Institute," and the second lab he sets up there is sophisticated for its time, sporting all the trappings one would expect in this type of movie. Present, and key to the plot of the movie, are two separate rooms with a chair (which looks like an electrocution chair) for the mind transfers.

The Ape (1940)

Dr. Adrian, like so many scientists of this cinema era, has a lab in his home. Visible are various pieces of glassware, flasks, beakers, ring stands, funnels, etc., along with rows of chemicals, reagents, test tubes, boiling liquids in flasks, the proverbial lit Bunsen burner, microscope, condenser tubes, columns, basins, surgical tools, syringes, and storage cabinets. All in all, quite a sophisticated setup for 1940 and one of the better equipped labs for its time and filmmakers' budget.

The Devil Bat (1940)

Dr. Carruthers has two labs in his home. His main lab is where he does all his experimental work on the perfumes, creams, and lotions he makes for the cosmetics company. In this lab are a couple of benches that contain several test tubes, elaborate glassware (appropriate for a cosmetics chemist), a lit Bunsen burner, a bookcase, volumetric flasks, retorts, beakers, boiling liquids, chemicals, and reagent bottles.

His second, secret, lab houses numerous elaborate electrical apparatus and devices for "training" his bats, plus a vivarium where he keeps his bats. Several bats are seen hanging upside down from their resting posts.

The Man with Nine Lives (1940)

Though a hospital operating theater is seen in a few scenes, it is mostly unremarkable. All the juicy stuff is saved for "Dr. Kraval's secret laboratory," which is located in the basement of a cabin near the Canadian border. Furthermore, this basement lab also has an underground chamber with a connecting tunnel! Kraval went to a lot of trouble to construct his "secret lab." Present in the lab are elaborate glassware and various apparatus, graduated cylinders and flasks, the proverbial lit Bunsen burner (where did the gas come from?), thermometers, a nice microscope, and other nondescript items hidden away in the shadows. All in all, it looks quite effective, secretive, and definitely sinister.

The Monster and the Girl (1940)

Dr. Parry has his own lab/operating room(!) in his home. The lab is large and sophisticated, with all the latest (by 1940 standards) apparatus and instruments, all related to clinical activities, such as EKG, EEG, and x-ray machines. It also contains copious surgical instruments, an autoclave, a very nice microscope, etc. Also present are two standard issue operating tables. Very little "chemistry" apparatus is visible.

Man Made Monster (1941)

The lab is that of Dr. Rigas. Present are the usual benches of glassware, columns, interesting looking pieces of apparatus and equipment, microscope, generators, retorts, chemicals, ring stands, books, notebooks, and beakers and flasks filled with assorted liquids. Also present are assorted electrical apparatus ("elecstrick fadden" stuff. Strickfadden is the man who created all the amazing electrical trappings for Universal's *Frankenstein*, among others) Rigas uses on his patients (i.e., victims), the centerpiece of which is an examination table (the "electrothermostatic table") he straps McCormick to for his doses of electricity; it is an impressive device. It is interesting that there are no tops to the liquid-containing glassware, which makes me wonder about the level of sterility and cleanliness, since all sorts of bacteria germs, dust, particles, and other minute chemicals could enter and cause problems.

The Undying Monster (1942)

Here is a question to ponder. How many Scotland Yard agents have a well equipped lab in their home? Well, there is at least one, and he is in this film. Robert Curtis' home lab contains a couple of nice benches, with multiple flasks, lit Bunsen burners (yes, that's plural), assorted glassware, test tubes, copious chemicals and reagent bottles, retorts, ring stands, boiling liquids, plus an impressive array of non-descript equipment and apparatus.

Curtis' lab at Scotland Yard contains a flame photometer, which obtains a key piece of information to advance the plot. This is the only example of the use of flame photometry in SF cinema.

The Ape Man (1943)

Brewster's lab is in the basement of his home. The entrance to the lab is hidden behind the fireplace (why are all these labs hidden and so difficult to get to?). In the lab are various benches, chemicals, shelves, a desk, books, numerous reagent bottles, test tubes, a mortar and pestle (used for grinding and mixing chemical powders), a lit Bunsen burner, boiling liquids, secret doors, cotton plugs in the necks of flasks (a nice touch for sterility), and a cage for a gorilla. Every respectable scientist has a corner cage just for gorillas, in case they need one.

House of Dracula (1945)

Dr. Edelman's lab is in his castle/home. The lab is extremely well equipped and stands out as one of the best of the decade. Present are copious pieces of glassware, benches, chemicals and reagents, instruments, a nice binocular microscope, many storage shelves, an autoclave(!), a walk in warm room/incubator (a humidity chamber filled with shelves of two liter Erlenmeyers with cotton plugs, several flowering plants, and "spores"), countless test tubes and racks, examination tables, elaborate organic chemistry columns, evaporators, titration columns, Bunsen burners, trays, pans, full carts, tables, books, notebooks, a pan balance, and on and on. The lab benches, tables, and carts are well packed with an amazing assortment of laboratory and medical supplies. Also visible are wires, tubes, overhead lights, various instruments, apparatus, and other large, non-described pieces of equipment.

Donovan's Brain (1953)

Dr. Corey has a lab in his home. Present are an operating table (all respectable cinemascientists have an operating room in their homes), various reagents and chemicals, shelves, another examination table, stainless steel sinks, carts, elaborate glassware, a lit Bunsen burner (under a flask with a dark liquid), lamps, oscillographs, and various electrical apparatus.

When Donovan's body is brought to Dr. Corey's lab, Corey administers both adrenaline and plasma. It is remarkable that Corey has these two items in any quantity at his home lab!

Them! (1954)

Though no formal laboratory is shown, we do see the scientific method in action. By this I mean the asking of precise questions, the careful analysis of available data, testing hypotheses, and making absolutely certain of theories before formulating conclusions. What I especially like are the careful observations made by the cinemascientists in this film. By their hypothetical-deductive reasoning they come to some interesting conclusions about what confronts them. It would have been too easy to just show the gi-ants killing and destroying. The cinemascientists shown here are true to form and act in the manner of their training. Science is better understood by observing it than by trying to create a precise definition, and the cinemascientists in this film do just that.

The Creature Walks Among Us (1956)

The lab is located inside a large boat. Visible are an examination table, various cabinets with surgical and medical instruments (syringes, scalpels, forceps, cotton balls, etc.), a clinical table-top centrifuge, a nice binocular microscope and slides, an x-ray unit(!) with film developing and viewing capabilities, shelves with books, reagents, many bottles of chemicals, an overhead surgical lamp, EEG instruments, chart recorder, surgical respirator, gas cylinders, and assorted glassware. On a boat this is all astonishing.

Indestructible Man (1956)

The lab shown is that of Dr. Bradshaw. Though he is a biochemist, his lab is no biochemist's lab and looks more like that of a physicist/chemist. Very little glassware is visible, and there are no columns, no visible microscopes, and no lit Bunsen burner. However, there are copious "Strickfadden-like" electrical devices all over the lab. Also present are an x-ray fluoroscope (an instrument biochemists do not use), a chemical and reagent storage room, and such accouterments as syringes, an intravenous bottle, etc. Implied, though not seen, is a nearby vivarium to house laboratory animals.

Giant from the Unknown (1957)

Though we see a simple setup of Prof. Cleveland's up in the mountains, this is more of an archaeologist's field station, so it is beyond the scope of this book. We do, however, see Wayne Brooks' lab, which is, of course, located in his home. Present are multiple shelves filled with various artifacts, a table/bench holding a single(!) volumetric flask filled with a dark liquid, one ring stand, the proverbial lit Bunsen burner, a few chemicals and reagents, and, finally, one mortar and pestle. Upon seeing this, the Professor says the lab, "is very complete," when in fact the lab is sparse.

The Incredible Shrinking Man (1957)

No specific lab, as such, is seen, though a number of bona fide lab procedures are seen being performed in the hospital and a doctor's office. These lab procedures involve test tubes, some glassware, microscopes, a nice paper chromatogra-phy tank (a first in SF cinema history), various x-ray procedures, a fluoroscope, Geiger counter, and EKG and EEG tests. Quite an impressive list of tests, with accurate supporting equipment and instrumentation. Everyone should have physical exams as thorough as what Carey went through in this film.

The Monster That Challenged the World (1957)

The lab looks like a typical 1950s version of a laboratory. Present are various test tubes, shelves, a nice microscope, sparse glassware, a monkey bar setup to hold glass tubes, rubber tubing, notebooks, separatory funnels, a vivarium (which houses rabbits), and an unusually large vat. Though the vat is used to house one of the giant mollusk eggs, there is no explanation given for its presence. Scientists, even cinemascientists, do not keep equipment around unless there is a practical reason for its use. Lab space is scarce, and items not used are not kept around very long. To have this vat there would imply some other use, one *not* involving giant mollusk eggs.

Not of This Earth (1957)

The main laboratory seen is that of Dr. Rochelle, the physician who analyzes the blood Johnson consumed. Visible are all the typical trappings and bench top dressings one would expect from a 1950s SF film, such as beakers, flasks, test tubes, various pieces of equipment and apparatus. Since this is a 1950s reel lab, the omnipresent lit Bunsen burner is seen under a flask containing a dark liquid.

20 Million Miles to Earth (1957)

The lab seen here is located in a warehouse large enough to hold the fully grown Venusian Ymir creature. The creature is on an elevated platform, and all sorts of apparatus and scientific gear surrounds him.

Present are multiple tables, assorted glassware, electrical devices, generators, stocked cabinets, chemicals, reagents, and other lab paraphernalia. Also visible are multiple white-coated scientists, all walking around looking busy and important. Everyone seems to know what they are doing, and everything has its place and purpose.

The Brain Eaters (1958)

Shown is the laboratory of Dr. Kettering. Kettering can do it all. He is fantastic. He is a physical scientist, a biological scientist, a biochemist, *and* a physician! He must have more degrees than a thermometer!

His lab is a '50s lab, with a couple of benches sparsely cluttered with glassware, ring stands, chemicals, some small electrical equipment, a smallish microscope, the perennially lit Bunsen burner, dark liquids in flasks, a dissecting tray, assorted tools (like a scalpel, tweezers, forceps, etc.), a file cabinet, and a blackboard. With just that he does everything!

The Fly (1958)

We have some interesting contrasts in this film. On the surface, everything in Delambre's home lab is electronic in nature; and, as his brother (played by the incomparable Vincent Price) says, "There's over $200,000 of equipment here" (and in 1950s money!). Nowhere to be seen are test tubes, flasks, beakers, microscopes, nor the proverbial lit Bunsen burner. However, there are loads of large pieces of equipment with numerous dials, switches, wires, electrodes, flashing lights, etc. It's unusual that a remarkable biological entity results from a purely electronic procedure. A nice touch is the presence of a chalkboard, which has several equations written on it.

Frankenstein's Daughter (1958)

Dr. Morton's home lab is entered through a door adjacent to his living room. Present are various shelves with numerous reagents, a monkey bar setup holding assorted (sparse) glassware, the expected lit Bunsen burner (see below), benches, glass funnels, test tubes, flasks with (colored) boiling liquids, a file cabinet, electrical equipment, an operating table, clipboards on a wall (a nice touch), and a lab coat rack.

The lit Bunsen burner is prominently shown several times because the creators of the film use it as a major plot point. During the final moments of the film, the she-male monster's arm, during a struggle, comes so close to the burner that her/his/its arm catches on fire, causing the creature's death.

Finally, Oliver does all his work in a secret lab, behind a movable wall in Dr. Morton's own home lab! This one really stretched the credibility of Morton's sanity since how could he not know there is a secret lab in his own house!? (And Oliver's assistant in the film is Dr. Morton's gardener! A wonderful combination — mad lab assistant and gardener.)

The Angry Red Planet (1959)

There are two labs in this film. The first is a very simplistic one on the Mars spaceship, and operated by Dr. Ryan. Present are some glassware, a nice binocular microscope (which Ryan spends a lot of time cleaning), a couple of nondescript pieces of equipment, and not much else. Ryan actually types up her notes on an old Royal typewriter. Also present on a wall is a periodic table of the elements chart!

As a sign of the times, to do any calculations the crew uses a slide rule. (Many of you gentle readers have never used such a device. I still have the ones I used during the "B.C." era; that is, *before* calculators.)

The second lab belongs to the launch base doctors who examine Ryan and O'Banyon. They too have a sparsely equipped, cheesy lab, with test tubes (some containing multicolored liquids), a centrifuge, colored liquids in various beakers and flasks, a metal monkey bar setup that holds glass columns and tubes in place, a small cheap monocular microscope (probably purchased at a local swap meet), a gas cylinder, sink, one(!) shelf, a volumetric measuring flask, and some white metal trays. All in all, not much to do anything with.

The Head (1959)

Abel has a lab and surgical operation facility in his home. Present are assorted and elaborate glassware, numerous apparatus, rotary mixer, large beakers with fluids, chemicals, a lit Bunsen burner, and assorted surgery related pieces of equipment. All in all, a rather eclectic assortment of gadgets and gizmos that any respectable cinemascientist would have in his home. He even has an elevator(!) that opens directly into the operating room, so he is prepared for just about everything.

The Killer Shrews (1959)

In keeping with the small budget, the lab of Dr. Craigis is also small. (Cheesy is probably a better word.) There are a few pieces of glassware and other items scattered here and there in his lab, like a near-empty table and a ridiculous bench. There's nothing even remotely useful to the nature of the work Craigis is doing. On top of all this, Craigis has a pitiful looking microscope, which is an embarrassment.

The Leech Woman (1959)

The lab/office of Dr. Talbot is sparsely decorated. There is a decent microscope visible (all doctors and scientists need good microscopes!), some chemicals (fewer than one would expect, considering the work Talbot is doing), a few pieces of glassware, a patient's examination table, and *one* ring stand. That is essentially it.

The lab budget for this movie must have been about $10!

Terror Is a Man (1959)

Getting all the expensive lab and surgical equipment onto this fairly isolated island is no mean feat. Also, Gerard has his own generator put on the island to supply him with the power to do his work. This is often an overlooked aspect of these films, and the writer is to be commended for including this source of electrical power.

Gerard's lab is located in the basement of his island house. Present are an operating table or gurney, a large overhead lamp, an x-ray machine (and a light box for viewing x-ray films), various test tubes, vials, chemicals, glassware, titration columns, side-arm flasks, evaporator columns, hot plates (used for heating up liquids, sort of like a stove), and an upright, top-loading autoclave, which is unusual, since most are horizontal and load from the front, not the top.

Also present are several wash basins where Gerard thoroughly washes his hands and arms in preparation for surgery, which he does quite accurately. He first scrubs his hands and forearms with soap and water, then dips his hands into two separate basins to wash off the soap and cleanser. He sprinkles powder onto his hands, then puts on rubber surgical gloves. He then opens another (sterile) container using his elbow and gets more sheets and surgical gowns. Even though he wears a surgical mask while operating, he does not wear anything over his hair. It would only take one strand of hair to fall onto an open surgical wound to cause a massive infection, thereby negating all his hard work.

Finally, for a surgeon, no EKG apparatus nor heart/lung pumps are visible. I would attribute this more to budgetary limitations than errors by the creators of the film, since the accuracy of the sterilization of the hands and surgical gowns are quite effective.

The Wasp Woman (1959)

There are two labs seen in this film. The first is in the "field," where Dr. Zinthrop experiments on extracting wasp royal honey; it consists of elaborate organic purification glassware on a monkey bar setup. The glassware and columns are all hooked up with various tubings and pumps. It's authentic looking for the purposes of analyzing and purifying small organic compounds, such as those found in royal jelly.

The second lab is assembled at Starlin's company. Here are shown several shelves filled with various bottles of chemicals, high quality organic synthesis glassware and columns (better and more complex than that shown earlier), flasks, distillation apparatus, animal cages, and an adjacent "wasp room." The elaborate glassware looks very authentic and quite impressive. The cheesiest thing seen, and in striking contrast to the obvious care and attention shown with the glassware, is a dime store-style microscope. After all the money put into the other lab trappings, it is unfortunate that its verisimilitude is ruined by this ridiculous looking thing.

The Brain That Wouldn't Die (1962)

At the start of the film the operating room looks authentic and realistic for its time. Like many of the main scientists in these films, Dr. Cortner also has a lab in his home, and this one is located in the basement (is there any other place?). Present in this lab are various monkey bar setups that hold numerous flasks, tubes, etc. On the walls are several anatomy posters. On another nearby bench are flasks with boiling liquids (with a lit Bunsen burner) and ring stands. There are shelves with chemicals, and a sterilization unit (which is a hot[?] water bath). Overall, there is a remarkable lack of sterile conditions for the type and nature of "open body" and exposed tissue work going on.

Atom Age Vampire (1963)

Professor Levins' lab is, naturally, located in the basement of his house. The lab is spacious, with lots of equipment present, flashing panel lights (which are always cool looking and suggest sophistication), machines with dials, radiation chambers, a bench with lots of glassware (flasks, columns, synthesis flasks, colored liquids), an oscilloscope, animal cages (mostly dogs and rabbits), a centrifuge (very few cinema labs show one of these), storage cabinets, fume hoods, desks, the ever-ready lit Bunsen burner, and a chalk board with various organic chemical reactions and formulae scribbled on it.

The Flesh Eaters (1964)

I am always amazed by the type and nature of the labs these cinemascientists have. Moreover, they have the most elaborate and unusual equipment and supplies at the most remote and inhospitable locations. This film is no exception. Dr. Bartell has his lab on a remote island in the southwestern Atlantic. His lab is located under a pitched tent! If that doesn't seem enough, he has an inventory of equipment that would make even Dr. Moreau jealous. Bartell has all the usual scientific gear at his disposal, such as test tubes, assorted glassware, vacuum traps, electrical meters, pumps, tubing all over the tent, a nice monocular microscope, some books, clipboards, and a jaw-dropping 10,000 volt solar generator! How do these cinemascientists get this stuff to these locales? Just amazing!

Frozen Alive (1964)

Dr. Overton has a large, spacious, well-equipped, authentic looking lab. Present are examination tables, metal casework (which indicates to me that they filmed the scenes in an authentic lab), shelves with copious bottles, reagents, and chemicals. Also visible are physiology equipment and instruments, sinks, an autoclave, desks, cabinets, elaborate glassware (which is somewhat puzzling, since they do no organic chemistry work), evaporator columns, assorted flasks, a fluorescent microscope (this is a *very* expensive piece of equipment, which is another reason why I suspect the movie was filmed in an actual lab; this microscope is probably worth the entire budget!), and various glass columns. Finally, we have the centerpiece of the whole set, the cryo/freezing chamber, which has multiple gas cylinders attached to it, as well as numerous dials and sensory gauges.

One hard-to-believe aspect of this set is the means of entrance and exit from the lab, which is through a large, circular, bank vault-like door. Why the security?

Last Man on Earth (1964)

Morgan is a scientist working at the "Mercer Institute of Chemical Research," and his lab is interesting. Present are cluttered lab benches (the best labs I have seen in my professional life have *all* been cluttered, indicative of active, ongoing work), numerous flasks, assorted apparatus, a precision balance for weighing out very small quantities of chemicals, a nice microscope, some shelving, and a spectrophotometer. (Technically, a spectrophotometer is an instrument used for measuring the intensity of light of specific wavelengths transmitted through a solution, giving you precise quantitative measurements of the concentration of substances within the solution. In other words, it's an instrument that measures concentrations of substances in solution by light scatter; the higher the concentration, the more the light scatter. For example, the amount of protein in serum. In the old days, these instruments were called colorimeters. Spectrophotometers are in every biological lab all over the planet, and can be very simple or very complex. They

are a true workhorse in biology and chemistry. I am pleased to see one in Morgan's lab, indicating someone [set director?] wants as accurate a lab as possible. Good job!) Also present are a clinical centrifuge, file cabinets, a pH meter, and an oven. All in all, a rather impressive lab setting.

Fantastic Voyage (1966)

There are two laboratories seen in this film. The first is the underground "CMDF" ("Combined Miniature Deterrent Forces") facility where all the miniaturization and "clinical" work is staged. The CMDF facility has several "clean rooms" where the main action takes place. One room is the operating theater in which the agent is located, along with his attending staff of nurses and physicians. Quite a lot of supportive equipment is present, not only to monitor the medical condition of the agent but also to track the miniaturized team. Another adjacent clean room is where the actual miniaturization work takes place.

The second "lab" is the living lab of the agent's inner body, where his physiology and anatomy are seen in action. Here are the arteries, veins, and other cells and tissues visited by the search team. Much of this "living lab" is accurate (for 1966) and much is not, primarily due to the scale of particular scenes and the (practical) limits of the effects budget.

Island of Terror (1966)

The main lab seen is that of Dr. Phillips. This is a well stocked lab, with lots of equipment with various gauges and dials. There are several monkey bar setups with plenty of attached glassware (such as evaporating columns containing various interesting looking red liquids), a nice microscope, file cabinets, copious general glassware on benches, casework, lab chairs, shelves of reagent bottles, and water tanks filled with clear/opaque orange liquids (cell culture medium?).

Astro-Zombies (1967)

The first lab seen belongs to De-Marco. Shown are what looks to be elaborate electronics equipment, a small power microscope, cotton balls, a (hot) water bath, plastic jugs with large non-sterile openings containing a red (Kool-aid?) nutrient (and a total lack of sterility), various test tubes and small reagent vials, bubbling colored solutions in flasks, tweezers, a metal pan, a brain(!) in a glass case with attached electrodes, eye droppers, and a titration column. In DeMarco's lab are storage units for blood (acceptable), eye banks (not acceptable), livers and kidneys for various transplantation procedures (no way), and heart/lung machines. He has it all!

The second lab seen is that of Petrovitch and Porter. Present are benches/tables, glass columns with multi-colored liquids, a small (cheesy) microscope, file cabinets, a large glass vat (which serves no explained purpose, other than that of "eye candy"), and assorted bottled chemicals. Petrovitch is seen building a toy "Visible Man" model and appears exhausted when finished! All mind-numbing craziness.

Dr. Jekyll and Sister Hyde (1971)

Jekyll, a gentleman of means, has a lab in his own home. The lab has elaborate glassware, columns, flasks, etc., containing many multi-colored boiling liquids, and found attached to a metal monkey bar setup. The expected lit Bunsen burner is clearly visible on a bench. A nice late 19th Century microscope is also present, as is a sizable personal library (of books rather than journals).

The Creeping Flesh (1972)

Professor Hildern's estate home has its own lab. Present are benches with assorted glassware, ring stands, flasks, animal cages (with monkeys!), the skeletal remains of various species, shelves, anatomy posters, a microscope, a Bunsen burner, and various beakers and test tubes. Also, strewn about are various lab utensils and other paraphernalia, such as syringes, pans, trays, forceps, etc.

Horror of the Blood Monsters (1972)

Dr. Rynning has his lab inside(!) the Earth rocket ship. Visible are multicolored liquids in flasks, assorted test tubes, a sink with a faucet (unbelievable, but true!), some instruments, a microscope, numerous books (dead weight on a rocket ship!), ring stand, lit Bunsen burner, a ridiculous looking "distillation unit" (described as "brilliantly constructed" by one of the crew members!), and various other general pieces of glassware. Also, while in his lab inside the rocket ship, Rynning wears a white lab coat. So much for astronaut attire.

Sssssss (1973)

Dr. Stoner, a herpetologist, has a large and spacious lab designed for reptile research. On top of multiple benches are numerous cages containing various snakes, rabbits, and a mongoose. Also visible are a warm oven, shelves, refrigerator, cabinets filled with chemicals and reagents, jars, tubes, vials, containers, metal pans, surgical instruments, ring stands, clipboards (for each animal cage), incubators (for snake eggs), sinks, an anteroom for "venom storage" with a microfuge (a small, high speed centrifuge, ideal for small sample sizes), a hot plate, and an upright freezer (full of vials, tubes, etc.). No significant "chemical glassware" is visible, and which shows that Stoner's lab is indeed for reptiles.

The Island of Dr. Moreau (1977)

Shown are various animal cages with bears, boars, panther, tiger, leopard, jaguar, lion, monkey, hyena, water buffalo, etc. The lab looks early 20th Century, with operating and examination tables, assorted glassware, flasks, running water (where is the reservoir for fresh water and how is it purified?), shelves, pans, a nice microscope, numerous reagents on shelves, and specimen jars on a table. No respectable scientist would be without his trusty microscope (like a cowboy with his trusty six-shooter!), and the one shown is typical for its era and quite adequate for the work performed.

Space: 1999—"Space Brain" episode (1977)

The various labs of Moonbase Alpha are interesting and composed of all sorts of glassware, columns, support structures, equipment, and other assorted apparatus. What set this series apart from most others is the dominant use of computers. They are everywhere and extensively used. This is called automation. As time goes on, more and more experimental work will become increasingly automated. The labs of the future will be highly computerized and automated.

Humanoids from the Deep (1980)

The only real lab seen is that of Dr. Drake, and very little is actually shown. Visible are the standard flasks, bottles, and test tubes of multicolored liquids. Some nondescript equipment and a few shelves are also scattered about. Also present are a number of aquatic specimens in preservation jars, indicating that Drake is an ichthyologist (studies fish).

Since Drake is also a molecular biologist (I would categorize her as a molecular ichthyologist), her lab is remarkably empty of anything even remotely resembling what she would need to study salmon DNA (or any DNA, for that matter). This is disappointing and poor form for a cinemascientist.

Zombie (1980)

Dr. Menard runs a "hospital" and lab located in an abandoned church on the island of Matule. Overall, the sterile conditions are abysmal and very inadequate. This hospital has about 10 "beds" (more like old cots that even beggars and the homeless would not want) with "patients" (i.e., those just about ready to turn into zombies). The lab is located in the same open area as the hospital beds. Present are various shelves stuffed with books, some glassware, chemicals and reagents, a decent microscope, and other trappings and paraphernalia appropriate for backdrop fodder. The top areas of the church cum hospital/lab are completely open for ventilation and could be a conduit for incoming infectious and contaminating particles.

The Thing (1982)

What little we are able to see of the lab looks pretty good and, even for 1982, is contemporary. All the usual trappings are visible, except for a lit Bunsen burner, which is nowhere in sight. The lab is sufficiently cluttered to easily pass for what it is intended for. This lab also serves as a pseudo clinic, since the base physicians do their clinical work in the same area.

One item present in the lab/clinic, however, does deserve special mention. At this military base, which houses perhaps no more than two dozen men, is a sizable blood supply! I can believe this in a hospital, or perhaps out in the field during a military campaign, but in the Arctic Circle?! Furthermore, this copious supply is way out of proportion to the number of personnel at the base. Leave it to the military to be needlessly exorbitant and excessively largess in their supply items. No wonder their budgets are so outrageous.

The Fly (1986)

Like the original 1958 movie, this version also has very little of a biological lab, but rather a lot of electrical and mechanical apparatus scattered about. No benches are seen, nor are any types of chemicals, reagents, etc. With all of the DNA work done, I would expect some sort of related testing and analysis apparatus to be visible, but none are found. Dials, switched, and flashing lights are in abundance, as are all sorts of heavy cable wires snaked across the floor. One significant piece of equipment is a centrally located miniframe computer that does all of Brundle's calculations and analyses. Brundle's lab is located in some type of warehouse, which also contains his living quarters. This is interesting because Brundle says that "Bartok Science Industries" finances his work (i.e., they own it), so why would a company put a key lab (not to mention an interesting scientist) in such an unusual location? I would think they would have his lab located at the company headquarters—not only to maintain a lower overhead expense but also to keep a close eye on a top scientist.

The Serpent and the Rainbow (1988)

The lab seen is that of Dr. Allen's and is quite authentic looking, with all the right pieces of equipment and apparatus strewn about. The brain scan data and computer analysis scenes are interesting to watch. Computerized Axial Tomography (CAT) scans are "state of the art" in brain analysis, especially in 1987; its presence demonstrates cutting edge thinking by the creators of the film.

Darkman (1990)

This film contains two labs. Dr. Westlake's first lab (the nicest) is located on the floor above a restaurant! An amazing setting and quite inventive by the writers. This lab is a well equipped '90s version, with Formica benches, chalkboards with all sorts of interesting things written on them, gas cylinders (an important set piece for the later explosion), cell incubators, both large and small computers, nice microscopes with multiple lens objectives (a

major expense here; I hope the movie's producers donated them to some worthy lab after they finished the film), and the proverbial lit Bunsen burner under a beaker. Also present are loads of assorted bench top accouterments, like petri dishes, pipettes, flasks, beakers, pH meters, mixers, etc. The set designer definitely knew his lab lore!

The second lab of Dr. Westlake is a sort of bastard son of his first. After he escapes from the hospital burn unit he returns to his destroyed lab and takes some of the surviving equipment to an abandoned warehouse and sets it up. Apparently, no one notices all of this, not to mention the significant use of electricity. (Wouldn't someone notice the huge increase in their electrical bill?) It is amazing that much of the sophisticated computer hardware and software Westlake needs survived the large explosion and remained somewhat intact. This shows how easy it is for cinemascientists to establish a new lab.

Watchers II (1990)

The genetic and recombinant DNA work takes place at a biotechnology company called "Anodyne." The first lab seen is large and spacious, with well-stocked shelves and an assortment of equipment, such as floor style centrifuges, x-ray light boxes, and interesting looking doodads. Also within the same large room is a vivarium with many cages, housing cats, dogs, rodents, rabbits, and monkeys. Normally, each type of animal is housed within a separate room to minimize the spread of disease and germs from one species to another. Regulatory agencies, such as the FDA and animal welfare activists, would find this totally unacceptable.

The second lab room seen is of moderate size and is essentially barren. All that is present are an examination table (for the creature), a largish refrigerator-styled container (similar to beverage containers seen in convenience stores), and the "creature container" that looks suspiciously like a large autoclave (a piece of equipment used to sterilize bulky items like large amounts of liquids), awkward and odd-sized glassware, and disposable biohazard trash.

Project Vampire (1992)

Though implied, there is no real laboratory visible at Dr. Klause's headquarters, which is located in what appears to be an abandoned warehouse in a run down part of town. In the "pre-DNAge" era (i.e., pre-cloning) cinema labs have a certain look to them and are usually located out of the way in the main protagonist's house. In the "DNAge" era, these labs seem to be located in dilapidated and rundown parts of towns. These scientists want to have their labs in out of the way places to minimize prying eyes and hard to answer questions. This gives the main scientist maximum control over his work and staff. In other words, he can carry out his work in secret, the equivalent of having the lab in your home basement.

We do get to see the small lab of "genius chemist" Dr. Fong, which is located in his apartment! That is a first. Visible are multi-colored liquids in glass containers (beakers, flasks, etc.), a pH meter, a computer, chart recorder, warm oven, and centrifuge tubes (the orange top kind, which means they came from a company called Corning, and some of the blue top variety, which means they came from a company called VWR; both of these are real and I have personally used thousands of each in my research). The most interesting item of all is a "laboratory safety" poster on a wall in his apartment! (I still chuckle to myself when I think of that.)

Carnosaur (1993)

We mostly see Dr. Tiptree's office surroundings and a few quick glimpses of her lab. What is seen looks okay by contemporary standards. Some glassware, generic equipment, a microscope, etc., are visible. Also seen is a dino egg chamber with several eggs being incubated. This chamber should have been encased to maintain better control of the temperature.

Jurassic Park (1993)

The laboratory at Jurassic Park is a well equipped 1990s lab, meaning there are copious instruments, such as microscopes, computer monitors, incubators, water baths, hot plates, analyzers, etc., throughout the lab. Some of the microscopes are nice stereo dissecting scopes, and one in particular — a Carl Zeiss top-of-the-line imaging microscope with all the attached gizmos and gadgets — is the most elaborate seen in any SF film to date. Also visible are shelves with large jars and bottles, large Nalgene-style plastic containers, lab stools and chairs, carts stocked with disposable (orange and blue top) 50ml centrifuge tubes, a floor model top-opening ultra cold freezer with a radioactive sticker on it (a nice touch, indicating an eye for detail), hand held microliter fluid dispensers, a box of "Kimwipes" (*the* standard wipe cloth in labs throughout the world), three-ring binder notebooks, and several digital recorders and monitors. In addition, there are several work stations with automated and robotic equipment. The employees all wear total body covering clean suits that zip up to the neck, leaving the head totally exposed. All in all, it's one of the best equipped and laid out labs in SF cinema.

Skeeter (1993)

We see two "labs" in this film. One is a sort of "portable lab" carried by Mr. Perry, from the "Advanced Geological Inspection Agency." He comes to the town to analyze the water table, looking for a cause of the unusual deaths of livestock (all caused by skeeters). Perry uses some test tubes and chemicals in a shoulder carrying case to take water samples and look for minerals, chlorine, and toxic chemicals. These tests are simple to perform and do not require a lot of fancy equipment. Perry is a good water chemist for the "AGIA."

The second "lab" belongs to Mr. Hopper (as played by one of my favorite character actors, Michael J. Pollard) and is located in his home. Hopper is a mental case, and he keeps a few of the skeeters in a cage. Strewn about are some nondescript minor pieces of equipment and some glassware. The interesting part here is how he feeds his "pets." He puts his arm into the cage and lets the skeeters "feed" by sucking his blood.

Ticks (1993)

The lab seen is located in a barn deep in the woods and serves as a place to grow, cultivate, and process marijuana. Rube Goldberg would have been proud to see this lab in action, because there are all sorts of contraptions, gears, and devices present. Tubes feeding plants, harvest traps, distillation apparatus, wires and pulleys are all strewn about in some semblance of home horticulture. The lab is a nice economical use of many items commonly found at home, so you really do not need elaborate or fancy materials, as is so often portrayed.

Deep Red (1994)

The lab seen is that of Dr. Newmeyer. This visually impressive set is well equipped with all the trappings of a '90s lab. Equipment is everywhere: stainless steel containers, benches, shelves, cabinets, all sorts of exotic glassware, tubes, chemicals, solutions and reagents, testing apparatus, and sophisticated computers that display a variety of physiological and biological parameters related to the "reds." This lab set had a healthy budget.

Not of This Earth (1995)

The Dr. Rochelle in this film version is a remarkable scientist who can do it all. His lab is definitely a '90s lab, with all the fancy equipment, apparatus, and lab bench detail of contemporary times. He has the necessary computers, blood analyzers, molecular biology equipment, microscopes, etc., necessary to do his work. In addition to this, he is a practicing physician. With all this going on he probably never sleeps. As he says, "Science never sleeps," nor do cinemascientists!

Outbreak (1995)

This film has several labs present for our evaluation, and all of them are first rate! I would personally be quite happy and content to work in any one of them.

The first lab seen is the "United States Army Medical Research Institute of Infectious Diseases," located at Fort Detrick, Maryland. This is a real facility and considered one of the best biosafety labs in the world. The labs within this facility are very authentic looking and contemporary. All the right "trappings" are visible. Four levels of biosafety labs are seen, which do exist in real life. Biosafety Level 1 is a minimal biohazard lab for the study of low risk infectious agents, such as pneumococcus and salmonella (in this lab a glass panel of a forced air containment hood is missing and probably removed for photographic purposes to prevent excessive light glare during the filmed scene). Biosafety Level 2 is for moderate biohazard infectious agents, such as hepatitis, Lyme disease, and influenza. Here the personnel are wearing cloth face masks. Biosafety Level 3 is for high biohazard agents, in which the personnel would be vaccinated against whatever they are working with, such as anthrax, typhus, or HIV. The personnel are seen wearing bio containment "moon suit" gowns with more elaborate face mask filters, though some facial skin and hair are showing. True (i.e., real) laminar flow hood containment cabinets are seen in the labs. Some personnel are seen walking in and out of the room without protective suits—a definite no-no. Furthermore, one person actually takes off his face mask *before* exiting the room! Biosafety Level 4 is for extreme biohazard agents, requiring maximum security. Such infectious agents as Ebola, Lassa, and Hanta viruses are studied. The personnel are completely covered with protective suits, which are air pressurized. A sign on the door to this room in the film reads, "Highly virulent. No known cures or vaccines." The personnel gown up, enter an anteroom, close the doors, then enter the "Level 4" room. The interior of this room looks authentic, with all the proper procedures followed. (It looks like the film crew actually went inside real labs; however, no crews with their equipment would ever be allowed in actual Level 4 biosafety rooms. The set decorators did a marvelous job to simulate such authenticity.)

Some of the labs at the "Center for Disease Control" in Atlanta, Georgia, are also seen, and these too look authentic. Quite impressive.

Next is seen a mobile lab the army deploys in a small (fictitious) seaside town on the Pacific Coast of California. This lab is located inside a bus-sized room brought in by a truck. This lab too is impressive and completely stocked with all the modern materials and equipment. With a military budget, it *should* be impressive!

Finally, some smallish labs in a few hospitals and clinics are seen that also look real and authentic. All of this must have kept the set directors very busy.

Proteus (1995)

Several labs are seen within the oil rig complex and they all look good. All the right pieces of equipment and devices are present and in the places they should be. In addition to the genetic engineering related equipment (nothing here to make "environmentally friendly oil"), some medical and physiological apparatus is seen, indicating that human specimen work is also being done. On a wall of one of the labs is a series of light boxes with x-ray films showing DNA-profile sequence data on them, clearly indicating the nature of the molecular biology work being done here. Also visible are a series of specimen jars with preserved organisms inside and a large water tank. One particular nice touch is the presence of a small cardboard radioactive waste disposal box in a corner. It even has the correct yellow radioactive symbol on it. Someone had their wits about them to go to the trouble to have that visible.

Species (1995)

The main lab, where Sil is created and developed, is a large spacious facility with all modern equipment. The containment structure that houses Sil is first rate and quite convincing. A key instrument seen is a micromanipulation device, an apparatus used to insert genetic material into a cell, and often used in artificial insemination and cloning procedures. These scenes are very realistic. It is also a pleasant surprise *not* to see a lit Bunsen burner nor boiling liquids anywhere.

The technicians and personnel in this laboratory facility are dressed in complete body covering suits, implying that strict sterilization procedures are followed. Though unnecessary, it is a nice touch and indicates that the creators of the film wanted to make this set as real as possible.

Dark Breed (1996)

The main lab belongs to Dr. Kline, a pathologist. Present are all the necessary benches, tables, and associated clutter of that profession one would expect to see in the 1990s. There's a very nice microscope, all sorts of surgical instruments, shelves of chemicals, glassware, etc. When Kline is doing an autopsy she wears gloves on her hands, something sadly missing in most of the films discussed in this book. Finally, no lit Bunsen burner nor flasks of colored, boiling liquids are seen anywhere.

The Island of Dr. Moreau (1996)

The main lab is very modern, well equipped, quite 90s looking, and the best seen in the three versions. Copious pieces of equipment and various apparatus are visible. Also present are radiation waste boxes (a nice touch; on an island, how do you get rid of radioactive and biohazard waste?), cold rooms (like a walk-in refrigerator to keep various chemicals and liquids cold and better preserved), numerous reagents and chemicals, stainless steel cabinets and casework, drying racks, carts, various portable lamps and lights, automated DNA and protein sequence machines (impressive!), etc. And nowhere in sight are green or blue colored bubbling liquids, nor a lit Bunsen burner. Inside one of the camp barrack buildings are an operating table and various cages with exotic animals, such as a llama, panther, monkeys, camel, etc.

My only complaint is the close proximity of the animal cages to the operating area. This would make the necessary "sterile conditions" required for Moreau's work non existent.

The Relic (1996)

Since most of the action takes place within the confines of a natural history museum, we are able to see some impressive lab sets. Everything is accurate and well put together. The pieces of equipment, the machinery, the storage areas, the lab benches, even the computers used are what you would find in a modern '90s lab. During the scenes in the labs I kept looking around at all the displayed items, looking for something wrong, and I could not find anything. Most impressive.

Mimic (1997)

The main lab present in this film belongs to Dr. Susan Tyler. Hers is definitely a '90s lab. Present are not only multiple vivariums with assorted insect species, nests, and living environments, but also various assorted electronics gear and apparatus, video cameras and monitors focused on nest activity, diplomas and posters on the walls, file cabinets, file boxes, a bench top autoclave (to sterilize those "problem" insects), and appropriate clutter of an academic professor. It is one of those labs to which, at first sight, you say, "cool," and not give a second's thought about anything being artificial or out of place. I would be very comfortable working there.

Index

291